Symbols and Sentiments
Cross-cultural Studies in Symbolism

Symbols and Sentiments

Cross-cultural Studies in Symbolism

Edited by

IOAN LEWIS

London School of Economics and Political Science
Houghton Street, London, England

1977

ACADEMIC PRESS

London   New York   San Francisco

A Subsidiary of Harcourt Brace Jovanovich, Publishers

ACADEMIC PRESS INC. (LONDON) LTD.
24–28 Oval Road,
London NW1

United States Edition published by
ACADEMIC PRESS INC.
111 Fifth Avenue
New York, New York 10003

Library of Congress Catalog Card Number: 76 016980
ISBN: 0 12 446650 8

PRINTED IN GREAT BRITAIN BY
J. W. ARROWSMITH LTD
BRISTOL

Contributors

I. M. LEWIS, *Department of Anthropology, London School of Economics*

ALFRED GELL, *Department of Anthropology, Australian National University, Canberra*

GILBERT LEWIS, *Department of Anthropology, University of Cambridge*

PAMELA CONSTANTINIDES, *Department of Anthropology, London School of Economics*

SERGE LAROSE, *Centre de Recherches Caraibes (Université de Montréal), Sainte-Marie, Martinique*

ABNER COHEN, *Department of Anthropology and Sociology, School of Oriental and African Studies, London*

CHARLES RYCROFT, *18 Wimpole Street, London*

STANISLAV GROF, *Esalen Institute, Big Sur, California*

JOHN PAYNE, *Student Health Service, London School of Economics*

DAVID STARKEY, *Department of International History, London School of Economics*

VIEDA SKULTANS, *Department of Mental Health, University of Bristol*

AUDREY CANTLIE, *Department of Anthropology and Sociology, School of Oriental and African Studies*

PAUL HERSHMAN† *School of African and Asian Studies, University of Sussex*

† *Deceased*

Preface

Within anthropology as well as outside it, current trends in the study of symbolism bear testimony to the pervasive influence of French Structuralism and Communications Theory. This tradition treats symbolism quasi-linguistically as a kind of arcane sign language, inscribed in challenging codes, with which the symbol cipher-expert must wrestle if he is to discover their secret cerebral messages.

Despite its many impressive achievements, this excessive emphasis on thinking and cognitive processes neglects, or seriously underestimates, the powerful emotional charge which all effective symbols carry. If it is to do full justice to its subject matter, the study of symbols must include the study of sentiments. This is our aim in this book which, bringing together work in social anthropology, history, psychoanalysis and psychotherapy, seeks to elicit the *emotional* as well as cognitive meaning of symbols in a variety of settings—individual and collective. In this process we also endeavour to renew that natural dialogue between those who study symbols in different cultural and temporal contexts, and those who analyse them in the lives of individual patients which, for reasons examined by several of our contributors, has so long been neglected in Britain. In the belief that current preoccupations in both sets of disciplines increasingly centre on common problems, we envisage a new rapprochement, capable of transcending traditional barriers and of progressing beyond the ethnocentric limitations of much that is written under the high-sounding title of "trans-cultural psychiatry". These are grandiose ambitions which can scarcely be realised in an exploratory volume. If the studies presented here encourage further inter-disciplinary work along these lines they will have more than served their purpose.

In this spirit, though not necessarily unreservedly endorsing all my personal ecumenical enthusiasm, other anthropological contributors explore spells and smells in New Guinea; the symbolism of a Sudanese women's spirit possession cult; the symbolic meaning of Africa in Haitian Vodu; seminal retention in Hindu asceticism; and the ambiguous image of Virgin and Mother in popular Hinduism in the Punjab. Moving from genital to anal symbolism, a historian throws new light on those most intimate of royal body-servants, the Grooms of the King's Stool, who enjoyed much power in England until the Revolution of 1688. Two further essays by anthropologists consolidate this inter-disciplinary bridge-head. One reviews the dynamic nexus in which personal identity is sustained in interaction with others; another demonstrates how contrasting views of the nature of madness in early and late nineteenth century England reflect corresponding changes in the dominant ideas of these two periods. From the psychoanalytic side, Charles Rycroft provides an encouragingly ecumenical re-assessment of Freudian constructs which should help those anthropologists who still have difficulty in deciding whether symbols must, or should be unconscious, emotive or cognitive, or whether they can be all or only some of these at the same time. Another psychoanalytically orientated psychiatrist shows how violently symbolic behaviour in adult life may recapitulate childhood traumas. The perennial importance of body symbols, drawn from our common biological experience, which forms a recurrent theme in all our contributions is examined in uniquely rich phenomenological detail in an important appraisal of material derived from LSD psychotherapeutic practice.

In this summary outline of the book's contents I have for convenience categorised contributions according to the discipline of their authors. The ordering of the chapters is not based on this principle, but on that of subject matter and treatment of material. The pattern that emerges is, I think, some indication of the extent to which the study of symbolism defies disciplinary boundaries, requiring the kind of inter-disciplinary approach advocated here. Most of the papers included were originally presented at an inter-collegiate seminar held at the London School of Economics in the Michaelmas term, 1973. In seeking to reopen a constructive debate on this front between psychiatrists and psychoanalysts on the one hand, and social scientists on the other, I am especially grateful to the ready co-operation and encouragement of John Payne, Charles Rycroft and Vieda Skultans. It is a matter of deep regret to have to record that Paul Hershman died suddenly while this book was in press robbing social anthropology of a young scholar of great promise. The memory of his unforgettably vigorous expository style will be cherished by all who knew him. Finally, I have to thank Katie Platt for compiling the index and my secretary, Isabel Ogilvie, for so much meticulous editorial typing.

London, December 1976   I.M.L.

Contents

I | Introduction

I. M. Lewis

The pervasive use of symbols is one of the most distinctive of all human attributes. By "symbols" we mean, of course, something more than signs. Unlike the latter which may be so, symbols are in principle never fully self-explanatory, self-sufficient or fully autonomous. As with Henry VIII's intimate representatives discussed by David Starkey later in this book, symbols act characteristically as agents, deferentially "standing", as the phrase has it, "for something else". They both reveal and conceal, pointing towards, if not fully disclosing, a different order of reality and experience. Symbols thus are by definition mysterious.[1] As with that epitome of the essence of the symbolic, perfume (see Gell, below p. 25), they are at once evocative and suggestive, redolent with significance. Symbolism consequently becomes a kind of sign language or semaphore, a code which is only intelligible once you have discovered the key. In our mass-media obsessed world, it is not surprising that this quasi-linguistic character of symbolism should have received so much attention. Thus following the linguist Saussure's pioneering work, in anthropology, Lévi-Strauss's light-footed structuralism and its ponderous American counterpart, *Cognitive Anthropology*, have assumed the burden of decoding the precious messages concealed in arcane symbolism. In the wider world of literature, art and philosophy, fortified by a liberal infusion of phenomenology, the same approach is celebrated in the fashionable craze for Semiotics.[2]

That symbols possess a cognitive aspect which is legitimately explored in this fashion is not in question. But the danger is that, infatuated with this

1. For a valuable conspectus of definitions and approaches to the study of symbolism, see Firth 1973.
2. It is a measure of the extent of this vogue in England that in the winter of 1973 that discreet arbiter of literary taste, the *Times Literary Supplement* should have devoted two successive issues, filled with appropriately opaque disquisitions, to this topic.

style of analysis, we should forget that the ultimate force of symbols depends at least as much on their power to stir the emotions, moving men to action and reaction. To follow the anthropologist, Victor Turner's (1964) terminology, we need, indeed, to try to explore the nexus which binds together the cognitive and affectual meaning of symbols. Otherwise as Abner Cohen reminds us later in this volume (p. 117), we shall never understand the hold symbols exert on the hearts as well as on the minds of men. Symbols and sentiments feed upon each other and their fruitful interplay lies at the heart of social behaviour. This is the central theme of this volume which we explore in the light of anthropological and historical contributions on the one hand, and psychoanalytic and psychiatric studies on the other.

II

The need for a dialogue of this sort between those who study the culturally standardised symbolism of societies and those who study the idiosyncratic personal symbolism of individuals seems obvious. It is certainly widely accepted in America where, indeed, collaboration between social (or cultural) anthropologists and psychiatrists and psychoanalysts has spawned the new inter-disciplinary specialisation known as trans-cultural psychiatry. But if this seems the natural path to follow on the other side of the Atlantic, the case is very different here, where, indeed, such a marriage would at the present time be almost unthinkable. In fact, the rather limited fruits which this new venture has so far produced, merely provide for British social anthropologists additional confirmation of the undesirability of all liaisons of this sort.

Although this is clearly not the place to attempt an exhaustive history of the phobic reaction of British social anthropologists towards psychoanalysis and psychology, a brief outline of some of the main precipitating circumstances is instructive and will help to identify some of the difficulties involved in exploring the relationship between symbols and sentiments.

As is so often the case, the hostility which British social anthropologists display towards these allied disciplines, masks an earlier state of co-operation and harmony. Malinowski's predecessors, W. H. Rivers (1865–1922) and C. G. Seligman (1873–1940) were not affected by this debilitating complex. While Rivers remains a respected anthropological ancestor, his name also still figures in psychology text-books where he is remembered for his pioneering cross-cultural studies of visual perception. C. G. Seligman daringly sought to apply Jung's concepts of introversion and extraversion and some of Freud's ideas on dreams in interpreting his rich store of ethnographic data drawn from research in Melanesia, Ceylon and the Sudan. He even had the temerity to deliver the 1923 presidential address to the Royal

Anthropological Institute on: "Anthropology and Psychology: A Study of some Points of Contact". In this modest, tentative manner Seligman can, I think, be said to have helped to lay the foundations for the American Culture and Personality school which we generally associate with the names of Ruth Benedict, Margaret Mead, and later, Whiting and Child. In Britain, however (many would say: Thank God!), these provisional attempts to apply individual personality types to whole cultures fell, for the most part, on deaf ears and largely fizzled out.

Later, Freud's theories had some influence on Malinowski who examined the Oedipus complex in the light of his research among the matrilineal Trobriand Islanders where, as he pointed out, the incest taboo referred to relations between siblings rather than mother and son, and the primary centre of intra-family friction was not between father and son but mother's brother and sister's son. If his field material thus seemed to challenge the universal validity of the Oedipus complex,[3] Malinowski did, however, follow Freud in acknowledging the significance of the unconscious in myth and symbolism and in common with so many other writers on the subject stressed the fear of death as a major spur to the elaboration of consoling religious rituals.[4]

Again, however, these limited cross-fertilisations (which were accompanied by extensive reciprocal borrowings *from* anthropology by Freud, Jung, Roheim and others), did not produce any vigorous innovatory current within the mainstream of British Social anthropology. Psychoanalysis and psychology became increasingly remote realms, into which only the brave (e.g. John Layard[5] and Gregory Bateson[6] who has recently become very fashionable)—or very foolish (if not "mad")—dared to venture from time-to-time, preferably in secret. Psychology (with psychoanalysis) was well on its way to becoming a "taboo" subject (as Audrey Richards once put it) for the British anthropological fraternity. Only such blithe spirits as Audrey Richards, S. F. Nadel, Monica Wilson, Meyer Fortes, Edmund Leach and a few others had the audacity to partake of the forbidden fruit—and then only in moderation and usually as discreetly as possible. The parochial British social anthropological establishment had resolutely turned its back on these "scare" topics (as Raymond Firth recalls his colleagues felt them to be). As we shall see, however, various clandestine liaisons occurred from time to time.

3. See *The Father in Primitive Psychology* (1927) and *Sex and Repression in Savage Society* (1927). Predictably enough, Freud's disciple Ernest Jones and other analysts retorted that the hostility evinced by Trobriand sisters' sons for their mothers' brothers could be seen as a displacement of that felt for the father.

4. More generally, Malinowski's theory of culture as a response to basic biological needs has a Freudian flavour. For Freud in Malinowski, see Fortes, 1957.

5. See his *Stone Men of Malekula*, 1942.

6. See *Naven*, 1936; and 1973.

III

How can this estrangement be explained? Many factors are involved. An important consideration was the anthropologist's justified irritation and alarm at the psychoanalyst's doctrinaire application of his often glaringly ethnocentric (or culture-bound) theories to the whole of mankind. So many Freudian and Jungian analysts were too ready to interpret exotic tribal customs, about which they were often strikingly ill-informed, in terms of their own, neccessarily limited clinical experience. If they found anthropological parallels helpful in understanding the problems of their patients, that scarely entitled them to explai then former by the latter! Vienna was not, after all, the whole of the world; and as Charles Rycroft observes below (p. 134) in his sensitive appraisal of Freudian apologetics, such dogmatic rigidity was scarcely conducive to mutual understanding and harmonious collaboration between the two camps. Such glaring examples as the following speak for themselves: the equation of religion with infantile obsessional neurosis; of witchcraft with paranoia; of witchdoctors and shamans with psychotics whose "hallucinations" provide the "origins" of religion.[7] As Rycroft rightly reminds us, much of this has to be understood in terms of the prevailing evolutionary assumptions, from which if social anthropologists were already attempting to extricate themselves, psychoanalysts had still to escape.

Unfortunately, however, these bizarre anachronistic associations still flourish in contemporary psychoanalytic as well as psychiatric literature. So, for instance, we find such an experienced psychiatrist as Carothers (1951) writing: "The native African in his culture is remarkably like the lobotomised Western European, and in some ways like the traditional psychopath in his ability to see individual acts as part of a whole situation, in his frenzied anxiety, and in his relative lack of mental ills." In similar vein, in a tradition going back at least as far as that pioneer of transcultural psychiatry George Devereux,[8] Silverman (1967) claims that tribal shamans (inspired priests and healers) are usually "acute schizophrenics", exhibiting "the most blatant forms of psychotic-like behaviour".

Nor is it only analysts and psychiatrists whose ethnocentric naïveté shocks the social anthropologist. Some of the modern research in child development, cognition and perception (e.g. on time-perception) carried out by psychologists on non-European subjects strikes the anthropologist as betraying a marked lack of insight into the culturally specific, and therefore parochial character, of human experience. This seems to me evident in some of Witkin's work, to name one leading figure in this field. Here

---

7. This claim is repeated in, and is indeed the central theme of Weston La Barre's recent book, *The Ghost Dance* (1970).

8. See Devereux, 1956 and for a more recent statement of his position, 1970.

there is no criticism like self-criticism: and so we may join two American psychologists in complaining that: "the laboratory psychologist still assumes that his college sophomores provide an adequate base for a general psychology of man" (Campbell and Naroll, 1972). There is the additional difficulty that as Roger Brown, a prominent social psychologist, phrases it: "Hypothesis-testers are not interested in total cultures or the total minds of respondents, but only in those fragments that figure in theory." (Brown would thus, apparently, like western investigators to think in the fashion which, in Africans, Carothers judges signifies insanity!)

More significantly, the growth of the American Culture and Personality school, with its prostitution of anthropological ideas and material, has proved an even greater irritant to British social anthropologists—partly of course because it is presented as a form of anthropology. I refer, of course, principally to the work of Abram Kardiner (from whom Abner Cohen suggests later in this volume it may still be possible to rescue something of value), Whiting and Child. As is well known, indeed notorious, these researchers purport to explain whole cultural systems in terms of child-rearing practices on the analogy of the significance attached to early childhood experiences in the etiology of neurosis by psychoanalysts.

This approach is as simplistic as it is ambitious. First, it is generally claimed that harsh parental treatment during infancy leads to a belief that the spirit world is equally stern and aggressive. This assertion is "supported" by exhaustive statistical tests on a wide range of data selected from that notorious treasure trove of misinformation—the Harvard Area Relations files. The truth, of course, is that none of the communities for whom we possess comprehensive information have as starkly simple cosmologies as this. All, to the best of my knowledge at least, include spiritual forces which are *both* aggressive and non-aggressive, whatever the prevailing pattern of child-rearing! There is the more fundamental objection which, indeed Kardiner (1945, p. 119) himself ultimately acknowledged—although he shied away from its discouraging implications—that this whole approach is as circular as it is simplistic.[9] It can just as plausibly be argued that it is the *religious beliefs* rather than the child-rearing practices that are primary; for such beliefs inevitably enshrine a morality and imply the local equivalent of a Dr. Spock compendium of prescriptions. The stern injunction "Spare the rod and spoil the child" proceeds from as much as prefigures a particular view of divinity. Moreover as Gustav Jahoda (1972, p. 34) more charitably observes, the trouble with Kardiner type studies of culture and personality is that: "Field material is collected in accordance with the major variables postulated by the theory. The findings are then interpreted

9. For some recent examples of work in this genre which are still open to the same objections, see Muensterberger and Esman, 1972.

in terms of greatly oversimplified causal linkages, ending up invariably and not surprisingly with conclusions in harmony with the theory. This is because the theoretical framework has to be very loose, so as to accommodate highly complex data: at the same time the looseness practically guarantees some kind of fit between theory and data and one gets out what one has put in . . .".

To these negative influences we must add a further, and I think ultimately decisive factor: the mixed legacy of the French social theorist Emile Durkheim and our precipitate acceptance of his arbitrary distinction between *psychology* as the study of *individuals* and *sociology* as the study of *groups*.[10] As is well-known, in all his major works, Durkheim maintained that social phenomena possess a unique reality of their own, distinguishing them totally from individual (i.e. psychological) phenomena, thus protecting the domain he was in the process of establishing from the threat of psychological reductionism. The whole is always greater than the sum of its parts: and according to Durkheim, only the "social" can explain the "social". This is the fundamental parsimony principle in sociology and in social anthropology. However, Durkheim was careful to acknowledge also that his own sociological approach constituted a special psychology with its own object and distinctive method. Hence without undue logical embarrassment, Durkheim could unfold his sacred trinity of society, sentiments and symbols as three, interdependent and mutually sustaining forces. In a manner that can be reconciled (for those who wish to do so) both with contemporary learning theory (Stimulus and Response) and with transactionalism, Durkheim considered that group behaviour created sentiments of loyalty and solidarity which, in turn, were reflected in such collective symbols as national flags or clan totems. Rituals, centering on symbols, served to recharge and maintain the corresponding sentiments and so enhance collective identity. Society, narcissistically regularly celebrated itself, eternally contemplating its own navel.

Durkheim's main proseletyser in England and the immediate source of the Durkheimian tradition in British social anthropology, Radcliffe-Brown, applied—with due acknowledgement—the same style of analysis, with a similar terminology, to the religious beliefs and sentiments of the Andaman Islanders in his classic monograph, *The Andaman Islanders* (1922). These simple hunters and gatherers possessed little formal social organisation and their sentiments of mutual dependence (at a level of social grouping which he did not specify) were, according to Radcliffe-Brown, focussed by what amounts to a sort of displacement, on various symbolic objects (e.g. foods, fire, body paints, etc.) whose ceremonial use and veneration thus sustained

10. Cf. Murdock, 1971, p. 30. For a comprehensive assessment of Durkheim's shifting position on this question, see Lukes, 1973.

group identity and cohesion. Here, recapitulating a long philosophical tradition, Radcliffe-Brown sought to explore the nature of social obligation and the sentiments binding the individual to other members of his community —a problem of perennial concern as Abner Cohen's contribution to the present volume indicates. For, as Radcliffe-Brown put it, "no society can exist without the presence in the minds of its members of some form or other of the sentiment of moral obligation" (Radcliffe-Brown, op. cit., p. 402). Such "sentiments or motives", like the Englishman's dog, required regular exercise if they were to retain their vigour and vitality. Ritual fulfilled this crucial constitutional function, allowing the sentiments of mutual concern on which sociability depends to be kept in good repair. Unlike so many derivative accounts by subsequent writers, this analysis is characterised by a refreshingly frank and profuse use of psychological terms, appropriate enough in one writing so assertively about the inner feelings of his informants. Later, however, perhaps recalling the stern (if conflicting) admonitions of Durkheim, Radcliffe-Brown evidently had doubts about the wisdom of so blatantly advertising the true nature of his enterprise. For in his own corrected version of the first edition of *The Andaman Islanders*, he systematically expunged all references to the increasingly offensive word "psychology".[11] Why subsequent editions never contained these drastic amendments remains a matter for conjecture. I suspect, however, that the preparation of a suitably bowldlerised version would have required too extreme and traumatic amendment and that ultimately Radcliffe-Brown was as confused (or undecided) as his master Durkheim on this sensitive issue.

IV

As his pupils have been only too eager to proclaim, Radcliffe-Brown's other early work is equally psychological in tone. We find the same reliance on the explanatory power of sentiments in his famous elucidation of the striking difference which occurs in many patrilineal societies between the relationship of father and son and mother's brother and sister's son (Radcliffe-Brown, 1924). The friendly warmth which distinguishes the latter from the cold formality of the former can, in Radcliffe-Brown's view, be traced to the contrasting relations between a child and his two parents. The mother's brother is, on this argument, in effect a male mother-figure, sharing the same warm maternal feelings towards her child as his sister. The sentiments which the mother feels and the child reciprocates are "extended" to embrace the maternal uncle. Although Radcliffe-Brown does not couch this in the Oedipal terms a Freudian might apply, there is nó doubt that his

11. See Stevenson, *Man*, 1969, p. 135.

analysis is grounded in psychological affect. The term "sentiment" is also used here in its traditional English sense to signify feelings which are independent of, and may be opposed to, both duty and interest.

The emphasis placed upon *feelings* in understanding relationships is equally evident in the logical extension of Radcliffe-Brown's theory proposed by Homans and Schneider (1955). As every anthropology student of kinship knows, the latter postulate that in societies where cousin marriage is customary, the choice between marrying a *maternal* or *paternal* cousin will depend upon the distribution of "jural authority". Where, as in patrilineal societies, fathers firmly control their sons, the latter, will be moved by sentiment to seek brides from their mother's side of the family, marrying maternal cousins (as Radcliffe-Brown's interpretation of the patrilineal complex would lead us to expect). Conversely where, as in matrilineal societies, authority lies with the maternal uncle rather than the father, sister's sons will marry girls from their *father's* side of the family. As Homans (1962, p. 33) writes retrospectively, this is a "structural proposition stating a relationship between two kinds of institution—the locus of jural authority and the form of unilateral cross-cousin marriage". The "sentiments" which provide the emotional (or motivational) bridge here are generated from the kinship matrix and parental authority structure described. It is consequently sharply ironical that the final punchline in Rodney Needham's polished polemic, *Structure and Sentiment* (1962), which tendentiously and in places disingenuously attempts to demolish this argument is the famous quotation from Durkheim: "Whenever a social phenomenon is directly explained by a psychological phenomenon we may be sure that the explanation is false" (Durkheim, 1901, p. 128). Needham studiously refrains from mentioning Durkheim's other descriptions (referred to above, p. 6) of his own work as a "kind of psychology". For naturally as a good British social anthropologist, Needham is well aware that if one wishes to discredit a fellow anthropologist, the most effective method is to accuse him of arguing "psychologically".[12] That is most damning.

The sentiments extended so liberally in these examples (from son to mother, to mother's brother, to mother's brother's daughter) are stretched even further and given a different twist in Meyer Fortes' talmudic treatment of Tallensi and other ancestor cults (Fortes, 1945; 1949; 1959; 1965). In this case the sentiments mirrored are those on the side through which descent *is* traced (i.e. paternally in a patrilineal system) rather than those on the other "extra-descent" side. Here, according to Fortes, the filial piety which paternal authority evokes is kicked upstairs to the supernatural plane to animate the ancestors. The reverence parents receive when they

---

12. For an admirable analysis of the logical deficiencies in Homans and Schneider's thesis and those in Needham's counter-attack, see Spiro, 1964.

are alive becomes a religion when they die. But of course in this patriarchal setting filial feeling is not untouched by ambivalence, and hence the ancestors may be capricious and "persecutory" as well as benevolent. As Professor Fortes has from time to time hinted and frankly acknowledged in his recent Ernest Jones Memorial Lecture to the Psychoanalytical Society (Fortes, 1972), his projective analysis is in the best Freudian tradition.[13] He has recently added the traditional Chinese ancestor cult to his collection (Fortes, 1965), apparently oblivious of the fact that Francis Hsu had already in 1948 *explicitly* employed Abram Kardiner's family authority projection theory in interpreting the same material!

Professor Max Gluckman's treatment of issues which he clearly felt to be acutely prone to psychological pollution is even more intriguing. For over forty years—the major part of his long, distinguished career—Gluckman wrestled valiantly, if as it seemed to some critics inconclusively, with the foul fiend psychology. The ethnographic origins of Gluckman's (1962) celebrated cathartic theory of "rituals of rebellion" which permit people to let off steam periodically relatively harmlessly, can be traced back to a paper published in 1935 with the unassuming title: "Zulu women in hoe-cultural ritual". This modest work argued quite straightforwardly that the unexpected prominence of women in certain Zulu ritual contexts was to be seen, with their virtual monopoly of the position of spirit-possessed diviner, as a form of feminist protest in a male-dominated society. Since then in a long series of revisionist treatments of the same theme, Professor Gluckman has gone to inordinate lengths to deny that his theory is in any way psychological, although he continues to employ the provocative and suggestive term "cathartic". He stoutly maintains that when he speaks of people acting in cathartic rituals he does not mean that they are "acting out" (Gluckman, 1962; 1963).

In the same fashion, Gluckman stubbornly insists it is entirely wrong to regard as psychological the well-known anthropological interpretation of accusations of witchcraft as expressions of social tension and conflict. He therefore counsels his colleagues to avoid such controversial terms as "projection" in case they give the wrong impression (Gluckman, 1964). Here it might be added parenthetically, Gluckman continued the tradition of his illustrious teacher, Evans-Pritchard, who similarly regularly

---

13. So pervasive is this psychoanalytic emphasis that as David McKnight (1967) has noted in a lively critique, even Jack Goody's (1962) economically based revision of the Fortesian approach suffers from the same fatal taint. As McKnight demonstrates, both Fortes and Goody are on particularly difficult ground when they attempt to account for the marked malevolence of ancestors on that side of the family through which descent is *not* traced. Such "extra-descent" ancestors pose a problem which McKnight explains in terms of their membership of an external and therefore hostile group. This "stranger-danger" theory is itself, perhaps, not entirely innocent of psychological allusions.

inveighed against psychology and psychoanalysis, although his own brilliant account of the fail-safe circularity of Zande witchcraft beliefs (Evans-Pritchard, 1937) seems strongly influenced by Freud's notion of "secondary elaboration". And so it goes on for, in his turn, Gluckman's pupil, Max Marwick (1970, pp. 16–17) with exquisite subtlety, similarly distinguishes between "psychological theories" referring to the "projection" of "conflicts", and "sociological theories" involving amongst other things "retrospective projection for feelings of guilt" and "social tension". How *social* tension has to become before it ceases to be *psychological* is not explained!

It seems to have entirely escaped the attention of these anthropologists that over the years psychologists, psychiatrists and even psychoanalysts (see, e.g. Rycroft and Grof below) have come a long way to meet us here. The modern psychodynamic approach which analyses neurosis in terms of interpersonal tensions is very close to the "anthropological" or "sociological" tension theory of witchcraft which, as I have argued elsewhere (Lewis, 1973, p. 20), is actually drawn directly from the witchcraft beliefs of the peoples studied by anthropologists. Such indeed is the degree of coincidence here between anthropological (and native) theory on the one hand, and that of modern psychiatry on the other, that a leading transcultural psychiatrist (Kiev, 1972, pp. 171–2) warns of the potential dangers which may result from the premature introduction of the psychodynamic approach in societies where people traditionally believe in witches!

Of course, we must quickly add that the British social anthropologist's difficulty in perceiving and acknowledging this correspondence between "psychological" and "sociological" theory here is reinforced rather than reduced by the more bizarre interpretations proposed by some writers of the Culture and Personality School. For example, Whiting and Child (1953) initially found themselves unable to decide between the behaviourist view that fear of sorcery derived from repressed aggression and the psychoanalytic explanation that its basis lay in sexual inhibition and latent homosexuality. More recently, however, Harrington and Whiting (1972) have proposed the compromise theory that *sorcery* is associated with inhibition of aggression, while *witchcraft* is connected with "conflict in the area of sex". The trouble with this ingenious synthesis, however, is that in most cultures where people believe in witches or sorcerers they do not distinguish absolutely between these two malevolent figures which merge into a hybrid entity employing *both* magical spells and malign psychic power. And where the distinction is made, both beliefs often co-exist within the same culture with a common pattern of child-rearing. The psychoanalytically inclined American anthropologist, Melford Spiro (1969, p. 256) makes the astounding claim that in Burma it is not paranoid to believe in witches—as long as you don't actually accuse anyone of bewitching you. It is only apparently when you activate your cultural beliefs that in Spiro's view you become paranoid! No wonder so many British social anthropologists should behave similarly when they encounter such implausible assertions.

But, as might be anticipated, the very violence of our righteous indignation masks out continuing if covert flirtation with psychological and even more dubious assumptions. An outstanding contemporary example here is provided by Mary Douglas's (1970) popular analysis of religion. This returns us directly to the familiar Durkheimian psychological tradition in its authoritarian, Stimulus-Response mode. Religious feeling, we are told, simply mirrors or mimics the prevailing social conditions following the sacred "principle of symbolic replication" (Douglas, 1970, p. 82). The idea here is not that illustrated so admirably in Vieda Skultans' contribution below (p.225), that we should expect to find some consistency between the leading assumptions of a given period or culture, but rather that the same simple parallelism should also extend to feelings. States of bodily dissociation in trance and possession provide Douglas with what she calls a "test case" for her theory of symbols and sentiments. Such abandoned behaviour is, she contends, symptomatic and so symbolic of social dissociation, being the product of loose, permissive social conditions. Tightly integrated communities will, she considers, regard possession and trance as dangerous states to be avoided at all costs. Weakly integrated communities will have no such compunctions and welcome trance with open arms.

Three well-known southern Sudanese peoples, the Nuer, Dinka and Mandari, are cited in support of this thesis, along with a more esoteric ethnic group—the "Bog Irish". "Among the Nuer", Professor Douglas discerns, "trance is held to be dangerous" whereas among the "Dinka it is held beneficient". The Mandari, she considers, display an intensification of the Nuer hostility and fear for trance and possession. Thus, the three peoples can be arranged in the following order of increasing aversion to bodily abandonment: Dinka, Nuer and Mandari.[14] This ordering, Professor Douglas considers, is the same as that in which the three societies stand in terms of increasing social integration: or to employ her own terms, in order of increasing stress on "group" and "grid".[15] Hence, on this eclectic interpretation of the evidence from these three Sudanese tribes, the more loosely organised the society, the greater the bodily abandonment. The "Bog Irish"—the immigrant building site workers of Camden Town, North London—are dragged in to round out the argument. They are held to represent a tightly structured community, living under oppressive social

14. Douglas's sources here are respectively: Lienhardt, 1961; Evans-Pritchard, 1956; and Buxton, 1968.

15. I hesitate to gloss these rather esoteric terms which are best examined in the context in which Douglas discusses them. They are meant to provide a way of measuring comparatively the hold which different communities exert on their members.

conditions, and not given to bodily abandonment—an assessment which I must confess does not entirely tally with my own observations of the Friday-night pub behaviour of those concerned.

In this fashion in company with a number of other writers on possession (e.g. Eliade, 1951; de Heusch, 1962;[16] and Bourguignon, 1967; 1973), Douglas naïvely supposes that there is a *direct coincidence* between religious experience and social structure, and more specifically, that "negative" evaluations of trance behaviour are to be taken at face value as signifying encounters with malevolent mystical forces and hence require different treatment and even different social conditions from those associated with positively valued ecstatic experiences. This approach which is strongly reminiscent of the gross over-simplifications of the Culture and Personality School, ignores the familiar experience of "bad trips", the basic psychological principle of ambivalence, and, for that matter, the old cliché of the agony and the ecstasy. The truth is rather that, as Pamela Constantinides and Serge Larose show later in this book, ecstatic experiences regularly assume a highly conventional character. They also typically include both "negative" and "positive" episodes or phases, as Grof's rich phenomenological exploration of LSD-therapy emphasises. Hence, what begins as a fearful "unsolicited" intrusion by a spirit, often indeed as an illness or psychic trauma, regularly achieves its climax in a glorious communion with the divine (cf. Lewis, 1966; 1971).

Thus the "negatively" and "positively" charged forms of ecstasy are frequently successive phases in what is ultimately a continuous spectrum or fugue of religious experience. Moreover, much of the evidence indicates, contrary to Douglas's view, that the ecstatic style of religiosity is typically a response not to lack of structure, but to an oppressive excess of it. The psychological assumptions involving a compensatory response (of *reaction* rather than passive acquiescence) are here drawn more explicitly and seem, on the whole, more securely founded. Certainly they accord well with the psychiatrist's notion of "secondary gains" accruing to the manipulative "patient" responding to stress in contexts of deprivation (see, e.g. Yap, 1960). However, in the final analysis, these contradictory views of the social precipitants of ecstasy are not necessarily entirely incompatible. It appears to me possible that, in certain circumstances, the experience of extreme indeterminancy and of chaotic disorder may indeed be overwhelmingly oppressive and so produce the same grounds for mental and bodily dissociation as those engendered by an excess of order and structure. As is so often the case, the extremes meet, as the gamut of paradoxical sensations reported by Dr. Grof implies.

16. Luc de Heusch has since revised his position, recognising the ambivalence of such experience (see de Heusch, 1972).

A similar conflict of psychological position can be seen to underlie that noble explanatory edifice of Mediterranean anthropology summed up in the phrase "honour and shame". Some of those who use this portmanteau formula as an analytical device, clearly imply a confirmatory view of honour as the prize that falls naturally to those who succeed in the battle of life (e.g. Friedl, 1962, p. 84). Others, however, see honour as a consolation which the weak and the powerless receive as a compensatory virtue (e.g. Cutileiro, 1971, p. 294).[17] On a much wider theoretical front, the first position broadly corresponds with that informing the fashionable interactionist/transactionist (game theory) approach represented in social anthropology by Barth, Bailey, and in his earlier political work, by Leach. This clearly depends upon an Adlerian paradigm, assuming a universal motivation to maximise political power. Much the same Adlerian view of political man seems to be implied in the social psychologists' new version of the Protestant ethic—"achievement motivation"

Finally to conclude what might otherwise become a long catalogue of psychological correspondences, we may note with some interest how French Structuralism and American Cognitive Anthropology have close, if generally unrecognised connexions with Kelly's Construct Theory (Kelly, 1955) in psychology and have both been similarly criticised for being excessively mentalistic.[18] At a deeper structural level, of course, Structuralism borrows heavily from Freud and also, which is not so well known, from Géza Roheim (e.g. 1930). It has indeed been well said of Lévi-Strauss that he is a cosmic analyst whose patients are myths. It is ironical that while it took a Frenchman (Durkheim), acting through a British intermediary (Radcliffe-Brown) to banish (at least officially) psychology and psychoanalysis from social anthropology, it has taken another Frenchman (Lévi-Strauss), with another local counterpart (Leach)[19] to reintroduce them in such a subtly disguised form that they pass unnoticed into our everyday theoretical currency.

V

Even from this brief record it should be plain that, despite the ambiguous legacy from Durkheim, British social anthropology has for long been living in sin with psychology and psychoanalysis. One of our major aims in this symposium is to urge that the time has come to regularise the relationship:

17. I am indebted to Katie Platt for pointing this out to me.

18. Anthropologists will find additional food for thought in the fact that Kelly appears to relate emotion to the perception of anomalies and hence shares common ground with Festinger and his theory of cognitive dissonance as well as with the work of Douglas and Leach on taxonomic classification.

19. Despite his frequent disavowal by the master, some credit must also be given here to Rodney Needham's painstaking interpretations of Lévi-Strauss.

there seems little chance that we shall ever otherwise achieve that "coming to terms with psychology" so forcefully advocated by Raymond Firth (1951, p. 485) over twenty years ago. It is simply no longer good enough to pretend that the protective posture of blissful ignorance towards the findings of psychology and psychoanalysis recommended by Gluckman (1964) still entitles us to ignore what our colleagues in these adjacent fields have to say about the emotions and motives we so carelessly impute to our informants. Whether we are concerned with witchcraft, ritual or symbolism when we assert that customs and institutions significantly modify people's feelings or exert specific effects on their emotions we must be prepared to seek the best possible independent evidence. Our traditional defence mechanism has worn threadbare and it is time that we abandoned it altogether. As the earlier discussion shows, we must also be much more explicitly aware of the psychological status of our own interpretative assumptions and so better equipped to assess their value and plausibility.

As I have stressed, the eclecticism that is here proposed should not in my opinion entail the uncritical acceptance of stock psychoanalytic interpretations or their wholesale and indiscriminate application to exotic ethnographic data which are then tortuously manipulated to fit and further legitimise ethnocentric theory. General psychoanalytic theories and mechanisms cannot in themselves provide necessary and sufficient causal explanations of *particular forms* of exotic customs or beliefs. Since they cannot thus satisfactorily explain causally (or explain away), our particularistic cultural data—although they may help to elucidate them, as Audrey Cantlie suggests in her contribution on Hindu asceticism—we have nothing to lose and everything to gain by considering in an unprejudiced fashion whether their application to our material enhances our anthropological interpretation.

Conversely, we might also reflect that, as anthropologists, we have a duty to scrutinise the culturally specific case material of psychiatrists and psychoanalysts in the light of our broader cross-cultural experience. Just as I have argued elsewhere (Lewis, 1971, p. 193) the comparison of psychiatrists and psychoanalysts with shamans and "witch-doctors" throws as much light on the former as on the latter, so our psychic experience should be set in a much wider cultural perspective if we are to identify what is universal and what is culturally specific in the inner life of men. If, for instance, as Serge Larose reports below of Haitian Vodu and as others have elsewhere, parallel cultural conceptions to the Freudian constructs of id, ego and super ego, we must register these correspondences and carefully weigh their implications. This is the only way in which we can ever hope to achieve a valid cross-cultural psychology of the human personality. This is what transcultural psychiatry should be, but is not. If anthropologists are not prepared to play their part here they must accept some of the blame when items from their ethnographic inventory are appropriated piecemeal and interpreted out of context by psychiatrists and psychoanalysts.

As others have observed before, one of the most intractable problems here is to know how to treat and what value to place upon ethnographic parallels in symbolism. The difficulty is increased rather than diminished when a symbolic motif in one culture is implicit, or unconscious whereas in another it is explicit and conscious. Prime examples are those "natural symbols" connected with the universal biological life of man in copulation, birth and death to which Freud attached such importance and which we today glibly identify as Freudian. Although, as Charles Rycroft reminds us, they need not always be so, these tend to be erotic in content. We can readily understand (and so potentially misunderstand) the use of genital sexuality (and its products, e.g. semen) as a symbol for power or energy in the Punjab or in Hindu asceticism generally. After all, as Vieda Skultans reminds us, our ancestors were almost as obsessed by the virtues of sexual continence as the Hindu ascetics Audrey Cantlie discusses. Nor can we fail to be struck by the remarkable Freudian character (this time at the anal level) of the late English medieval institution of the Groom of the Stool presented in such rich detail by David Starkey. We have, however, in these three examples already moved from an explicit to an implicit (or conscious to unconscious) level of analysis; for if the Hindus in question are well aware of the mundane sexual allusions of these highly charged symbols, it is far from clear that Henry VIII's contemporaries understood the Freudian allusions of the royal stool (i.e. excreta) in the way that a modern psychoanalyst would.

Thus some peoples (none more blatantly perhaps than the Australian aborigines)[20] seem to treat their arcane sexual symbolism explicitly in the manner of a Freudian analyst. Others, however, lack this insight and the Freudian interpretation has to be teased out in an elaborate (and often unconvincing) exegesis. Are then those explicitly recognised conscious symbols in the first case less significant than their unconscious, covert counterparts? This, of course, is what the conventional Freudian wisdom teaches and the anthropologist also is apt to feel that, as soon as a symbol can be completely distilled into its component elements, it melts away becoming little more than a conventional gesture or a figure of speech (which is roughly equivalent to the degraded popular concept of a symbol as something signifying nothing).

Here Charles Rycroft's incisive and undogmatic explication of the levels of symbolic expression seems particularly timely. Rycroft challenges the

---

20. Compare for instance the analyst Roheim's interpretations of these data with those by anthropologists (e.g. Berndt, 1951, and McKnight, 1973).

orthodox Freudian view of "true symbols" which are predominantly sexual and unconscious. Symbols, as he wittily illustrates, may be more or less conscious or cognitive and carry a highly variable emotional charge. It is absurd to suppose that some are "true" and others "false"—even if we enlarge our range of examples to include the deliberate symbolising of the mass media and advertising agencies. What is much more significant is the nature of the emotional loading associated with a given symbol in a given context. Here in psychoanalytic parlance we are concerned with the distinction between "modified" and "unmodified" affect, and so return to our primary theme: the nexus binding symbols and sentiments. As Rycroft's picturesque examples from individual case histories show, for psychoanalysts as for anthropologists there is ultimately no invariant, universally valid equation linking particular symbols with particular feelings in all cases and cultures. There are common symbolic motifs: but their cognitive and affectual significance is not given *a priori* and can only be discovered by painstaking, particularistic investigation. Here the anthropologist who is prepared to make discriminating use of psychoanalytic and psychiatric insights has as much to gain as those analysts who return the compliment.

VI

These preliminary remarks will perhaps serve to set the essays which follow in an anthropological context. Alfred Gell opens our discussion with an incisive examination of that highly evocative symbolic essence—perfume—which, as he so well puts it, is halfway between a thing and an idea, ideally suited to mark an end or a beginning. The symbolic significance of smells and their association with moods and feelings—as in "good" and "bad" smells (including those of success and sanctity)—which is firmly embedded in our own folklore is a curiously neglected theme in the comparative study of symbolism, although Radcliffe-Brown (1922) long ago called attention to it, referring picturesquely to the Andaman Islanders' "calendar of scents". In the New Guinea culture discussed by Gell, the words "smell" and "dream" are semantically closely related and the hunter who seeks to secure success in the hunt places *oktesap* perfume under his pillow at night. The ensuing sweet dreams should include the conquest of women. Since success in the chase requires sexual chastity (after the manner of the chaste huntress Diana), this dream has a hidden meaning. Love-making in the dream state signifies its opposite—catching pigs and eating them—in the waking state.

Gell thus calls attention to the insubstantial character of symbols and their not fully determined relation to the thing they stand for. The limits of the symbolic equation, again in a New Guinea context, are further explored by Gilbert Lewis who points out that if "symbols" acquire a genuine life of their own and true autonomy, they cease to be understudies and become substitutes and hence alternatives to what may originally have been signified. Hence, if for the actors, the lethal rituals employed by outraged maternal uncles against delinquent uterine nephews are as effective as the actual physical murder which they mimic they can hardly be aptly characterised as "symbolic" action (except by ethnocentric anthropologists). Yet as Gilbert Lewis acknowledges, the issue is not quite as simple as this. For there are varieties of effectiveness and different degrees of belief in the efficacy of the same spell or rite. There are moreover, circumstances in which what is felt to be a problematic and conditional course of action may seem more appropriate than a definitive, irreversible act.

The extent to which the "symbolic" curse examined by Gilbert Lewis constitutes something more than an assuaging expression of righteous indignation seems debatable. In the case of the Sudanese women's healing cult discussed by Pamela Constantinides it is clear that symbolic action not only affects the inner psychic life of the spirit-possessed devotee but also provides a means of modifying her domestic circumstances. The symbols involved, readily invoked with the aid of incense (known appropriately as the "key to dreams"), are seemingly autonomous spirits which, however, speak for their human hosts in that most persuasive and irrefutable language of all: "tongues". These powerful forces which announce their intrusion in the lives of women through illness and domestic crisis both summarise and recapitulate the history of the Sudan and refer directly to the perennial, timeless problems of fertility, life and death. Their demands, through the sickness they inflict upon their female victims, ultimately reach the latters' husbands and male kin. The effect of this feminist cult of affliction, as with so many others elsewhere, is thus to enable the "weaker sex" in a male-dominated Muslim society to achieve what Dr. Constantinides calls a "subtle adjustment of position" and to overcome problems that prevent women from conforming adequately to the ideal norms. The domestic focus of the cult is strongly reflected in the pervasive marital symbolism employed. The patient is referred to as the "bride" of the spirits which in turn are known as "threads", suggesting that the human host is conceived of as a kind of puppet. Other aspects of the power imagery that appears to be involved here (as in the word *dustuur*, "constitution") are hinted at in Dr Constantinides suggestive account and clearly merit further research.

Serge Larose's novel contribution to the study of Vodu demonstrates how possession cults may, in contrast, also play a dominant, authoritarian role at the centre of society, in this case as part of the ancestor cult of the Haitian peasantry. As in the Sudan, here too the spirit pantheon reassembles the past, a past in which Guinea, symbolising the proud African heritage, is the corner-stone of the spiritual universe. Of course, as Larose brings out brilliantly, the unchanging character of the spirit world is an illusion: all is really flux. What were originally sinister sources of self-seeking anti-social magical power (literally "points"[21] and some "skin-head" spirits) are, as they pass into a family's spiritual heritage, trans-formed into sedate, benevolent, and socially acceptable *loas* and are in time admitted into the ultimate spiritual establishment, the sacred kingdom of Guinea. The conflict and tension between self-interest and group-interest to which Abner Cohen and other contributors to this volume direct atten-tion is thus here expressed directly in the most dramatic symbolic form. As Larose sums it up: "By magic one separates his own private destiny from his ancestral background, looking forward to his own descendants, to his own establishment in opposition to all others." Thus the developmental cycle of religion is closely tailored to that of the families it represents. Nurture (magic) constantly becomes nature (religion).

The way in which the dialectic between self and group is treated sym-bolically is the central theme in Abner Cohen's thoughtful contribution. The identity of the self, Cohen reminds us, is continuously created and re-created through symbolic action. Here in line with Victor Turner's analysis of ritual (Turner, 1969), but also harking back to the preoccupations of Radcliffe-Brown himself, Cohen contends that ritual and symbolism pro-vide the means by which irksome duties and tasks are disguised and mysti-fied and so sanctified and made to seem desirable. Ultimately, he argues, the moral sense of obligation is rooted deep in the human psyche and should be explored in terms of the structure of the self, of personal identity and integration. We must thus discard the strongly entrenched sociological stance that treats the members of a community as if they were all equally effectively socialised. We must be prepared to take account of variations in motivation (which are, after all, even recognised by sociologists under the unhelpful label "deviance") and in the extent to which individuals are sensi-tive to and actually honour the obligations thrust upon them by society. A possible line of advance here, Cohen suggests, would combine a bio-graphical approach, network analysis and entail the co-operation of psychologists and psychoanalysts. This prescription comes close to the epidemiological approach which I and others have recently found valuable in the study of spirit possession and ecstatic cults.

For reasons that have been discussed above, these recommendations will not readily commend themselves to the more conservative of British social anthropologists. However, if anything is capable of swaying anthropological

---

21. Notice the same imagery is employed in Hindu mysticism; see below, Cantlie, p. 259.

opinion it must surely be Charles Rycroft's generous ecumenical essay in which he subjects the basic structure of Freudian symbolism to searching criticism. As we have already noted, Rycroft's presentation of symbolism as embracing a wide spectrum of cognitive and affectual elements helps to clarify the ongoing debate in anthropology about the effectiveness and meaning of conscious and unconscious symbols. Equally welcome is his open-ended, undogmatic exploration of the cognitive and emotional signi-ficance of symbols in their specific contexts which, as with Hadfield's work on the interpretation of dreams (Hadfield, 1954), is very much in the prag-matic anthropological tradition. At the same time, few anthropologists would now want to dispute Rycroft's contention that "human beings are much more preoccupied with their biological destiny and with their intimate personal relationships than most of them realise".

This considered, if subtly modified stress on "natural", biologically linked symbols is amply confirmed by the rich phantasmagoria of symbolic themes culled from LSD therapy by Dr Stanislav Grof. Here therapy has become religion and we confront an extraordinary diversity of psychic experience, centering on the womb, birth and death. Grof argues that this material challenges established psychoanalytic categories, suggesting a new system of analysis which would subsume Freudian, Jungian, and (I would add) Kleinian, assumptions. Professional analysts will be better equipped than anthropologists to assess the intriguing analytical construct of Con-densed Experience Systems (a kind of long-hand for symbols), and Peri-natal Matrices, as heuristic rather than causal principles, which Grof proposes. (In this context, the term matrix, which etymologically means womb, seems particularly apt.) From an anthropological perspective, the "deep parallel between biological delivery and sexual orgasm" which Grof registers seems highly suggestive, indeed it parallels exactly those shama-nistic rites in which the summit of ecstasy is conceived as an incestuous uterine orgasm. His finding that, phenomenologically, the "agony of death becomes indistinguishable from the ecstasy of being born" is again in har-mony with much anthropological evidence on rites of passage and limina-lity. It is fascinating to learn too that in the course of LSD therapy women often could not tell whether they were giving birth or being born them-selves. This, I suspect, may throw new light on the frequently reported "psychological pregnancies" observed in spirit possession and so contri-bute, from a somewhat more earthy angle than usual, to the rather rarified anthropological debate about virgin birth. More generally in relation to the central theme of this book, Dr. Grof's contribution is of great importance in so thoroughly demonstrating phenomenologically the paradoxical oscil-lation of extremes which is so characteristic of the deepest emotional experience. This evidence is all the more telling since, as its presenter acknowledges, it defies his neat expository scheme. The relevant implications for anthropological attempts to identify styles of religiosity with particular feelings and emotional states have already been noted above (p. 121).

Grof does not claim (although at times he seems to imply) that these perinatal experiences have a causal force on later life. John Payne's carefully controlled exploration of the roots of symbolic violence in cases drawn from his own psychiatric practise explicitly seeks to establish a causal nexus, although the origins are not traced to such an early point in life. Rejecting Freud's notion of the death instinct (*pace* Hayley) Payne shows how violently aggressive reactions (of the baby-bashing type), directed at objects of affection and love, recapitulate suppressed earlier experiences of rejection and oppression. Here, in contrast to the situation discussed at length in Gilbert Lewis's paper, it is real violence that is unquestionably symbolic rather than symbolic violence that is questionably real.

David Starkey's paper presents material which will intrigue anthropologists and psychoanalysts as much as historians. He examines the very important role played in fifteenth and sixteenth century politics by those shadowy and usually neglected figures, the Grooms of the King's Stool, who through their intimate body service more than anyone else participated in the royal charisma which, in this period, was most powerfully expressed in his physical body—"his lively image". These royal lavatory attendants, the nearest thing the monarch had to friends, could represent the king more completely than any other dignitary in the realm. The unsettled political conditions of fifteenth and sixteenth century England, necessitated frequent royal military intervention if the monarch's authority was to be successfully sustained. The consequent demand for unswervingly loyal royal representatives and ambassadors who could act as "agent symbols" for their monarch, Starkey argues, favoured the development of the institution of the Groom of the Stool and the rise of the Privy Chamber, with a membership drawn from the middle and upper gentry. The revolution of 1688 dealt a mortal blow to the concept of divine kingship, and so the office of the Groom of the Stool declined accordingly. Anthropologists are familiar with the West African notion of a "stool" (i.e. seat) as embodying the power of a person or office, and psychoanalysts need not be reminded that the faeces symbolise money or power. Starkey's intriguing contribution brings these two facets together, posing for further research the whole question of the contemporary attitudes towards bodily excreta in this period of English history.

Vieda Skultans' paper moves us forward from anal to genital symbolism. Her thesis is that the ebulliently optimistic conditions of the first half of nineteenth century England fostered a view of mental illness which could be cured by self-mastery. The less mobile world of the second half of the century, in contrast, prompted a fatalistic view of mental disease as a hereditary curse from which there could be no escape. Nature had irrevocably reasserted her authority over nurture. While some will read Dr. Skultans' contribution as a parable on the contemporary psychiatry/anti-psychiatry debate, in the present context we should note how this nineteenth century obsession with the pernicious evils of masturbation and seminal loss can be seen to reflect the prevailing emphasis on self-control and self-management. The most persuasive demonstration of self-mastery was below the belt.

The symbolic significance of semen as power is a central focus of Audrey Cantlie's sensitive appraisal of Hindu asceticism. Here, as we have noted earlier, there is an explicit theory that bases ascetic virtue and power upon seminal retention, a cultural theme which she considers is a kind of mirror image of the (Kleinian) psychoanalytical concept of the breast that feeds itself. Audrey Cantlie also proposes that the ascetic stress on renunciation of the world and return to the primordial beginning (cf. the return to the womb in Grof's material) represents a disguised (and perhaps modified) expression of Freud's death instinct. This bold thesis which will certainly arouse controversy leads Cantlie to argue that, in the Hindu caste system, it may be more illuminating to define purity negatively in terms of lack of impurity rather than vice versa.

Paul Hershman pursues these issues further and with a different emphasis in the context of Sikh religious symbolism where, as he says in a phrase pithily recalling one of our recurrent themes in this symposium: "What is most powerful is most dirty." The problem here is that perennial issue of reconciling the diverse, contradictory aspects of female sexuality. Like so many other peoples, Punjabis place a high value on virginity and motherhood, but abhor the sexuality which transforms the former into the latter and the attendant pollution associated with childbirth. They want the baby, but not the bath water. This dilemma is clearly expressed symbolically. They worship as a mother figure, generously bestowing her fertility on humans, the capricious virgin goddess *Mātā*. The sacred cow, the "mother of men", constitutes a second and more placid maternal image whose benificent ministrations neutralise the polluting sexual exhudations which otherwise threaten to overwhelm men. The fiendish goddess *Mātā*, astride her tiger, with her hair unbound and "powerfully free", clearly represents unbridled lust—raw sexuality which has to be tamed and domesticated by that familiar ruminant, the cow. So, in this sprightly elucidation of the sanctity of the Hindu cow, Hershman argues that these two dominant symbols—the mother goddess who is a virgin, and the cow which is a "mother of men"—by their mutual collaboration resolve for the Sikhs the problems posed by the contradictory values of positive fertility and mother-hood on the one hand and negative female sexuality and birth on the other. This discussion of the symbolic expression of contradictory ideas and feelings thus fittingly returns us to one of the abiding common preoccupations of anthropologists and psychoanalysts: the conjunction of opposites.

Bibliography

Bateson, G. 1936. *Naven*, Stanford University Press, Stanford.

Bateson, G. 1972. *Steps to an Ecology of Mind*, Chandler, San Francisco.

Berndt, R. 1951. *Kunapipi: A Study of an Australian Aboriginal Religious Cult*, F. W. Cheshire, Melbourne.

Bourguignon, E. 1967. World distribution and patterns of possession states. *In* R. Prince (ed.) *Trance and Possession States*, Montreal.

Bourguignon, E. 1973. (ed.) *Religion, Altered States of Consciousness and Social Change*, Ohio State University Press, Ohio.

Buxton, J. 1968. Animal identity and human peril: some Mandari images, *Man* (N.S.) **3**, 35–49.

Campbell, D. T. and Naroll, R. 1972. The Mutual methodological relevance of anthropology and psychology. *In* F. L. K. Hsu (ed.) *Psychological Anthropology*, 435–68, Schenkman, Cambridge, Mass.

Carothers, J. C. 1951. Frontal lobe function and the African. *Journal of Mental Science*, **97**, 12–48.

Cutileiro, J. 1971. *A Portuguese Rural Society*, Clarendon Press, Oxford.

Devereux, G. 1956. Normal and abnormal: the key problem of psychiatric anthropology. *In* J. B. Casagrande and T. Gladwin (eds.) *Some Uses of Anthropology: Theoretical and Applied*, Washington.

Devereux, G. 1970. *Essai d'Ethnopsychiatie Générale*, Flammarion, Paris.

Devereux, G. 1972. *Ethnopsychanalyse Complémentariste*, Flammarion, Paris.

Douglas, M. 1970. *Natural Symbols: Explorations in Cosmology*, Barrie and Rockliff, London.

Durkheim, E. 1901. *Les Règles de la méthode sociologique*, Alcan, Paris.

Eliade, M. 1951. *Le Chamanisme et les techniques archaiques de l'extase*, Payot, Paris.

Evans-Pritchard, E. E. 1937. *Witchcraft, Oracles and Magic among the Azande*, Clarendon Press, Oxford.

Evans-Pritchard, E. E. 1956. *Nuer Religion*, Clarendon Press, Oxford.

Firth, Raymond. 1951. Contemporary British social anthropology. *American Anthropologist*, **53**, 474–89.

Firth, Raymond. 1973. *Symbols Public and Private*, Allen and Unwin, London.

Fortes, M. 1945. *The Dynamics of Clanship among the Tallensi*, Oxford University Press, London.

Fortes, M. 1949. *The Web of Kinship among the Tallensi*, Oxford University Press, London.

Fortes, M. 1957. Malinowski and the study of kinship. *In* R. Firth (ed.) *Man and Culture: An Evaluation of the Work of Bronislaw Malinowski*, 157–88, Routledge, London.

Fortes, M. 1959. *Oedipus and Job in West African Religion*, Cambridge University Press, Cambridge.

Fortes, M. 1965. Some reflections on ancestor worship. *In* M. Fortes and G. Dieterlen (eds.) *African Systems of Thought*, Oxford University Press, London.

Friedl, E. 1962. *Vasilika: a Village in Modern Greece*, Holt, Rinehart and Winston, New York.

Gluckman, M. 1935. Zulu women in hoe-cultural ritual. *Bantu Studies*, **9**, 255–71.

Gluckman, M. (ed.). 1962. *Essays on the Ritual of Social Relations*, Manchester University Press, Manchester.

Gluckman, M. 1963. *Order and Rebellion in Tribal Africa*, Cohen and West, London.

Gluckman, M. (ed.). 1964. *Closed Systems and Open Minds: The Limits of Naivety in Social Anthropology*, Oliver and Boyd, Edinburgh.

Goody, J. 1962. *Death, Property and the Ancestors*, Tavistock, London.

Hadfield, J. A. 1954. *Dreams and Nightmares*, Penguin, Harmondsworth.

Harrington, C. and Whiting, J. W. M. 1972. Socialization process and personality. *In* F. L. K. Hsu (ed.) *Psychological Anthropology*, Schenkman, Cambridge, Mass.

De Heusch, L. 1962. Cultes de possession et religions initiatiques de salut en Afrique. *Annales du Centre d'Etudes des Religions*, Brussels.

De Heusch, L. 1971. *Pourqoi l'épouser?* Gallimard, Paris.

Homans, G. 1962. *Sentiments and Activities*, Free Press, Glencoe.

Homans, G. and Schneider, D. 1955. *Marriage, Authority and Final Causes*, Free Press, Glencoe.

Hsu, F. 1948. *Under the Ancestors' Shadow*, Stanford University Press, Stanford.

Jahoda, G. 1972. A psychologist's perspective. *In* P. Mayer (ed.) *Socialization: the Approach from Social Anthropology*, Tavistock, London.

Kardiner, A. 1945. The concept of basic personality structure as an operational tool in the social sciences. *In* R. Linton (ed.) *The Science of Man in the World Crisis*, Columbia University Press, New York.

Kelly, G. A. 1955. *The Psychology of Personal Constructs*, Norton, New York.

Kiev, A. 1972. *Transcultural Psychiatry*, Free Press, New York.

La Barre, W. 1970. *The Ghost Dance*, Doubleday, New York.

Layard, J. 1942. *Stone Men of Malekula*, Chatto and Windus, London.

Lewis, I. M. 1966. Spirit possession and deprivation cults. *Man* (N.S.), **1**, 307–29.

Lewis, I. M. 1971. *Ecstatic Religion*, Penguin, Harmondsworth.

Lewis, I. M. 1973. *The Anthropologist's Muse*, S.E. London.

Lienhardt, G. 1961. *Divinity and Experience: the Religion of the Dinka*, Clarendon Press, Oxford.

Lukes, S. 1973. *Emile Durkheim: his Life and Work*, Allen Lane, London.

Malinowski, B. 1927. *Sex and Repression in Savage Society*, Kegan Paul, London.

Malinowski, B. 1927. *The Father in Primitive Psychology*, Kegan Paul, London.

McKnight, D. 1967. Extra-descent group ancestor cults in African societies. *Africa*, **37**, 1–21.

6cKnight, D. 1973. Sexual symbolism of food among the Wik-Mungkan. *Man* (N.S.), **8**, 194–209.

Muensterberger, W. and Esman, A. (eds.) 1972. *The Psychoanalytic Study of Society*, V, International University Press, New York.

Roheim, G. 1930. *Animism, Magic and the Divine King*, Kegan Paul, London.

Marwick, M. (ed.) 1970. *Witchcraft and Sorcery*, Penguin, Harmondsworth.

Murdock, G. P. 1972. Anthropology's mythology. *Proceedings Royal Anthropological Institute* (1971), 17–24.

Needham, R. 1962. *Structure and Sentiment*, University of Chicago Press, Chicago.

Radcliffe-Brown, A. R. 1922. *The Andaman Islanders*, Cambridge University Press, Cambridge.

Radcliffe-Brown, A. R. 1924. The mother's brother in South Africa. *South African Journal of Science*, **21**, 542–55.

Seligman, C. G. 1924. Anthropology and psychology: a study of some points of contact. *Journal Royal Anthropological Institute*, **54**, 13–46.

Silverman, J. 1967. Shamans and acute schizophrenia. *American Anthropologist*, **69**, 21–31.

Spiro, M. 1964. Causes, functions and cross-cousin marriage: an essay in anthropological explanation. *Journal Royal Anthropological Institute*, **94**, 30–43.

Spiro, M. 1969. The psychological function of witchcraft belief: the Burmese case. *In* W. Caudill and T-Y Lin (eds.) *Mental Health Research in Asia and the Pacific*, East-West-Center Press, Honolulu.

Stevenson, H. N. C. 1969. Psychology and social anthropology. *Man* (N.S.), **4**, 135.

Turner, V. 1964. Symbols in Ndembu ritual. *In* M. Gluckman (ed.) *Closed Systems and Open Minds*, Oliver and Boyd, Edinburgh.

Turner, V. 1969. *The Ritual Process: Structure and Anti-Structure*, Aldine, Chicago.

Whiting, J. W. M. and Child, I. 1953. *Child Training and Personality*, Yale University Press, New Haven.

Yap, P. M. 1960. The possession syndrome—a comparison of Hong Kong and French findings. *Journal Mental Science*, **106**, 114–37.

2 | Magic, Perfume, Dream ...

Alfred Gell

I

The Umeda[1] term which corresponds most closely to our word "magic" is *sap* (ginger). Besides referring to the varieties of *zingiber*, both wild and cultivated, that Umedas use in their magic, *sap*, as a suffixed element, means "the magic of such-and-such" thus: *oktesap*—the magic of pig-killing, *kwisap*—the cassowary-hunters magic, and so forth. It's on the first of these, *oktesap*, the magic of killing pigs, that I want to focus attention here. The ethnography involved is very simple, no spell, no cult, no ritual of any kind being involved. Yet the manner of operation of this *oktesap*, is, in its extreme simplicity, revealing in a way which many more complicated magical procedures are not. The problem of "magical efficacy"—the underlying problem with which this essay is concerned—is not one, I think, which will be ultimately clarified by more field research. The factual material available is plentiful and of high quality. Unfortunately, it is also paradoxical, and the difficulties of interpretation only seem to multiply the richer the material is. Hence the usefulness of restricting oneself to the simplest possible examples.

But there is also another, more immediate reason why I want to look particularly at the *oktesap* example. In a famous paper, Evans-Pritchard (1929) commented on the ephemeral nature of the Zande spell, as contrasted with the highly standardised incantations characteristic of Trobriand magic. The Trobriand word for magic is *megwa* "spell" and the material element "is of minor importance", whereas, in Zande, the word for magic is *ngwa* which really means "wood" but which Evans-Pritchard says refers to the "strange woods and rare roots" used in magic. Now I would like to make two suggestions in this connection: (i) that there is a complementarity between (standardised, formulaic) spells and *magical substances*; and (ii) where the "bias" of the system is away from spells (Trobriand-type) and toward substances (Zande-type) we will find a corresponding increase in the importance of the *olfactory* element in magic. Evans-Pritchard, it is true, does not single out scentedness as one of the characteristic features of the "strange woods and rare roots" used in Zande magic, thereby preventing us from pursuing this idea further in relation to the Zande material. Fortunately, I can be fairly explicit on this score where my own New Guinean material is concerned. In Umeda, at least, odoriferousness and magical significance were closely correlated, though not, to be sure, exclusively so. In numerous contexts, informants explicitly stated that it was the *smell* of a magical preparation which endowed it with its efficacy (*zingiber*-based medicines are prime examples of this). *Oketesap*, a common medicine consisting of a variety of *zingiber*, plus turmeric and perhaps some other ingredients which were not revealed to me, kept in a tightly bound sachet of bark (the porous underbark of *gnetum gnemon*) is entirely typical of Umeda magic as a whole. *Oktesap* works by smell, that is, the sachet containing the medicine is kept in the net-bag of the owner, gently infusing both the bag itself and the surrounding atmosphere with the special *sap* aroma. *Oktesap* is, in short, a magical perfume, attractive to the wild pigs which are the most highly sought-after local game animals. There would seem to be very little to explain here at all. Perfumes are attractive, and this is simply a perfume supposedly attractive to pigs. In fact, there is rather more to it than this, since as I will describe later, the *oktesap* has a more subtle effect via the influence it has on the dream-experiences of the hunter who possesses it.

But for the present let me restrict myself to the straightforward problem of perfume as an attractant, here a means of attracting wild pigs, or, in a more general sense, attracting *good hunting*. There seems to be no problem here only so long as we do not speculate on the specific character of olfactory experience in general, including our own. Once we begin to do so, I think it will become immediately apparent that the olfactory domain is one of the least explored aspects of human symbolic experience, but not, for that reason, one of the least significant. Just how, and in what sense does perfume "attract"? The semiological status of smells is indeed highly ambiguous, for it would seem that we are dealing neither with a system of "chemical communication" which could be handled within a purely ethological perspective, nor yet with a "sign-system"—since the smell-aspect of the world is so intimately bound up with its purely physical and physiological constitution that it can in no sense be considered conventional.[2] Somewhere in between the stimulus and the sign a place must be found for the restricted language of smells, traces which unlike words only partially detach themselves from the world of objects to which they refer. However fragmentary, a phenomenological analysis of the olfactory domain would, I think, be a great help in coming to understand the cognitive basis of magic, because it is here that our own experience is most congruent with that of practitioners of magic—at least, the "magic of substances" to which I have alluded. Nor is this the only reason: for it would seem that this semiological ambiguity of the smell-sign, which does not properly detach itself from the world, points directly to an analogous ambiguity in the status of the magical sign, which refers to, and also *alters* the world. The phenomenon of magic confronts us with a situation in which matter and meaning become miscible fluids, a scandal, of course, from the standpoint of scientific method. Looking at all this from the angle just indicated—the olfactory dimension which is both part of, and a reference to, the world—assists us not only in coming to grips with magical techniques which make direct use of odoriferous substances, but also in understanding, in a more general way, how this paradoxical "mixing" takes place.

II

A colour always remains the prisoner of an enclosing form; by contrast, the smell of an object always *escapes*—it is an active principle. But if a further contrast is drawn between smell and sound—another quality which shares the ability to escape from the object—smell is distinguished by formlessness, indefinability and lack of clear articulation. Smells are characteristically incomplete. They are completed, in the first place, by their source, which is where they become so highly concentrated that they cease to be smells and become substances. Apart from this a smell is completed, not only by the actual source, but also by the context. Because smells are so intimately bound up with the world, the context of a smell is not other smells (in the sense that the context of a linguistic sign is the rest of language, only in relation to which it outlines its distinctive meaning)—but simply the world. We do not discover the meaning of a certain smell by distinguishing it from other smells (we have no independant means of codifying these distinctions) but by distinguishing contexts within which particular smells have a typical value.

This incompleteness, this extreme determination of olfactory meanings by non-olfactory contexts, means that for us, olfactory sensations are in the main only tangential to the business of living. For each and every kind of experience, there is a characteristic olfactory accompaniment, yet it is rare for an experience to be dominated or thematised by this particular sensory mode. Eating and drinking, parties and country walks all involve a dimension of olfactory pleasure, yet it is true of none of them that they are worthwhile on that basis alone (to be able only to *smell* food, without any prospect of eating it is torture, not pleasure). The pleasures of this sense only adumbrate those of richer sensory content. This is to say that just as the smell only acquires definiteness in relation to a context, so the pleasures that this sense confers rarely appertain to the olfactory dimension *per se*—rather to the context with which a particular smell is typically associated. In this respect, though, the very impalpability of olfactory pleasure is also its special advantage, because a smell may give access to a pleasure more intense than could ever be realised in practice, albeit the access given is only vicarious. Many more wines promise to be reasonably drinkable, than actually are. Because all wines of a certain type smell broadly similar (to my inexpert nose at least) the smell of a wine is, for me, the smell of *absolute wine*—a wine I have not tasted once. As soon as I have begun to drink I can tell good from bad readily enough. Perhaps this observation can be generalised: our response to smell is typical rather than specific, general rather than particular. And this is not without importance when one comes to consider the olfactory aspect of magic.

Another thing one can readily see is that the pleasures of the sense of smell tend to be anticipatory, or retrospective, rather than being climactic. The sense of smell comes into play most when the other senses are in suspense, at moments, one could say, of *materialisation* and *dematerialisation*, the coming into being and passing away of things, situations, circumstances which hold our attention vividly while they are present (suppressing olfactory awareness, whose role is restricted to announcing them prior to their arrival, and commemorating them when they are gone). For example, a merely prospective meal is heralded, and its specific nature is somewhat suggested, by wafts of cooking smells coming from the direction of the kitchen, gradually assuming an ampler and more concrete character . . . Or alternatively, where other standards are in operation and diners are sedulously isolated from the kitchen area with its suggestive aromas, the same function (of olfactory anticipation) is performed by the distribution of scented aperitifs, whose minor alcoholic importance is secondary, surely, to their role as aromatic stimulants to hunger (hunger becoming frankly desirable only because the aperitif provides an olfactory context which promises its speedy satisfaction). The smell of something cooking or the tang of an aperitif mark a transition from concept, expectation, to fact—a notional meal to the actual one—and conversely the standard and familiar postprandial aromatics, nuts, cheeses, coffee and cigars set a seal of finality on the dematerialisation of a meal, now only an insubstantial trace. A mere aroma, in its very lack of substance is more *like* a concept than it is like a "thing" in the usual sense, and it is really quite appropriate that the olfactory sense should play its greatest role at junctures when it is precisely this attribute of a meal (meal-concept or meal-fact) which is in the balance.

III

To manifest itself as a smell is the nearest an objective reality can go towards becoming a concept without leaving the realm of the sensible altogether: as such, the dematerialisation of the concrete thing as the evaporated essence of itself serves as the model for exchange between this world and another, disembodied one. In a poem entitled *All Souls' Night* Yeats writes that it is:

> *. . . a ghost's right,*
> *His element is so fine*
> *Being sharpened by his death,*
> *To drink from the wine-breath*
> *While our gross palates drink from the whole wine.*

These lines suggest, not only the familiar idea that it is the smell of an offering which is the portion of its unworldly recipient, but also that the recipient (. . . *his element is so fine/being sharpened by his death* . . .) is different in nature to the part of the offering he receives, only in being if anything still more tenuous. There is a profound connection between the olfactory dimension and the dimension of other-worldliness, which is only inadequately expressed in the phrase "odour of sanctity". The very words "spirit" and "essence" reveal the fact that the vehicle for an ideal or absolute truth which would be, at the same time, concretely within reach, would have to be something like a vapour, a distillate of more mundane reality. Platonism, idealism, spiritualism, seem to haunt any discourse which concerns itself with the sense of smell and the kind of experience it gives us access to, and I will show that this is no less the case when we come to consider the concept of smelling among the Umeda villagers of New Guinea, for whom smelling is intimately connected with dreaming, and for whom dreaming means having access to a higher truth. But all this must be related back, I would argue, to the incompleteness, the disembodiedness of smells as such, which makes them the model for the ideal which hovers on the edge of actualisation, something not quite in being but which announces itself as an odour which corresponds to a context within which the ideal *is*. The olfactory exchange between the gross and spirit worlds can be understood not only in the sense of the subtle sacrificial portion ascending skywards, but also in the other direction, as the presentation, in the vehicle of an impalpable but distinctly perceptible odour, of an ideal order which could be real.

This idea may not carry much conviction. But consider the facts which surround the apparently simple institution of perfume-wearing, as familiar to us as it is the New Guinians of whom I shall speak later. It does not seem to me that the wearing of perfume is to be accounted for either as the attempt to trigger an innate ethological mechanism—if the mechanism existed so would the means of triggering it without recourse to artifice— nor yet as a purely customary signal, since there is no consistent meaning encoded in perfume, as there is, say, in wearing black (for mourning) or white (for the bride). Perfume does not have a discrete communication function (though I do not say that it does not communicate). It does not say "I love you" "I am available"—these are messages which imply a recipient, and the message of perfume is not specific as to its recipient. Some perfumes say "I am rich", but only by implication, for the message really is "I am wearing a perfume that rich people also wear", i.e. the meaning of perfume is a function of context, and it is characteristic of smells, as I said earlier, that the context dominates the sign. Perfume-wearing is resorted to routinely, like tooth-brushing (also not devoid of magical overtones), with the result that its "message" is weakened by the absence of diacritical weighting: "wearing perfume" is not much more "marked" than "not wearing perfume". The language of code, message, sender and recipient is inappropriate to perfume—the real meaning of the custom of wearing perfume lies less in the communicative ends it may contingently serve, than in the *act* of putting it on. It is not sufficient to say, simply, that this is auto-communicative; since, just as perfume does not have a diacritical meaning for others, it may lack one also where the wearer himself or herself is concerned. Perfume is not a language or a substitute for language. Nor yet is it a technique, efficacious in a straightforwardly instrumental way. It is a symbolic presentation.

What the characteristic atmosphere of expensive perfume enveloping a woman can do is give us access to an ideal which is perhaps only lamely expressed except by that precise olfactory sensation. Perfume is symbolic, not linguistic, because it does what language could *not* do—express an ideal, an archetypal wholeness, which surpasses language while language remains subservient to the more or less worldly business of communicating (I agree that language can be used symbolically as well as communicatively: poets and magicians do this). Perfume has to do with the transcendent, the transcendence which, while always inaccessible, can thematise the experienced world. I said earlier that a smell is always incomplete by itself, that it acquires a meaning not by contrast with other smells, but by association with a context within which it is *typical*. Where perfume is concerned this completion is contextual also: the perfume is not completed by the idea "roses, pachtouli, musk, alcohol . . ."—or whatever the actual constituents of the perfume may be (they are probably quite unfamiliar) but by the idea of the perfume *situation*. The constituents of perfume as substance are not the constituents of perfume as experience: just as an odour permeates a place, an occasion, a situation, so.the context comes to permeate the odour-sign and becomes inseparably part of it. But if we try to define what that context of perfume, the perfume situation, really is, it is apparent that this is an instance of an odour-sign giving vicarious access to a kind of experience not really matched by anything in real life.

At any rate, perfume advertisements of the kind which commonly occur in the glossies, notwithstanding the combined efforts of the most expert copywriters and photographers, sometimes achieve a quite egregious degree of bathos, even for advertisements. Trade-names like "Nuits d'amour" or "Stolen Kisses" linearise the essentially indirect relationship between perfume and sexual happiness in a way which, seeming to lay bare the motives of perfume wearers, exposes them to ridicule.[3] A perfume does not seduce: it sets up a context of seduction. This context is not the mundane one, the actual tangible elements of the scene, only a kind of aura which, enveloping everything, assures us that the scene is typical, that it is the realisation, in the here-and-now, of a pre-ordained scheme. Perfume evokes a transcendence (of the world but not in it)—it could be called *the transcendence of the sweet life*. But because it *is* perfume (spirit, halfway between thing and idea) it almost partakes of the nature of the transcendence (otherwise dimly adumbrated in images, musical sounds, vague feelings and desires) while still remaining part of the world.

In real terms, the transcendence of the sweet life is inaccessible, but while we are content to remain under the spell cast by perfume, so redolent of everything that is typical of that life, it seems that the otherwise separate spheres of the actual and the transcendent merge together partially, the communication between the two having been established in the olfactory domain. This is really having access to a charmed universe in which good fortune is the law of life. This possibility or actuality of the charmed universe in which the good happens, not contingently, but typically and as a consequence of something pre-established is what perfume communicates, or better, appresents. This is what I wished to indicate when I said earlier that the significance of the custom of wearing perfume lay less in the socially communicative ends it served than in the act of putting it on. For to open up a channel of communication between these domains (the real world and the transcendence of the sweet life) is extremely propitious. A shift of boundaries, of contexts, has occurred, and the ideal intersects with the real, or rather, it should be impossible to tell which is which.

It is surely correct to say that wearing perfume is a *magical* act.

IV

An Umeda man will sleep with his net-bag beside him on the bed, or may,

for want of anything better, use it as his pillow. In waking life the bag
hardly leaves his shoulder, and its contents (tools, ornaments, magical substances and food) summarise his life and its activities. This is the bag which
contains the sachet of the magical perfume *oktesap*. It is believed that the
sleeping man, imbibing the magical aroma of *oktesap*, will thereupon
dream a dream which betokens good hunting according to the system of
dream-augury followed by the Umedas. *Oktesap* has, therefore, two distinct modes of operation: it is, first of all a perfume used by hunters, used
in the same vaguely propitiatory way as perfumes are in the west (*oktesap*
creates a context of good hunting)—and secondly a means of so influencing
a hunter's dreams that hunting success follows *necessarily*.

It may be of interest to say something at this point about Umeda dream
augury. The Umeda word for "dream" (*yinugwi*) is, in fact, very close to
the Umeda word for a smell (*nugwi*). Umedas were very sensitive to both.
They were brilliant at detecting the faintest hint of the smoke from a camp-
fire in the depths of the forest, or at distinguishing (by the freshness or
otherwise of the scent), whether pig-tracks were new or old, or where a
cuscus might be concealed aloft. They were always on the alert for olfactory
clues which might lead them to discover things otherwise kept hidden.
Their attitude towards dreams was only a more complex instance of the
same thing: a dream was always a clue giving access to something hidden—
the world of spirits, ghosts, or the future fate of the dreamer and/or his
immediate associates. Some dreams simply reflected accurately a state of
affairs which would duly come to pass (unless avoided by counter-action).
Others were interpretable by means of a standard set of symbol-identifica-
tions. The dream which foretold the killing of a pig was one such dream;
for it did not take the form of a direct representation of the event (to dream
of killing a pig was an evil omen, an indication of illness and death in the
local community)—the dream indicative of hunting success was dreaming
of making love to a woman.

The substitution of "making love" for "killing a pig" is not arbitrary.
Eating, violence (hunting), and sexuality, are alternative "modes" of a
single basic activity which the Umeda language expresses by means of only
one verb (*tadv*). In dreams, the modes are switched round—"hunting"
becomes "lovemaking", and "lovemaking" becomes "eating" (the dream
which prefigures the successful consummation of a love affair is "your
sister comes and give you some food"). It is as if the displacement of the
action from the plane of real life to the plane of the dream brought about a
systematic shift in *tadv*-modalities, for it is by no means the case that hunting and lovemaking are substitutable as activities in normal existence. In
fact, they are regarded as being mutually inimical to the highest degree: the
actual practice of lovemaking robs the hunter of his luck—pigs can smell

a man who has been in contact with women, particularly those who are menstruating. The ideal hunter is a chaste bachelor, who, shunning contact with women, makes an ascetic vocation of the chase. Such a young man will, however, dream of the women from whom he has absented himself: and having been aroused by his dream he will take his bow and arrow and slip away into the forest, speaking to nobody, emboldened in the belief that a pig must come his way. It is not hard to surmise the psychological value of the incentive to hunting the dream must provide, nor the continuous stimulus of the wafts of *oktesap* perfume issuing from the hunter's net-bag. The "focusing" power of magic has been discussed elsewhere (Tambiah, 1968; Douglas, 1966, ch. 4). What interests me particularly, though, is the relation between the perfume and the dream-augury, and the light they conjointly shed on the question of the efficacy of symbolic action.

It would appear, both from the fact that the *oktesap* perfume is believed to be conducive to the pig-killing dream, and from the very marked similarity of the words for smelling and dreaming in Umeda (both being based on the element *nug* "smell") that the connection between smell-experiences and dream-experiences in Umeda is very close. They could, I think, be seen as two aspects of a single faculty or activity—the faculty of having cognizance of things at a remove—just as the various modes of eating, sexuality, violence, etc. referred to previously are "aspects" of a single basic activity. Seen in this light the *oktesap* perfume no longer need be seen as having two separate ways of working (as an attractant and as a dream-stimulant)—but only one, in that the kind of access to the ideal order possible in the dream state is only an intensification of that already present in the "perfume state".

Perfumes, in their disembodiedness and typicality serve as the vehicles for symbolic awareness of an ideal order: the "perfume state" is a state in which perfume becomes for the wearer (and for others under its spell) much less a sign of good fortune or happiness or the sweet life, than a condition for that life. That is to say that the context has permeated the sign, and has become so inseparable from it, that what might be—from the standpoint of one outside the system—an "association" endowed with only contingent significance, has acquired in the light of "perfumed consciousness" the force of something inscribed in the fabric of the world. Perfumed consciousness grasps the world as something emanating from the sign, ordered according to necessities imposed by the sign, because the sign and the idealities which are the context of the sign are inseparable. The dream-state is more complex than this, but is also, analytically, more familiar. The similarity between the two is possibly most apparent in the way in which a dream colours subsequent waking perception of events, so that the day following a memorable or fateful dream gains a characteristic feeling-tone corresponding to the tenor of the previous night's dream. This "atmospheric" modulation of waking experience by dreams is not unlike the effects achieved by perfumes. But dream consciousness is autonomous in a way in which perfume-experiences are not. Except where special techniques are employed, as they sometimes are, to direct the course dream experiences will take—the *oktesap* magic I have mentioned is one such technique—the worldly interests of the dreamer are not in play on the plane of the dream. The splendours or abasements of the dreaming soul do not "count" in the sense that the erotic or hunting feats achieved under the propitious influence of perfumes, magical or otherwise, obviously do. Their value in terms of real life is only indirect, monitory, prognosticatory, or inspirational as the case may be. At the same time the relative fullness of the dream experience contrasts with the tenuousness of perfume, however vividly suggestive. The dream seems to hold out the possibility of direct access to the transcendent, mitigated only by forgetfulness, and the barriers to understanding posed by elliptical symbolism (such as the "shift" from "hunting" to "lovemaking" and "lovemaking" to "eating" described above). In the dream transcendence is revealed as fully constituted, leaving little enough room, usually, for the subject's manipulations. Perfume, on the other hand, while it can only dimly prefigure what the dream vividly shows, admits readily of intervention by the subject in pursuit of certain ends. It is not a surprise to find the value of the dream, in the Umeda system, is that of infallible augury, while the value of perfume is as a means of manipulating transcendence actively.

Perhaps, one might go on to say, a fully developed magical technique is always founded (like the *oktesap* technique I have described) on a conjunction of two such elements, an element of constituted transcendence (the world as it ideally, typically, is, "in the light of eternity") and on the other hand a symbolic technique for making this eternal order part of an integral situational reality, by so using signs (magical perfumes, incantations, gestures) that the transcendence invoked comes into being naturally as the implicit context of the signs used. Divination and augury, for instance, presuppose the existence of a pre-given, authentic, "truth of the world" by seeking access to it: where the historian *reconstructs* the past, the diviner tries to re-establish contact with it directly as an eternal present, and augury, similarly, reposes on the idea of prediction not from "observed regularities" but from messages emanating from a future already enacting itself but out of our sight. Divination and augury respect the pre-givenness of the world "as it really is" and only try to achieve as direct as possible intuition of the totality of which the current situation affords us partial glimpses only. Magic differs from these, "passive", forms of ritual action only in actively seeking to condition the occurrence of events in the immediate situation by specifying their symbolic context in the light of the pre-established totality or the "truth of the world".

Magic—or purposive ritual generally—can be viewed as *manipulated augury*. Spells (e.g. the familiar example from *Coral Gardens* "The belly of my garden leavens, the belly of my garden rises . . . reclines . . . grows to the size of a bush hen's nest . . . etc.") depict a favourable outcome as a means of bringing it about. But the depiction—the description—is not of this or that actual garden, canoe, etc. but of the lineaments of an essential one (just as the smell of roses is not the smell of this or that particular rose, but *the*, typical, absolute rose-smell . . .). The factor of *standardisation* in the morphology of the spell corresponds to the factor of typicality in smells, which makes them magically efficacious. There is no room for idiosyncracy, for anything merely personal or improvisatory, in magical language, which must evoke not a contingent, situational reality, but that reality "as it really is" stripped of everything inessential: the spell is standardised because the reality it evokes is no less so.

The lesson of the example I have considered seems to be that magic seeks its effect neither in miracles, nor yet in technical manipulations of a would-be rational kind, but by means of a rhetoric which annuls the distinction between the contingent situation and the regularities of the overall pattern of meanings which the rhetoric evokes. While the magician speaks, he is every magician: the garden he addresses is the epitome of all gardens. He normalises the situation. In the same way, I have tried to suggest, perfume could be said to normalise the situation of seduction, by placing it in the context of the transcendence of the sweet life, a generalised pattern of pre-established harmonies latent in every contingent encounter; the real intersects with the ideal and a happy outcome is assured.

Notes

1. Umeda village (pop. *c.* 200) is one of a group of four known as the Waina-Sowanda villages situated in the West Sepik district of New Guinea. A monograph on the Umeda (*Metamorphosis of the Cassowaries*) is in press. Further information on the culture is contained in an article published in *Man* (Gell, 1971) devoted to Umeda penis-sheathing practices. The Umeda are a small, relatively isolated group, maintaining themselves by small-scale shifting agriculture, sago palm culture, collecting and hunting. Fieldwork in Waina-Sowanda was carried out in 1969–70, supported by a grant from the Social Science Research Council and the Horniman Scholarship Fund.

This paper replaces my original contribution to the seminar organised by Ioan Lewis, a study entitled "Prehending the Occult" which the editor deemed "too theoretical" for inclusion in this volume. The rejected paper appeared in *Radical Philosophy* (Gell, 1974). The reader is referred to this publication for a more detailed and technical formulation of many of the ideas presented here in an intentionally impressionistic style.

2. Objections might be raised here on the score of my too-ready assumption that "smell" is not an in-built communications mode in man, as it may be in other mammals. An article by Alex Comfort which appeared in the pages of the *New Scientist* a few years ago (Comfort, 1971) might be cited in this connection. Comfort's piece, entitled "Communication may be Odorous" adduces some evidence to suggest that the presence of the hormones androgen and estrogen may exert subliminal influence in activating or supressing sexual behaviour in animals including man. He goes on to suggest that the use of deodorants, especially of the kind insidiously named "intimate" may be interfering with a basic mechanism of sexuality itself. I would not dispute Comfort's point where deodorants are concerned. However, it is clear that none of this data affect the points I shall be making here. First of all (cf. the subsequent correspondence in the same periodical) these hormones have no detectable smell at room temperature, and it is not certain that it is by olfaction or by some other means that the effects observable in animals are actually caused. Female rats, it is said, become more sexually receptive after *removal* of the olfactory bulbs—evidence which suggests, for what it is worth, that perfumes cannot be the most efficacious means of bringing the sexes together. What is more to the point is the admittedly "subliminal" character of the posited olfactory communication, which, *per se* I would not wish to discount altogether. What happens "subliminally" is here treated as extrinsic to a consideration of perfume as a cultural phenomenon. It seems to me quite likely that a perfume such as musk, which is a molecule similar in shape to naturally produced human sexual hormones may, in perfume, operate on two levels at once, i.e. as a subliminal stimulus, consciously perceptible not "as a smell" but directly in the guise of sexual desire, and, simultaneously as a symbolic presentation "as a smell" of the *idea* of desire. It is only on the latter aspect that I shall be concentrating here. It would require a fresh approach and a considerable amplification of theoretical apparatus to deal with the delicate question of the dialectic of conscious and cultural *versus* unconscious or "subliminal" factors in erotic experience and behaviour.

3. The most polished satirical assault on the latent absurdities of the perfume trade was that of the artist Anton—a woman, significantly—whose cartoons used to appear regularly in the pages of *Punch*. A typical example of her work is the following, selected after only a cursory examination of some back-numbers of *Punch*, and by no means vintage Anton, but very much in line with the argument here being elaborated:

Shy Girl (on being proffered a perfume called "After Midnight" by a fierce-looking perfume-counter assistant) "But I'm not allowed out after eleven" . . .

Here the joke turns precisely on the "misplaced literalism" which haunts all perfume publicity material, which we must supress if we are to respond as intended. Actually perfume trade-names are a study in themselves. Hardly one of them has anything to do with the actual smell of the product (one has only

"Fleurs du Monde" and "Wild Musk")—reinforcing our point that it is the *context*—not the smell—which matters above all. But a context of what?—most frequently eroticism is implied rather than stated outright for the very reason that the greater the degree of explicitness, the greater the danger of misplaced literalism and the resultant bathos. Names like "Aphrodisia" or the elegant graphemic pun "Y" (the name of a perfume marketed by Yves Saint-Laurent) go quite far in this direction however. Standard practice is to adopt a name less suggestive of desire, strictly speaking, than of its satisfaction: "Je Reviens" promises to recapture past experiences in a succession of eternal returns, for instance.

Taken together, perfume-names contrive to suggest a vast scenario of romance conducted on an epic scale. One has a heroine in her middle years ("Tosca") conducting a tumultuous affair with an opposite number whose outline is only faintly but massively delineated ("L'Aimant") against a background which shifts between vertiginous peaks ("Sikkim") tropical skies ("Fidji") and locations altogether mythical ("Xanadu"). The affair is perpetually threatened by the interventions of exotic temptresses ("Mitsouko", "Kiku") but never fatally, for one suspects that these temptresses are only facets of the many sided personality of our heroine herself, who can be, by turns, "Hypnotique", "Primitif" and "Electrique". Meanwhile, between spasms of frenzied romantic intrigue ("Vol de Nuit") the heroine has moments of tranquility and reflection ("Je Reviens") —she breaths "L'air du Temps" while reviewing her "Memoire Chérie". She recalls her virginal days as "Miss Dior", her sweet old chaperone with her tales of calmer and more formal loves ("Quadrille") and her Scotch governess beneath whose rugged exterior lay concealed a heart of gold ("Tweed"). As "Sandrine" her red hair set the boulevards aflame, and among the students on the "Rive Gauche" not a few expired for love of her. Now, however, her "Capricci" lie mainly in the past, and her heart is consumed by a great and only love "Imprévu", of course, for calculation is foreign to the spirit of one whose "Joy" and "Exuberance" are bought only at the cost of incredible "Audace"—her motto in life being "Vivre". Yet, amid all this activity, one encounters in the end only the stillness of immortality, the shifting mid-point of a biography which by its nature can have no beginning and no end, and we are not forced to choose whether we will leave her murmuring "Forever" or still more thrillingly, perhaps, "Nichevo"— Russian for "Nothing". For in her vocabulary, if in no other, these words can be taken to mean approximately the same thing.

It is the elements of this archetypal biography which together make up what I call in the text the transcendence of the sweet life.

References

Comfort, A. 1971. Communication may be odorous. *New Scientist*, **49** (25 Feb.).
Douglas, M. 1966. *Purity and Danger*, Routledge, Kegan and Paul, London.

Evans-Prichard, E. E. 1929. The morphology and function of magic. *American Anthropologist*.

Gell, A. 1971. Penis sheathing and ritual status in a West Sepik village. *Man* (N.S.) **6**, 165–81.

Gell, A. 1975. *Metamorphosis of the Cassowaries*, Athlone Press, London.

Gell, A. 1974. Prehending the occult. *Radical Philosophy*, **9**.

Tambiah, S. J. 1968. The magical power of words. *Man* (N.S.), **3**, 175–208.

3 | A Mother's Brother To a Sister's Son

Gilbert Lewis

Introduction

I choose the kinship relation between mother's brother (MB) and sister's son (ZS) among a Sepik people (New Guinea) named the Gnau for this discussion of symbols and feelings about them. Under the head of symbolic acts, I will consider different things not all of which stand out as conspicuously symbolic. Some only seem so when looked at in a certain light. As the theme is the interplay of symbol and sentiment, I will not try to present an overall picture of the relationship in this paper. Here at the beginning it might be best to indicate one thread I will be following among others it may become tangled with.

Customs, social rules and laws change some of what would otherwise be arbitrary in social dealings. What should be done in certain circumstances is specified. The characteristic of custom is that it refers its precepts to a tradition or to ancestors to explain or justify them. If someone should say, it is our way to do it like this, not primarily because it is the only sensible way to do it, nor primarily because a king, a god, or a law decrees it so, but because we are people of this kind, and our forefathers always used to do it like this, then we should say it was their custom. It involves recognising whether you are one of those who should follow the custom, whether the tradition applies to you. For with custom there is also recognition that the ways of my people may not be the same as yours. Of course in Rome it may seem wise to do as Romans do, and it would be wise in Rome partly because the significance that attaches to many actions, for instance, shaking hands, sticking out the tongue, rubbing noses, may be misunderstood.

It is characteristic of rules of custom that they are practical: they specify the kind of person and situation and say what should be done by him then.

Often the form of the rule is of the sort: "A sister's son must not speak the name of his mother's brother"; it says what must or must not be done but leaves the reason why unstated. The rules are cited often, but not always, as imperatives without conditional clauses to explain the motive or rationale or symbolism that lies behind them. "Why do you do this?" asks the field-worker; "We so-and-so have always done it like that", or "It is the way of our fathers and forefathers", comes the unenlightening answer. Yet the rules in many cases are connected closely with ideals and beliefs which the people feel strongly about. If the rules be flouted, witness the response. Even though the links may not be spelled out in answer, many customary rules are to belief and morality as practice is to theory. If it is good and right to be polite and respectful or pious, I shall still require to know how, in given circumstances, I may show my good intentions by my conduct. A rule of custom may tell me how. To speak or to avoid a name, to cover or uncover the head—I do not know which conveys respect or reverence except that some rule tells me what is proper.

As certain things to do are spelled out in rules so the duty and ideals are directed into forms of outward conduct that show them. Of course the rules for conduct are few and the details of actual particular circumstances scarcely possible to count. The ideal or belief may apply as general to the situation, but there may be no rule to say exactly what should be done. Choice and interpretation of action are more free and less certain. As the rules of custom are at least clear about some features of the conduct of relations between MB and ZS, so the rights and duties tend to seem crystal-lised in them. They epitomise what is required and proper. To fulfil them shows recognition: the actions stand for something beyond what is done in plain matter of fact. But it is possible to carry out such rules with attention to the very detail of the letter, to do it with punctilio, yet feel inwardly something quite different from what should be felt. Preserve the outward forms and hide one's inward face. If moral sentiments about the good relationship between MB and ZS are strong in the society, one problem of interplay between sentiment and symbol is this: can the token actions re-quired by custom substitute for the sentiments that are expected and held appropriate to it? If not, what is the part of these actions that in one light may seem symbolic?

The problem might be put more briefly by example. The mother of a woman I knew in the village was killed by her father, i.e. the husband killed his wife. The daughter I knew said, as did others in the village, the reason was that her mother spoke the names of the husband's parents (a wife should not speak the names of her parents-in-law). How was I to take this reason? That to say their names was really believed so foul a crime that whatever of affection and ties lay between the man and his wife,

he had to kill her? Or that, at least, in public terms such a reason will do to
explain, or even justify, why he killed her? Or that it does so but only by
implying much not mentioned that she must have done to provoke him to
murder?

Metaphors and Symbols for a Relationship

The relationship between MB and ZS in Gnau society is an important one,
signally important. So many customs to do with it indicate that. It is not
left to chance and spontaneity. We are used to think of kinship terms to
name either end of a relationship, but not so used to think of verbs which
mean the relationship. In Gnau I can think of only three verbs so specific
to kinship that if they were used, I could tell the kinship terms that must
be at either end.

    A. *Dəg'əbasila* "I bore her" (I=*dakao*, "father": her=*niŋgi*, "daugh-
        ter")

      Li wɔbasiləg "she bore me" (She=*maŋkao*, "mother": me=*nəŋganin*,
        "son")

The root—*basil*—means to "give birth or beget" and also to "carry in the
arms".

    B. *Dəg'arəpa* "I married her" (I=*muŋgan*, "husband": her=*ulma*,
        "wife")

      Li wɔrapəg "She married me" (She=*ulma*, "wife": me=*muŋgan*,
        "husband")

The root—*rəp*—means "to marry" and also to "take over or to take
possession of".

    C. *Dəg'atəglən* "I—*təgl*—him" (I=*mauwin*, "sister's son": him=
        wauwi, "mother's brother")

      Lin natəgləg "He—*təgl*—me" (He=*mauwin*, "ZS": me=*wauwi*,
        "MB")

The root—*təgl*—specifies the relationship between MB and ZS, but how
should it be translated? If the verb for to "bear" also means to "carry in
the arms", and the verb for "to marry" also means to "take over" or "take
possession of", is there another use too for—*təgl*—likewise suggestive?
There is, but I can find in my notes of casual speech only one instance:
someone said a woman was ill and thin, *tapi'it watəgla* "her backbone
stood out on her". Instead of saying now what word of Pidgin English they
use for—*təgl*—, I will begin by introducing some metaphors and customs
which are connected with the relationship. It has been said that symbols
may serve as instruments for the discovery of mysteries so perhaps they
may help here.

1. The evening star (*gə'uwan*), they say, climbs first into the sky and then goes before the moon (*gə'unit*) to pull it along its path: the evening star is *wauwi* (MB) to the moon who is *mauwin* (ZS).

2. The sulphur-crested cockatoo (*igambati*), they say, first excavates the holes in trees in which nest other parrots, like the eclectus parrot (*məlangəti*): the cockatoo is *wauwi* (MB), the eclectus parrot is *mauwin* (ZS).

3. A metaphor heard in use. A young man had asked for help with his bridewealth in a way that the man asked thought would have been appropriate if he had been *wauwi* (MB) to the young man: but he was not. As comment on this, what someone literally said was: "A banana plant but one in the bush, but if instead a *lyimʌŋgai* banana (of the village), yes, you plant it in your ashes; but this banana, one belonging to the bush". To explain the metaphor: only certain kinds of banana, among them the *lyimʌŋgai*, are planted inside the hamlets, and the people who plant them bring and put ashes from their house fires on the ground where they plant them to make the ground fertile and the plant grow well. Bananas planted in bush gardens are not fertilised like this. The metaphor assimilates the sister's son to the *lyimʌŋgai* banana planted in the village in ashes from the house fire. The young man in question—he was a banana belonging to the bush garden.

4. The *mauwin* (ZS) cannot eat the *lyimʌŋgai* banana or any banana planted in ashes at his MB's hamlet. He can eat bananas from other hamlets, or bananas from his MB's bush. The metaphor I quoted above assimilated the sister's son to the *lyimʌŋgai* banana. It may sound silly, but the Gnau hold a view that you must not eat yourself: it appears in the rule that you must not lick or eat your own blood, from a cut, for example: that a man's own blood is said to be somehow in whatever he kills with an arrow, and therefore he cannot eat anything he shoots; nor can his father eat it, because the father's blood is necessarily in the son; nor can the MB eat what the ZS has shot if, and only if, that particular MB is the one who has given and fed his blood to his ZS (in puberty rites), who therefore has it in him too, and therefore the blood must be in the kill and the kill therefore forbidden to that particular MB. The mother's brother may give blood to his ZS; he may put ashes to make the banana he plants in his hamlet grow well.

5. The ZS must not eat such a banana. Nor may he eat any bird, bat, snake or lizard, or furred animal, that nests, has its home, or lives, *in a hole,*

if it was killed by anyone on the land of his *wauwi*. I saw many instances of
the care people took to find out where such food was killed, and who killed
it, before they ate. One day, I asked someone to come with me to the bush.
He refused, he said his MB had asked him to stay in the village, because
he was going to cut down a tree on his land in which he had seen a hole
where bats were roosting. He wanted his sister's sons to stay in the village
while he cut down the tree lest (and this was what the sister's son explained
to me) the bats should fly from the hole when he cut down the tree and
escape him.

6. Although I anticipate the issue of good relations broken, I will quote
here for their symbolism a text on the *wauwi*'s revenge. The text comes
from a long response given to me when I asked a man to tell me the duties
and obligations between MB and ZS. He explained them to me by describing imaginary situations, among them bad ones.

Wauwi speaks to his sister to make her take away the children (*ta'aŋ*)—to his
sister who has died—(in the subsequent part of the text he changed the spirit
addressed to the *wauwi*'s father)—he speaks to his dead ancestors about the children, saying, You, So-and-So (i.e. naming the ancestors) come, stand at my
back while I cut down this tree and call out the name of the son of So-and-So
(his sister). He (ZS) went to the coast (the plantations), got things and earnings
there, and came back. But he gave me nothing. He came back, he hunted and
killed pig, animals, birds, but he gave me nothing. He did not know me (ignored
me). I shot game, I gave it to him. He got things but he kept them to himself.
He planted yams and taro, bananas, pit-pit. He kept them to himself. Now I call
out his name and may he die. (The *wauwi*) takes the skull of his father or ancestor,
he goes, puts marks on it, and places it up resting here like this (i.e. just behind
him), he makes an offering platform, breaks a branch of betel nut, prepares sago
jelly, gets a coconut and puts it on the platform. The tree stands here like this
(in front)—a great tall tree (on the *wauwi*'s land). Then the *wauwi* goes and
makes marks for the eyes, nose, lips and chin (of his *mauwin*)—marks on the tree.
He speaks, "Father! Ancestor! I cut down this tree and I name the son of So-
and-So. He got things and he kept them to himself, (put) nothing for his mother's
brothers and their sons". Then he stands here like this, he put things on the
platform. He puts the sago jelly, the meat with it, the betel nut, the dead spirit's
skull, and the coconut, he prepares tobacco in a leaf, he breaks off some betel
pepper leaves, puts them out and some lime. Then he speaks to his spirits, saying, "Father! I am giving you this coconut, the betel nut, I have prepared sago
jelly for you, cooked you this possum and you must draw the son of So-and-So
to you. You two together can eat the sago jelly. You can cook him the meat, give
him coconuts, get him betel nut, and prepare his tobacco for him, and the betel
leaves for him to put in his string bag. The two of you can sit together now. I am
going to cut down this tree: you hold him fast and wait. In a little you will see
the tree about to fall, then you throw him first (in front) and follow him—hold

him well! You can look after the son of So-and-So now. He gave me nothing. If
he had not been like that, then we might have stood together still. But I send him
to you now. He is not mine but yours. You look after him now. Strike him down!
Draw him to you so that he may learn to shoot game and give some to you." The
tree crashes over, destroying the image (*malət*) of the ZS. Later in the night, the
(*wauwi*) sleeps and dreams of his father who speaks to him, "I have drawn your
mauwin to me and gone away with him." The *wauwi* answers, "He's yours! Pull
him to you and go off—he's not mine but yours! I have sent him to you."

The chief analogies in these images are the tree which grows up from
the earth, the creature which shelters in a hole, the banana plant nourished
by ashes, the moon led by the evening star. In each case the stress of the
analogy or metaphor is on the first term, to which the sister's son is assimilated, and on the benefit he receives. There are not clear images for the
wauwi (MB) except as the star; unless you choose to take him as the earth,
or the hole; but I think the accent is rather on the benefit he provides (supporting growth, shelter, nourishment, showing a path). Gnau translate—
təgl—into Pidgin as *kamap long* (*em i-kamap long en* "he, ZS, comes up
from him, MB": it might be possible to translate this as "he grows him",
for *kamap* is used of the growth of plants, however *kirap* is the usual verb
used of a man's growing). Certainly the ideas of benefit, of indebtedness to
the *wauwi*, of help in growth, nourishment and the idea of shelter are quite
clearly associated with the relationship between ZS and MB. The only
plural form for the kinship term *wauwi* is interesting. Like other Gnau
kinship terms, its form is quite unrelated to that of its singular, however it
can also be given another meaning (and the other kinship terms are not
like this): the plural form is *wigət adji*, or more briefly *wigət*. And *wigət*
means "home, place, hamlet, village"; *wigət adji* means "your home".

Right and Duty in the Relationship

But where one's *wauwi* lives is not one's home. During childhood and after
marriage, a man lives in the hamlet of his father. This is where he builds
his wife's house and he sleeps in the men's house where his father slept or
sleeps. He does not garden on his *wauwi*'s land; neither does his mother
inherit any of it (except in special circumstances). Her son's house and
hamlet is that of his father; his land and trees, the magical knowledge he
gradually acquires for gardening and hunting should all come to him from
his father and men of his clan, not from his *wauwi*.

But his *wauwi*, in other ways, has much to do for him. What he does is
seen at once both as right and duty, if right is taken to suggest something
desirable and worth preserving while duty implies something burdensome
and constraining. Here there is a question of balance and correlation. A

right is usually correlated with a duty. Broadly speaking, in this relationship the *wauwi* (MB) has rights and the *mauwin* (ZS) has duties. The debt is asymmetrical. The *mauwin*'s mother was taken from the home of her birth beside her brother when she married. Her son belongs in her husband's home. The asymmetry is to be found in many features of the relationship between MB and ZS, and most sharply in the ideas of how a *wauwi* may kill his *mauwin* by magical techniques which are special to the relationship. The *mauwin* can not counter these; and he has no similar or comparable power to deal death to his *wauwi*. He must not speak his name but call him *wauwi*; even when his *wauwi* is dead; even if the *wauwi* died in childhood before the *mauwin* was born; even should the name be in some song, having no reference to the person of his *wauwi*, he still may not sing the sound. But the *wauwi* (MB) calls him freely by his name. And should the *mauwin* (ZS) speak his *wauwi*'s name, it is not his *wauwi* who will suffer but himself. These are their assertions.

Given a broad asymmetry of right and duty in the relationship, there is still the balance of right and duty to consider in details of the relationship. And as one looks at the details, it becomes much harder to decide whether the stipulated action is felt to be a right or a duty. The compound of attraction and constraint is characteristic of moral sentiments. The attraction of what is ideally good also involves ideal in its other aspect of that which ought to be, "ought" implying both the duty and the difficulty, for ideals go beyond what it is easy to attain. The *wauwi* has the right (or should I rather say the duty and responsibility?) to foster the growth and health of his sister's son. As a man might put his housefire ashes in the ground so that the *lyimʌŋgai* plant grew well, so a *wauwi* hunts game and gives meat to his sister's son. To find and kill much game is hard. To give a great amount, such as is given with ostentation at certain stages of the life of the sister's son, is demanding. If it should seem a duty and a burden to do it, as in a way it does undoubtedly to some, it is also for most their right which they would not willingly see usurped. It is not that the father provides no meat for his children, but there is a special virtue or benefit in what the *wauwi* gives. If they grow into fine upstanding men, they are a credit to him. The finery of the *wauwi*'s dress will come from them; the plumes of birds of paradise in his head dress, the hornbill at his back, the torque of pig tusks round his neck, the trophies on his hunting bag, his belt of cassowary quills—if he can wear these things and say my sister's son killed and gave me them, it is good. Not only is his sister's son a good and dutiful *mauwin*, but it is also good that he has become such a man because his *wauwi* hunted well and gave him meat for him to grow and gave him the ability through health, strength and steadfastness to hunt and kill. There is certainly an aspect of repayment in the giving of these things though they are the finery of dress rather than valuables in the sense that shells (*miŋgɘp*) represented wealth. And the *wauwi* (MB) also hangs up on a line in his men's house or at his garden house, the skulls of pigs and the breastbones of cassowaries which his *mauwin* has shot, and they show off the prowess of his ZS. These things are given to the *wauwi* as his due, even though he does not teach his *mauwin*, or perform on him, the rites which are most closely connected with achievement in hunting and killing: these rites and knowledge are transmitted within the clan, that is, within the father's clan to which a young man belongs.

The point which I am trying to disentangle, perhaps seeing a subtlety beyond the warrant of my evidence, is this: if the trophies were given to repay the benefit of hunting magic, they should be given to the killer's father and to other men within his clan; if they were given to repay the benefit of health, growth, strength, steadfastness, they should be given to the *wauwi*. In practice, men can and do wear trophies that they have shot themselves, or that their sons and grandsons have shot, as well as those their *mauwin* (ZS) have presented to them. But it is best to be able to say that this which I wear my *mauwin* gave me. If you ask what is the rule for giving plumes of paradise, boar's tusks, cassowary quills, you are told "You give them to your *wauwi*" But in practice there are alternatives, it is a matter of some freedom of choice, of recognition, sentiment and responsibility, in complex interplay. To give to the *wauwi* is both right and good, and the reasons for his satisfaction are complex.

In the important rituals for stages of the social and physical development of the ZS, the MB should perform a decisive part. But they can be done, and sometimes are, without him. The Gnau attribute to the *wauwi* a power to bring disaster to his sister's son who either himself, or through his parents, fails to respect the *wauwi*'s rights. In the main rituals for the stages of development, what the *wauwi* should do is laid down explicitly, but the rationale or reason for it is not so clear. It is not necessarily stated. In keeping with a general view that success in hunting and killing, health and strength, are desirable in a man, that this is a great part of virtue in a man (a view which recalls the Roman concept of Virtue as strength and the ability to achieve a set and freely chosen end by exercise of will), so whatever special benefit may come to the ZS through performance of the ritual, the benefit is also said to include that general one of health and strength and success in hunting.

On these major occasions in the *mauwin*'s development, the *wauwi* received a payment of shells, wealth. Shells are now devalued—they call them in Pidgin *rabis-moni*, or even just *rabis* (rubbish) and payment is made with money. The shells lost their value because men brought back box loads of them from plantation labour. Before then the people had had few shells.

The problem of how to accommodate an upsetting new situation faced the Gnau very soon after their first contact with white men. The problem was that by two years' work, young men could acquire enough shell wealth for bridewealth and independence. By the time that the glut of shells began to turn treasure into rubbish, they had a solution to the problem. They had to dispossess the young men of their wealth. The solution lay in the parallels they could see between plantation labour and their Tambin initiation rites. In the Tambin initiation rites, the young men were secluded in the men's house for many months: inside they talked in whispers or whistles, they could leave it only by a secret hidden path, their heads and trunks hidden by a thick leaf-frond covering. From the public point of view they disappeared as though they had died. They were fed and fed. And they reappeared at the culmination of the rites, fat, shining, in finery they had not worn before. They made a great gift of wealth to their *wauwi* who had hunted meat for them during their seclusion. Plantation labour was two, or even sometimes three, years long. The men who went were lost to sight and sound. But they came back; and came back dressed in shirt, laplap, shorts, sleek, well fed, their hair peroxided, their skin shining and scented with the pink perfumed oil of the trade store. And the wealth in their *pinis* —*taim paus*, a bright red box with a lock? Well, here is a text on the disposal of plantation earnings from that long response I quoted before:

> His (the *mauwin*'s) father speaks, saying he must tell his *wauwi* to come to see the things brought back by his *mauwin*. He has gone to the coast and they will honour their obligations. The *wauwi* looks at the things, then he says "You can keep the bushknife, I will take the axe". Or if there are many *wauwi*s— the older one will take the axe, the younger one the bushknife. And the boy's father says to his brother-in-law (i.e. the *wauwi*) "You take your money, take the axe. You decide, you say whether to leave me some, or if you will take it all yourself—if all for you—that's all right, I shall not be angry with you. I am good (generous). It is as you wish, give me some only if you choose to".

The text describes an imagined situation and indicates the ideal. In practice, the *wauwi* (MB) usually gets (gets perhaps rather than takes) only about half of the total money brought back. But given that a man goes only once or twice to work at the plantations in his life, and that there is no other way for people in the village to earn so much money, it is a great gift.

I would like to quote now two letters from a father to sons at the plantation. I served as scribe in the village. The letters are terse, to the point, and they come from a man of no practice in composing letters. They were dictated in Pidgin. To his son:

Dear Seri,
    When you are ready to come back, you must not throw your money away

on things. Bring it all back. Buy an axe for Maitata who "washed" you (a euphemistic reference to penis bleeding), and buy one for Dukini (the younger brother of the sender), but don't buy finery and things. Your "finish-time" box, that's all right, you can buy it. Your monthly clothing issue, get it and then put it away to bring back to the village for gifts.

Give it to your mother's brother. Now, as everyone knows, the *wauwi* gets his *mauwin*'s stuff. They get the *mauwin*'s stuff in the finish-time box. These are the things you will bring back with you and your *wauwi* will get them. I have got what Dabasu brought back. We got £18. Well Paitu got £3, Dukini £5, I got £6 and Pɔalen £4. Of this they are putting aside £5 to go to Paitu (Paitu belongs to the generation following the sender's; Paitu is in the same generation as Seri, the sender's son) and I gave my £6 to Belei (Belei is Seri's wife). That's what we did with the money from Dabasu. Tukri didn't get any. Later perhaps we can change it and put a small part for him. We are waiting for when Weiri dies (Weiri is the sender's sister, a redoubtable, spry widow voluble and in excellent health), and when we bury her, then we will get the money and share it all out. I, your father Sɔlaukei, I am telling you what to do about the things you are going to bring back.

To a classificatory son:

Dear Lelei,

I, Sɔlaukei, write to you. Your uncle Wɔgwei has arrived back at the village. When you and Seri return you must not land at Nuku. You must land at Yankok. Recently coming through Nuku, Dalukil's son Waimo, got back. He did not come and give the money well (generously, properly—*em i-no kam gipim moni gut. Nogat! haitim long en*). No! he hid it for himself. His father took it and hid it away, put out £5 10s for us, and we also got a mosquito net, a towel and a laplap. That's all for now, Lelei.

The first letter presents duty in a brighter light—what it is good to do and to receive. It is hard but right to give. The second letter indicates that people do not always do right, the money and the things may not be offered entire, and there can be suspicion that a part is hidden, a portion granted but begrudged.

But if we paused to ask about Dalukil's son, we would find a whole involved story and a tragedy behind it. Dalukil as a young woman of about 19 years old, loved Wɔlaku, though he was already married. Her father was fiercely against the idea of her marrying him especially because he believed the spirit of Wɔlaku's father (the man was dead) had caused his own wife's death. His wife had fallen from a *tulip* tree that Wɔlaku's father had planted. So there was a row between Dalukil and her father over the young man Wɔlaku. She ran off in the night to Mandubil, the next village on the other side of the river Galgɔbisa. In the early morning, her father found she had gone. He followed after her crying and weeping out loud that she must come back because he needed her help to look after her younger brother and sisters. The village she came from and Mandubil were at the time involved still in the long series of killings between them, but her father supposed he could go there as he had many clan kin at Mandubil who would give him safe passage. Perhaps he did not stop to care. He carried only his axe. But three young men had gone out from Mandubil to ambush him close to the river as he came crying. The one who shot first was the one who had decided to marry Dalukil, and he did. He is the father that Səlaukei suspects in the letter of hiding the plantation earnings. Dalukil after her flight that night did not make the two-hour journey of return to the village where she was born for many years, perhaps as many as fifteen years, not until her children were well grown.

Her father's death was revenged in the eyes of her "brothers" when they killed a Mandubil man but not until a few years after her father's murder. Her children grew up, but not because Dalukil's "brothers" in her natal village made any move to benefit them. Had she come with the children to seek such a thing for them, the children might have been killed: I was told of an instance which had happened at about that time—the child was a baby pulled away from the breast, held upside down by a leg, and stabbed through with a big arrow in front of the desperate mother.

What I wish to consider is this: the man who married Dalukil, though he murdered her father, and by so doing orphaned her brother, yet sent shells in bridewealth for her soon after through a woman intermediary to her remaining kin. Though her brothers did no service to grow or benefit her son, they got some of his plantation earnings. Of course great changes had occurred in the time lying between Dalukil's flight and her sons return from the plantation—killing had been stopped and the villages could visit each other freely.

The Symbolism in Duties and the Point of It: Uncertainties and their Resolution

Their idioms and customs indicate some of the sentiments that they expect between a MB and his ZS. The significance someone can find in some event or thing depends in part on the attention he chooses to give it. A detective may find clues where the casual passer-by would see only litter and hardly notice it. Certain rules or duties in a relationship are spelled out and people note whether the requirements are met or not. Their attention is more focused on them because they know what should be done. The acts are taken in part as tokens of the type of attitude and feeling that should prevail generally in the relationship. If the duties by their particular content also indicate some attribute proper to the relationship or desirable in it, even if only a hint or a clue, the people may see it because they pay attention to the performance of these definite duties. As the focus is on a duty linked specifically to a given relationship, it is likely that the set content of the duties is so set because it is in some way appropriate as an epitome, or summing up, of the desired character of the relationship.

The people who find themselves in a given relationship develop more or less complex feelings about each other from their various contacts. These develop and differ in the detail of each case. Left to grow quite unguided from circumstance and character, there would be great variety in the sentiments of different people who chanced to stand in that relationship. Alternatively, its desired quality might well be known. If this were known only as some precept such as "Love and respect your mother's brother", it would still be difficult for the individual to know what to do about it. Without any teaching or rules to say what kinds of action showed love and respect, the actions of one man are open to another's misunderstanding. The question is how clearly the desired sentiments are formulated and how clearly they are linked with particular actions. If it is clear, the action can be used to show the sentiment. But a particular action may be set as a duty without establishing a dogma about what sentiment it shows; this then remains open to individual supposition. Custom can determine how some actions should be done, but in terms of kind and detail, it says little about the vast variety of circumstance in which people may face each other in everyday life. The push and pull of their interests and personalities in this is bound to be accompanied by assessment of each other in terms of the values associated with the relationship. Doubt or resentment built of various small things, complicated, hard to judge, hard to make public because their significance would not be generally accepted, may be set to rest or forced out into the open by making use of the attention given to performance of certain duties and their accepted significance. It is easier and clearer to throw down and break a ZS's gift, asserting it to be too small, than to try to explain and list a whole string of minor snubs or derelictions which taken singly are not serious and even taken together could be construed in various ways.

The performance of set duties can serve to show up or indicate with objects and actions what otherwise might remain amorphous, uncertain or petty. Something about the state of relations can be objectivised; but only in specified and restricted terms which tend towards all-or-none, black-or-white, statement. This statement is clearer, less ambiguous, but only if, or because, the terms by their fixity and formal ruling allow for little in the way of qualification or shading. What should be done by the ZS when first returned from the plantation is decided in bold outline, not in minute terms that say act for act, object for object, what obligation is recognised

in each and what feeling it bespeaks. Money by its divisibility makes it possible to measure and finely grade the wealth presented in a way that was
not possible with shells. Differences in amounts stand out so clearly, money
is counted, but what such differences shall mean is not established.

Dalukil's son gave £5 10s. of his plantation earnings, a mosquito net, a
towel and a laplap. Dabasu, the other ZS in the first letter gave £18. What
sort of titration of recompense, sentiment and duty is this? Does £5 10s.
represent what is due to some irreducible principle of Gnau kinship and
the £12 10s. of difference represent £10 of recompense and £2 10s. of
affection? Had he made over all that he brought back, would he have fulfilled some ideal? Given what had happened in the past, why did they
bother to give anything at all? To Dalukil's husband and Dalukil's son did
£5 10s. seem generous, a gesture full of good intentions? To Dalukil, a
gesture of remorse and desire for reconciliation? How did they expect
Səlaukei or more precisely, Dalukil's brother to receive the gift? Səlaukei
and Dalukil's brother took it ill, which I doubt Dalukil's son intended them
to do, though he may have guessed that whatever he would do there was
some risk of this, because the action was bound to make them think again
about what had happened in the past. The feelings they had about all that
past infected their judgement of his action. There were no rules to say just
what he should do to make his intentions clear to them.

Other people said they expected that Dalukil's brother might use one of
the ways to harm his sister's son which was described in the text I quoted
earlier about a *wauwi*'s revenge. The money affair made them think again
of what could be done. I learned of nothing from which to suppose the
brother did in fact try to use the method. But the suggestions that he might
use it are interesting. Did the people who suggested it not stop to think
that surely he must have tried to work this technique for dealing death in
the past when he had reasons more sharp and bitter for doing so then than
now—the wound was not so old then? If it had not worked then, why
bother with it now?

Beliefs, Actions and Illusions

We talk of the beliefs of another people and it is a catch-all phase. Belief is
used not only of absolute faith and unalterable conviction. The things
someone says, what he feels, what he does, do not have to stand in any
simple relation of consistency to each other. Words come easily, they are
said quickly and cost small effort in the saying. While human actions can
and do change even the inanimate world, doing things is harder and slower
than speaking about them. By a direct act of violence, a Gnau man might
kill his sister's son (as the baby was killed), but the Gnau also say he could

have killed him by words and actions which are not so direct as stabbing, spearing or shooting him.

In the statements about revenge by magical murder, the words and actions are said to lead to the death of the sister's son. The man who would do these things must know that too. In the bare light of this knowledge, it must be judged that he intends to kill. Why kill by magic where one might kill by violence? It is true that to kill with the arrow or the spear is now forbidden; that to kill by magic might be kept secret; that to kill by magic makes a shade of one's dead accomplice to the act and part responsible; that to kill by magic does not carry the immediate danger and difficulty of the violent act. But what of its certainty? Surely the hate so hot and bitter as to spur a man to try to kill his ZS would seem enough to fix his attention on the effects of his actions, and make him face the question of delay and his intention unfulfilled?

In asking why a man would seek to kill by magic, when he might kill by violence, I want to know about his choice. He says that he would kill, but between that and the act on the one side, of attempted violence, or on the other, of spoken phrases and cutting down a tree, is there just one self-same will to kill linking what he says to what he does?

This is a lurid way of asking a question about belief and symbol. If we take their statements literally, and if we presume a true intent to kill, our answers on the actor's choice will have to do with the relative economy of effort, the secrecy, responsibility, and the dangers that decide him in his choice. In magical revenge, it happens that I suppose he will almost surely face a failure and that the strength of his intent to kill should force him to try and explain why the magic failed. But that is an issue on one side. If we assume his true and literal belief, either the violence or the magic must seem to him equally effective ways to satisfy his desire. Before that ferocious desire, there are two ways open, and to our assumed literal and convinced believer, it is not that his words and his cutting down the tree are symbolic, because to him they would not be a symbol (however they may seem to us) but a substitute for the act of violence. For secrecy, the safety of his skin, shame, difficulty and danger, he might prefer to substitute magic for violence.

Now suppose we slacken the certainty of his belief, impute less of the literal to his statements, allow him some measure of recognised and voluntary illusion, a half-belief, then the magical action may become that much more an act that stands for what he would like to do but does not really dare, or does not wholly desire. It is a substitute but a partial substitute. It does not bear quite the same relation to fulfilling the desire as setting out to kill the man with a bow and arrow. It is in part symbolic to the man himself. There is a difference in the recognition of symbolic action as one looks from outside at the beliefs, makes tentative play with exotic materials, knowing that one's own beliefs are not involved, or instead seeks to grasp and understand the experience of someone for whom these things are part of the real business of his life and involve his own knowledge, the things he learns and is asked to believe. It seems evident to me, if I think about the implications of the things people sometimes said to me that there is some voluntary illusion recognised in their assertions about these beliefs. For example, a younger man, who happened to be the one who first told me about one of the forms of a *wauwi*'s revenge, ended his brief account by saying that he had such a hole on his land, that some day he might do the magic, not because he wanted to kill his *mauwin* but because he wondered whether it would work. Of course, he said, if his ZS did fall ill, he would immediately unstop the leaf in the hole and end it. People must vary individually in how they view the truth of what they assert in common with the others of their community, and vary too in their inward reflections as impulse and motive wax or wane to allow them a degree of detachment which is inconstant, and alters how they think about it.

Assertion, Affirmation and Promise

Some kinds of conviction involve assertion only. To believe that a God has set the stars in their courses and therefore they must move as they do and so for ever, does not present a believer with the same possibilities for doubt as does a belief that entails a promise or a prophesy. If you do this, then that will happen. There is an infinite and complex gradation in the particulars of belief between those of pure assertion and those affirming the promise of immediate and material effect. The complexity lies partly in the strength, closeness and detailing of the link which binds the affirmation to its promise. The link may be defined clearly or not so clearly—this is part of the matter —but feelings may also affect how individuals regard the link. These may vary. It is one thing to talk in an airy or theoretical way about what is possible in vengeance, but another to brood with aching unappeased spite on what to do.

Conviction and False Knowledge: The Part of Reason and the Part of Feeling

Evans-Pritchard showed why he could not prove to Zande people that what they said about witchcraft was false. He unravelled and ordered the premises and logic that would defend those beliefs by reason rather than sentiment. Indeed he put the case for the defence by reason so well that a defence on grounds of sentiment might seem superfluous. Sentiments and

individual feelings are clearly involved in such beliefs. Some anthropologists (Evans-Pritchard was one of them) have said or implied that such
matters of sentiment and feeling lie in fields belonging to the psychologist—
a bridge leads to these fields but only the asses of anthropology would
cross it.

I have no wish to find myself with hairy and long ears, yet I would give
attention to the part of sentiment and feelings in belief. These contribute,
as well as reason, to the preservation of false knowledge and the incorrigi-
bility of shared illusions. My concern here is with the variable interplay of
reason and feeling, and to see how it is complicated when we speculate or
ask about the individual's private attitudes to prevailing public beliefs. I do
not suggest that one aspect of explanation (through sentiments and feelings)
should supplant or displace another (through reasons): the one does not
exclude the other, but they interact in various, inconstant ways, particular
to circumstance and occasion. The relations people have to their assertions
are psychologically complicated, and these relations are not solely dominated by reason. As outsiders, our curiosity is especially drawn to those
assertions sometimes made by members of another culture which we regard
as errors or false knowledge. We see these errors according to the knowledge which we share with members of our own culture. In seeing them,
we do not have to take a view that isolates us as an individual with an understanding no one shares. The errors we see as outsiders are errors that
within another culture are common to everyone, i.e. socially shared, normal,
and openly asserted, indeed perhaps sanctioned as right thinking. The
individual, within that community of knowledge, is faced with real events
which may put doubts into his mind. To bring these forward he must be
prepared to separate himself from what everyone else says they believe.
And it requires courage to assert oneself against the others of one's whole
world, and stand alone confronting them with doubts. Whether it is worth
doing depends a great deal on what is at stake for the individual—this is
a matter for his feelings and interests as much as, or more than, cool
reason.

Whether some belief tends towards pure assertion or an affirmation
linked to a promise can alter for the individual as his feelings weigh down
the balance on one side or another. To an individual faced with some particular situation in which his immediate interests are at stake, the weight
may fall rather on the promise entailed than on the assertion, but not for
other people. As their concerns are not involved, they may not share his
grounds for doubt. The issue of shared assertion as against an entailed but
empty promise can be seen in a Gnau belief linked with the rules against
speaking a *wauwi*'s personal name. I stumbled against the requirements of
this rule almost every day of my fieldwork. I knew their stated belief and

I must have been the casual witness of thousands of situations in which some individual had to interpret the rule in his conduct.

The rule is tacit, part of common knowledge, imperative and unconditional: do not speak the name of your *wauwi*. In the ordinary dealings of life, no one needs to talk about it. Everyone lives by it. As a child begins to speak, the rule is already in force for him. The child still stammering, imitating noises, people round about repeating *"wauwi"*, smiling, pointing, encouraging so that, for the child, *wauwi* comes among its first and most loaded words. As for the infant so for me, it was only later after I had sensed the rule as something imperative and almost absolute, that it came to have anything conditional about it. I learnt that someone who spoke the personal name of his *wauwi*, might be fixed by a certain little snake (*bulti malwati*) as he walked along a path. He would be fixed, unable to move before the little snake unless he gave it all his shell valuables and finery, stripped himself bare. It was suggested to me that nowadays, for instance, I or someone like me wearing shorts, should empty his pockets of any money and drop his shorts down before it. *Bulti malwati* is not, they say, poisonous. Nor did I discover or hear of any man who had had to face this disturbing predicament.

But countless times, I have pressed someone in another predicament, that of identifying a name to me which was his *wauwi*'s. Obtaining genealogies was the problem. There were ways round it: someone else present might say the name for him; or he might say something like "you know— thingumme, the father of X, or the husband of Y, or the son of Z"; or he might begin the name and hint "Wei . . . Wei . . ."; or say it dropping out a consonant or two "Wei . . . Wei—il"; or he might twitter it very soft in whistle talk: or he might put his mouth right up to my ear and breathe it out just audible, we two in secret at my house. There were some men who could be pressed to say the name in private to me, and others who would not budge and we just had to leave it until someone came up who could tell me. I do not know for sure, but I doubt strongly that any of these men put by me in this predicament gave a thought to the possibility of trouble with a little snake on a path in the future. Their attitude about speaking the name I would assume was close to what some people in our society feel about saying four-letter obscenities, except that the sentiment complex involved had to do with respect and moral duty, not sex and filth. The prophesy or promised condition about the snake which they can assert as a reason for obedience carries little or no emotional weight. It is mere assertion. But the act of speaking the name does do something to the speaker's feelings. We may reason that an obscene word refers to a bit of the body, or to sex in action, which we forbid people to dare expose in public; that to say the word is a bit like showing the thing or doing it, but of course it is not quite so bad, though still offensive to the more delicate-minded. We know that just about everybody else knows the words. We know that if a newspaper were to print "The Hon. Member said 'F . . . the Minister'," then every reader would know what foul word he was supposed to have uttered. But all this reasoning and recognition, does not convey that shock which the word spoken straight and clear can produce in the right circumstances. An account of the rules and beliefs about the wicked speaking of forbidden words which concentrates only on reasons and cognition and leaves out sentiment and affect fails to convey what such beliefs and rules *mean* to those who try to live by them.

The Significance of Symbols in Real Life

I have asked whether it would be right to call the actions of a *wauwi* who tried to kill his *mauwin* by saying words and cutting down a tree, symbolic to him (the *wauwi*) if we supposed that he truly believed they were as fully a way to kill as hunting the man down with a bow and arrow. If the two ways were seen by the *wauwi* purely as alternative techniques, the one able to be substituted for the other, there need be no difference of intent to kill behind a choice of one or other technique. But if we suppose his actions are recognised by him as symbolic, we must in turn recognise that his choice of the magical revenge involves some alteration, perhaps a deflection or a hesitation, in his intent to kill.

The issue here involved can be made more general. The issue is that of symbols and their significance in real life. When we use the word "symbol" we refer, at the very least, to one thing which *stands for* something else. I have argued that if one thing can fully serve in the place of another, it is not that one thing *stands for* the other, but that one thing *substitutes* for the other. Symbolic equivalents are not so equal as substitutes.

In metaphor, the illusion of identity is voluntary. The Gnau know as we do that on many grounds neither the banana plant, nor the bats, nor the tall tree, are the same as a sister's son, but they are prepared to neglect many conspicuous differences for the sake of one (or a very few) attributes in which they see an identity. Indeed it is because there are so many differences to be neglected or discarded before the metaphor makes sense that the sole or few attributes of that identity in metaphor stand out so clear— more clear, and so metaphor may serve as an instrument for discovery.

What the metaphor is in the sphere of speech, the symbol is in the sphere of things, i.e. the sphere of objects and actions. There may be mere symbols too in the sense of mere metaphors, where the illusion is voluntary and passes for unreal. Both the terms metaphor and symbol stand for something which is not used in its barest literal sense or for its proper purpose. Both describe methods which are used to give concrete expression to ideas. An object that can be seen may be transferred to an entirely different concept that cannot be directly perceived. Our reason thinks of something for which there is not any corresponding direct object or action to perceive. But to say that there is no corresponding concrete object or action to perceive, is not the same as saying that the thing thought of is not real. The subject of this essay has been the relationship of MB to ZS. It is not easy to point to an object or an action and say *that is* a relationship. But the relationship is there.

By certain rules of recognition, the Gnau can assign two persons to certain relative positions, one termed *wauwi* and the other *mauwin*. The rules of recognition allow them to predict that if a male person is born to a certain woman then he will be *mauwin* to certain men. If none of these men survive, or even if none of them happened to have been born, it is still known who (where) would have been his *wauwi* if they had been alive or born, because they would have occupied the specified position. To know the terms for the positions and rules to decide when they are occupied by persons, does not yet entail any knowledge of the nature and content of the relationship between them. In Gnau society, persons in these two structural positions should have a relationship of a particular and valued kind. The relationship is a complex, desired, and enduring thing which I believe they think of as a kind of whole or entity or thing. It is not the kind of thing which can be seen, grasped, touched or smelt, or heard as a whole. It can be thought of in terms of the qualities of the relationship and its particular duties and attributes. It is enduring. It exists also at other times than solely those when a particular duty is done and seen to be done. The relationship is given or axiomatic, its desired qualities are formulated in ideal terms by people who see them as good and right. As ideals, they go beyond what can be simply pointed to and seen. The nature of the relationship is not shown directly in a single concrete experience, but it may be more accessible in symbolic form. When we take the particular symbols, and ask "of what are they symbols?" we find no actual object or action referred to except in the form of the ideas of the relationship. The enduring qualities desired in the relationship are moral and involve sentiments of concern, love, respect, and recognition of the special value of the other person. These are things which cannot be simply or directly seen and described. The symbols help to make them known. Human ideals and values and counter values are pre-eminently the sort of things for which people require symbols, because they are insubstantial and abstract. They are hard to grasp and apprehend. But the values and ideals are felt as real, they have personal validity for the people who hold them. Symbolic thinking amounts to more than just thinking in images. When we consider other people's symbols from the outside, our own beliefs uninvolved, make play with exotic material and images, we are liable to miss their true seriousness. If it were suggested that I might be able to build up from the detail of many observed situations, such accurate, well-witnessed and vivid scenes of daily life, that a reader might approach an understanding of the sentiments involved similar to that of the people themselves, I should point out a great difference in his second-hand understanding compared with that of the first-hand actors: that seriousness of real life, that experience of feelings which one's own real life involves, would be missing.

The symbols help people to apprehend these sentiments and values. The sentiments and values have personal validity for the people in the society; they are real to them but not simple or directly graspable things. The symbols or symbolic actions are concrete, actual objects and actions. They help them to understand the ideas which the objects and actions stand for. But people are prone to take the symbolic objects or actions for the reality they stand for (the felt reality of the sentiments and ideas). In other words they mistake the concreteness and substantial nature of the objects or actions for the reality of the sentiments and ideals they feel. They take symbolic reality as if it were the reality of direct apperception. So the symbols come not to stand for something else (an ideal or sentiment that goes beyond the object or action), but to be equal to the sentiment or idea itself. That is, instead of being a symbol, it becomes a substitute for the thing itself; to our outsiders' view it becomes for them an object of superstition. From our external standpoint, we may still call these things symbols, but for the actors they are not any longer.

Part of the purpose of my paper has been to bring this issue forward, and to suggest that people do not take the material performance of their duties as substitutes for the moral sentiments and ideals desired in this relationship, but do indeed see them as symbols or tokens of something that goes beyond the materiality of these required actions. Despite the face value of what people say, we can perhaps see better why the *wauwi* chooses the magical mode revenge, desiring not wholly the death of his sister's son but that he should come to heel and return what he owes. The *wauwi* may cut down the tree and the secret may out; and rumour or suspicion scare a ZS into a sense of his duties derelict but so endangering that he will turn and seek to make them good. There can be appeal against the curse; but the arrow loosed from the string is irrevocable. There may be much subtle and individual variation in how particular people regard their beliefs. Belief is not always a matter of absolute conviction: emotion and feeling as well as reason enter in the link between assertion and conviction: emotion and interest can alter that detachment which might enable someone to see certain objects or actions as symbolical or instead mistake them for reality.

Notes

1. For nearly all the substance of this paper, I first must thank the people of Rauit village especially, and of Mandubil village, Lumi Sub-District, West Sepik District, New Guinea; for support of my field work, my thanks to Anthony Forge of the London School of Economics who supervised it, and to the Social Science Research Council who financed it.
2. For the view of custom: J. Ladd (1967).
3. For the view on substitutes instead of symbols: E. H. Gombrich (1965, the title essay, and 1966, pp. 393–401).
4. For morality in general as attraction and constraint, almost any text on the philosophy of morals, but conveniently, M. Ginsberg (1961, Chap. VIII).
5. For the moral nature of kinship: M. Fortes (1953, pp. 35–6) and (1969, Chap. V and XII).
6. For the view on binding words to actions; assertion, affirmation and promise: Pierre Janet (1927). I used the summary of Janet's work contained in H. Ellenberger (1972, pp. 331–417).
7. For the view on false knowledge and voluntary illusion (as well as the idea for an analogy with four-letter obscenities): F. Kraüpl Taylor (1966, Chap. 11).
8. For reason but not sentiment: E. Evans-Pritchard (1937, especially pp. 475–8). For the *pons asinorum*: E. Evans-Pritchard (1951, p. 46).
9. For the view on symbols in real life: K. Jaspers (1963, pp. 330–40).

References

Ellenberger, H. F. 1972. *The Discovery of the Unconscious*, Allen Lane, London.
Evans-Pritchard, E. E. 1937. *Witchcraft, Oracles, and Magic among the Azande*, Clarendon Press, Oxford.
Evans-Pritchard, E. E. 1951. *Social Anthropology*, Faber and Faber, London.
Fortes, M. 1953. The structure of unilineal Descent groups. *American Anthropologist*, **55**, 17–41.
Fortes, M. 1969. *Kinship and the Social Order*, Routledge and Kegan Paul, London.
Ginsberg, M. 1961. *The Diversity of Morals*, Heinemann, London.
Gombrich, E. H. 1965. *Meditations on a Hobby Horse*, Phaidon Press, London.
Gombrich, E. H. 1966. Ritualized gesture and expression in art. *In Ritualization of Behaviour in Man and Animals* ed. J. Huxley, *Phil. Trans. Roy. Soc. London*, Series B, **251**, 393–401.
Janet, P. 1927. *La Pensée Intérieure et ses Troubles*, Maloine, Paris.
Jaspers, K. 1963. *General Psychopathology*, transl. J. Hoenig and M. W. Hamilton. Manchester University Press, Manchester (First Edn. in German 1913).
Kraüpl Taylor, F. 1966. *Psychopathology*. Butterworths, London.
Ladd, J. 1967. Art 'custom'. In *Encyclopedia of Philosophy*, Macmillan and Free Press, New York and London.

4 | "Ill at Ease and Sick at Heart": Symbolic Behaviour in a Sudanese Healing Cult.

Pamela Constantinides

The quotation contained in the title of this paper is taken directly from a description given by a Sudanese woman as she related the sort of physical and emotional state she was in just prior to joining the spirit possession cult which ultimately gave her some relief from her symptoms.[1]

She went on: "I became frightened and anxious about everything, always feeling that death would happen to one of my family. My heart was beating hard and I had short breath . . . I was upset all the time. I was pregnant and afraid that I might lose my baby. I became anxious about my house and every small thing . . ."

This woman's personal symptoms and sentiments, and the dreams that she had at that period, were to lead her to accept a culturally appropriate diagnosis that her troubles were caused by her being possessed by spirits called *zaar*. And acceptance of this diagnosis was, in turn, to lead her to participate in an ego-centred group ritual of spirit appeasement, rich in personal significance and in dramatic, historical and symbolic significance to all those taking part.

The concept of spirit possession, and curative ritual associated with it, touches directly on some of the main themes raised in this symposium. It is right at the interface between private and public symbols and sentiments, and forms a most pertinent starting point for any analysis of the nature of

1. The field research on which this article is based took place from April 1969 to July 1970 and was financed entirely by the Social Science Research Council.

Thanks are due to the several colleagues who commented on an earlier draft of this paper, and most especially to Professor Ioan Lewis and Dr. Pat Caplan for detailed and helpful advice.

these and the relation between them. It is precisely this thesis which leads Mary Douglas, when discussing natural symbols, to use cases of spirit possession as "test cases" in formulating her concepts for describing "the way that social pressures reach an individual and structure his consciousness" (Douglas, 1973, p. 112). Her hypothesis is that societies, or sections within a society, which indulge in ecstatic and effervescent forms of ritual and symbolic behaviour, are expressing their "lack of strong social articulation" and that their practices amount to ". . . a fair representation of the social reality they experience" (Douglas, 1973, pp. 114 and 110).

Approaching the same sort of phenomena from a somewhat different viewpoint, Ioan Lewis argues rather that spirit possession may provide an outlet for those who are too rigidly circumscribed by their alloted status-roles; that it allows a form of contained protest to those who are the controlled, rather than controlling, members of structurally "tight" societies. Specifically, in his Malinowski lecture (Lewis, 1966) and in his later, more widely-ranging work on ecstatic religion (Lewis, 1971), Lewis has linked certain manifestations of spirit possession to feelings of absolute and relative deprivation experienced by those, especially women in "male-dominated" societies, who find themselves in a peripheral position *vis à vis* the sources of power and authority in their societies.

A close look, then, at one active curative cult which exists to treat individuals diagnosed as suffering from spirit possession, should help us towards a greater understanding of the phenomenon. It should help to demonstrate the sort of symbolic and emotional synthesis which allows an individual not only to express, in an atmosphere of group support, the social pressures impinging upon him, but also to experience a sense of relief from, and hopefully to come to terms with, these pressures.

It is my contention that the ritual of the *zaar* spirit possession cult of the northern Sudan provides individuals under a variety of forms of stress with a standardised and acceptable means of expressing the position in which they find themselves. At the same time, both the ritual act, and membership of the cult group, are instrumental in allowing subtle adjustment of their position.

Furthermore, since ego-centred curative ritual sensitive to, and indeed in part a product of, social change, allows for a two-way symbolic dialogue between the individual and his society, in examining such ritual we may also be able to gain some insight into the degree and extent to which the society is prepared to utilise the mystical experiences and dramatic and innovative abilities of its individual members.

In discussing a wide variety of inspired cults and religious movements, Victor Turner observes that however personal seeming the initial inspiration upon which they have been founded, "their mythology and symbolism is borrowed from those of traditional rites de passage, either in the cultures in which they originate or in the cultures with which they are in dramatic contact" (Turner, 1974, p. 99).

This is certainly valid for the *zaar* spirit possession cult, now an established but once an innovative cult in the Sudan.[2] What is interesting is the manner in which such "traditional symbols" are re-deployed, and it is here that we broach the complex relationship between individual and group sentiments, private and public symbols.

Before going any further, it is necessary to set the cult in its ethnographic context. This I shall attempt to do in the briefest possible manner.

The Social Background

The cult groups which I am going to discuss here are urban and suburban and involve mainly women of the sedentary riverain tribes of the Muslim northern Sudan.[3]

Marked sexual segregation is a dominant feature of northern Sudanese society. There is a clear sexual division of labour. Households are separated into men's and women's quarters, and in almost no instance do men and women who are not closely related mix at any public gatherings. Weddings, child-naming, circumcision ceremonies, and mourning, all take place with two separate, sexually segregated congregations.

One point at which this division breaks down to some extent is during personal and family crises of illness. A woman may, in complete privacy, consult an unrelated male Quranic healer or *feki*, either on her own behalf or on behalf of a member of her family, male or female. Similarly a man may resort for treatment to what is considered to be the essentially womens' cult of *zaar*.[4] Some men are regular participants at cult rituals, and a few become cult group leaders. Of this male minority some are overt homosexuals, while others may initially have symptoms, such as bleeding from the anus or penis, which tend symbolically to classify them with women. The majority of both cult group leaders and followers are women.

2. For an attempt to trace the history of the cult in the Sudan, and to demonstrate its adaptive potential in situations of rapid social change and increasing urbanisation, see Constantinides (1972).

3. Another, in some ways similar, cult called *tumbura* exists in the poorer areas of the towns and appears to involve both men and women with no claim to Arab descent.

4. It is noteworthy that these excursions across the usual boundaries of sexual propriety are sometimes marked by deep sexual suspicion. Men are likely to joke, irreligiously, that certain *fekis* much resorted to by women to cure infertility "do the job on the women" by more direct means than the latters' husbands suspect! Men who attend *zaar* rituals regularly are suspected by both men and women of being homosexual, or conversely, may be thought by men to be somewhat too heterosexual, dishonourably gaining access to women by feigning illness.

It is virtually impossible to estimate with any accuracy the proportion of women who are initiated members of the numerous cult groups, but most women, members or not, attend more than one ritual, in some capacity, at some stage of their lives. The number of mature women in the urban and suburban areas who have never attended such a ritual I would reckon to be small to negligible.

Taking the society as a whole, for men the main rituals are those of the life-cycle crises—male circumcision, marriage and death; and the formal religious rituals of Islam and the various religious brotherhoods. The main womens' rituals are similarly those of the life cycle—female circumcision, marriage, birth and death; and the rituals of the *zaar* womens' cult. Women do not generally attend the formal group rituals of Islam, but carry out their prayer and worship individually. Their participation in the *zaar* cult, however, in many ways parallels men's participation in the religious brotherhoods, and it could be said that the cult groups are in the religious and social life of the women what the brotherhoods are in the religious and social life of the men.[5] Significantly, certain aspects of usage and terminology are the same. Among many similarities of detail I shall mention here only the following: that *zaar* cult groups, like the brotherhoods, celebrate the major annual festivals of Islam with sacrifice and the display of standards and flags, often bearing the names of popular saints; that both begin and end their proceedings with long incantations calling for the blessings of God, the Prophet Mohammed, and the saints; that the leader of a brotherhood is entitled *shaikh* and the leader of a *zaar* cult group is called *shaikha*; that both are said by their followers to *arif al tariqa* or *arif al sikka*, literally to "know the way", to have access to the mysteries of the supernatural. The *shaikh* of a brotherhood usually passes on, in the male line, his office and the blessing and power, *baraka*, associated with it. While there are several instances of a *zaar* leader passing on her office to a female relative, the position is most usually achieved by means of an initial experience of severe illness followed by a period of discipleship to another cult group leader.

In considering the whole ritual life of the northern Sudan it is evident that, in terms of duration, expense, and symbolic elaboration, spirit possession ritual is probably most closely comparable to the ritual surrounding marriage, from which also, as we shall see, some of its terminology is borrowed. In terms of pure drama, it is the most elaborate of all. As both ritual and drama, it draws upon a set of symbols which form a pattern throughout the total ritual of the culture.

5. In Morocco certain religious brotherhoods with ecstatic practices appear to be combined with spirit possession, as in the case of the Hamadsha described by Vincent Crapanzano (see Crapanzano, 1973).

Within the spirit possession cult groups a person suffering from an individual syndrome of physical, emotional or social malaise, becomes incorporated in an elaborate group ritual process, during the course of which she is encouraged to express her reaction to her symptoms in terms of a fairly standardised pattern of symbolic behaviour which has meaning to all the members of the group. I say "fairly standardised" because sometimes dreams, and nearly always trance, form parts of this process. Now these latter might be thought to be experiences whose meaning is highly specific to the individual concerned, but in fact how far is this so? How far can we go in predicting that both the symptoms she expresses, and her dream and trance experiences, will be culturally determined?

In order to come to grips with these and other problems, I shall now describe the typical process whereby a woman becomes a member of a spirit possession cult group.

Diagnosis of Spirit Possession and the Role of Dreams

The primary basis for recruitment into the group is illness. Illness in this culture is a broad concept, and includes individual symptoms of all the local endemic diseases and a whole range of other organic ailments, as well as behavioural symptoms and a variety of social distresses such as anxiety about conflicts or problems in the home. To give just one example of the latter: a woman who has been worried because a husband or son is out of work, or drinking heavily, will describe herself as "sick". This is quite close to the notion one occasionally hears expressed in our own society: "I worried myself sick over him!" A cult leader will take on most complaints, excluding, however, severe behavioural disorders where the behaviour of the person concerned has become totally socially unacceptable. These are classified as possession by another class of spirits called *jinn*. The word for mad in Arabic is *majnuun*, literally, "*jinn*-possessed". Treatment is given by a male Islamic healer or *feki* and may involve the spirit being beaten, bullied, starved or tricked out of its unfortunate host. Milder behavioural symptoms, those which would probably be termed neurotic in Western cultures, tend more to be ascribed to possession by a *zaar* spirit—also referred to by the synonyms *rih al-ahmar* or "red wind" and *dastuur*.[6]

---

6. The etymology of the terms *zaar* and *dastuur* is obscure. Some writers assume the essentially non-Arabic form *zaar* to be a corruption of an Arabic term meaning "he visited". Yet others believe the word to be a borrowing from either Amharic or Persian. As it exists in Sudanese Arabic it has no meaning outside its spirit possession context.

With regard to a possible "visit" or "visitation" meaning, it is interesting to note that the word *dastuur* was apparently used in Egypt as a warning cry to a household's womenfolk to conceal themselves when a male visitor approached the threshold.

Dastuur also bears the commonplace meaning of "door support" or "door jamb" in the

Whereas the aim is to exorcise *jinn*, *zaar* spirits are merely placated and remain bound to their hosts for life.

Many women consciously link their illness symptoms to remembered antecedent personal crises, and these are overwhelmingly to do with emotional distress at the death of a relative, or with problems of childbirth or fertility, and to a lesser extent with problems of marriage, or with adolescent and pre-adolescent problems such as circumcision and the onset of menstruation.

Indigenous healers tend to treat the total patient. I have been present at several diagnostic sessions, and in all of them the striking fact was that, even in cases of seemingly trivial organic complaints, all aspects of the patient's life were taken as relevant background. Thus for example, one person would volunteer the information that the patient had once had a baby which was still-born, another that she had been divorced twice before, another that she had conflicts with her present husband's mother, and so on.

So, the first criterion is illness, and when I refer to "the patient" I am adapting the Arabic term used, *al-ayana*, literally, "the sick one".

When a new patient consults a cult leader to ascertain whether or not she is spirit possessed, the diagnostic procedure may take one of two forms. Either the patient herself may act as a medium for the spirits which express through her their demands, or the cult leader, after what are said to be spirit-inspired dreams, or meditation, will convey to the patient what the spirit requires to cease troubling her. In the initial interview the attempt is always to encourage the patient herself to express the wishes of her invading spirits. What usually happens is that after some preliminary attendance at spirit possession rituals, after the urging and recommendation of her female kin and neighbours, and possibly after trying other available types of diagnosis and treatment, the patient, or her kin acting on her behalf, will arrange a formal consultation with a cult leader.

After taking the hand of the patient, calling down the blessings of God, and uttering soothing reassurances, the cult leader will then proceed to administer, one after another, the different blends of incense particular to each classificatory group of *zaar* spirits. This may or may not be accompanied by rhythmic drumming.

Any person may be possessed by a multitude of different spirits, but there are always a few who are considered to be the principal possessing agents, and it is to these that a patient will dedicate a ritual. These principal

---

Sudan, and this ties in with much of the liminal terminology used in the spirit possession songs, which include much reference to doorkeepers, thresholds, doorways and so on.

In the Sudan no conscious conceptual link with the similar Arabic term *dustuur*, meaning "constitution" (in a governmental sense) is made, but it is interesting to note that a similar cult in Somalia bears the name *mingis*, an Ethiopian term meaning government.

spirits are said to be those which reveal themselves first in the diagnostic session. Others may manifest themselves during the course of the patient's first ritual, or at later stages in her possession history. As the cult leader administers the different types of incense, the patient may go into or assume a state of trance and begin to tremble and to groan or weep. This indicates that the first spirit has, as they say, "descended". The cult leader begins to question it: "who are you?"; "tell us your name"; "what do you require?"; "why are you troubling this woman?"; and so on. The patient answers in a "spirit voice", or by miming gestures interpreted by the cult leader, as the spirit indicates its requirements. These are usually stereotyped—a standardised spirit costume and the mounting of a ritual and sacrifice in its honour.

The cult leader begins to bargain with the spirit manifested in the patient: "take this illness from her and we will make a ritual for you and bring you all that you require". Relatives of the patient, usually visibly impressed by this point, add their assurances that they will provide everything possible.

The appearance of the first spirit marks the diagnostic breakthrough. After that several other spirits may reveal themselves one by one as their particular incense is administered. The first spirit, it is said, "stands locking up the door". After it reveals itself and receives promises that its demands will be met, then any other invasive spirits within the patient may also express their own particular characters and demands.

It is important to note that in general it is rare for a previously unknown spirit to reveal itself during these early sessions. The patient-medium is operating within a choice range of well-known spirit forms whose characteristics and demands are fairly uniformly conceptualised. As I said earlier, there are very few women who have never been to a spirit possession ritual. Most have some contact with, or knowledge of, cult groups. Many have been familiar with the spirits from their early childhood, having been taken along as infants and small children by their mothers to rituals, and later imitating the dances and costumes of the participants in their play. They may be directly under a cult leader's influence as her kinswoman or neighbour. Moreover it is not unusual for an ill patient to spend several days or weeks at a cult leader's house before undergoing formal diagnosis, thereby being fully exposed to a *zaar* atmosphere and to the ideas and suggestions of the cult leader and her colleagues.

The accuracy and success of this diagnosis by means of incense is measured by the degree of recovery of the patient, and to this extent the proceedings are highly pragmatic. Either immediately, or within a reasonable time afterwards, she should feel some relief from her symptoms. This is taken as a sign that the spirits are prepared to keep their side of the bargain and that she must start making preparations to keep hers. This is why to call the actual ritual itself curative, is to some extent misleading. The "cure" may have taken place earlier, and a perfectly healthy and contented woman who sponsors a ritual is seen as merely fulfilling her vow to the spirits.

But sometimes the administering of the incense does not evoke a response from the patient, and she does not straight away become the medium for her intrusive spirits, even though general concensus insists that she is spirit possessed. When this happens the cult leader acts alone in a further diagnostic procedure.

The patient or her relatives bring to the cult leader a garment or cloth worn close to the patient which has her bodily smell upon it. The cult leader sprinkles perfume on it and holds it over an incense burner, before putting it beneath her head when she sleeps at night. She may wrap in it other objects, brought as gifts by the patient, such as palm leaves, perfumes and sweets, which are referred to as "keys of dreams". Before the cult leader sleeps she concentrates her thoughts upon the patient. If she has no dreams that night, she will tell the patient that there is no spirit possession involved. More often, not surprisingly, she says that she has dreamt of the spirits and their requests, and she instructs the patient accordingly.

Dreams, and their interpretations, play an important part in the *zaar* cult. Strange or unpleasant dreams, especially those involving unknown or foreign persons, will often be the factor that stimulates a woman who is unwell to seek a diagnosis in terms of spirit possession. They may also serve to confirm in the patient's mind the accuracy of a diagnosis already made.

These dreams, at least as they are remembered and told, are often remarkably clear in their reference, both to the dreamer and to anyone familiar with the culture. One example will have to suffice here:

This concerns a married woman now in her thirties. Like the majority of women of her age group and rural origin, she has had no formal education. She has been married for sixteen years to a father's brother's son (the preferred form of marriage) and the marriage has been affectionate and stable despite the fact that the couple are childless. Out of regard for his wife, and for their close links of kinship, the husband has resisted suggestions that he take another wife to bear him children.

At the time in question the woman had been married for five years. Her husband had gone abroad to study for a period of some years, returning only in the vacations, and had left her in the care of a group of kin living in a town far from her natal village. While there she started to suffer from continual headaches and dizziness. She began to have vivid dreams, and one particularly stimulated her to have recourse to a spirit possession cult leader. She dreamt that she was ill, sitting on a chair, and unable to speak. An uncle of hers, a religious leader and a strict orthodox Muslim, opposed to spirit possession practices, appeared in the dream carrying a ram and saying it must be slain and she must be given its blood to drink, whereupon she says, she awoke feeling a heavy pressure in her chest and back and began to spit blood.

Now here we have a girl who has been feeling wretched and unwell. Her childlessness after five years of marriage makes her an object either of curiosity, not necessarily charitable, or of pity to her fellow women. Her husband is not there to boost her status by demonstrating loyalty to her as a wife, and she is away from the protection of her natal family. The move from a village, where she can claim some tie of kinship with most of the inhabitants, to a town largely composed of strangers, has undoubtedly restricted her social range and freedom, controlled as these are by the moral obligations of Islam. Furthermore, her husband's absence ensures that there is no immediately foreseeable chance of alleviating her central problem of childlessness.

In her dream she is sitting on a chair, speechless and therefore unable to express the nature of her illness. The "chair" refers directly to *zaar* spirits. The tray of offerings made to the spirits is called their "chair". During the course of spirit ritual the spirits are believed to come down and stay on their "chair". They are also said to "descend" onto the patient and "sit on her", so that she herself in a sense becomes a spirit "chair". A ram sacrificed in the course of a ritual as a specific patient-substitute, is first sat upon, and sometimes rode around the room, by the patient when she is in a state of trance and has the spirit within her. The ram patient as an offering is also then a "chair" for the patient spirit.

In this dream a strict uncle, who was in fact opposing her interest in the possession cult, now insists that this is the only way she can be cured. The sacrifice of a ram and annointment with its blood is the climax of a spirit possession ritual. In earlier times the blood was also drunk, and this has been one of the principal objections to the cult made by local Islamic leaders. So in this dream the uncle is not merely neutralised but transformed, and his religious authority is used to encourage his niece's participation in the cult.

Sometimes it is not the patients themselves who dream of the spirits, but their relatives. Kin who are already part of a spirit possession circle particularly, use the evidence of their dreams as a mechanism for recruiting their kinswomen to their cult group. Men sometimes dream of the spirits, and their dreams, or the interpretation of them by their womenfolk, have been known by their own testimony to force reluctant fathers, brothers and husbands to finance the ritual for which their women have been asking.

It is interpretation which counts in channelling an individual's dream processes along the culturally possible courses. For example, if a dream is by no means as clear as the one above, and the dreamer is already, shall we say, spirit-prone, she will go to a cult group leader who will draw, like the psychoanalyst, on a specialised store of esoteric knowledge to give an interpretation in terms of the dogma of the cult.

Dreams may be the means for the genesis of new spirits, or at least for the appearance of ones said to be previously unknown, since in theory all the spirits are supposed to have existed from ancient times. However, it is admitted that sometimes either a cult leader or a patient may dream of a new spirit form which they do not recognise—sometimes the wife or lover of an existing spirit. This spirit will teach them in the dream the song and drumming style it requires, and will convey its particular demands as far as costume is concerned.

It is not very easy to get a new spirit established. One has to persuade the cult leader and the others of the group of the validity of the dream apparition. One has to be able to describe in detail tangible characteristics and demands of the spirit, and to be able to provide a distinctive song and drumming rhythm. The song and costume may be tried out at a ritual sponsored by the innovator, but this is still a long way from its gaining general credence and acceptability, so that others begin to be possessed by the same spirit. What seems to happen much more frequently is that old spirits become slowly endowed with additional characteristics and demands, or with greater sophistications of costume. Thus Hakiim Baasha, a long established doctor spirit, now has two manifestations. One is a Turkish doctor wearing the costume of the Turko-Egyptian period of rule in the Sudan (1821–1880). Another has a modern medical uniform—long white coat, pocket pencil and stethoscope.

Working alongside the innovative and imaginative tendencies of individuals within the cult groups is the overall tendency to conservatism in belief of the group as a whole. Rituals should be performed in the "correct" manner if they are to have the desired beneficial effect. The trend therefore is for pre-ritual discussions between the patient, the cult leader, and other devotees, to attempt to reach a concensus on what is the correct and proper way to please a particular spirit or spirits. These decisions are drawn from a common pool of existing ritual knowledge. It is the well-known pattern whereby what was, in its early history, undoubtedly an innovative cult (see Constantinides, 1972, ibid.), gradually becomes more and more establishment, particularly when it models itself on existing religious institutions, as this cult has in many ways modelled itself upon the various mystical religious brotherhoods.

But a survey of the cult since the years of its introduction to the Sudan shows that new spirits, and hence new segments of ritual action, have been introduced from time to time in the cult's history, and gained general credence. This appears to happen when an individual's notions strike a chord of recognition in the wider group of which she is a part, and where the expression of private sentiments coincides with a cultural readiness to accept symbolic expression of that sentiment.

Spirits of Sickness

Let us now look more closely at the nature and characteristics of these *zaar* spirits.

The dogma of the cult has it that there are seven groups of spirits and seven blends of incense, one for each group. However, this appears merely to be one of several devices for incorporating the cult within the overall belief system of popular Islam, the number seven having some prominence in Muslim theology and hence considerable mystical value. In fact, although the spirits are classified into groups, the classification is fairly flexible and varies slightly from one cult leader to another. There are usually more than seven groups, and the individual spirits whose classification is not clear-cut may be differently assigned according to the notions of individual leaders.

The main groups distinguishable are:

The Holy Men—a collection of Muslim saints, teachers, founders of religious brotherhoods, and pilgrims.

The Ethiopians—purportedly an ethnic group: it includes both anthropomorphic spirits such as "The Little Ruler of the Ethiopians", and the spirits of places and things associated with Ethiopia.

The Pashas—spirits of early government administrators and doctors, several distinguishable as historical figures, others apparently cultural stereotypes.

The Arabs—spirits of the nomadic desert tribes of the Sudan.

The Europeans or Christians—this group includes the spirits of Jews, Copts, Greeks, Armenians, French and British. General Gordon of Khartoum is there, and so is Lord Cromer, as well as the spirit "Electricity". The Europeans are known particularly for their excessive fondness for alcoholic beverages.

The Ladies or Daughters—an ethnically mixed group, including the daughters of all the above mentioned categories. The daughters of the Holy Men especially, typify a sort of ideal womanhood.

The Blacks—this includes spirits of all the peoples and areas from which the northern Sudanese have in the past obtained slaves, as well as the peoples of the Western Sudanic regions.

The Fellata—Muslim West Africans begging their way on pilgrimage to Mecca. Some of these may be alternatively classed as Holy Men, or as Blacks.

The Grandmothers—the spirits of old women, sometimes included with the Ladies, or some of them with the Blacks.

The Tumburawi—spirits from the previously mentioned Tumbura cult. This is a small group of spirits thought to be particularly savage in their effects, and may include spirits of animals, such as the crocodile, as well as the spirit of death and the graveyard.

There does not appear to be any marked status association in being possessed by one type of spirit rather than another, whatever the prestige of the ethnic category it represents, and the degree of significance of the possession lies rather in the severity of the illness inflicted. Certain individual spirits from a variety of groups are, however, more popular in terms of frequency of occurrence than others. Cult participants are normally possessed by more than one spirit, and it is not unusual for a person to have one or more from each of the groups.

Taken as a whole, the classification provides a fairly consistent view of all the cultural influences which have penetrated the Sudan from without, especially during the last one hundred years or more, and in this sense can very much be viewed as the spirits of social change.

When we come down, however, to the level of the individual spirits, we find remarkably little elaboration of character. Though each has a song and drumming sequence particular to its name, and a colour and costume association by which it can be recognised, these are usually little more than variations on a highly stereotyped theme. Cult members are much less interested in the nature and character of the spirits *per se* than they are in how any individual spirit is affecting them, or their close friends or kin. Spirit demands are worried over simply to "get it right" so that the ritual will be efficacious. In other words the spirits stand for, or symbolise, something else.

While in one sense, then, the spirits represent a panorama of the recent historical past, if we look closely at the ritual addressed to them, we find throughout the symbolic expression of timeless realities—fertility, life and death, and the individual's fears, failings and inadequacies in the face of these.

Now before I give a gloss on the ritual, I must make it clear that, as is so often the anthropologist's experience, the participants themselves are not interested in problems of meaning. They simply do not think about the ritual in these terms. Questions about meaning are meaningless questions, and tend merely to draw forth in answer re-descriptions of actions.

I remember vividly on one occasion being made to feel rather like a dim pupil hauled before the class for consistently failing to perceive the internal beauty and logic of some self-evident mathematical formula. I was attending the ritual of a cult leader whom I knew well, and had in the intervals been persistently pressing her about the meaning of what I was seeing. Finally she threw up her hands in exasperation, turned, and announced to the whole assembly "time and time again we tell her, and still she doesn't understand!" However, she then proceeded to give me nothing more than a blow by blow re-description of all that had just taken place, finishing "and we do this because this is what the spirits want!" Cf. Wittgenstein: "don't ask for the meaning—look and *see*!"

So my answer was clear. The meaning lay within the action. The hypothesis then must be that the participants do not find it necessary, or perhaps even possible, to express the meaning explicitly, because it is self-evident at some level, conscious or unconscious, to members of the culture. This necessitates looking at the other, equally unexplained, rituals of the culture and drawing comparisons.

But firstly a brief outline of a typical *zaar* ritual held for the benefit of an individual patient.[7]

Possession Ritual

This will take place either in the patient's home, or at the house of the cult group leader. It lasts from one to seven days and involves considerable expenditure in relation to income. It is attended each day by, on average, thirty to one hundred women, according to the wealth and status of the main participants. Some of those attending are the patient's own female kin, affines, neighbours and friends; some of the others, followers of the cult leader and invited by her. The patient is referred to as "the sick one" or, alternatively as "the bride". When not dancing or in a state of trance she should maintain the modest and downcast expression of a bride. She is also dressed as a bride with red *henna* dye applied to her hands and feet, a new dress and as much gold finery as she can muster, and a new white outer garment, the all-enveloping, sari-like *tobe*. The clothes should be new and clean because, as the cult leaders say, "as the ritual cleanses one of illness, so one should be clean and have clean things". She must remain in these clothes, apart from costume changes, throughout the length of the ritual. She must sleep alone in a special room designated for the ritual, and which contains all the ritual objects and offerings, and she is secluded from contact with the men of the household, especially from any sexual contact with the husband. A woman who breaks the ban about male visitors, even for adolescent sons, will be admonished "do you want to lose your health for the sight of men!"

---

7. This very generalised description is based on the thirty-six rituals, given at different times by a total of eight different cult leaders, which in whole or in part I attended.

The patient will have spent a great amount of time and effort in preparing a series of costumes for the different spirits possessing her, a tray or "chair" of offerings, and a ram and goat to be sacrificed. The money for all this, as well as for the cult leaders fees, will normally be provided by a woman's husband, or by her close male kin—father, brothers or son. The head of a household should provide for the ritual needs of those former slaves who still work there as servants. Some women are able to finance themselves with the proceeds from inherited property, or from goods produced by them in the home, such as clothing and special foodstuffs, and sold to other women. If a woman is very poor a cult leader will often treat her and lend her the appropriate costumes, in return for general domestic services.

After the patient and gathering have been liberally applied with incense, especially at the bodily orifices, the points of entry and exit for the spirits, the drumming of a whole series of spirit songs will begin. This is called "pulling the threads". The spirits are referred to as threads and the drumming is said to pull them to "descend" into those who "have", that is, are possessed by, them. These latter are then also referred to as "descending" as they enter into a state of trance and become the spirit. Here is a cult leader's description of the process:

> the odour of the incense is smelt by the spirits, and it draws their attention to the person who is applying it. And the song calls them as I would call you— "Hey! Come here!" Group by group they come, like people, into the room and into the people. And when the farewell is drummed they leave. The thread descends into people. Into some it goes quickly and others slowly. When the spirit descends into a person's body, they do things that they could never normally do.

Although the main focus of attention is on the patient, anyone fully initiated into the cult, who has given her own ritual, may rise to dance. Habituées arrive with hold-alls packed with their own spirit costumes, and will don them at the music appropriate to their own possessing spirits. During the course of the dancing several women may achieve, or assume, a state of dissociation, the drumming, incense, rhythmic bodily jerking, and over-breathing, all being employed as techniques. Trance allows for considerable bodily and emotional abandon. The same women whose culture normally demands of them sedate, restrained behaviour, may weep, tremble, rage, shriek, yelp, beat themselves violently against the ground, smoke and drink openly, or strut about arrogantly. However, this abandon occurs in remarkably controlled circumstances. Different states of bodily abandon are suitable to different groups of spirits. Even in trance, a woman possessed by the spirit of a Muslim saint would be expected to act in a dignified manner appropriate to the saint. She would not, for example, display the violence and self-abuse suitable only to the spirits of the Blacks. If sometimes individuals behave inappropriately to the spirit in question, they are pulled up sharply by the cult leader and publicly chastised. So the apparent abandon is in fact carefully controlled and not necessarily spontaneous.

The drumming and dancing continues for several days and is punctuated by certain ritual highlights. Of these I will describe here only the most important, the sacrifice. This forms the dramatic and ritual climax of a whole sequence of symbolic actions. Any ritual of three days or more normally involves the sacrifice of two animals—a black male goat and a white or reddish-brown male sheep, depending on the colour association of the class of spirits predominating in the patient.

The word for slaughter may be used in referring to the sacrifice, but the most common word used is *karaama* or thanksgiving. This is a word used at life-cycle rituals, for sacrifices made at the principal Muslim festivals, and also for the occasion when a sheep is killed to provide food for guests who come to congratulate a person after they have recovered from some form of illness, or made good some misfortune. The word is often used to describe the *zaar* ritual itself, indicating the focal nature of the sacrifice. Thus a woman, when asked how many spirit rituals she has given, will reply for example, "I have made *karaama* three times".

On the day before the sacrifice an assistant carefully washes down the animals and applies red *henna* dye in a line from the head to the tail along the spine, and then at right angles across the body, leaving a cross-shaped red stain.

At the time of the sacrifice the animals are led into the centre of the dancing area. They are covered with cloths, white for a white sheep, red for a reddish one, and fumigated with incense. If the goat is to be sacrificed at the same time it is covered with a black cloth and placed side by side with the sheep. The patient, dressed in the appropriate spirit costume, sits or rests briefly upon the sheep, and is then prepared to go in procession around the animals. An assistant leads the procession, bearing aloft the incense burner. Behind her comes the patient, and any others who have themselves already made a sacrifice to the spirits. They carry lighted candles as they go around. Dates, nuts and cereals may be tossed to the assembly during the course of the procession.

At first the patient wears white as the drumming and chanting invokes God, the Prophet Mohammed, and the Holy Men. She may then change into red. Soon the rhythm of the drumming increases and the patient and others in the procession may go into trance. The whole sequence may go on for up to half an hour as spirit after spirit is invoked. The attention of all the spirits must be drawn, lest any feel "jealous" at being left out and inflict further illness on the patient. As one cult leader put it: "All the threads are to come. All of them are to be called from different directions, and all hear it. So that one spirit would not say it had not seen the sacrifice. All of them are invited, threads after threads, so that no one of them would say 'I have not seen the sacrifice'."

Finally, with the patient in a state of trance, the animals are led into the courtyard and all follow after. A large canopy is made from white cloth; beneath it stand the patient and the sacrificial sheep. The animal's throat is slit and some of the fresh blood that spurts out is quickly caught in a bowl by the assistant. Perfumes are added to the blood. The patient then steps or jumps over either the stream of blood or the body of the slaughtered animal seven times. The cult leader then proceeds to annoint the patient with the blood on her forehead, temples, hair parting, base of the neck, armpits, belly, hands and feet, paying particular attention to any part that aches or has been a seat of illness. New spirit costumes are marked with a spot of blood "so that the spirits will recognise them". A red handkerchief may be annointed with blood and tied about the patient's right wrist as a sign to the spirits that the patient has made a sacrifice. The patient is also given the blood-stained knife of the sacrifice to grasp in her right hand. Both knife and handkerchief will stay with her until the final riverside purification ritual.

Parts of the sheep are served as food to all the guests. Its head is kept aside and roasted or boiled in preparation for a further ritual sequence called the "Opening of the Head".

This takes place on the day following the sacrifice of the sheep. During a break in the dancing the cooked head of the sheep is placed, mouth pointing upwards, on a round tray, together with the four hooves, and brought before the cult leader. The whole assembly is ordered to observe silence. The cult leader adminsters incense to the patient and then she and three assistants ritually cleanse their hands in the incense smoke. Each takes a corner of the tray and they lift it seven times from the ground, and then lower it seven times onto the head of the seated patient. While the assistants continue to hold the tray in that position, the cult leader takes both jaws of the sheep firmly in her hands and forces them open. The tray is again lifted seven times from the patient's head, and she is then fed parts of the meat of the head, especially what are known as the sensitive parts, those where the essential being of a creature is thought to reside—the eyes, ears, brain and tongue. The cleaned skull of the sheep, together with its hooves, are kept aside to be thrown into the river.

The grand finale of this curative ritual is marked by a symbolic purification with water—where I worked, the waters of the river Nile.

Throughout the preceding days remnants from the various ritual sequences have been stored in a large rush basket. These include the head and hoof bones of the sacrificial sheep, the head, hooves and intestines of the goat, dates, peanuts, sweets, a handful of the mixed cereal grains used in the course of the ritual, candle ends, perfumed oils, *henna* dye, and the blood-stained dishes. This rather malodorous collection stays in the room with the patient.

On the day following the last day of the ritual the cult leader and her assistants call at the patient's house for the final riverside sequence. The patient is still secluded in the spirit room in her blood-stained clothing, attended by her close female kin. The household will have hired a market bus, or taxis, to take the patient, the cult leader, and a small group of assistants and kin to the river bank, together with the basket of remains. On the way to the river the patient still clutches the blood-stained sacrificial knife in her right hand.

On arrival at the river bank, cult leader and patient stand in the water at the edge. The cult leader may throw handfuls of cereal grains towards the land and the water. Leader and patient then raise their hands in a salutation to the female spirits believed to reside in rivers. The contents of the basket are then hurled into the river, the assistants having taken the knife and bowls of caked blood which they proceed to wash in the river water.

Cult leader and patient wash their hands and faces in the river water. The leader then removes the red handkerchief from the patient's right wrist and washes it, after which she splashes handfuls of water into the faces of all those attending the ceremony. This marks the occasion for general rejoicing and merriment and the trip back from the river is rather a joyful affair.

Once back at the house, the patient is told that she may now go and wash and change into clean clothing, and perfume herself. The matting is rolled up from the floor and the patient may now sleep on a normal bed, though she is still secluded for a further number of days equal to the number of days of the ritual itself, and should continue not to see her husband during this time.

Context and Meaning

I will now attempt to elucidate some of the symbolism used in these spirit possession rituals. In spite of the paucity of indigenous exegesis, it is obvious that the symbolism *is* meaningful to those taking part. In ritual action and preparation, in discussion, in the interpretation of dreams thought to be spirit-inspired, both cult and non-cult participants draw on a common pool of symbolic expression. Victor Turner (1968, p. 7) says: "Even when symbols are not explained in linguistic terms, they tend to appear in contexts which, to a person reared in the appropriate culture, abundantly elucidate them". So let us now turn to the wider culture of our spirit possessed women for insight.

Both men and women of the Muslim northern Sudan regard the reproductive power of women as their most important attribute, and most of the rituals of the life-cycle are to do with control, socialisation and protection of this power. Before puberty, usually between the ages of five and nine, young girls undergo so-called Pharaonic circumcision, which involves cutting away the external genitalia and sealing together the scar tissue to leave one small orifice for the passage of menses and urine, and later of course, though it may have to be incised for this, for sexual intercourse.

Without this operation it is said that young girls would become wild and disorderly. It marks the beginning of the girl's social maturity, her transition from being a young animal free to roam and play with all her age mates regardless of sex, to being a responsible member of society, adhering to the mores and modesty required of members of her sex. The circumcised girl will now be increasingly restricted to association with female kin, she is expected to assist in and master all the jobs culturally appropriate to women, and will begin to cover her head and shoulders.

The circumcision is thought to ensure her good behaviour sexually, and to ensure that the sexual passions of women, often otherwise thought of as urgent and uncontrollable, are kept in order. It is supposed to guarantee her virginity on first marriage. Not to be a virgin when she first marries is totally unthinkable. So the girl's potential fertility, bounded and controlled by circumcision, is given over to the husband at marriage, so that through her he may perpetuate his lineage. The genital orifice has to be cut open to allow the birth of a child, and the circumcision is subsequently re-rendered and the woman re-presented as a "bride" to her spouse.

The overall ideal to which a northern Sudanese woman aspires, if I may be allowed to generalise very broadly here, is a marriage suitable to the status of her lineage, a household of her own which she is given free reign to manage, the exclusive affectionate and economic attentions of her spouse, and the demonstration of her fertility in the birth of many children, especially sons. Through all these she gains enhanced status, security in marriage, and ultimately a considerable degree of authority over her fellow women as the recognised "grandmother" of a lineage section. But many things may threaten the achievement of this ideal: her own physical illness or infertility; her personal and emotional inadequacy in the face of what is socially required of her; conflict with the other women among whom she must live and work; death of the close relatives who support or promote her interests; inadequacies in her spouse; the possibility of his taking another wife, or divorcing her, and so on. All these find expression as symptoms of sickness, and seek relief, in spirit possession.

Against this background then, we may take as our starting point in the interpretation of spirit possession ritual, its pervasive marital symbolism.

The patient is called a "bride of the *zaar*", though there is no accompanying notion of her actually marrying the spirit.[8] She is carefully groomed and perfumed as a bride; her hands and feet are stained with the red *henna* dye of a bride; she is dressed in fine new clothing and wears gold ornament and a new white *tobe*; she is bound with a red cloth; a sheep is sacrificed for her; and she is purified at the river.

Now there are other occasions in the course of a woman's life when she is called a "bride" and is similarly adorned and treated, with a sacrifice made for her and a very similar riverside purification held. This happens at circumcision (or did before this was made illegal and its practices became more secretive and restricted), first marriage, and after the birth of each child.

In fact nearly all the main symbolic themes present in spirit possession prove on examination to be recurring themes throughout the total ritual of the female life cycle.

A great many of them have to do with protection from the forces of evil believed to be ever present and menacing, but especially at these life-crisis danger points, when the principal actors are on display and are open to the malevolent envy of both man and spirit. Some are expressive of the condition of the person. Yet others are generalised symbols of life, fertility and regeneration.

Let us take for example the use of the colour red. The *zaar* spirits themselves are, as a class, said to be "red winds". Red is thought of as a hot colour, and the spirits are also described as "hot" and as "heating" people. The blood association of the colour is obvious. The spirits are counted responsible for many ailments classified under the indigenous sytem as "diseases of the blood". As recipients of the sacrifice they are called "the owners of the blood". The Ethiopian spirits who are all associated with the colour red, are said to be especially "hot" and to "bring bleeding". The popular sub-group of Ethiopian female prostitute spirits are often held responsible for either excessive or non-existent menstrual bleeding and by association for all sorts of genito-urinary ailments and problems of fertility. Blood and fertility and therefore red and fertility are closedly linked in the total social and ritual system. A woman bleeds at circumcision, the circumcised woman bleeds at first sexual intercourse and at childbirth. Regular

8. My frequent enquiries as to whether the patient was actually marrying the spirit were scorned as quite absurd. "How?" I was asked by one cult leader. "Can she marry *al-Tomsa* (a crocodile spirit) or *Waldi Youra* (a child spirit) or *Muna* (a female spirit)? Of course not! She is called a bride because she is *like* a bride."

monthly bleeding is overtly recognised as a sign of on-going fertility. As against this socially desirable, socially controlled situation, we have the threat posed by the irregular bleeding/uncontrolled sexuality/prostitution association of the female Ethiopian spirits.

Red is also a colour which indicates "importance" and status within the culture. In the Turko-Egyptian Sudan, the presentation of a red gown of honour and a red fez, such as are now required by the Ethiopian spirits, marked acknowledgement of the power and authority of the recipient. So we have the series of associations red/blood/fertility/importance/status.

For both men and women status is both ascribed and achieved. In part it is derived from the standing of the lineage into which one is born, and in part from the lineage which one creates through marriage and the birth of children. Although individually a man may achieve some degree of recognition for his religious piety, knowledge, military or political prowess, economic skills, or a combination of all these[9] to maintain the reputation thus gained he needs sons who will support him in his endeavours and carry on his line, and daughters with whose co-operation he can create alliances through marriage.

The achieved aspect of a woman's status, at least until recent years, is derived only through full exercise of her reproductive powers in socially appropriate circumstances, preferably in the context of a stable and on-going marriage with a man of equivalent ascribed lineage status. So, fundamental to a woman's aspirations, as indeed to a man's, are first of all her own health and fertility, and the health, fertility and potency of her spouse. Moreover, she needs to be able to exercise considerable social skills in securing and marshalling support for her goals, and in controlling and containing conflict which may threaten them. In part she will obtain this support from her husband and male kin, and indeed their willingness to bear the financial burdens of a *zaar* ritual is public affirmation of her importance to them. But we must not forget that this is a sexually segregated society, and that the constant day-to-day contact of any woman is with her female peer-group. It is her fellow women among whom she competes for, and displays, status, with whom she is in potential conflict, and among whom she seeks her strongest supporters. And when a point of crisis is reached in a woman's life, its definition in terms of *zaar* spirit possession demands that all the women with whom she is in contact—kin, affines, neighbours, servants and patrons, allies and enemies—join together in a series of ritual actions stating symbolically their unified desire for the restoration of her wellbeing.

The red/blood theme is of crucial importance at the sacrificial stage of

9. See Barclay (1964, p. 135) for factors influencing achieved status in a modern suburban Sudanese village.

the spirit possession ritual. The release of the blood of the sacrificial animal is considered as the first and most important step to health and well-being for the patient, and this is readily symbolised by her stepping or jumping seven times over either the body of the sheep or the blood. The sheep is alternatively viewed as an obstacle in the patient's path from illness to normality over which she can now step, or as a repository of the illness itself, a patient substitute, and in leaping over it she leaps away from the illness. The sheep is, as it were, a scape-goat! This is made quite explicit in such formulae as "the soul of this sheep is given up for your peace" or "you owners of the blood, this soul is sacrificed for you", which the cult leader utters as she annoints the patient with the fresh blood. A further sign to the spirits that a sacrifice has been made to them is the red handkerchief which is dipped in the blood of the sacrifice and then worn upon the right wrist until the final ritual and curative stage of the purification at the river. At the same time that this is washed in the river, the remains of the sacrificial animal are hurled into the water. This was specifically compared by one cult leader to the throwing into the river of the afterbirth which used to take place at the ritual following the delivery of a baby. "The river takes the afterbirth and leaves us the child." The implication is of course that the river takes the remains of the sheep and a cured patient is restored to her proper place in society.

The two other pervasive colour themes of the spirit possession ritual are black and white.[10] As we have seen, black is the colour associated with the group of spirits who induce violent and uncontrolled behaviour. Throughout the culture black is seen as an undesirable colour. It is associated with sorcery and the evil eye, with severe illness leading to death, and with madness. Spirits which bring madness and fatal disease are classified as black spirits. Black is contrasted to white in belief and popular expression. Devils are black. God is white. White indicates divine blessing and purity, a state of grace. The spirit holy men, as also their real-life counterparts, wear white and are expected to act with dignity and control. White is the colour of mourning because it signifies spiritual re-birth, as against earthly birth, the colour association of which is red.

So we have a whole series of contrasts: black is to white as the devil is to God, as evil is to blessedness, as violence is to calm and dignity, as disorder is to order.

I would suggest red as an intermediate colour between black and white, as indeed it seems to mediate between them in spirit ritual and sacrifice.

10. Possible significances of the almost universal ritual usage of the colour triad red/white/black have been postulated by Victor Turner (1967, p. 81 ff.). Many of the colour meanings prevalent in Sudanese ritual are directly comparable to their associations in Ndembu ritual (ibid., pp. 69–71).

God, the Prophet Mohammed and the saints, association white, bring a state of blessedness, wellbeing and order. Red spirits bring cureable illness and milder forms of behavioural disorder. Black spirits bring severe behavioural disorder and death. Red, I would suggest, can go either way. We have already seen that it can be associated either with irregular bleeding/ uncontrolled sexuality/low status, or with regular bleeding/controlled sexuality/high status. A person who is ill because she is under attack from the red *zaar* spirits is in a ritually dangerous liminal position. If she ignores warnings and refuses to placate the spirits in ritual, it is believed that she will get progessively worse, possibly even mad or fatally ill. A correctly carried out *zaar* ritual however, is designed to restore her to a state of white/blessedness/and order.

The ambiguities of the red/blood/fertility association is recognised in women's discussion of their gynaecological ailments. Regular menstruation indicates on-going fertility, but also the absence of conception. Cessation of the menstrual flow may indicate pregnancy, or the *absence* of fertility.

Conclusion

It will have become obvious to those acquainted with the literature on spirit possession that in emphasising same sex support, conflict and competition, and in de-emphasising cross-sexual hostility, I am approaching the sort of analysis advocated by Wilson (1967, pp. 366–78). He argues that "the social epidemiology of possession . . . suggests that by far the greatest proportion of persons involved have some sort of ambiguous status identity . . ." (ibid., p. 375) and that "spirit possession and similar states seem more closely correlated with social situations which regularly, though not necessarily, give rise to conflict, competition, tension, rivalry or jealousy between members of the *same* sex rather than between members of opposite sexes" (ibid., p. 366). However, it *is* only a matter of emphasis, and should not perhaps be taken too far.

In the sexually segregated society that exists in the Muslim northern Sudan, particularly in its urban and suburban areas, cross-sexual hostility does of course exist, and men may frequently be held responsible for thwarting the aspirations of women, and vice versa. The fact that the symbiotic relationship between the sexes is the recognised basis for society, does not stop each sex holding negative as well as positive stereotypes of the other, nor does it prevent each sex from attempting to manipulate the other to its own advantage.

My point is merely that, on the whole, women do not tend to evaluate themselves *vis à vis* men, but rather in relation to other women. They live in an enclosed and feminine world, with very much its own cosmology, where men are indeed necessary, and frequently manipulated to serve the goals of women, but tend to be peripheral to their day to day concerns.

Women associate principally with, and are interested principally in, women. They see their main claims to status and security as resting in their re-productive power, fundamental to society, which, though it can only be given expression in properly sanctioned relationships with men, is unique to their sex. In this context it is highly significant that all the ritual designed to control, transfer and protect this power, is very largely in the hands of women. It is they who organise and supervise all the ritual trappings surrounding circumcision, marriage and birth, usually against a background of bitter complaints by the men about female extortion, as they pay out heavily to get their daughters and wives through each ritual stage. Similar male complaints are levelled against the restorative ritual of the spirit possession cult, also overwhelmingly organised and run by women. It is noteworthy that the only two full-time professions dominated by women in the traditional society are those of circumciser/midwife and *zaar* cult group leader.

So really I am suggesting that through spirit possession cults women who, for internal or external, physical or emotional reasons, are not adequately approximating to their culturally defined potential, express the nature of their problems through the symbolic behaviour of the cult's activities.[11] But it seems to me that the cult ritual achieves more than this, that it is, to use the established terms, both expressive and instrumental. It not only allows the individual to express, *vide* Douglas (1973, ibid.), the nature of his social reality and, *vide* Lewis (1966, ibid.), what is wrong with that reality, but also promises that things will get better, that problems will be overcome.

Cult ritual requires the individual members of a woman's social network to participate together in a standardised but dramatic enactment both of her own, and of each others, problems, inadequacies and anxieties. The atmosphere of mutual support and confession, the symbolic assurances of a better life to follow, the very nature and scope of the hospitality offered at the ritual, all allow for definition or re-definition of the status of the patient.

To summarise very briefly: the evidence of the cult groups which I have studied seems to me to support the far from novel hypothesis that individuals' attitudes, sentiments, needs and also stresses, are to a considerable extent shaped by the culture into which these individuals are born, and that therefore reaction to stress, although in one sense highly

---

11. Among the external factors impinging upon the women I would of course include social change and contact with other ethnic groups with different value systems, as symbolised in the very nature of the possessing spirits themselves.

individual, is bounded and given form by the sentiments of the culture which have been internalised in the individual since infancy. The particular material presented here attempts to demonstrate some of the mechanisms through which these individual attitudes, sentiments, needs and stress reactions, are capable of finding expression in culturally appropriate symbols through the group rituals of spirit possession. At the same time, it seeks to demonstrate that the fact that those rituals are largely ego-centred allows for a certain degree of adaptive exchange whereby the individual can subtly adjust his position in relation to the instruments of social pressure.

References

Barclay, H. B. 1964. *Buurri Al Lamaab: A Suburban Village in the Sudan*, Cornell University Press, Ithaca and New York.

Constantinides, P. M. 1972. *Sickness and the Spirits: A Study of the Zaar Spirit Possession Cult in the Northern Sudan*. Unpublished Ph.D. thesis, London University.

Crapanzano, V. 1973. *The Hamadsha: A Study in Moroccan Ethnopsychiatry*, University of California Press.

Doulgas, M. 1973. *Natural Symbols: Explorations in Cosmology*. Penguin, Harmondsworth.

Lewis, I. M. 1966. Spirit possession and deprivation cults. *Man* (N.S.), **1**, 307–29.

Lewis, I. M. 1971. *Ecstatic Religion: An Anthropological Study of Spirit Possession and Shamanism*, Penguin, Harmondsworth.

Turner, V. W. 1967. *The Forest of Symbols: Aspects of Ndembu Ritual*, Cornell University Press, Ithaca and London.

Turner, V. W. 1968. *The Drums of Affliction: A Study of Religious Processes among the Ndembu of Zambia*, Clarendon Press, Oxford.

Turner, V. W. 1974. *The Ritual Process: Structure and Anti-Structure*, Penguin, Harmondsworth.

Wilson, P. J. 1967. Status ambiguity and spirit possession. *Man* (N.S.), **2**, 366–78.

5 | The Meaning of Africa in Haitian Vodu

Serge Larose

To Haitians, Vodu denotes the whole range of beliefs and superstitions held by the peasantry in its dealings with the supernatural. However, among the peasants themselves, it has a much more precise meaning: it designates a specific ritual concerned with the so-called Vodu spirits. These spirits are worshipped within cult-groups which take much pain to point out the differences between them and other groups mainly pre-occupied with other sets of powers, all more or less related with the practices of sorcery, the "Petro" and the "Zandor" and the "Matok". I shall use the term "magic" to refer to the latter. Haitians do. The pre-eminence of Vodu societies over the magic ones is expressed in terms of fidelity to *l'Afrique Guinee*. Guinea stands for tradition, unswerving loyalty to the ancestors and through them to the old ways and rituals they brought from overseas. It forms what Turner would describe as a dominant symbol by reference to which spiritual power (1967, p. 28) is legitimated.

There have been very few attempts to relate these ritual distinctions to the functioning of social groups. Most studies of Vodu have tried to interpret it as a result of history, a mixture to be accounted for in terms of re-interpretations of Catholic beliefs by an African mentality (Herskovits, 1941). Whatever the usefulness of such an approach, it tells us little about the present function of such beliefs; it is clear that Vodu is not only the end-result of historical contact, but expresses itself a conception of history by which present behaviour is explained and evaluated. Lewis (1971) has shown how spirit possession can embody moral values held by the society where it occurs. I shall try in this essay to show how possession forms in Haiti an idiom in terms of which individuals and groups compete for power and morally evaluate one another. Such moral evaluations presuppose a set of shared assumptions about what is ultimately good and bad and are rooted in this opposition between Guinea and magic; the more Guinean one is, the better. However, when applied to concrete situations of competition between groups, these concepts are likely to form an idiom of dissent; everyone is Guinea in his own way and everyone denigrates his neighbour for having added to and thus diluted the inheritance.

The Creoles and their Fathers

In a paper on the theatrical aspects of possession in Haiti, Alfred Métreaux (1955, p. 23) saw in the freedom left to the worshippers, a sign of degeneration: "This may be seen in the overall absence of external controls surrounding the possession syndrome compared with what may be observed in Dahomey and even Brazil, where possession occurs in a mood of hieratic stiffness and where initiates are appointed in advance and receive a single spirit for their whole life and avoid any excess in the hysterical mimic. The Vodu worshippers may incarnate as many spirits as they like. It is this freedom left to the believers and the relative anarchy of their conduct which announce the decline of these cults." Vodu seems to indulge in hysterical outbursts of energy that would be considered out of place in other possession cults. Most observers have noted this spectacular character of possession in Haiti; possession is quite often preceded by a sudden explosion of excitement that may last quite a long time. The possessed person jumps in the air and falls violently to the ground, rolling all over the place, or literally throws herself into the arms of attendants with frantic movements of the shoulders and the hips, sometimes locking up a partner in his arms and pulling him to the ground in a sexual embrace.[1] This initial phase of possession is called *djai* by Haitians (from the French, *jaillir*, meaning to spring). As one moves into the domain of magic rituals, possession becomes more violent; the spirits may burst through the thin mud walls of the cult-houses or, standing on their heads, shake their legs to the lively rhythm of the drums or jump, head first over a fire. Usually, it is only after such an outbreak of energy, often quite furious, that the possessed person assumes the character of the god he is impersonating. These hysterical fits, deplored by Métraux as signs of anarchy, are simply traditional means by which the cleavage between the sacred and profane is expressed. This cleavage has to be over-dramatised in the absence of explicit rules by which religious authority is transmitted and religious power controlled; there is a need to

1. Spirits always form a pair, a male and a female counterpart. The sexual embrace is explained by the pleasure a male spirit feels when it meets its female partner. While possessed, a person still knows on whom its complement may fall and will often trigger off the expected possession by embracing his usual partner.

convince, to persuade by extravagant gesture, which is not a sign of degeneration but an attribute of the system itself. The same can be said of this
freedom left to the individual. As early as 1885, an Haitian scholar (Trouillot, 1885, p. 19) had made similar observations and predictions: "The
increasing number of local spirits and saints, between which hierarchical
relations are ill-defined, is an indication of regression; the old African ways
are forgotten." The continuous invention of new spirits seems rather to be
the traditional way in which Haitians have always manipulated their social
environment, and still do.

I would not refer to these recurring statements about the disappearance
of Vodu if they were not shared by the believers themselves. I suspect that
anthropologists have been more or less misled by the way Vodu practitioners look at their beliefs and this brings us back to the central issue of the
meaning of Guinea. All worshippers agree that Vodu is disappearing; this
may be explained partly by a natural tendency to beautify the past—
economically, it is certainly true—but there are other reasons which are
part of the ideology we have to describe. The Ancients, those who were
born in Africa and brought as slaves to Haiti, had tremendous powers and
almost boundless knowledge. With a few gestures of the hand, they were
able to make food appear before them; with a stick they made springs come
out of rocks. An informant told me how, one day, his ancestor, Gabriel,
went to visit a friend; under the pretext that he felt cold, the latter entered
the stove and came out through the chimney, unharmed; in reply, Gabriel,
feeling suddenly too hot, decided to bathe in a large caldron full of boiling
water. These men served also in a simpler way; they did not need all the
ritual elaborations and complexities one finds today; a simple word could
drive an enemy mad; three leaves picked up in the garden healed the worst
diseases. To worship in a Guinean way often means in a simple way: "a
small chicken killed at the gate for Legba, every year and this is all. No
drums, just the family; simple". The history of Vodu is the history of the
constant erosion of these powers, a loss of this original simplicity.

When one asks how this original science has been lost, one is likely to be
given two kinds of answers. The fathers did not hand over their secrets to
their children; they knew that they would be the first on whom their children would test them. They transmitted a part of it but kept the most
important tricks for themselves. It is a common saying in Haiti that the
receiver of a secret will first test it on his teacher. "An Haitian always keeps
an extra trick in reserve, a secret he will tell to no one, not even his children.
Just in case, one day he may be in trouble." This idea of a primordial science
of which only a part still subsists, is well illustrated by the following dream
through which the spirits appointed the leader of a cult-house in the area
where I was working. A beautiful lady appeared to his sister and told her:

"Lucy! Lucy! The caldron is empty. It is broken. But there is still a piece of it you will find behind the mango tree in the garden. You may take it; it still can be used to grill coffee." The following day, Lucy went to the garden and found a beautiful polished stone behind the mango tree, just where the lady had told her. She took it and, being a woman, she gave it to her younger brother who then assumed responsibility for the family cult-house. This stone is a "Guinea stone", a share in the original powers of the ancestors, a portion of this power. Guinea may thus be represented by the simplest object; such a stone would probably pass unnoticed in the corner of the small shrine, an unremarkable object scorned by visitors and yet it was considered by its owner as the most valuable piece of all his religious paraphernalia; to him, the paraphernalia were just to attract clients, but the stone embodied his own inner convictions. Sometimes it is a stone, some-times a small cross transmitted by the great-grandfather, sometimes a frag-ment of an antique cane-juice boiler. But these objects are surrounded by the deepest veneration.

The second type of explanation attributes the loss of power to the numer-ous ritual innovations themselves, to the lack of fidelity to the Guinea principles and the multiplication of "magic" associations. "Today God has cursed our country; Haitians have deepened too many mystical subjects. Everything has become more complicated." And one immediately points out these groups, the "Hairless societies" (*Sans poils*) worshipping demons and presenting themselves as the children of Lucifer, walking all night throughout the country and performing strange ceremonies at the cross roads and in the cemeteries. These groups, whose existence was doubted by Métreaux, are not just a product of the imagination; they exist and conduct specific rituals. Everyone ascribes their emergence to the very recent past; it is a "new fashion". However, if one inquires a bit further, he is likely to be told that similar groups existed a long time ago; but they had different names. They were called Bizango, they were called Vlindebindingue. By attributing these rites to the recent past, one denies their Guinea status and at the same time underlines their transient character. In spite of this, Guinea needs and always needed magic as its ground-figure, but by pro-jecting it into the recent past, it refutes its essential nature. The magic societies, mainly linked with landless peasants and the poor living in town, have heavily borrowed from European esoteric traditions. "You have to study very hard if you want to become a cult leader. Every step you take tells you: 'come on. Another step.' It all depends upon your own courage; there are things one would be better to ignore. But if you listen to the voice, you soon pass through all the Great Books. Ti Albert, Grand Albert, Ti Dragon, Grand Dragon, the 'Black hen', the 'Three Ladies of Egypt'." Such research is said to be very dangerous since Guinea spirits, the family spirits, do not mix with these entities and could withdraw their protection. All innovations are assimilated to magic. Of course there are many novelties which are accepted by society; however, as they are legitimated in terms of constancy to the Guinea traditions, they are not seen as innovations by the worshippers; if seen as such they are likely to be subsumed under the labels of magic and sorcery.

Both sets of explanation can be related. Since the fathers did not transmit all their knowledge to their children, the latter, the "Creoles", were more or less forced to look elsewhere, to create new rituals and new spirits. This idea is expressed in a Vodu song:

> Creoles say:
> There is no more Guinea,
> They will do whatever they like.

Guinea is thus associated with a particular form of social authority. On the one hand, the loss of primordial science is linked with the necessity for the ancestors to maintain their authority over their children by keeping to themselves the secrets of their powers; on the other hand the ritual elaborations and innovations can be seen as a kind of indirect rebellion against the authority of the fathers, embodied in the concept of Guinea. Of course, such an interpretation is not held by the voduist who simply opposes the ways of Africa to other practices considered as innovations and judged morally wrong. There is no myth about a Promethean rebellion of the sons against their fathers. It is only through the careful observation of overt behaviour and the way tension between the fathers and their children are expressed, that one is led to make such assumptions. To illustrate this, I give the transcription of the following argument between a Vodu priest and his child. I was lucky enough to record it on my tape recorder.

Thomas is a Vodu priest of about seventy years old. In spite of his age, he has not appointed any successor, partly because he fears to create dissension among his children, partly because he is reluctant to hand over the control of the cult-house and go into retirement. The argument arose as Thomas was "tying up the wanzins", a ritual conducted by the Vodu priest out of sight of the attendants and whose secret is transmitted together with the "asson", the rattle which stands as the symbol of Vodu priesthood. Two persons were allowed in the room where the ritual would be performed, together with myself. As the door was being closed however, Leon, one of Thomas' sons, more or less forced his way into the room to the evident displeasure of his father. He probably wanted to know how his father operated. Without raising his eyes from his work, Thomas asked him, harshly and ironically:

Are you baptised?

Meaning, are you old enough and mystically strong enough to intrude like that. A bit puzzled, Leon answered that of course he was. His father repeated the question and he replied:

If I am baptised? I father! A big chief as I!

Leon was a Makoute, a member of the political police of the regime. Thomas muttered:

—Fool.
—Father! It's me! A man who walked the whole country over.
—Follies!

—How that, follies!
—Well, you have become hairless. You walked the whole country.
—Father, there is no beast I am not.

Leon was referring to the powers sorcerers have to transform themselves into any animal they like. Nodding his head in disbelief, Thomas added:

—You are searching, so you will find.

Then Leon came to the main issue of the argument, saying that his father was too old, that he was unable to retain responsibility for the cult-house and that he had to appoint him as his successor. Thomas did not give him any encouragement:

—So you say that I am unable to keep the house. Well build up your own.

Leon said that he had already built it up. One of the attendants decided to intervene and explained to the ambitious young man:

—When your father asked if you were baptised, he meant baptised above your father.

Leon seemed to pretend that he knew more than his own father, that he was thus older than his own father. Pluming himself on what he had learned elsewhere, Leon reaffirmed that he was baptised and to prove it that his father could let him conduct the whole ritual in his place. He knew everything about the "tying of the wanzins".

—Leave it all to me. I shall conduct everything in the correct way. I am not stupid.

A bit irritated, Thomas said:

—Follies you will do. You never had any talent. What I know is not what you know, son.
—I did not work with you only, father.

—That is what I am saying. Follies that make you sleep anywhere, with any vagabond.

Undisturbed, Leon went on saying that in the northern part of the country, they considered "wanzins" a trifle. Vexed, Thomas replied:

—So I will come and ask you to teach me. Enough is enough. "Gangan" Leon, you are a bad "gangan", true.

("gangan" means priest.) One of the helpers tried to reason with the boy:

—Thomas is your father. What he knows, even if you come to know more than he does, you never know more.

Leon said that he did not mean that, but that his father had welcomed him in a rather rude way.

—No, Leon. That is no reason to behave like that before your father.

Leon said that he was on too good terms with his father to be treated in such a way. The helper replied:

—The way you are talking, it sounds as if you are going to test him.

(Testing or sounding means in Haiti putting the mystical force of a person to test.) Leon replied:

—I would not sound him. I would just listen to what he tells me.

Bent over the pots he was tying up, Thomas muttered:

—Should I trust him where I drink water?

(Referring to the possibility that such an ambitious child would not hesitate to poison him to take over his place.) And threatingly:

—Once there was a man, named Azar, who proclaimed himself houngan before Zilma . . .

Zilma was Thomas' own father and Azar had provoked him in the same way Leon had. For that, he had died. Leon mumbled a few words and was told to shut up. Thomas then said to him that he should have waited for his father to invite him before intruding like that.
Such conflict between a father and his children is by no means an isolated occurrence. I was told of four cases concerning children who had "sounded" their father in a similar way. The whole argument shows how Leon, being denied access to his father's expertise, had tried to compensate for it by travelling all over the country and even entering a "hairless society". Leon confronting his father, is magic confronting Guinea.

It is this opposition between a ritual Guinea, reassuring and transmitted from generation to generation, associated with the benevolent authority of the ancestors, and other spirits, more frightening but often ephemeral, linked with the rebellion of the children against their father's omnipotence, with all the guilt feelings it may arouse, which divides the supernatural world in two morally opposed categories, by which groups and individuals oppose one another. The idea that a concrete group could embody a pure Guinea tradition has no foundation and no such group should be looked for in Haiti. God is always "on our side", and Guinea is a similar concept, a complex figure through which power is legitimated. I shall now consider the main categories of spirits and the way they are integrated into cult-groups.

The Spirits

Haitian spirits are called *loas*. They are known literally as the "invisibles" one compares them to air, to winds. Everyone has a personal *loa* as his protector; he is identified with the Catholic guardian angel. This protector is inherited either on the father's or the mother's side. Every family, the family (*fanmi*) being a large bilateral group of kin, worships its own spirits. It is mainly in relation to land that it emerges as a bounded group, living within the framework of the "habitation"; the "habitation" is a piece of land that has been bought by an ancestor whose name still remains attached to it. The ritual group includes all the descendants of such an ancestor, membership being defined through male or female links. The family is the group within which the spirits have power and exercise authority; they do this mainly by "catching" a member of the group, meaning causing him some kind of affliction. The *loas* act only within the family. They may manifest themselves in many ways; in dreams, by assuming a human or an animal form (e.g. as an old man, a dog, a pig, a barn-owl) and finally in a privileged manner by possessing a member of the family.

How is possesion explained? Man is said to consist of three parts. The first one is the body. It is the corpse which is buried at death. It is animated by two spiritual principles; the "big angel" and the "little angel". Both may be seen as two shadows projected by the body on the ground (the umbra and its penumbra). The "big angel" is the seat of consciousness, emotions and sentiments, the source of all mental and physical energy. It is described as crude, heavy, unrefined, mainly because of its fleshy nature. It is more or less subordinate to the body functions, a kind of Freudian "id" principle. At night, it leaves the body and floats in the open all round the country thus accounting for dreams. Haitians are well aware of the compensating character of dreams; a proverb says that what you are unable to do in the daylight you will at night. But this is the main weakness of the "big angel"; if you go to bed while still hungry, your "big angel" just wanders around, looking for food, instead of doing more useful jobs such as seeking the next winning-number at the national lottery or spying on your enemies in the neighbourhood to warn you against their malicious intentions; such dreams are a sheer waste of time since they do not provide any guideline for future action and may even delude oneself into misrepresentations. The "big angel" is that part, located in the head, which is vulnerable to magical attacks. It may be displaced by a "dead" sent by a malefactor. It may even be trapped by a sorcerer who then substitutes his own will-power for his victim's. This explains why it is the object of many rituals, the purpose of which is to strengthen it. The head is simply given food; a mixture of wine, white flour, groundnuts, cassava, maize and chicken, is tied up in a white handkerchief over the head for a few hours. At death, the "big angel" is particularly vulnerable. It sticks to the body and becomes a kind of disembodied force wandering here and there, looking for employment; it has turned into a "zombi".[2]

The "zombi" has to be captured by a near relative and hidden in a bottle before any scream announcing the death to the neighbourhood be uttered; otherwise, it is feared that it would be seized by a sorcerer and put to work in the latter's gardens or used to harm the living.[3] After a year, the bottle is crashed over the tomb of the deceased; the "zombi" has changed into a harmless butterfly and can no more be captured.[4]

2. The word "zombi" always refers to the big angel. However, a person whose big angel has been captured by a sorcerer while he was still living, is himself named "zombi" a kind of walking corpse that can be materially seen. Of course the "zombi" of a deceased person has no such material appearance; it may be a stone taken from the cemetery ("you can put a zombi into your pocket"). It may be a skull, a bone or any other part of a corpse. In all magical operations, zombis play an important role. Candles are made with the bone-marrow of the skull; the burning flame of the candle is said to re-animate the dead which is then instructed to go and harass someone (such a procedure is called "expedition"). By grating the skull with a knife, magicians obtain a white powder which is used as a powerful poison as well as counter-poison. Most cult-leaders who also conduct healing rituals, have "zombis" they acquire by paying three or four dollars to any needy person who is ready to enter a cemetery at night to get them. Such practices are frowned upon but are fairly common, at least in the area I have been working in (Léogane).

3. Elaborate precautions are taken to prevent such a kidnapping. They all have a common theme. The "zombi" is given a never-ending task to perform, like counting a handful of sesame seeds that has been sprayed into the coffin, or passing a thread into the eye of a needle whose threadhole has been cut away. The "zombi" is then so busy doing that job that it does not listen to the voice of the one who comes at night to raise it from the tomb. It is also a usual practice to make the deceased drink a pint of gas in order to debilitate it and make it unfit for work. The corpse may be "arranged"; a dagger is put in the hands of the deceased and it is instructed to strike the first one who would attempt to seize it. A salted herring may be put in the left hand of the dead so that, having already something to eat, it will not be attracted by the food the sorcerer could present it to trap it.

4. Butterflies are said to bear news to the living. There is a complex set of meanings

The second shadow, the "little angel", is immune to mystical attacks. It is often described as if it was the *loa* itself. However, everyone agrees that the *loa* is external to the individual; it comes from Guinea and "enters one's head". The "little angel" seems rather to denote the capacity a person has to be possessed by such a spirit. In contrast with the "big angel", the "little" one is pictured as a small innocent whose presence at normal times is quite hard to perceive. The following analogy can be used: "Imagine that you are going up a very steep hill. You have become so tired that you feel you are going to faint, and yet you are going on. This is the 'little angel' that draws you forward; the 'big' one completely exhausted, has abandoned you." In ritual possession, the little angel displaces the big angel; it takes its place. The possessed person thus becomes the "horse" of the god. The first time one is possessed, he usually cannot stand the shock and keeps rolling on the ground, shouting terms of abuse or unable to say anything. This is described as the *bossale* stage of possession. (Under French colonial rule, the *bossales* were the newly arrived Africans, un-baptised, unable to speak Creole and not yet integrated into Haitian society.) The spirit has first to be baptised. The head of its horse is thoroughly "washed" with a number of leaves and then given food in order to fortify it and make it able to bear the shock of this intrusion. As long as the spirit has not been baptised and the head of its horse washed, there are doubts about the healing powers of the spirit and the relevance of its communications. By baptism, the *loa* is "fixed into one's head" and a permanent relationship is established between the spirit and the one it has selected.

The first possession by no means occurs only in contexts of illness; a spirit may claim someone during a dance without having caused him any affliction. One may be mounted by a number of spirits, but the first to possess a person is considered the "master of his head". At death, the "little angel" is sent "under the waters"—meaning Guinea—whence it will be removed a year later,[5] ready to mount another member of the family. Not all spirits are sent under the waters however; it is the controlled retention of this ability which distinguishes the Vodu society from other cult-groups identified with the magic rituals.

Though there is no common word to designate the benign possession by a *loa* and the evil possession by a "zombi"—both were considered quite

---

attached to them. A butterfly entering the house and going out immediately announces visitors. A black butterfly, resting upon the wall, inside the house, announces death and so on.

5. Often the ritual may be delayed until enough money has been collected to meet the expenses of the ceremony. The lapse of time referred to here is not to be taken literally.

distinct by all my informants—the parallelism is evident. Both displace the "big angel" and on both occasions, the head is similarly washed and given food to strengthen it. The *loa* and the "zombi" are said to sit down at the same place, behind the neck of the possessed person, though the "zombi" is easily identified by the inability of the possessed to raise his head. A permanent accommodation is looked for with the former but the latter has to be expelled. At death, both entities are set aside; one is concealed in a bottle till it loses its power to harm, the other is sent back to Guinea. It is only after a certain period of time that the ambiguity surrounding the deceased is removed; when his capacities have been ritually recovered by the society and his evil aspects have been exorcised.

The ambivalence surrounding the dead remains attached to an important class of spirits; the spirits of the cemeteries and of the graveyards. A brief consideration of these spirits will illustrate the way the dichotomy Guinea-Magic may work in practice. The first man buried in any burial ground is the master of that cemetery; his name is "Baron" (he has a wife, "Grande Brigitte", who is the first woman buried in the same cemetery). All those who have been buried after him are his followers and form together a group of *loas*, the *guedes*. There are as many "barons" as there are cemeteries but all are represented in the same way; a cross in the middle or at the gate of the burial yard. "Baron" is chief of the dead in both aspects; as "zombis" and *loas* (*guedes*). It is usually an ancestor. One may ask anyone in what way he is related to any particular "baron" in the area and be told that he is one's grandfather or one's own father. As an ancestor, it is part of the Guinea heritage and as *loa* it may ritually possess one of its children. But "Baron" also shares the attributes of "zombi"; it can be sent "on an expedition" by any of his descendants to avenge a wrong suffered by the latter at the hands of a non-kinsman. An argument between two peasants sometimes leads to such a threat by both contenders to bring the matter before their own respective "baron" and let it settle the quarrel. Often such a threat is never actualised; but if it is, one then comes before the cross that stands in the family cemetery and, lighting a black candle before it, asks "Baron" for a "little help" sending it to harass his adversary. In these cases, the sending of a "baron" is synonymous with the sending of a corpse. This is still a Guinea practice. The right to light a candle in any cemetery goes with family membership; family membership could be defined in terms of the cemeteries one can enter and where one can perform what is called an "illumination". These burial grounds are located within the "habitation" and there are always a number of them to which one has access either on his father's or his mother's side. They are guarded with great concern to prevent any stranger from entering at night. Such an intruder would be immediately suspected of trying to capture zombis and would be promptly arrested and led before the authorities. Peasants often point out with pride that, at least in their own burial ground, one can rest in peace. "Nobody would ever dare to come in here and seize your zombi."

But there are other kinds of "barons". Haitians say that they all have the same name but that it is not written in the same way. These are the "barons" of abandoned cemeteries, those of public cemeteries and the dead who have been interred along the road, most of them beggars with no family-ties who were buried where they happened to die. These are the ones used by sorcerers and magic groups such as the "hairless". Public cemeteries in towns are particularly unsafe since anyone may get in at any time of the day or night and address the particular "baron" who is chief of the place. This explains why supernatural diseases in towns are usually attributed to the sending of the spirit of a deceased person, while in rural areas, they are more likely to be interpreted as demands from neglected family spirits. Many Haitian governments have tried to convince the peasants to bury their dead in common cemeteries where it was said it would be easier to prevent the stealing of "zombis"; all these efforts failed, because public cemeteries, being open to anyone, have always been considered the most exposed place to bury one's dead. This illustrates how the contrast between Guinea and magic may divide what appeared at first sight to be an homogenous category, and at second sight, a category full of inconsistencies. The works of the spirits and their moral value always refer to the definition of the concrete social groups within which they operate. The worshipping of "baron" as an ancestor and the sending of such a "baron" against an enemy is considered a Guinea practice; the use of "barons" in public or abandoned cemeteries, of socially unattached "barons", is related to the stealing of zombis, classified as magic and said to attract divine wrath. The social context is part of the definition and always contributes to the meaning of any of these concepts.

"Baron" appears as a close equivalent of the African ancestors' shrines. But while in Africa, only the Elders have access to these, in Haiti any member of the family has direct access. There is no formal allocation of authority within the group which would restrict or control the private demands of the individuals to the dead. This may be related to the fact that a "baron" can only be sent out against a non-kinsman and thus cannot be used for personal advantage within the family. Baron provides the family with teeth, but these are directed against outsiders. If such a spirit catches a member of the family, it is not because it has been sent deliberately by any one of its members but because the spirit itself tries to attract the attention of the group as a whole.

The status of any spirit is linked with the question of its origins. In practical terms, the contrast between Guinea and magic is expressed through

the opposition between the ancestors and the "points". Before considering
the cult-groups themselves, I have to explain the meaning of this fundamental opposition.

Where do the spirits come from? They are either ancestors or medicines
that have turned into spirits. As an ancestor, the spirit is inherited within
the family group; it is called *loa*. As a medicine, it is bought by an individual who wants to prevent mystical attacks by witches or sorcerers or to
obtain a change in his own economic position; it is then called "point".
The point is an individual affair; however, it will be inherited by the
buyer's children, so that "point" constantly moves from generation to
generation into the Guinea category. Many worshippers are well aware that
some spirits they have inherited were probably originally, "points"; but
since worshipping in a Guinean way is to worship in the same way as your
father did, without trying to change or add anything, they will describe
these spirits as "Guinea" spirits. The buying of "points" is socially dis-
approved; it is a mark of ambition. So it often happens that the buyer
conceals it; this is why they are so dangerous for their children; they will
inherit a spirit without knowing how to serve it. Anyone climbing the
social ladder is likely to be accused of having bought such "points"; anyone having bigger pigs than his neighbours or harvesting bigger potatoes,
is similarly suspected. *Loas* can also be bought and they may be stolen; but
if the buying of "points" is open to anyone, the buying of *loas* defines a
sphere of competition restricted to the priesthood.

The Ancestors

The basic cult-unit is called *démembré* ("dismembered"). It is a portion of
a larger estate, acquired by its founder, and left by him for all his descendants to live on;[6] a piece of land, in the middle of which stands a little
house, the "first house", where he kept his religious possessions and conducted specific rituals. While the estate is equally divided between the
children, both males and females, this particular spot is never partitioned
but remains the common property of all the descendants. Any member of
the family, anyone who can trace actual relationship to that first ancestor,
is entitled to come and build his house there. The *démembré* is a well
shaded area where all the family spirits "rest". A number of trees, some of
them very tall and ancient, surround the little house; each is the repository
of a group of spirits; together they form the spiritual heritage of the family
as a group. No one would ever dare to cut down such a tree without incur-

6. Such estates may vary from an infinitesimal quantity of land to as much as 100
hectares.

ring the punishment of the spirits which reside in it. The founder of such
an establishment is himself a *loa* and may even possess one of his children;
as a spirit, he is the "master of the land". *Démembrés* vary widely in aspect.
Some are empty; the children have moved out and tempted fortune elsewhere. Others form large domains, literally covered with homesteads,
called *lacou*. These differences are partly accounted for by differential pressure on land; as land pressure increases, the scattering of the children
become more or less inevitable. But they also result from the way problems
of succession to the leadership of the founder are solved.

The cult house is generally well-kept, but it may or may not have a
leader. Usually the one who takes responsibility for it, the "burden" as it
is called, is the best off member of the family; as long as he recognises his
ritual duties of course. But that does not make him a *houngan*, meaning
someone who can use his spirits and knowledge to treat clients for a fee, or
will conduct ceremonies for outsiders. Such a person presents himself
as a modest servant of the spirits, like any other member of the family,
worshipping them in exactly the same way his father did and calling in a
specialist whenever he feels that something exceeds his competence. To
become a *houngan*, one has either to have been taught by another specialist
(in the case of a *démembré* it is often one's father and we have seen the
problems linked with that kind of co-operation), or to have been instructed
in dreams by the spirits themselves. Such pretensions are likely to raise a
lot of suspicion and jealousy within the group. The reluctance of the father
to appoint a successor while he is still living, does not ease the finding of a
solution. Quarrels over succession often lead the contenders to build up
their own installation on another piece of land they may have bought elsewhere or in their own share of the inheritance. Each of the new establishments defines a new *démembré* for the children of its founder. Unless there
is some kind of agreement within the family, the first cult-house is likely to
be abandoned. Each member of the family will recognise its pre-eminence
but will relate to it individually. One will go on receiving his family spirits
where he lives. The family spirits, being ubiquitous, are said to leave their
original residence to come and attend any ritual performed in their honour,
on any of their descendants' new establishments; but as soon as the ceremony is over, they return to their first abode. Unless the spirits themselves,
either in dreams or through the mouths of their horses, appoint the successor, the cult-house may soon collapse, no one daring to look after it, for
fear of being accused of wanting to take it over for himself.

As one may guess, the number of *démembrés* rapidly increases from
generation to generation, since each of the children is potentially the
founder of a new one centred upon his own establishment. Moreover, one
equally inherits the ritual duties of both parents; both sides have to be

given equal consideration, otherwise the neglected spirits would soon be jealous and would "catch" the offender. How are all these obligations reduced to a manageable size? It is generally agreed that one is heir to the *démembrés* left by the four grandparents. He may even not be active in all of them restricting his participation to those which are near his place of residence, unless he has some valuable piece of land in a more distant area which would justify frequent contacts and active membership, mainly by contributing to the expenses of the various ceremonies which may be held on the *démembré*. Practically, it is this question of land which defines one's duties. As long as one "feeds on spirits' land", the family estate of which the *démembré* is part, the *loas* of that *démembré* have power over him. But if one abandons one's rights to the piece of land to which he is legally entitled on the estate (it is often too small to ensure its owner a decent standard of living), such power seems to disappear, or at least, it becomes a very remote possibility that such a spirit would ever "catch" him. It is a common way for anyone, anxious to free himself of his ritual obligations to any particular cult-house, to sell his share of the inheritance to another member of the family (family land should always remain in the family) or simply not claim it. In spite of all this, however, one never gets rid of the grip of the family *loas*, since the power of these is not simply a reflection of land tenure but is usually defined in terms of ancestry, of "blood" relations. Confronted with an illness resisting all kinds of treatment, one is likely to enquire about the forgotten installation, his parents used to talk about, but where he himself may have never gone, a "deep ravine with a lot of trees and a source, a refreshing place somewhere in the North" and where he may have been told by a spirit, he would find some relief. In times of hardship, the number of *démembrés* is likely to increase as one is desperately looking for the cause of an enduring misfortune; this number usually contracts as soon as one gets better, to the great despair of the spirits which always complain about the lack of gratitude of their children. "When they do not need me, they call me shit. But when they do need me, they call me father" says a song.

The *démembré* is not only a piece of land where the family spirits reside. It is also a set of rules (*reglement*) and rituals, laid down by its founder, which should theoretically never be changed. Here the family may celebrate, every year, a night of songs and prayers on the eve of Good Friday; here, a stump of wood has to be regularly burned down, in the middle of the courtyard; here, a lamp has to be lit every Saturday on the small family altar, in honour of the dead. There is a large number of these devotions, varying from one individual to another and from group to group. But more important is the way each *démembré* is related in its own way to a specific "nation" of spirits.

All the *loas* come from Africa. Haitians say Guinea: "We are the children of Guinea." Guinea consists of a large number of "nations", the original ethnic groups of which Haitians are the descendants. Vodu, Rada, Wangoles (Angola), Mondongue, Nago (including all the Ogu), Ibo, Congos, Petro, Zandor . . . There is no agreement upon their number, neither are they given equal importance from one area to another.[7] All these spirits have to be regularly fed, otherwise they are said to become weak and unable to do anything for their children. A "nation" can be defined as the set of all spirits sharing a common ceremonial meal and exhibiting the same type of behaviour when possessing their horses. The word applies to all levels of abstraction. The *loa* Damballah is a snake; a person possessed by such a spirit, creeps on the ground, hissing and is usually presented with an egg placed in the middle of a small quantity of white flour on a porcelain plate. It then delicately sucks it just as a snake would do. All damballahs, since there are many of them related with discrete family groups, form together a "nation". This "nation" is itself a sub-group of a larger class, the "White spirits", which all share a common fondness for town and foreign goods; French perfumes, soft drinks, white bread and sugar, silver cutlery and porcelain plates. As a member of the "white nation", Damballah fraternises with a number of other spirits which share the same cult-house: Erzuilie, the beautiful long-haired and very snobbish mulatto girl; Agwet Royo, the master of the oceans and many others. The "white spirits", often identified with the Rada "nation", are classified as Vodu spirits which are said to come from Dahomey. It seems an easy task to arrange all these spirits according to their "nation" of origin. In practice, this is far from being the case. On some *démembrés*, Erzulie may be received as a Zandor spirit; on another, it may be considered as a Petro spirit. The "nations" do not constitute discrete categories of spirits either. They rather define discrete sets of ritual rules, each one named after a "nation", and to one of which all the spirits of the same *démembré* are subjected, whatever their own particular nation of origin is. An Erzuilie may thus appear on a *démembré* where there stands a Zandor cult-house, and may be given recognition, or asks itself for

7. In Port au Prince, the Petro nation includes the following spirits: Ti Jean, Marinette, Ti Kata, Grand Bois. All of these are wild spirits, spirits of the bush. They all share a violent temperament and a predilection for fire and strong drinks; they are "hot" spirits. In Port au Prince, the Zandor nation stands apart, as an isolated and undifferentiated group of spirits, particularly dangerous since they "eat" the ones they "catch" (meaning, they kill them). In Léogane, only thirty miles away, the same spirits which are Petro in the capital are worshipped as members of the Zandor nation and it is the "petro ' group which stands apart as an undifferentiated set of spirits. Moreover, the importance of a "nation" may vary in time. All the spirits mentioned above were worshipped as members of the Simby-kita "nation" sixty years ago on the plain of Léogane. Zandor rituals then scarcely existed. The fate of any given nation is largely a function of the success of the family groups which worship it.

recognition, not as a Vodu spirit but as a Zandor entity, and is served accordingly. Haitians explain this in terms of mixed ancestry.

Peasants see the *loas* as distant ancestors to which they are related through their parents and grandparents. When the "nations" came to Haiti, they mixed with one another, so that every Haitian is the child of all the "nations" and every "nation" of spirits has to be served. It is this idea of mixed ancestry which explains how a black Haitian may be possessed by a "white" spirit; and how, after Independence (1804), a number of French landowners were transformed into *loas* which are said to have come from Guinea.[8] There is thus both myth and history here. Nearly all African ethnic groups contributed to the slave trade. But the bonds of ethnicity were crushed forever by the new society they had to assimilate into. French slave-owners did not like having "crews" of workers composed of people from the same ethnic background; their very diversity of custom and language was the best way to divide them and so maintain their authority, unquestioned. Maintenance of ethnic identity was discouraged by the slaves themselves. On the plantation, status was no longer a function of one's position in a lineage or in a tribal group, but simply followed the division of labour. The more one was assimilated to Haiti, the more likely he was to be given a high status job on the estate. Negro-drivers, domestics and artisans, were usually Creoles, born in Haiti, or at least, liked to pass as such, and they were all well acquainted with the operations of the sugar or coffee plantation to which they were attached. Newly-arrived Africans, the "bossales", were usually employed as field labourers, hard work in which no distinction could be gained. Under colonial rule, there were already a number of stereotypes which characterised the different ethnic groups, mainly in terms of their general capacity to absorb the new values and ways of living defined by the multi-racial and slave society they had to live in. Ibos had a reputation as "loners", and were said to adapt only with great reluctance to their new environment, often preferring to kill themselves (Moreau de St-Mery, 1876). Still today, Ibo spirits are lonely spirits;

8. The incorporation of French ancestors into the genealogies of many peasant groups, is related to the emergence under colonial rule of the mulatto class out of illicit unions between free white fathers and their black concubines. Mullatoes had often been freed by their father and given some property. Many had opened coffee plantations in unpopulated areas of the hills and mainly on the virgin lands of the South, where they formed compact and tightly knit groups, before the war of Independence. Many white landowners, before leaving the country, had left their properties in the hands of their mulatto children, hoping to get them back when things had settled down. After Independence, mulattoes often evidenced their claims to vacant estates with such deeds of transfer—many had actually been forged, while the newly freed, the black generals who had emerged during the war of Independence, relied on the lands that had been seized by the government, hoping to be awarded the rental of a property as a recognition of their war exploits. The question soon led to a civil war. But the incorporation of French into the genealogies of many groups is no pure fantasy. Behind it is a claim to land.

they eat alone in the corner of the cult-house and do not share with any attendant. Mondongues were reputed to be cannibals (Debien, 1941, p. 96); Mondongue spirits are still today described in a similar way since they "eat" the people they "catch". Radas were considered the most intelligent group: hard workers they were said to learn easily and to be good domestics, which quite agrees with their present status as "white" spirits. No doubt these vague ideas, held by slave owners and traders, were passed on to the slaves and contributed largely to the present definition of the "nations". The idea of "nation" is thus a complex result of real ethnic traits which were transmitted by slaves of different origins to their children, and of the colonial ideology itself which reformulated these ethnic differences on a scale of acculturation, a continuum along which the different tribes could be plotted in terms of their ability to assimilate the values of civilisation, identified with French and White values, as opposed to African barbarism, expressed through the usual cannibalistic imagery.[9] After Independence, the concrete "nations" had disappeared. The "ritual Nations" were however to provide an ideology in terms of which the new basic social units of Haitian society would oppose one another. The family is by no means an ethnic group, but through its particular *démembré* it states its identity as if it was one. Each *démembré* is linked with a specific "nation" or a specific combination of these. Here one finds a Vodu cult-house, here a Petro cult-house; there a Zandor house. Family spirits are thus defined with reference to a dominant nation, to the dominant ritual structure to which they are subjected. However, we have seen that Haitians still present themselves as the children of all the "nations". How is this achieved in practice? Mainly by giving to all other "nations" not identified with a particular *démembré*, a peripheral position.

Thomas is a Vodu cult leader. He does not serve Zandor spirits; he usually associates them with magic and sorcery. He says that he is unable to receive them since both his father and grandfather, did not. Thomas's father himself was killed by a Zandor spirit, called Marinette, which had asked him in vain for recognition. While he was going to town, one day, he was hit by a small stone behind the neck, a stone probably projected from under the wheels of a passing lorry; he had died a few hours after. Marinette had come, possessing an aunt of Thomas (Haitians say, "dancing in the head of someone") and explained that she herself was responsible; she had killed him because of his stubbornness in refusing to serve her. The family had then decided to give the spirit the ritual meal it was asking for and also to "bind" him, meaning ritually put it into chains, so that it would no more

9. After Independence, this opposition between French and African values changed to the contrast between town and countryside; the town elites now embodying the idea of civilisation and "enlightenment" as opposed to the "illiterate and supersitious" peasantry.

harm any member of the group. However this ceremony could not be held on the *démembré*; it was feared that all the Vodu spirits would at once leave the property. So Marinette was received but in the ruins of an old abandoned sugar house, which dated from the colonial period. This peripheral position granted to Zandor spirits by Thomas, is again clearly expressed when he gives his own Vodu spirits their annual meal, on the twenty-third of December. Such a ceremony is always preceded by the recitation of a long litany (the "Guinea prayer") in which all the "nations" without exception, together with the dead, the ancestors are asked to attend. The Zandor spirits are said to come; but they do not enter the *démembré*, staying out at the gate; they are said to be ashamed, to be too shy to mix with spirits from another "nation", having different tastes and manners. As the cult leader comes to the gate of the property to greet Legba, the "gatekeeper spirit", he always throws out a handful of maize and groundnuts for all these "nations" which are present but do not dare to enter the *démembré*. Moreover, at midnight, an assortment of roots ("all kinds of food for all kinds of spirits") are sliced into pieces and put into a calabash which is sent out, to be laid down at a crossroads, for all the Zandor spirits and other nations which cannot enter the property. On a Zandor *démembré*, the Zandor spirits would come freely and possess their horses to take their meal, which would be much more elaborate. There, Vodu spirits would never come in; they would feel out of place in the middle of such an uncultivated and savage group.

We have already mentioned how such peripheral spirits may be accepted on a *démembré* but then treated as if they were members of the dominant "nation" which defines the ritual structure of that particular *démembré*. This brings us to a discussion of innovation and the way new developments may be legitimated. The mixing of "nations" is clearly a function of the bilateral transmission of ritual duties; the recognition of all lines of descent as being equally relevant, explains how one may relate himself to all the "nations" while still being able to define discrete groups of these through the *démembré* he is an heir to. In that case, change is structural change and results from the process of fission that goes on within the family from one generation to another.

When the children of a chief ancestor live on the family estate he had left, let us say on their father's land (but the same would apply to mother's land), it is possible for them to "pick up" their mother's spiritual heritage and to receive the mother's *loas* on their own share of their father's estate. They may build up a house for them on the plot they have inherited from their father. This is likely to be the case when distance prevents them from having any contact with their mother's country of origin, or if, for one reason or another, they have relinquished their rights to their share of their mother's inheritance. Such a house forms a *démembré* for all the children by the same mother, living on land left by their father. Besides a common allegiance to the "first house", the different "branches" living on the same family estate, have distinct ritual duties defined in terms of their respective complementary filiation. It has already been mentioned that the family spirits may leave their original residence to attend any ceremony stated on any of these secondary installations. In ritual possession, such a spirit always makes the following stereotyped entry; he has made a long journey to get there and he is tired, even breathless if he had come in a hurry; he first asks for the meal which should have been prepared for such a distinguished visitor coming from a distant area, and also to sustain him on his way back home; if nothing has been prepared, he then complains loudly that he has been called for a trifle, threatening never to come back again. There is a large element of comedy in this and the threats are rarely taken seriously. The dialogue follows traditional lines. In time, the family estate becomes spotted with a number of similar secondary *démembrés* surrounding the "first house". The latter always retains its pre-eminence and defines the largest group of kin, the family; the secondary ones define groups of a lower segmentation order, the "branches".

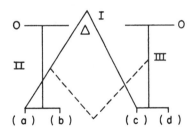 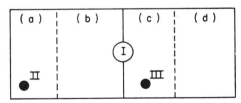

The above piece of land has been equally divided between the four children of its buyer. The latter left two groups of children by different mothers. A portion of the property (I) has not been shared and forms the first "démembré". Each sub-group of children has decided to pick up their mother's spirits, and to build a small cult-house for these on their respective share of the inheritance (II, III). While (a) and (b) serve in II, (c) and (d) serve in III; but all serve in I.

If one moves out of such an estate and buys a piece of land elsewhere, he may receive all the "nations", both his father's and mother's nations, within the confines of the same *démembré* of which he is the founder. "Nations" which were linked with discrete family properties in one generation, thus come together in the next one. If one's father worshipped Vodu spirits and one's mother, Zandor ones, he will receive them on the same piece of land he has bought. In such a case however, the two groups of spirits are too different to simply fuse; two cult-houses have to be built or at least the cult-house is divided into a number of separate rooms, each one accommodating a "nation" of *loas*. Moreover these nations will be received on different days, the Vodu being usually served in December, and the Zandor spirits, during the summer. Such a *démembré* will be defined by more than one "nation".

There are many other possibilities which cannot be discussed here. The main point is that all these are not seen as change. One's motivation is always to worship the spirits in the same way as one's ancestors did. This shows why, the more ancient an establishment is, the nearest it is assumed to be to historical Guinea and the largest potential membership it has; thus the more prestige it is endowed with. Change also comes from that relative lack of external control over ecstasy which was underlined by Métreaux. It often happens that a new spirit, their number is never specified, "mounts" a member of the family and asks for recognition, legitimating its claim by identifying some distant ancestor it used to possess. As the group often knows nothing about it, it is up to the spirit itself to define the way it should be served, thus opening the door to a constant inflow of private symbolism into the ritual structure. This is not seen as change but simply as the re-appearance of what had been forgotten.

Moreover, Haitians recognise the importance of training in explaining the specific behaviour of any given spirit and the way it may evolve in time. I had always been told that "Marinette", being a spirit of the bush (a Zandor spirit in Leogane), used to eat at midnight, with her hands, pork meat which was given to her in a calabash which was laid down on a mat or a banana leaf. Once I saw one, eating in a very civilised manner, with a fork, a meal which had been presented to her on a porcelain plate placed on a table, behaviour any outsider would immediately attribute to a "white" spirit. If it had not been for the initial phase of this possession, when the "horse" mounted by Marinette, balanced himself on his feet, stooping forward to the ground, both arms projected backwards, twisted upside-down, and the hands distorted, claw-like, in a very sinister way, it could have been mistaken for an Erzulie, the beautiful Mulatto girl. I was told that such a Marinette was received in a "white" way and that it was finally just a question of training; a spirit always asks for the same kind of treatment he has been accustomed to by those who receive it. In ritual possession itself, there is usually some haggling between the spirit and the group; the *loa* is never quite satisfied with the way it is received and makes demands upon the group which decides if these can be met or not. It may be a new dress, or two red handkerchiefs it would like to be tied to its arms. The Marinette in question had asked for a fork; she disliked eating with her hands and the cult leader had agreed to her request. Another one could have refused fearing that one day, they would forget about the fork and then they would be in trouble. But once such a demand is accepted, it becomes part of the way a particular spirit should always be served; it has been accustomed to it.

This shows how the spirits themselves appear to move from one category to another. Many of them exhibit traits which seem to have been borrowed from a number of distinct "nations". Every *démembré* has its own idiosyncrasies. These changes, being defined by spirits whose Guinea origin was never doubted, are never seen as true innovations. Innovations appear in another kind of context; the buying of "points" and the "buying of *loas*".

The "Points"

The word *point* is used in a wide variety of contexts. It has the general meaning of personal advantage, an ability in which one surpasses others. A child whose complexion is clear, has a good "point", an advantage over a darker one, since it is said that people always look at him first; he is more beautiful and bound to have better opportunities than others. But "point" also denotes specific powers which can be bought at the hands of a *houngan*. The power to disappear (*point disparaitre*), the power of ubiquity (*point déplace*), the power of immunity to bullets (*point balles*), the power to steal without being caught (*point Haoussa*). Other powers are more closely related to ordinary economic operations in a peasant society; it may be a recipe to have bigger bulls and pigs (*point gardinage*), or better crops (*point jardin*), or better sales in the market (*point la vente*). A large number of these powers are simply protections against all kinds of mystical attack (*point protege*). These powers are said to be looked for by the ambitious; such a pursuit (*chaché*) is morally wrong. Whenever one says that he serves Guinea, he always stresses that he did not look for any of these and that if he is relatively better off than the others, "it is not magic, it is a gift", an ability given to him by God. All "points" are means by which an individual tries to manipulate his environment to his own individual profit, usually at the expense of others. Individual and social inequality as well as social mobility are explained by this opposition between "points" and "gifts" which is another way to oppose Guinea and Magic. The family *loas* are inherited, but the "points" are bought. The *loas* have been created by God, while "points" are man-made. However, a "point" is no simple material object. It is also a kind of spirit, since the making of any of these imply the insertion of a "soul" (*nam*) into it; it may be a "zombi" or it may be a spirit which has been bought specifically to do that kind of work. Such a "point" may possess its owner and has to be regularly fed.

How can such a spirit be made? This may be illustrated by the following confection of a garden "point". One takes a dark bottle and puts the head

of a dried herring into it. The use of a dried herring is particularly significant. Herrings are food for the spirits of the cemeteries and of the graveyards. It has already been mentioned that the dead offer two aspects:
"zombis" and *loas*. All the dead, those whose achievements were not
important enough to have their names remembered by the succeeding
generations, form anonymously the "guede" nation; these *loas* are given
salted herring to eat. Here, the use of a dried herring refers to the dead as
"zombis". "Zombis" do not eat salt; a few grains of salt dropped on the
floor is enough to send them away from the house. Moreover, peasants
when discussing presumed cannibalistic practices they attribute to some
groups of sorcerers, always refer to the corpse, to human flesh, as "unsalted
meat". The dried herring stands for the flesh of the "zombi" which is put
into the bottle. This clearly comes out from the next operation. One adds a
few drops of water, and a few drops of blood from a chicken which has been
killed for the occasion. The bottle is spoken to in these terms: "Now you
have water and you have blood; you are a living one. I want you to be the
soul of that garden and to kill any intruder." The mixture of blood and
water is a kind of chemical operation by which life is given back to dead
flesh, to the dried meat of the fish which represents the corpse of the "zombi". The bottle is finally sealed up with a copper thread. In tying it up,
one says, "This is to prevent you from harming any of my children." The
copper thread is the chain of the spirit. Such a "point" is particularly
violent and vicious; it could "catch" any of its owner's children and "eat"
them. It has to be "bounded", it has to be restricted. The bottle is then
buried in the ground. This is a "point"; it has to be given food; it may be
every year or every seven years according to the kind of agreement made
between the buyer and the spirit. The spirit may also possess its owner or
any of his descendants. The main object in putting it in one's garden is to
prevent theft. Peasants always complain about intruders who enter their
fields at night to steal their crops. After such an operation, there will always
be someone in the garden; at night, any passer-by will see a shadow in the
middle of the garden and eventual thieves will be kept away, thinking that
the garden's owner is not asleep but stands there, waiting for them.
"People will begin to whisper that such and such is a devil, that he never
sleeps." One's reputation will grow. This is what is meant by "taking a
zombi and putting it to work in one's garden".

"Points" are thus associated with the abhorred practice of "zombi"
stealing. They are a common explanation for social mobility. It is said that
all "progress" lies in the cemetery, and that "Baron holds the keys to any
advancement". During the last month of my field-work, it was very difficult
to find herrings in the country. Shipments from abroad had been delayed.
Everyone was joking saying that no more advancement was at the time

possible in Haiti. Anyone whose economic and social position suddenly changes for the better is suspected of having bought such a "point". It is morally wrong and seen as a mark of ambition. So it often happens that one conceals his acquisition, serving it alone in secret. The great danger in such an attitude, is that the children will inherit a spirit without even knowing of its existence. The "point" looking for food may then begin to eat all the descendants of the one who bought it; it turns into a *baka*. Usually however, one informs one's children and tells them how to serve it. But the very idea of secrecy surrounding the acquisition of "points" has the consequence that no one is above suspicion. Family groups, competing for status and power, are thus likely to accuse one another while at the same time stressing their own fidelity to Guinea tradition. As a "point" is inherited by the children of its buyer, it becomes in their generation part of the Guinea heritage. "It is something I was born with." Thus, the classical distinction between magic and religion is blurred.

"Points" specialised in livestock-breeding are similarly manufactured. When possessing their owners, they change them into beasts of burden, a donkey, a mule or a bull. The possessed person bellows, kicks up his heels, scratches his back against the trees or impatiently stamps the ground with his foot, as a bull does which is going to charge. The spirit is then led into the pasture to take its meal. These powers all have similar names: General Bull, John Donkey, Bossou.

All the "points" already described were buried objects. A very large number of these however, are medicines or drugs ("drogues") made out of a variety of leaves known for their specific powers, which are either infused in water and rum ("bain") or pounded into powders. A mixture is prepared and rubbed over the inside part of the upper-arm, which is then tied up with a handkerchief to allow the composition to "pass into the blood"; sometimes, an incision is made. These "drugs" are usually defences bought from a *houngan* in order to protect the buyer from various mystical attacks. The medicine can mount its owner whenever he feels in danger. These possessions are always violent but offer a wide range of variations. Sometimes, it is only the arm which stiffens and begins to shake as if it was an autonomous part of the body, no more controlled by the will. That kind of possession often occurs when one person is incensed at another. A neighbour of mine was mounted by such a "point" whenever he seriously quarrelled with his wife, most of the time out of jealousy, and there is no doubt that in his case, possession was triggered off by deep aggressive impulses, partly repressed, which found expression in the uncontrolled shaking of the arm. Such a trance is easily dealt with. The "point" is said to be thirsty; some rum is rubbed over the arm, where the drug has been applied, and everything comes back to normal in a few seconds. Similar medicines are made and sold to improve one's capacity to work. The finest drummer in Léogane was said to have two "zombis" in his arms. Some peasants "drug" themselves in order to increase their endurance and physical strength; when possessed by the "drug", one is said to be able to do twice the amount of work he usually does. Eventually, these "points" may turn into spirits.

A medicine may take a very long time before evolving into such a spirit. One of my informants had been very ill, when he was a baby. His father had gone off to the southern part of the country to buy a powerful medication to keep away the vampire-witches that were preying on his child at night. Children are particularly vulnerable to these witches, always females, who leave their body at night and fly through the air looking for babies whose blood they suck. A common way to protect a child is to "spoil" his blood, to make it so bitter that vampires will be repelled by it. A nauseating composition is prepared with leaves mixed with bile, fetid water and other stinking ingredients; the child is regularly bathed with it. As a result, "the witch stays away; your baby's blood smells nasty and tastes bitter. To you it does not make any difference; it is your child and you love him."[10] These medicines are not points and are in general use, even among Protestants who do not worship the *loas*. But if prepared with "zombis" or extra-powerful leaves, they are. The "point" is said to grow up with the child. My informant had been rubbed with such a powerful drug. It was not till he was fourteen years of age that he was possessed by it. The drug had become a spirit, named "Cross Danger" (*Jambe Malheu*). When receiving such a spirit, one must be very careful not to displease it; it has to be "caressed", constantly flattered, overpraised. An attendant may pass his perfumed handkerchief over its face to wipe off the sweat; another fans it with his hat in order to "cool" it; another may fondle it very slowly with the fingers, from the top of the head to the feet. If these "points" are known to "eat" people, no one would dare to make such a shocking allusion in their presence; on the contrary, attendants emphatically deny this. The appearance of such a spirit is the intrusion of absolute power into society, and the whole interaction is marked by an excessive submission on the part of the attendants, as if they were trying to tame a dangerous wild animal. If angered, a "point" could break down everything in the house; some are known for having suddenly run out and rooted out a whole garden of banana trees. These spirits are particularly fierce and tempestuous. A number of them keep rolling, and rolling all over the ground, for many minutes, before finally calming down and beginning to speak. Sometimes, the possession is too

---

10. Certainly the main cause of anxiety among peasants. The rate of infantile mortality is very high. Out of a random sample of 43 women in Carrefour Fort where I was working, 23 had lost at least one child before the age of two.

brutal for the horse who may be thrown on the ground, unable to move or speak, incredibly tensed, the arm locked behind the back at near breaking point, as if the whole bodily energy, instead of being channelled into dancing or jerking was intro-oriented, in an attempt at self-destruction. The "point" is said to be too hot for the horse and has to be sent away with water. Such a possession shivers on the brink of madness. But the extravagance of gesture is also related to the fact that these spirits have no legitimate position in the ritual system and have to overact in order to see their powers recognised. This overacting usually subsides with time. These spirits are what Haitians regard as innovations. One always speaks of them with mixed feelings of fear and admiration.

Perhaps the best way to express this opposition between Guinea and Magic, the ancestors and the "points", is to briefly describe the trees with which each domain is associated (tree symbolism is however much more elaborate since each "nation" has its own tree of predilection). Guinea is often said to live in the Calabash-tree while Magic and bad "points" dwell in fig trees. The calabash-tree is never very tall. Its gourd-like fruits are described as "the vessels of the first creation". But the important thing about them, is their underground root-system, which is always described as much more ancient and larger than the visible trunk would seem to suggest. A calabash-tree is like an iceberg whose larger part lies underground, invisible to the eye. One always stresses its ability to survive any cyclone; it may lose all its branches and yet the trunk never ceases to regenerate others. It is also a useful tree, planted a long time ago by some ancestor. One often passes from that tree to a discussion of his ancestors, as in the following comments made by a peasant who was trying to explain to me the meaning of Guinea. "God created an angel to protect you. Even if you are a Protestant, it is always there. Your mother dies; she becomes an angel (angel often is synonimous with *loa*). It is God who commands her to protect you on earth. She is dead; yet she is living. She can't die. As long as you have a good heart." Then pointing at a calabash-tree in the middle of the yard: "You see that calabash-tree. It protects you; it protects the yard. And it allows one to live. Here are three gourds that you can sell; enough to live. There is no need to go in crossroads, calling for bulls and other demons. These acts are satanic. As for myself, I live on a *démembré*; it is a father; it is a mother; after God." The calabash tree is perhaps the best representation of the way Haitians look at Guinea through their many ancestors and relate to it through generations and generations of them. The fig-tree connotes quite different values and provides sanctuary for demons and vampires. The following description from the Encyclopedia Britannica shows clearly why: "Some fig-trees (*ficus religiosa, f. Benghalensis*) commonly start life from seeds deposited by birds, squirrels, monkeys or fruit-eating bats, high up on a palm or other native tree. The roots grow downward attached to the trunk of the supporting plant . . . such figs are known as epiphytes or more accurately as hemicpiphytes as they pass their early life on the trunks of trees but subsequently become connected with the ground by their own root-system. The name of "strangler" has become attached to fig-trees which grow in this way since their descending and encircling roots become at length largely or entirely confluent, forming a pseudo-trunk, hollow at the centre through which the dead or dying host plant passes. These fig-trees are roots and no stems" (T. 9, 1967, p. 256) Points are similar to fig-trees; they are often qualified as "never ending roots"; like the fig, they are illegitimate power springing from nowhere. With its well-defined trunk the calabash tree, on the other hand, stands for legitimate power that originates from Guinea. *Loas* can finally be bought. Only *houngans* may be interested in making such an acquisition. In his case possession is the indispensable asset since the spirit is not bought for any specific goal but mainly because of its capacity to produce other "points" which will be sold to clients. These *loas* are most of the time Zandor or Petro spirits known for their violent nature and closely connected, being spirits of the bush, with leaves and thus well acquainted with their curative properties. Such a spirit may be put in a bundle which is buried in the ground till it claims a close relation of the buyer as its horse, usually one of his wives; but the spirit can also be deliberately "fixed into the head of a candidate" by a specialist. The origin of such a spirit is unknown. They are usually described as "vagabonds" who feed from the hands of anyone ready to serve them.

Whole "nations" seem to have originated as "points". Petro rituals were first mentioned by colonial writers in 1780. They were said to have been created by a fugitive slave from the Dominican Republic, called Don Pedro. The dance had been prohibited by the colonial administration; it was said to be so violent that it could kill the dancer. But the main reason for the prohibition was the military atmosphere which pervaded the whole ritual (explosions of gun-powder, ritual fighting, the drinking of animal blood) as well as its millenarian tone. From 1791 to 1792, a cult leader, Roman the prophet, terrorised the plain of Léogane. Presenting himself as the godson of the Virgin, he used an abandoned church as headquarters; he said the Mass before an inverted cross; he preached that God was black, that all whites had to be killed; those who would die during the war would return to Guinea where they would enjoy eternal bliss. Today Petro societies are mainly defined in terms of family allegiances (at least in the rural areas); the rituals have lost these millenarian themes but they still retain the original military atmosphere and their connection with particularly violent spirits. In Léogane, the Zandor "nation" was almost unknown when it began to spread out from the hills into the plain, about sixty years ago. On every Zandor *Démembré* one finds an iron bar, surrounded with heavy chains, called Lucifer and which has to be heated up whenever rituals are conducted (in Creole, the word is made up of two constituents: Luci-fer, the last one meaning iron). The word is a clear indication of the satanic origin of these spirits. Many informants still remember that when they were children, their parents did not allow them to attend Zandor rituals which were then assimilated with sorcery. But with the passing of generations, these spirits were transmitted to a large number of descendants, the children of those who had innovated. As these moved into the plain and began to get properties there, they brought their spirits and rituals with them. Inter-marriage with local people and the bilateral transmission of religious duties, soon resulted in the acceptance of these spirits by a large number of family groups. As they become more and more identified with family units, the spirits seem to lose a bit of their original demoniac character. Now, Zandor spirits are often said to have become more civilised. Peasants say that like the people who came with them from the hills, they have become more educated, more "enlightened" (*éclairés*). They used to eat at midnight; now many of them eat during daytime. Some of them, when "catching" an offender, gave festering sores; now, they no longer do that. I have already shown how many of these spirits are now being served in a "white" way. This illustrates how magic turns into religion. Like the fig-tree which, in time, becomes connected to the ground with its root-system, so "points", even if they always retain something of their evil origin, become for the inheriting generations, part of the so called "Guinea heritage". Born out of the private ambition of one man, they come to define, in the subsequent generations, the collective interests of family groups and are thus incorporated into society along traditional lines.

The Pre-eminence of Vodu

If in some contexts, Magic seems to be treated as Guinea, relatively, Vodu itself is Guinea, absolutely and all Haitians recognise its pre-eminence. This pre-eminence comes from secrets which make Vodu cult-leaders, the *houngans asson*, the only ones able to achieve the transformation of the deceased into a *loa*, an ancestor with whom descendants can safely communicate, without having to rely on such an improbable event as possession and such an unreliable medium as ecstasy. It is the privileged way by which Haitians relate themselves to an historical Guinea, through named ancestors with whom they were once closely related.

At death, Vodu spirits lose their "horse" and another one has to be provided. The "little angel" has to be sent under the water from which it will be removed a year later, to capture another member of the family. The ritual thus consists of two parts which I can only briefly describe here. The first one is called *dessounin*. The little angel is separated from the body and sent back to Guinea. Vodu spirits have to be sent back, otherwise they would be lost to the group. Two persons one male and one female, are appointed by the family to "lie down for the deceased"; it is to them that the *loas* of the deceased will be transmitted a year later. One lies down for his father or his mother or an uncle. These candidates are called *kanzos*. The little angel is given some food to sustain it during its long trip; the food is put into a clay pot. Then water is poured into the jar, over the food, a symbolic representation of the separation between the two worlds. The pot is wrapped up in calico, which in Haiti is the white mortuary sheet, and then passed over a flame; it is the flame which sets the little angel in motion. The *kanzos* have to keep the pot firmly over their heads, pressing it down, for a few seconds. The pots are then put aside till the time has come to enact the final part of the ceremony. A small tent, made with a white sheet, is put up over a source or a well; if none of these sites is available in the courtyard, a basin full of water is simply placed under the sheet. The *kanzos* dressed in white, come out of the cult-house, holding the jars upon their heads; they are laid down by attendants, at the entrance of the tent, heads and jars which they never cease to press down tightly on their heads, towards the entrance. The Vodu priest then disappears under the sheet. The whole ritual is conducted out of sight of spectators. The *asson*, the rattle which stands as the symbol of the Vodu priesthood, is shaken over the basin. One hears the sound of water and suddenly the voice of a *loa*. That spirit is the chief of the cult-house of which the Vodu specialist is the leader; it is also the master of his rattle. This spirit is the one which goes under the water to fetch the ancestors that the priest is looking for. At the same time, it keeps order among the dead since many of them not related to the family and forgotten by their own relatives, try to get out. Sometimes an unexpected relative appears, begging the group to take him out. There is always an extra number of jars to meet such an eventuality. One after the other, the dead relatives come out and speak; they are now called *loas*. They ask about their children, tell details of the way they died (many deaths in Haiti are caused by sorcery or are so suspected), enquire about old unpaid debts, about the goat they intended to offer to such and such a spirit. They finally move into their respective jar. Once all of them have been removed, the *kanzos* are put back on their feet. They have to be helped since they are said to be extremely weak. They bring the jars back to the cult-house, still holding them on their heads. But now the pots have become very heavy; many walk as if they were drunk. A few possessions may occur. These pots (*govis*) will be kept in the cult-house. From now on, the Vodu priest may call the dead upon them, whenever one of their children wishes to get their advice on any kind of subject.

It is the knowledge of this whole procedure which forms the Vodu secret. The Vodu specialist is not an inspired man. He has been taught the technique by another Vodu specialist, never a relative since that would spoil him. Thus the Vodu is transmitted on family lines (one can take the *asson* only if one of his ancestors, either on his father's or mother's side, had already done so in the past). Vodu cult leaders nevertheless seem to form a loose association, bound by a common esoteric tradition, which has nothing to do with the family; this is why I describe them collectively as a priesthood. One can see how Vodu tries to control ecstasy and transmission of religious leadership; only a Vodu priest can appoint the successor to the leadership of a cult-house, through the mouth of the deceased cult leader when he has been called upon the jar; it is the best way problems of succession can unambiguously be solved; by the authority of the deceased father himself.

By contrast, magic spirits (Zandor, Petro, Nago) cannot be caught in jars. "They are too hot. They would break the jars." Moreover there is no need to send them back to Guinea, though their "horse" himself can be removed from the water by a Vodu specialist and thus transformed into a *loa*. These spirits pass freely from one world to another and they select freely a successor to the "horse" they used to possess. Magic cult leaders legitimise their position not so much in terms of the historical Guinea as by referring to the subterranean world, the Guinea under the ground, to which they claim to have direct access either in dreams or in possession.[11] It is said that if one could dig a hole deep enough into the ground, one would arrive in that mythical continent and this belief is shared by Vodu specialists themselves since this is where they send back the "little angel". But many magic specialists pretend to have spent years under the ground where they have been instructed by the spirits themselves. Female cult leaders, who in rural areas are denied access to Vodu secrets (it is completely different in the Capital) may achieve quite an important position in this manner. In Léogane, one of them, who had succeeded in founding her own establishment, was said to have spent fifteen days in a well, "under the water";

---

11. One can understand the importance of springs, ponds and wells since they provide a channel through which the Guinea spirits pass from the underground to the upper world. Every source has a master, a *loa* called Simby, which acts as a kind of gatekeeper between the two worlds. When such a spirit mounts its "horse", the person has to be firmly held back by the spectators otherwise he would plunge into the water, head first; and it is only after a calabash full of water has been poured over his head and he is thoroughly wet, that he may sit down and begin to eat its ritual meal. Water is dropped on the ground at the beginning of any Vodu ritual; the *loas* are said to come "through the water". The baptism of the spirit refers to this conducting power of water and is not a simple copy of the Catholic ritual. (Rigaud, 1953, p. 356.)

everyone thought that she was dead when she suddenly reappeared, her hair untressed (sign of possession state) and with all her religious para-phenalia; cards, necklaces, rattles. The *loas* themselves had chosen her. When she died, these objects were not transmitted but returned where they belonged, disappearing under the ground. Guinea is that kind of mythical kingdom whence all power comes and to which it returns.

Vodu priests scornfully call these magic specialists *houngans makoutes*, which means more or less, self-appointed leaders. Unlike Vodu specialists who work "awake", they are said to have no personal knowledge; unless they are possessed by their *loas* or "points", they cannot do anything by themselves. On the other hand, *makoute* cult leaders defame the Vodu secrets; in their opinion, "calling the dead over jars" is sheer nonsense, a fraudulent trick; and they always stress that, in the end, all power comes from knowing the mystical and curative properties of plants and roots, another way to express their privileged connection with the underground.

Vodu cult leaders are usually better-off than the others and are to be found mainly within the landed peasantry which emerged in Haiti, after the collapse of the plantation economy, as a result of the war of Independence. The creation of this landed peasantry is certainly the crucial factor explaining why Vodu still persists in Haiti, as a coherent ancestor-cult of which one finds only fragments in the other Caribbean Islands. Magic specialists pullulate among the landless or quasi-landless peasant as well as in town areas. However, as a *makoute* cult leader achieves a more secure financial position together with landed properties, he usually steps up; he takes the *asson*, thus eventually becoming a Vodu priest and worshipping both Vodu and magic spirits, but in separate cult-houses. It is thus possible for anyone who can afford it, to move from one category to another.

I would like to conclude briefly by going back to the antagonism between the generations and the way this is expressed in the opposition between Guinea and Magic. Guinea spirits, the family spirits of whichever "nation", are said to be cold. They protect you in a passive way. They will not give you any money; just enough to survive. They will not allow you to move up. In the Guinea cult-house one remains a child with no authority; Guinea spirits do not have to obey your wishes. But magic spirits, the "points" and zombis you buy, are like slaves in your hands; they obey your orders without preoccupying themselves with the morality of the operation; they are efficient servants. A large majority of *houngans* thus are said to serve with "both hands". They will have two cult-houses. In the larger one, at the front of the yard, they serve their family spirits, as children. And in a corner of the yard, concealed to the eye, is a shaking straw hut where they will keep their "points" and zombis; it is there that one will treat clients or will make "points" for them, and collect fees. Only in the smaller house, can he be described as a "master" of the spirits. By magic one separates his own private destiny from his ancestral background, looking forward to his own descendants, to his own establishment in opposition to all others.

References

Debien, G. 1941. *Une plantation de Saint Domingue. La sucrerie Galbaud du Fort* (*1690–1802*). Presses de l'Institut français d'Archéologie du Caire.

Herskovits, M. J. 1941. *The Myth of the Negro Past*, Harper, New York.

Lewis, I. M. 1971. *Ecstatic Religion*, Penguin, Harmondsworth.

Métreaux, A. 1955. La comédie rituelle dans la possession. *Diogene*, **11** (July), 1–24.

Rigaud, M. 1953. *La tradition Voodoo et le Voudou haitien*, Niclaus, Paris.

St-Mery Mor. 1876. *Description de la partie française de Saint Domingue*, Paris.

Trouillot, D. 1885. *Le Vaudou, apercu historique et evolution*, Etheait, PAP.

Turner, V. 1967. *The Forest of Symbols*, Cornell University Press, Ithaca.

6 | Symbolic Action and the Structure of the Self

Abner Cohen

I attempt in this short essay to consider the nature of the hold that symbols have on men. By symbols I mean normative forms that stand *ambiguously* for a multiplicity of meanings, evoke emotions and sentiments, and impel men to action. They usually occur in stylised patterns of activities, such as the rituals of religion or the ceremonials of kinship.

Why do men everywhere, in developed as in underdeveloped societies, engage in symbolic activities? Why does Political Man—shrewd, calculating, utilitarian—also have to be Symbolist Man—idealist, altruistic, non-rational? And how are these two dimensions of man interrelated? How do they affect one another?

This is an essentially "meta-anthropological" issue which has eluded empirical and systematic scrutiny. But it is so crucial to our understanding of the nature of socio-cultural causation, on which the development of social anthropology depends, that any light, no matter how little, which can be thrown on it, will be of value. For we have now reached a stage in social anthropology where, unless we develop insights into the processes mediating between the symbolic order and the power order, no further advance in our analytical endeavour will be possible.

I shall first relate this issue to the wider philosophical problem of the nature of "ought", of obligation, both moral and ritual, and will then discuss a number of propositions, some of them derived from the formulations of the Symbolic Interactionists, about the sociology of the self. Central in the discussion is the concept of selfhood, particularly as developed by George Herbert Mead (1934). The main argument to be advanced is that selfhood is continuously created, recreated and maintained (in the face of subversive processes both from within and from without) through symbolic action. Symbolic action is by definition action that involves the totality of the self and not a segment, or a role, within it. We achieve selfhood through continual participation in patterns of symbolic activities. For the majority of people these patterns are provided by the interest groups to which they are affiliated: the lineage, the tribe, the caste, or the "class". These interest groups always attempt to manipulate and structure the selves of their members to further their own ends. The self reacts to this in a variety of ways, including the creation of new symbolic patterns that are free from utilitarian interests. In time these new symbolic patterns are exploited by new or old interest groups, and the search for new patterns will be resumed. The process here is dialectical and cannot be analysed in reductionist terms. The discussion will in due course be related to some current theoretical problems within social anthropology.

"Ought": The Categorical Imperative

The nature of moral obligation has been the subject of extensive discussion and controversy among philosophers over the centuries. The unique quality of obligation is highlighted most dramatically by the philosopher Immanuel Kant in his distinction between what he called the Hypothetical Imperative and the Categorical Imperative, between "must" and "ought". The hypothetical imperative is essentially utilitarian, contractual and rational. It states that if you want something you "must" do something else. If you want money you must do a certain job. This kind of imperative is fundamentally different from that governed by an "ought", which states unconditionally and in absolute terms that you "ought" to, for example, respect your father, help your friend, worship God. Here, there are no questions of likes and dislikes, of calculations of benefits and losses. What "ought" to be done "ought" to be done, whether pleasant or unpleasant. This kind of imperative, Kant maintained, can never be explained scientifically in terms of causal links. The imperative comes not from the phenomenological world, i.e. the world as it is structured by the "categories" of the human mind, but from the transcendental, "real" world which exists objectively outside our mind. Indeed, Kant elaborates this point to the extent of concluding that the categorical imperative is the only window, so to speak, through which man can experience the "real world".

Not all philosophers have accepted the absolute uniqueness of "ought", as advocated by Kant, and some have argued that "ought" can be ultimately explained, or rather explained away, in terms of "must". This has been particularly the position of those philosophers known as the Utilitarians. To put it briefly and bluntly, the Utilitarians hold that altruistic action can be accounted for in terms of egoistic calculations of consequences.

This controversy between idealists and pragmatists regarding the nature of obligation has appeared in various forms in human thinking throughout the ages. In social anthropology it can be detected in a number of significant theoretical issues. It is, for example, at the basis of the controversy during the last two decades about the nature of kinship relationships. The contention by Fortes (1949) that kinship is an irreducible principle of social organisation, that it is a system of relations governed by moral values, is challenged by Worseley (1956) and others who point out that kinship relations are only idioms that can be explained away in terms of economic and political interests.

The controversy is also implicit in the more fundamental issue regarding the nature of society and, consequently, the logical character of social anthropology itself. Radcliffe-Brown (1952) saw society as a natural system that could be studied scientifically. Evans-Pritchard (1951) on the other hand argues that societies are moral, not natural systems and social anthropology cannot, therefore, be an exact science.

During the last few years the utilitarian stand of the orthodox Marxists has received powerful support from the anthropologists of the "Transactionalist School" who tend to reduce moral action to egocentric strategies directed towards the maximisation of personal power.

An even more important support of the utilitarian stand has been implicit in the evolutionary formulations of The Great Sociologists of the turn of the century who have very plausibly argued that change has brought about a qualitative transformation of the nature of society, proceeding in one direction: from community to association, from relationships governed by status to relationships governed by contract. These formulations have greatly influenced a number of anthropologists who see everywhere in industrialising societies contractual, single-stranded, utilitarian relationships replacing moral, multiplex, altruistic relationships. Everywhere, "ought", the categorical imperative, is giving way to "must", the hypothetical imperative. And as a result, or as a concomitant variation in this process—Weber and others have even argued—the evolutionary trend is towards increasing rationality and secularisation in social organisation.

It is clear that I am grossly oversimplifying the issues here. Judging by what is implicit in their monographic studies and by the explicit pronouncements of some of them, most anthropologists are not reductionists. They recognise that both "ought" and "must", the obligatory and the contractual, are involved in nearly all social relationships, that in fact these are two dimensions of social action. Thus, kinship relationships have both moral and utilitarian elements.

For many anthropologists, the major theoretical problem has been the analysis of the nature of interdependence between the obligatory and the contractual, when these are considered throughout the extent of a social group. How are these two types of action mediated? How do they act one on the other? We see in various social contexts various types of obligation manipulated to serve utilitarian interests and we want to know how this is achieved. How is "must" transformed to "ought", the utilitarian to the moral? At what level and by what mechanisms do such transformations take place?

Our answers to such questions have so far been superficial. Operating within conceptually assumed synchronic systems, we have often juxaposed the moral and the utilitarian and said that the two are interdependent. I think that Geertz (1966) is right in complaining that the multiplication of studies showing repetitively, one after the other, that, for example, ancestor worship supports political authority, will not advance our analysis; that instead we should address ourselves to the question *how* this is achieved. How are purely political interests converted to the most intimate moral and ritual obligations which are capable of impelling men to action without any coercion from the outside?

Our coverage of the action and reaction between the two variables has so far tended to be tilted to one side. The influence of orthodox Marxism, of transactionalism and of the evolutionists, together with the traditional re-action of social anthropology against psychological and historical cultur-ology, has inhibited the study of the nature of the obligatory in social action. Generally, the whole tendency in the social sciences has been to "oversocialise" man.

Symbolic Techniques

Part of the difficulty has been created by the abstract and vague nature of obligation. To many of us, the obligatory is an innate, subjective and per-sonal experience and its study is therefore beyond the competence of the anthropologist.

But it is possible to go some way in solving this difficulty by turning our attention from the subjective and abstract experience of obligation to the symbolic forms and activities that objectify obligations. Norms and values do not exist on their own but are everywhere couched in symbolic forma-tions. They are developed and maintained within the psyche of the indivi-dual through continual symbolic activities. Often it is the objective symbols that generate the subjective experience of obligation and not the other way round. In terms of observable and verifiable criteria, what matters sociologi-cally is what people actually do, not what they subjectively think they are doing.

As our subjective life is shifting, vague and chaotic, we are only too happy to be assisted by the objective symbolic formulations provided to us by "experts", leaders, teachers or, generally, the culture under which we live. Symbols are essentially objective forms. They may be originally the spontaneous creation of individuals going through specific subjective experiences, but they attain an objective existence when they are accepted by others in the course of social interaction. What was originally subjective and individual, now becomes objective and collective. They develop a reality of their own, become obligatory and begin to exercise constraint on the individual.

So we come back to the question: What is it in symbols that can impel men to act altruistically? One answer to this question has been indirectly provided by Turner (1964) in his well-known distinction between the sensory and the ideological poles within the structure of the dominant ritual symbol. At the ideological pole, he points out, there is a cluster of meanings referring to moral values, principles of social organisation, rules of social behaviour, the ideals of corporate groupings, in short all the obligatory elements in social conduct. At the sensory pole, on the other hand, there are gross sensations, desires and feelings. The norms, values, principles and rules at the ideological pole are abstract and remote and their mere perception by the person is not sufficient to induce him to action. It is only when the person is emotionally agitated by the sensory pole of the symbol that he will be moved to action. In the action situation of ritual, Turner argues, the ritual symbol effects an interchange of qualities between the two poles of the symbol. Norms and values become saturated with emotion, while the gross and basic emotions become ennobled through contact with social values. The irksomeness of moral constraint is transformed into the love of goodness. Ritual thus becomes a mechanism which periodically converts the obligatory into the desirable.

This is a very illuminating formulation which goes a long way in explaining the manner in which symbols operate. But essentially it explains the working of *symbolic techniques* and not the obligatory in symbols. A symbolic technique can be literally mechanical, operating on the basis of a Pavlovian type stimulus-response formula. It may have nothing to do with the obligatory. We are familiar with advertisements showing, for example, a girl model standing beside a car. The girl has nothing to do with the car, but her image is thought by the advertiser to attract the attention of men, who are usually the buyers of such a car. By the repetitive experience of the advertisement, the potential male buyers begin to associate the particular brand of car with exciting and pleasant feelings. And this may persuade them eventually to decide to buy the car. Colour, music, dancing and the human body can certainly enhance the power of symbols. But they cannot by themselves account for the impelling power of symbols.

Action on the stimulus of symbolic techniques is essentially based on a hypothetical, not categorical, imperative. What the symbolic technique "says" is that if you want to have some pleasant sensations you must perform certain acts. It does not explain the nature of "ought". What is more, there are many symbols that are not particularly pleasant or desirable. For example, one of the most powerful symbols employed in many cultures is the human corpse which can fill the mind with revulsion and fear. These unpleasant feelings are aroused even when in a mock funeral in a political demonstration it is known that the coffin is empty.

A much more mechanistic explanation is implied by the structuralism of Lévi-Strauss and his followers, who would maintain that men behave symbolically in the way they do because their mind is structured, or "programmed", to do so.

The Structure of Selfhood

But the nature of obligation is rooted in a much deeper layer of the human psyche, well beyond what we call personality. The reference here is to selfhood, the sheer *oneness* of the person. This is a subject I have discussed (Cohen, 1974) elsewhere in some detail; here I give only a short outline of it.

In our contractual relationships we are essentially involved in roles whose performance formally involve only segments of our personality, not the totality of the person. An engineer is involved in his job only as an engineer not as a father or member of a political party. The relationship is instrumental, in the sense that the parties involved in it use one another as a means to an end and not an end in themselves. In our social life we come to perform different and sometimes discrepant roles of this kind. As a result, our life tends to become compartmentalised and our personality fragmented.

But there is a limit to which this segmentation of the person can proceed. Even in the performance of our most instrumental, contractual role, we have to involve the totality of our self though this is not formally required or recognised. Indeed, if we are too specific in adhering to the requirements of the contractual role, we may defeat the very end of that role. Thus Merton (1957) points out that the bureaucrat who disciplines himself to perform his task efficiently according to the letter of the rules, will in effect become unfit to perform his role, which requires flexibility in dealing with people.

This means that a man cannot live a normal life in society without having a self, or oneness, within which the various specialised roles or segments are integrated. This self is not a natural inborn feature of man, but is achieved through social interaction with other men. What is more, it is not a once-and-for-all achievement, but is continuously in the making. In the course of the developmental cycle of our life career and also as a result of changes of all sorts, we continually find outselves enmeshed in new constellations of disparate and often conflicting roles which threaten our oneness. The self will thus have to be continuously recreated and maintained.

Selfhood is achieved by a person when he interacts with other persons with the *totality* of his self. Social roles differ in their demand on the totality of the self. In the performance of a single, highly specialised contractual role, the totality of the self is least involved. On the other hand, maximum involvement of the self is achieved through non-contractual, non-utilitarian, non-rational roles and the patterns of symbolic activities associated with these roles.

Symbolic action is by definition action involving the totality of the self. Symbols vary in their potency. The more potent the symbol, the more total the involvement of the self. Nearly all social action has both symbolic and contractual elements, but some activities are more symbolic and less contractual than others. There is thus a continuum from the most symbolic and least contractual at one end to the most contractual and least symbolic at the other. These two elements in social action are psychically interrelated. They represent two psychic processes. The contractual element is subversive of selfhood; the symbolic element is recreative of selfhood. *It is in the symbolic act that we continually create and recreate our selfhood*, the totality of our person. Symbolic action is so essential to the existence of selfhood, that to say self is to imply automatically the presence of symbolic action. Selves exist in society; therefore symbolic action exists. There can be no self without the experience and periodical practice of the obligatory.

I believe that it is for these considerations that Fortes (1949) argued that kinship is an irreducible principle of social life. Symbolic interaction however is not confined to kinship but is an element in nearly all social relationships. Fortes (1969) has recently extended his concept of the irreducible principle of kinship to cover pseudo-kinship relationships, indeed all relationships that have what he calls "amity" as a common denominator. What I find difficult in some of these formulations is the psychoanalytic assumption that personality is formed in interaction within the family during the first few years of life and that the sentiments that are formed during those early years are later *extended* to cover other kin or pseudo kin. In recent years psychologists and even psychoanalysts have tended increasingly to view personality as an open system given to significant changes in adulthood as a result of continuous socialisation under changing sociocultural conditions. Selfhood is continually in the making.

The precariousness of the self is created not only by the discrepant roles in which the person is involved but also by the perpetual threats of anomie and marginality posed by the unresolved problems of human existence like misfortune, evil, sickness, decay and, above all, death. These problems have confronted man everywhere, in preindustrial and in industrial societies, past and present. They are *perennial* problems, i.e. problems that are by their very nature not given to rational explanation or solution. Almost everywhere they have been explained in mystical terms and dealt with by patterns of symbolic activities.

But men seldom meet these perpetual threats to the self, both from within and from without, entirely unassisted. For most of us, the major interest groups to which we belong provide us with explanations, sharpened by the work of expert ideologists and with remedies created by artists and visionaries. These interest groups attempt to prescribe for us a blue-print for living, including rules of conduct governing interpersonal relationships and patterns of symbolic activities aimed at making the mysterious, enigmatic, unpredictible, dangerous universe into a more familiar, predictible, habitable home.

In the course of developing, maintaining and strengthening their interests, these groups develop basic organisational functions for the effective co-ordination of their activities. When any of these functions cannot be organised formally and contractually, attempts are made to organise them informally, through the mobilisation and manipulation of the obligatory, moral or ritual, in conduct. To that extent, the pursuit of the group's aim, will be ensured, not by contractual mechanisms that operate on the individual from the outside, but by obligations, by "oughts", operating from "inside" and involving the totality of the individual self.

To take an example, an opposition group within a state will do its best to co-ordinate its activities effectively. If allowed, it will officially register as a formal association, with special regulations governing membership, communication, processes of decision-making, a structure of authority. The privileges and duties of the members will be formally laid out. Membership in general will be governed by a contract. The association will demand the individual members to play a few specific roles which involve only some segments of their persons. At least formally the association will not demand the totality of the selves of its members. Compliance with the regulations of the association will be ensured by the mechanisms of reward and deprivation. If however the group is not allowed to form an association, it will organise itself informally, say as a religious group or as a fraternity. Here membership is governed by ritual or moral obligations, by "oughts" that involve the totality of the self. Compliance with the aims and requirements of the group will be ensured by spontaneous impelling force from within the self.

These two types of organisation are the extremes of a two-dimensional continuum on which nearly all groupings can be located. Even the most formal associations make use of informal mechanisms in their organisation. Almost all organisations are two-dimensional, being partly formal and partly informal, combining these two elements in different ratios. They all make claims on the totality of the self, though in different degrees. The self is thus subject to a most intensive competition between interest groups.

The Heuristic Significance of the Concept of "Selfhood"

I have attempted to present this discussion in as dogmatic a form as possible. But the value for social anthropological enquiries of the concept of selfhood seems highly questionable. Can this concept be operationalised for empirical sociological research? Many sociologists and social anthropologists have succeeded in evading this issue. A few have confronted it and their verdict has, on the whole, been negative. Thus Dahrendorf (1968) states categorically that sociology deals exclusively with *homo sociologus*, not with the real, total person which, he emphasizes, has no place in sociology.

The whole issue hinges on whether selfhood is a variable and whether social anthropologists are competent enough to study it and to use it as a significant tool in their fieldwork and analysis.

If selfhood is taken to be the achievement of the sheer oneness of the psyche, by integrating within one unified psychic system the totality of the roles in which the individual has been involved, and if this oneness is always fully achieved by men, or at least by normal men, then the concept cannot be a significant sociological variable. At best it can only be naively conceived and its analysis left to the competence of the trained psychologist or to the more speculative endeavour of the psychoanalyst.

But there are two possible ways in which selfhood can be conceived as a variable. Firstly, oneness is never perfect in any man. It is, so to speak, essentially an ideal model. We learn from the psychoanalysts that men differ in the degree of their integration on a continuum. This variation in the structure of selfhood is explained in terms of individual differences that are related mainly to differences in family relationships during early childhood.

But, and here we come to the second sense in which selfhood can be a variable, there are different types of family orgnisation giving rise to different patterns of psychic conflict in different societies or in different groupings within the same society. Thus, as Malinowski pointed out long ago, the Trobriand family is very different in its structure of relationships from that of the middle-class Viennese family which Freud had in mind when he developed his views about the psyche. Furthermore, many psychologists today reject the Freudian assumption of a once-and-for-all formation of the psyche in early childhood. While conceding that a measure of continuity of the self exists, these critics maintain at the same time that socialisation goes on all the time in response to major changes in sociocultural contexts.

Thus, different role structures in different social systems can produce different types of conflict, or disjunctions, within the self. On the other hand, different cultures may provide different symbolic forms, that achieve different degrees of success, for the continual development and maintenance of selfhood.

As a case in point, reference can be made to Durkheim's (1951) concept of the *rate*, as against the *incidence*, of suicide. The rate of suicide in any one society at any period of time is highly stable, the same number of people destroying themselves year after year with a remarkable consistency. Different societies, or different groups within a society, have different rates of suicide. If one accepts the psychoanalytic view that absolute integration of the self is an ideal which is never fully realised by any man, then each man harbours conflicting tendencies within his psyche and is thus a potential candidate for suicide. In some socio-cultural systems this potentiality is minimised, in others it is strengthened. In the first, selfhood, or the degree of self-integration, is made strong and the suicide rate is low; in the others it is weakened or left unassisted and the suicide rate is high, with most societies falling in-between on the same dimension. Durkheim goes on to state that:

> ... the social suicide-rate can be explained only sociologically. At any given moment the moral constitution of society establishes the contingent of voluntary deaths. There is, therefore, for each people a collective force of a definite amount of energy, impelling men to self-destruction ... Each human society ... has a greater or lesser aptitude for suicide. (ibid., p. 299)

If selfhood *is* a variable, can anthropologists operationalise it in their study, in both fieldwork and analysis? A start can probably be made by confining ourselves to the analysis of the obligatory as it is manifested in symbolic activities. Selfhood is achieved through symbolic action, and in dealing with symbolic action we are dealing with objective phenomena.

An early attempt to study cross-cultural differences in self-integration was made by Kardiner and his colleagues (1945) when they developed the concept of "Basic Personality Structure", referring to patterns of conflict and to the institutions associated with them, that are shared in common by men living within the same socio-cultural system. But the attempt soon degenerated into the study of "national character", which became popular during the Second World War and the decade following it. Sweeping generalisations were made about colossal, complex societies like those of

Japan, Russia and Germany. And even when the studies were confined to small scale subsistence societies, no notice was taken of group and individual differences within the same society. But in principle the idea is a valid one and may be of some empirical value. For, if we concede that *individuals* differ in the degree of their self-integration, then it is plausible to think that individuals living under essentially similar socio-cultural circumstances will have some broad similarities in the structure of their selves. The main difficulty in maintaining this statement is that no two persons live under identical socio-cultural conditions and the larger the size of the group one studies, the more the differences between individuals and the less valid our delineation of the basic structure of the self. However, if we confine ourselves to the study of small, socially and culturally homogenous groups, and cover only broad similarities and differences, we may yet be able to make some progress in our endeavour.

One way of proceeding under these heuristic conditions is to combine our usual anthropological methods and techniques with the detailed study of the biographies of different categories of men and women, particularly in situations of crisis or rapid change, noting changes in roles and changes in the patterns of symbolic activities, against the general socio-cultural background. Of particular significance here will be the biographies of creative leaders and artists, which can be compared with those of ordinary people in the same groups.

Social anthropologists do collect biographies of individuals in the course of their research, but do so largely unsystematically. However, once the theoretical objectives are clarified, biographical studies can be developed and this will make it possible to have deeper insights into the structure of the self and the role of symbolic action in developing and maintaining that structure. The method can be further systematised by combining it with a modified form of network analysis.

The diagramatic representation of the individual social network, as developed by many anthropologists, has tended to be "uni-dimensional", with ego in the middle of the star and the relationships between ego and alters represented as lines. Most of these anthropologists have been aware that the lines stand in fact for different kinds of relationships. But the criteria they have suggested for differentiation have been expressed in quantitative terms, such as "intensity", "effectiveness", "strength", "extendedness", in addition to the distinction introduced by Bott (1957) between "loose" and "close" connectedness of the network. Kapferer (1969; 1973) came nearer to qualitative differention when he distinguished between multiplex and simplex relationships in the network. However, nearly all these anthropologists have found the mechanical, uni-dimensional, neat model to be more convenient to operate with, as it enabled them to introduce more and more sophisticated statistical and diagramatic techniques for studying, with only very limited sociological results.

In the light of discussion it is possible to conceive of the star-network as consisting of two principal types of relationships, that can be diagramatically represented in two different colours, the one contractual, the other moral or obligatory. These two sets of relationships are closely interrelated and form what may be called the structure of the self. Ideally we can conceive of the possibility of measuring their respective intensities and the balance between them, but this will perhaps require the specialised competence of the psychologist or psychoanalyst.

References

Bott, E. 1957. *Family and Social Network*, Tavistock, London.

Cohen, Abner. 1974. *Two-Dimensional Man: An essay on the anthropology of power and symbolism in complex society*, Routledge and Kegan Paul, London.

Dahrendorf, R. 1968. *Essays in the Theory of Society*, Routledge and Kegan Paul, London.

Durkheim, Emile. 1951. *Suicide*, The Free Press, New York.

Evans-Pritchard, E. E. 1951. *Social Anthropology*, Cohen and West, London.

Fortes, M. 1949. *The Web of Kinship among the Tallensi*, Oxford University Press, London.

Fortes, M. 1969. *Kinship and the Social Order*, Aldine, Chicago.

Geertz, C. 1966. Religion as a cultural system. *In* Michael Banton (ed.) *Anthropological Approaches to the Study of Religion*, ASA Monograph no. 3, 1–46, Tavistock, London.

Kapferer, B. 1969. Norms and the manipulation of relationships in a work context. *In* J. C. Mitchell (ed.) *Social Networks in Urban Situations*, 181–244, Manchester University Press.

Kapferer, B. 1973. Social network and conjugal role in urban Zambia: Toward a reformulation of the Bott hypothesis. *In* J. Boissevain and J. C. Mitchell (eds.) *Network Analysis: Studies in Human Interaction*, 83–110, Mouton, The Hague.

Kardiner, A. 1945. *The Psychological Frontiers of Society*, Columbia University Press, Columbia.

Mead, G. H. 1934. *Mind, Self and Society*, University of Chicago Press, Chicago.

Merton, R. K. 1957. Bureaucratic structure and personality. *In* Merton, R. K. (ed.) *Social Theory and Social Structure*, The Free Press, New York.

Radcliffe-Brown, A. R. 1952. *Structure and Function in Primitive Society*, Cohen and West, London.

Turner, V. W. 1964. Symbols in Ndembu ritual. *In* M. Gluckman (ed.) *Closed Systems and Open Minds*, Oliver and Boyd, Edinburgh.

Worseley, P. M. 1956. The kinship system of the Tallensi: a revaluation. *JRAI*, **86**.

7 | Is Freudian Symbolism a Myth?

Charles Rycroft

It has become a commonplace among the general public, and perhaps among journalists in particular, that some things are Freudian symbols. In the popular usage of this phrase, the word Freudian is synonymous with "sexual", the word "sexual" is synonymous with "genital", while the question "what does the word 'symbol' mean?" is answered, if it is asked at all, by saying that it is something that stands for something else. A pipe, a sword, a gun is held to be a Freudian symbol on the ground that Freud reputedly said that they stand for penises. In view of this widespread assumption, I thought it might be appropriate to start this paper by investigating whether the general public has in fact correctly divined and understood an essential part of Freud's thinking or whether some distortion of his ideas has taken place during their passage from the learned literature into the colour supplements.

Now, in one very simple sense, a distortion certainly has occurred. Freud himself was not the psychoanalyst who first attached central importance to sexual symbolism. As he himself said, he arrived late at a full realisation of the importance of symbolism of any kind. The first edition of his *The Interpretation of Dreams* (1900) contains only a few pages devoted to the subject of symbolism in general and only one dream exemplifying sexual symbolism. These few pages came at the end of a section entitled "Considerations of Representability", and the matter under discussion was not primarily "how are sexual ideas symbolised in dreams?" but two more general ones: How are thoughts, which are not necessarily visual, converted into the visual imagery characteristic of dreams? And how can forbidden, taboo ideas be expressed in dreams in such a way that the dreamer, when he awakens, will not understand them?; sexual ideas being only one of several classes of forbidden ideas which the "dream work" has to translate into imagery that will get past the censor.

Freud did, however, eventually get around to attaching great importance to symbolism in general and to sexual symbolism in particular, successive editions of *The Interpretation of Dreams* containing additions referring to sexual symbolism. But it was not until the fourth edition (1914) that Freud included a section concerned exclusively with symbolism. However, even in the present definitive Standard Edition, this section consists of only 55 pages in a work running to 623 pages.

Freud's reasons for taking fourteen years to attaching central importance to the idea with which his name has become most widely associated, are expressed clearly in the opening paragraphs of this section, and I should like now to quote extensively from them.

> The analysis of this last, biographical, dream (i.e. the one discussed at the end of the previous section) is clear evidence that I recognised the presence of symbolism in dreams from the very beginning. But it was only by degrees and as my experience increased that I arrived at a full appreciation of its extent and significance, and I did so under the influence of the contributions of Wilhelm Stekel (1911), about whom a few words will not be out of place here. (1925)
>
> That writer, who has perhaps damaged psycho-analysis as much as he has benefited it, brought forward a large number of unsuspected translations of symbols; to begin with they were met with scepticism, but later they were for the most part confirmed and had to be accepted. I shall not be belittling the value of Stekel's services if I add that the sceptical reserve with which his proposals were received was not without justification. For the examples by which he supported his interpretations were often unconvincing, and he made use of a method which must be rejected as scientifically untrustworthy.
>
> Stekel arrived at his interpretations of symbols by way of intuition, thanks to a peculiar gift for the direct understanding of them. But the existence of such a gift cannot be counted upon generally, its effectiveness is exempt from all criticism and consequently its findings have no claim to credibility . . .
>
> Advances in psycho-analytic experience have brought to our notice patients who have shown a direct understanding of dream-symbolism of this kind to a surprising extent. They were often sufferers from dementia praecox (i.e. what we nowadays call schizophrenia), so that for a time there was an inclination to suspect every dreamer who had this grasp of symbols of being a victim of that disease. But such is not the case. It is a question of a personal gift or peculiarity which has no visible pathological significance.

I should like now to make two glosses on this quotation.

1. It is apparent that in symbolism Freud encountered a phenomenon which was resistive to, and indeed incompatible with, his ideal of founding a psychology based on natural-scientific principles. Freud's original and

indeed life-long Grand Design was to construct a science of mind which would be analogous to the physical sciences, which used concepts such as force and energy, which was strictly determinist and in which all explanations were in terms of causation. But here in symbolism he encountered phenomena which required explanations in terms of meaning not of cause, and in which convincing explanations could be arrived at by "a method which must be rejected as scientifically untrustworthy" and by persons who possessed not a training in the rigours of the scientific method but a "peculiar gift for the direct understanding" of symbolic equations. It must have been all very embarrassing for Freud and one has to sympathise with his resistance against recognising the importance of symbolism.

It must, however, be remembered that Freud displayed similar resistance towards two other ideas which have become generally associated with his name: the idea that human beings are as affected by their phantasies as by their actual experiences (cf. his distress at realising that his female patients could not all have been literally seduced by their fathers); and the idea that psychoanalytical treatment is essentially a matter of transference—"finally every conflict has to be fought out in the sphere of transference" (Freud 1912).

2. It is evident that Freud must himself have had patients who possessed the "peculiar gift" of being able to translate symbols intuitively, that it would have suited his theoretical book if they had all turned out to be mad, but that in fact they often were not—but note his phrase "no *visible* pathological significance". It followed from *this* embarrassing observation that symbolism in the Freudian sense could not be either a pathological phenomenon capable of a causative explanation, or one of the so-called "primary processes" which Freud postulated were characteristic of unconscious mental activity. As is well known, Freud held that there are two types or principles of mental functioning, one discursive, verbal, conforming to the laws of grammar and formal logic, and characteristic of conscious thinking, the other non-discursive, condensive, iconic, ignorant of the categories of space and time, and characteristic of unconscious thinking. It would have been methodologically convenient and economical if Freudian symbolism could have been included in the latter, and most analysts other than Freud have in fact done so, but the existence of "peculiar" people like Stekel—and also, as Freud himself pointed out, of artists and jokers—makes it impossible to do so.

II

Having described Freud's rather reluctant acceptance of the fact that there is such a thing as what has come to be called Freudian symbolism, I must turn to the question as to whether this symbolism is exclusively sexual, as popularisations of psycho-analysis would have one believe. The answer to this question is equivocal. According to Freud's tenth Introductory Lecture (1916) "The range of things which are given symbolic representation in dreams is not wide; the human body as a whole, parents, children, brothers and sisters, birth, death, nakedness—and something else besides." This "something else besides" turns out to be "the field of sexual life—the genitals, sexual processes, sexual intercourse. The great majority of symbols in dreams are sexual symbols. And here a strange disproportion is revealed. The topics I have mentioned are few, but the symbols for them are extremely numerous." Freud then goes on to list over 30 symbols for the male genitals and over 20 for the female.

Reading this lecture one is indeed left with the overwhelming impression that in Freud's view, Freudian symbolism is predominantly sexual, but I must confess that I think that Freud reached the conclusion that "the great majority of symbols in dreams are sexual" by a mixture of logical error and intellectual sleight-of-hand.

The logical error consists in failing to appreciate that the topics which he designates "few" and the "symbols" which he designates as "numerous" are not of the same logical type, and cannot therefore be compared numerically with one another. The topics mentioned—birth, death, sex, etc.—are general ideas arrived at by abstraction, the symbols mentioned—umbrellas, revolvers, Zeppelins, cupboards, apples, etc., etc.— are specific objects, or, to be pedantic, concepts of a lower level of abstraction. It is therefore hardly surprising that there are more symbols than topics symbolised. The entities classified must of necessity be more numerous than the classes into which they are classified.

The intellectual sleight-of-hand consists of (a) asserting that the range of things which are given symbolic representation is not wide, when in fact the list of things which he says are symbolisable embraces almost the whole range of human experience, apart perhaps from work, intellectual activity and some kinds of play, and (b) detaching the sexual life from the other members of the list of things deemed symbolisable and treating it as though it had no intrinsic connection with them. But this is, of course, not so. To go through his list: we only have a body because our parents once had sexual intercourse; we only have children because we have had intercourse; we only have brothers and sisters because our parents had intercourse more than once; birth and death are the first and last members of the series birth, copulation and death; nakedness has obvious connections with both the sexual life and with the interfaces between the self as private and public being, as biological and social being.

What, it seems to me, Freud should have said was that the range of things which are given symbolic representation embraces all aspects of man's biological life-cycle, and that scrutiny of dreams reveals that human beings are much more preoccupied with their biological destiny and with their intimate personal relationships than most of them realise. Freud, strangely, seems always to have assumed that it is normal for human beings to be oblivious and obtuse about the importance of this emotional, poetic, mythopoetic, imaginative aspect of human experience, and that people who are aware of it are "special cases", with gifts that are "peculiar" in both senses of the word. As I have said elsewhere (Rycroft, 1962), Freud's conception of the normal person was "cast in the mould of the scientist at work". Hence, incidentally, his ambivalence towards artists, whom he both admired for their natural understanding of things that he had had to learn the hard way, and disparaged by trying to demonstrate that they were all neurotic. To be fair to Freud, I must add that late in his life he abandoned this attempt: "Before the problem of the creative artist analysis must, alas, lay down its arms" (Freud, 1928).

In parenthesis I must mention that I believe that Freud's insistence in 1917 that the great majority of symbols are sexual was polemical, and was an attempt to preserve the scientific purity of psychoanalysis from contamination by Jungian ideas about archetypes, which he regarded as mystical and irrational. He wanted psychoanalysis to remain grounded in biology, and genitals are more down to earth than mandalas.

The same concealed polemical motive can also be discerned in Ernest Jones's paper "The Theory of Symbolism" (1916), which remains to this day the classic statement of the psychoanalytical position, and which only a few analysts—in this country Marion Milner (1952), Hanna Segal (1957) and myself (1956)—have challenged. In this paper Jones makes two points which I should like to discuss in some detail, one because it has been largely responsible for the difficulties in communication which have notoriously always existed between psychoanalysts on the one hand and anthropologists and linguists on the other, and the other because it is highly germane to the general theme of this symposium, symbols and sentiments.

The first is Jones's argument, or rather assertion, that there is such a thing as "true symbolism", which is psychoanalytical and predominantly sexual and can be differentiated from what he calls "symbolism in its widest sense". According to Jones's distinction words, emblems, tokens, badges, charms, conventionalised gestures, etc. are not true symbols, even though they "represent some other idea from which they derive a significance not inherent in themselves", and are only loosely and vaguely called symbols by those ignorant of psychoanalysis. "The thesis will here be maintained that true symbolism, in the strict sense, is to be distinguished from other forms of indirect representation."

On the face of it, the claim that only Freudian symbols are true symbols is both arrogant and parochial. One would, after all, not allow a mathematician to get away with the assertion that the only true symbols are algebraic, or a linguist with the assertion that the only true symbols are words. But in Jones's defence it must be mentioned that in 1916 it was generally believed that the concept of evolution could be applied to human societies, and that it was, therefore, legitimate to equate phylogenetically the "infantile phantasies of civilised neurotics and the dreams of healthy civilised adults with the rites, folklores, myths, religions, etc., of primitives". As a result of this evolutionary assumption, Jones could without personal arrogance make remarks in 1916 which ring false in 1974, e.g. "Much more significant for the genesis of symbolism is the phylogenetic fact that in primitive civilisations an importance was attached to sexual organs and functions that to us appears absolutely monstrous." and "The tendency of the primitive mind—as observed in children, in savages, in wit, dreams, insanity, and other products of unconscious functioning—to identify different objects and to fuse together different ideas, to note the resemblances and not the differences, is a universal and most characteristic feature, . . ."

Now, given this assumption, that civilised Western Europeans are more evolved than lesser breeds, Jones was, of course, justified in postulating that symbols encountered in dreams and neurotic symptoms had some sort of evolutionary priority over other more sophisticated kinds of symbols such as words, emblems or crests, the use of which demands a considerable degree of ontogenetic and phylogenetic development. Jones's position assumes, incidentally, that civilised children dream and phantasise before they learn how to talk—which may well be true—and that primitives think while awake in a way that resembles the way in which civilised people think while asleep—which I presume is not.

According to Jones "only what is repressed is symbolised; only what is repressed needs to be symbolised" and true psychoanalytical symbols "represent ideas of the self and the immediate blood relatives or of the phenomena of birth, love and death. In other words, they represent the most primitive ideas and interests imaginable." Note again the curious use of the word "primitive" in a context which seems to demand "basic" or "fundamental". "The two cardinal characteristics of symbolism in this strict sense are (1) that the process is completely unconscious . . . and (2) that the affect investing the symbolised idea has not, insofar as the symbolism is concerned, proved capable of that modification in quality denoted by the term 'sublimation'."

III

I shall now consider these two cardinal characteristics separately. First, the idea that the process underlying symbolism is completely unconscious. This statement is, I think, capable of two interpretations. It could mean either (1) that an innate and unconscious sense of similarities determines whether particular objects are utilisable as symbols for other particular objects, or (2) that the person using a true symbol is unconscious of its true meaning. Both interpretations can be found in the psychoanalytical literature, the first to explain the apparent universal or constant meaning of certain symbols, the second to explain the difference between "true" symbols and metaphors. To make clearer what I am getting at, and to rescue myself from the morass of abstractions into which we have fallen, I shall now give four illustrative examples, all of which depend on the fact that the human mind is capable of conceiving a similarity between genitals and a violin or other stringed instrument. The two clinical examples are not my own; I have taken them from Hanna Segal (1957).

1. A male violinist was asked, while having a psychotic breakdown, why he no longer played the violin. He answered, quite seriously, "Why? Do you expect me to masturbate in public?", thereby implying that for him at that moment his violin *was* his genitals. The symbolism was fully conscious, but in a curious way, since he had temporarily lost insight into the fact that a symbol only *represents* something other than itself. He equated the symbol with its referent and could, therefore, no longer perform in public. I would remind you here of my earlier quotation from Freud in which he expressed his original suspicion that people with a direct understanding of symbolism were insane.

2. Another male violinist was having psychoanalytical treatment on account of, *inter alia*, inhibitions about performing in public. During the course of his treatment he reported material, including a dream in which he and a woman were playing duets together, which suggested that he unconsciously equated genitals and violins; after this had been interpreted to him, he resumed playing in public. In this case the symbolism was initially completely unconscious; only in dreams did he equate violins and genitals, and his analyst had to draw his attention to the fact that he did so. But after he had recognised his unconscious tendency to fuse, or rather confuse, violins and genitals—and after, presumably, his sense of guilt about sexual matters had been reduced—he could again perform in public.

3. The French novelist Honoré de Balzac, who died in 1850 and cannot, therefore, have read any Freud, is reputed once to have remarked that the love-making of many men resembled a gorilla trying to play a violin. In order to have been able to make this remark, Balzac must have been able

to conceive of a similarity between men of a certain type and gorillas and of another similarity between women as sexual beings and violins. Since he was awake when he said it, he must have been fully conscious of these similarities and have assumed confidently that his audience could also become conscious of them. He was in fact talking metaphorically, in perfect confidence that his audience would neither assume that he thought that clumsy men are in fact gorillas or that amorous women are in fact violins, nor that they would fail to appreciate that clumsy men can be likened to gorillas and that women can be likened to violins. According to Jones's formulations, such metaphorical statements are not truly symbolic, since the process is not completely unconscious. Yet it is difficult to see in what way the process of symbolisation differs when it occurs consciously and emerges as a metaphor, and when it occurs unconsciously and emerges as a dream-image. It seems to me more economical and logical to say that the process is identical in both cases and that symbolism, or rather the capacity to symbolise, is a general mental capacity, which can be used consciously or unconsciously, while awake or asleep, neurotically or creatively, with or without insight into its implications.

4. The sculptor Ossip Zadkine, who was born in 1890 and who may well, therefore, have read Freud, and whose work is characterised by a "flair for metaphor and transformation" and "a vocabulary in which voids replace solids, concavities replace convexities" (Jean Cassou in his Introduction to the Arts Council Exhibition 1961), has produced a number of works in which human bodies and string instruments, mostly violins and cellos, are fused. In some of these the strings of the instrument pass through the genital area, leaving the viewer in no doubt that Zadkine is equating string instruments and genitals—and string instruments as sources of music with human bodies as sources of erotic sensations. Here again the symbolism is patently conscious; sculptors are not asleep while they sculpt and must be presumed to reflect upon what they are doing. But since Zadkine could have read Freud, one would have to possess biographical information about him before deciding whether he spontaneously equated string instruments with genitals, or whether he was self-consciously exploiting the concept of Freudian symbolism. Personally, I suspect the former, but it is, I understand, a fact that artists who work for advertising agencies do consciously exploit the idea of Freudian symbolism, knowingly introducing Freudian symbols into advertisements, hoping thereby to add unconscious sex-appeal to the wares they are trying to sell. Whether such gambits are effective remains dubious and there is, I understand, some evidence that they may on occasion backfire. The slogan "there's a Tiger in my Tank" is said to have frightened some motorists off buying the petrol it advertised.

Surrealist painters also used Freudian symbolism self-consciously (see Ades, 1972).

Jones's second cardinal characteristic of "true" symbolism is "that the affect investing the symbolized idea has not ... proved capable of that modification in quality denoted by the term 'sublimation'." In other words, true symbols retain the emotional tone that is appropriate to the referent symbolised, while other classes of "symbolism in its widest sense" possess an emotional tone of some other quality, this other quality being only definable by reference to the concept of sublimation. The implication here is that images and actions are only true symbols if they are accompanied by, or evoke, the feelings naturally aroused by the phenomena of birth, love and death, but are not true symbols if they arouse some other more "sublime" affect. According to this view, violins were "true" symbols for the psychotic violinist I mentioned earlier since he conceived himself to be masturbating if he played one. They were also true symbols for the inhibited, neurotic violinist when he was dreaming that he was playing duets with a woman violinist, but ceased to be when, after recovery, he could again play in public. They were not true symbols for Balzac when he made his remark about gorillas playing them, since he and his audience were, presumably, amused not sexually aroused by it. And Zadkine must be presumed to have been having aesthetic not sexual emotions while sculpting his torsos.

It seems to me that this second cardinal distinction between true and other symbols is open to four objections. First, Jones has really made a distinction between two different kinds of affect, unmodified and modified, not between two different kinds of symbol. Secondly, there are too many intermediate phenomena which resist classification on the basis of Jones's distinction; for instance, obscene language, pornography, erotic art, intentional and unintentional double entendres. Thirdly, the propriety of using vivid sexual imagery in speech varies from generation to generation in a way that cannot possibly be explained by reference to the prevailing extent of sexual repression. The virgin Queen Elizabeth I could say without losing dignity: "If I had been born crested not cloven, your Lordships would not treat me so", but one cannot imagine either Queen Victoria or our present Queen speaking in such a way. And yet it is hard to believe that Elizabeth I was the least repressed of these three Royal Ladies. Nor, I think, could one safely assert that there is greater sexual repression in those parts of the English-speaking world where male gallinaceous birds have to be called roosters than in those parts where they are still cocks.

Fourthly, the essential nature of the distinction between unmodified, erotic and modified, sublimated affects remains obscure and mysterious. Indeed much of the obscurity and esotericism of contemporary psychoanalytical theory seems to derive precisely from the difficulties it has encountered in trying to formulate and explain the differences between instinctual and sublimated activities, and in establishing what kinds of childhood experience facilitate or compel the transformation of instinctual drives into sublimations. According to Heinz Hartmann, who until his recent death was the doyen of American psychoanalysis and the psychoanalytical theorist whose thinking was most akin to that of Freud, sublimations are "autonomous", i.e. immune from interference by changes in instinctual tension, occupy "a conflict-free area of the ego", and use "de-eroticized", "de-aggressified", "neutralized" energy, and their development is facilitated not, as early analytical theory maintained, by frustration but by experience of "delays in gratification". Now, although I have no doubt that Hartmann knew what he meant by such formulations—and, in fact, I do too, though I do not subscribe to them, since they seem to me to be the result of an heroic attempt to reconcile loyalty towards outmoded theory with respect for facts—they are hardly formulations likely to assist communication between psychoanalysis and the other humane sciences.

IV

It might be anticipated that abandonment by psychoanalytical theory of the idea that there exists only one "true" kind of symbolism, which is characterised by unmodified affects and is concerned only with representation of "the most primitive ideas and interests imaginable", would have important effects on clinical practice. But this seems in fact not to be so. Indeed, it would seem that the effect of the revision of theory suggested in this essay would merely be to legitimise changes in practice that have already occurred. Jones's classic paper was written nearly sixty years ago, and since 1916 psychoanalytical theories of all varieties have increased enormously in sophistication; and I doubt whether many, if any, analysts are deterred from making interpretations that occur to them by the thought or theoretical scruple that what they want to say would be only a metaphorical statement and not a truly symbolic interpretation. In any case the practical exigencies of clinical work make it inconceivable that any analyst would monitor all his utterances in order to ascertain what sort of metaphor or symbolism he was using at any particular moment. Furthermore, advances in ego-psychology since 1916 have made analysts much more aware of the interconnections between different levels or parts of the mind and less inclined to envisage their role solely as pointing out the "primitive", unconscious, infantile sources and meanings of what their patients tell them.

I suspect, indeed, that the original formulations by Freud and Jones have survived basically unchallenged for two, basically adventitious reasons;

because their emphasis on the specifically sexual appeals to the popular imagination, and because piety prevents psychoanalysts from criticising their Founding Fathers. The paper in which I first presented the view of symbolism proposed here (Rycroft, 1956) was written before Jones's death and he wrote to me expressing his general agreement and drawing my attention to the extent to which his earlier ideas had been presented as a reaction against Jung's flight into mysticism.

To summarise:

1. The concept of Freudian symbolism has passed into general circulation and refers to the idea that many, perhaps most objects are sexual symbols.

2. Although the idea is popularly believed to have originated in Freud's book *The Interpretation of Dreams*, published in 1900, Freud did not in fact attach paramount importance to symbolism, whether sexual or otherwise, until it was forced upon his attention by Stekel and by a number of peculiarly gifted patients.

3. Freudian symbols are not in fact exclusively sexual; they represent, to quote Jones again, "ideas of the self and the immediate blood relatives or of the phenomena of birth, love and death", in fact everything that comprises man's biological destiny.

4. Psychoanalytical theory has attempted to pre-empt the concept of symbolism by asserting that the only true symbols are those which analysts encounter when interpreting dreams and neurotic symptoms.

5. By doing so psychoanalytical theory has offended against common usage and has created well-nigh insuperable barriers between itself and other humane disiplines.

6. According to the view expressed here, these barriers could be lowered by recognising that symbolisation is a general capacity of the mind, which can be used both by the discursive, syntactical, rational form of thinking characteristic of waking, intellectual activity ("secondary process thinking" in psychoanalytical terminology) and by the non-discursive, condensive, affective form of thinking characteristic of dreaming, imagining, joking and creating ("primary process thinking" in psychoanalytical terminology); and by recognising that these two types of thinking are not necessarily opposed to one another, as most formulations of psychoanalytical theory imply, but can work in harness.

7. Since Freudian ideas have, after a fashion, passed into general currency, self-conscious, contrived and fanciful manipulations of the idea of Freudian symbolism have become possible. The artefacts produced by such self-conscious manipulations are meretricious, since they can be passed off as products of the creative imagination.

8. The revision of the psychoanalytical theory of symbolism suggested in the second half of this paper has less relevance to clinical practice than might be expected. It would probably do little more than legitimise changes that have already occurred in interpretative modes as a result of the increase in sophistication of theory that has taken place since Freud and Jones wrote their classic statements of the theory of symbolism sixty years ago.

References

Ades, D. 1972. Freud and surrealist painting. *In* J. Miller (ed.) *Freud*, Weidenfeld and Nicholson, London.

Freud, S. 1953. *The Interpretation of Dreams*, Standard Edn. Vols. 4 and 5. Hogarth (Originally 1900).

Freud, S. 1958. *The Dynamics of Transference*, Standard Edn. Vol. 12. Hogarth (originally 1912).

Freud, S. 1963. *Introductory Lectures on Psycho-Analysis*, Standard Edn. Vols. 15 and 16. Hogarth (originally 1916).

Freud, S. 1961. *Dostoevsky and Parricide*, Standard Edn. Vol. 21. Hogarth (original 1928).

Hartmann, H. 1959. *Ego-Psychology and the Problem of Adaptation*, Imago (original 1939).

Hartmann, H. 1964. *Essays on Ego Psychology*, Hogarth.

Jones, E. 1948. The theory of symbolism. *In Papers on Psycho-Analysis*, Baillière (original 1916).

Milner, M. 1952. Aspects of symbolism in comprehension of the Not-self. *Int. J. Psycho-Anal.* 33.

Rycroft, C. 1956. Symbolism and its relationship to the primary and secondary processes. *Imagination and Reality*, Hogarth (1968).

Rycroft, C. 1962. Beyond the reality principle. *In Imagination and Reality*, Hogarth.

Segal, H. 1957. Notes on symbol formation. *Int. J. Psycho-Anal.*, 38.

Stekel, W. 1911. *Dies Sprache des Traumes*, J. C. Bergmann, Wiesbaden.

8 | The Implications of Psychedelic Research for Anthropology: Observations from LSD Psychotherapy

*Stanislav Grof**

The use of psychedelic substances is probably as old as the history of man-kind; from time immemorial plants containing powerful mind-altering compounds have been used in various parts of the world for religious and magical purposes. References to hallucinogenic drugs can be found in Chinese history as early as 2600 years B.C. The legendary divine potion called haoma in the ancient Persian Zend Avesta and soma in the Vedic literature was used by the Indoiranian tribes several millennia ago. Pre-parations from the Indian hemp have been used under different names (hashish, charas, bhang, ganja, kif) in the Oriental countries for many cen-turies as folk medicine, in religious ceremonies, and for recreation and pleasure. In the Middle Ages potions and ointments containing psycho-active plants from the family of Solanaceae such as the deadly nightshade (*Atropa Belladonna*), thorn apple (*Datura Stramonium*), henbane (*Hyoscya-*

*This is a revised version of a paper presented at the Interdisciplinary Conference on "Ritual: Reconciliation in Change", organised by Margaret Mead and Catherine Bateson, and sponsored by the Wenner-Gren Foundation for Anthropological Research, European Conference Center, Burg Wartenstein, Austria, July 1973.

I would like to express my sincere thanks to Margaret Mead and Catherine Bateson, initiators and organisers of the conference on Ritual: Reconciliation in Change. They gave me the idea to write this paper, as well as the motivation and enthusiasm necessary for its completion. I also feel deep gratitude to the hosts of the conference, Lita Osmondsen and the Wenner-Gren Foundation for creating quite unique conditions for all the participants, conducive to a most meaningful exchange of ideas and information.

mus niger) and mandrake (*Mandragora officinarum*) were widely used within the framework of the witches' Sabbath and the black mass rituals. The use of psychedelic substances also has a long history in Central America where various hallucinogenic plants were well known in several Precolumbian Indian cultures. The most famous of these plants are the Mexican cactus Lophophora Williamsii (*peyote*), the sacred mushroom Psilocybe mexicana (*teonanacatl*), and several varieties of Ipomoea, source of the morning glory seeds (*ololiuqui*). Hallucinogenic plants have also been used by various tribes in Africa (e.g. *Tabernanthe iboga*), South America (*Banisteria caapi, Peganum harmala, Piptadenia peregrina*), and Asia (*Amanita muscaria*). The preceding list represents only a small fraction of psychedelic compounds that have been used in various centuries and countries of the world.

The long history of use of psychedelic drugs contrasts with a relatively short history of scientific interest in and study of these compounds. The first psychedelic drug that was synthesised in pure form and systematically explored under laboratory conditions was mescaline, the active principle from the peyote cactus. After the pioneering experiments with mescaline in the first decades of this century,[1] very little research was done in this most interesting area. Hofmann's sensational discovery of LSD, a semi-synthetic psychedelic drug active in incredibly minute quantities (gamas or micrograms), in the early forties started a new era of research in psychopharmacology.

During a relatively short period of time, the joint effort of biochemists, pharmacologists and psychiatrists has succeeded in laying the foundations of a new scientific discipline that could be referred to as "pharmacology of the human mind". The active substances from the most famous hallucinogenic plants have been identified and prepared in a chemically pure form. This made it possible to systematically study their effects from the experimental, clinical and phenomenological point of view. Even though this research was very severely curbed in the early sixties by irresponsible lay experimentation, a sufficient amount of observational data have been accumulated to allow for preliminary conclusions and tentative conceptualisations.

Psychedelic research has offered new insights into the experiential world of psychiatric patients and new revolutionary possibilities in psychiatric therapy. Equally profound has been the contribution of this research to the understanding of the psychology and psychopathology of art and religion. The significance of psychedelic drugs appears to be, however, much more fundamental than that. They seem to be unusually powerful tools for the exploration of the human mind in health and disease and of the human personality. Some of the observations from psychedelic research, if pursued and studied systematically, would probably not only revolutionise psychiatry and psychology but change our concept of the nature of man.

Since 1956, experimentation with LSD and other psychedelic substances has been my major professional interest. In this time, I have personally conducted over 3,000 psychedelic sessions with LSD and other compounds and, in addition, had access to records from over 1,300 sessions run by several of my colleagues in Europe and in the United States. The majority of subjects in these sessions were patients with a wide variety of emotional disorders, such as severe psychoneuroses, psychosomatic diseases, border-line psychoses and various forms of schizophrenia, sexual deviations, alcoholism and narcotic drug addiction. Another rather large category of these subjects was "normal volunteers"—psychiatrists, psychologists, students and psychiatric nurses who asked for psychedelic sessions for training purposes; painters, sculptors and musicians seeking artistic inspiration; philosophers and scientists from various disciplines interested in insights that the psychedelic experience has to offer; and priests and theologians willing to explore the mystical and religious dimensions of the experience. A small fraction of these sessions involved patients suffering from a terminal disease and facing impending death.

During the early years of my LSD research when I worked in the Psychiatric Research Institute in Prague, most of the subjects received repeated medium dosages of LSD (100–250 mcg.) within the framework of analytically oriented psychotherapy (the psycholytic approach). Since 1967 when I moved to the United States, I have been using high dosages of LSD (300–500 mcg.) in a special setting, aimed at facilitating a religious experience (the psychedelic approach).

Psycholytic therapy employs the administration of lower or medium dosages of LSD or other psychedelic drugs; the total number of sessions per series range widely between ten and one hundred. In theory and practice, this approach represents actually an extension and intensification of psychoanalytically oriented psychotherapy. The introduction of LSD results in a considerable amplification of all the effective therapeutic mechanisms operating in conventional psychotherapy, such as reliving and integration of traumatic memories from childhood, corrective emotional experience, abreaction, catharsis, emotional and intellectual insights and transference analysis. The specific characteristics of the LSD reaction require, however, substantial modifications of the conventional psychotherapeutic technique. It is necessary to abandon the orthodox analytic situation, in which the patient lies on the couch and is expected to free associate in the reclining position, and the uninvolved and indirect analyst sits behind his head and occasionally offers interpretations. In psycholytic therapy with LSD, the reclining position is preferred and recommended, but quite frequently the patients toss and turn, sit, kneel, pace around the room or even roll on the floor. The therapist is often confronted with acting-out behaviour rather than disciplined associating. Much more personal and sometimes even psychodramatic involvement is necessary, and actual physical support is occasionally used. By and large, the techniques of psycholytic therapy are very similar to those developed for psychotherapy of psychotic patients.

Psychedelic therapy differs from the psycholytic approach in several important aspects. It uses only one administration of a high or very high dose of LSD, sometimes aptly referred to as the "single overwhelming dose". The set and setting is specifically structured in order to increase the probability that the patient will experience deep religious and mystical feelings. During the preparation period, the therapist tries to analyse all the aspects of the patient's personality that might interfere with his willingness and ability to let go of his usual defences and surrender to the experience. An important part of the preparation for a psychedelic session is the therapist's emphasis on the growth potential of the patient and an effort to connect with the positive resources of his personality. Contrary to psychoanalysis, which usually dwells on detailed analysis of psychopathology, the psychedelic treatment generally tends to discourage the patient's preoccupation with psychopathology, be it symptoms or maladjustive interpersonal patterns. There is much more concern about how to transcend psychopathology; on occasions, the patient even receives direct guidance as to how he could function more effectively. Such a direct approach is very different from the undisciplined and random advising in important life situations, which the analytically oriented therapists warn against. It is quite consistent and systematic and is based on the life philosophy and hierarchy of values derived from observations of patients who were successfully treated with LSD psychotherapy. From the theoretical point of view, the basic principles of this approach bear a close resemblance to Abraham Maslow's (1964, 1968) description of the self-actualising person and his concept of metavalues and metamotivations.

The setting for psychedelic sessions has a strong aesthetic emphasis— tasteful furnishing of the treatment room; special choice of colours; use of flowers, pictures and sculptures; and beautiful natural scenery. An integral part of this treatment is the use of headphones and high fidelity stereophonic music. The choice of music in general, and in relation to different stages of the sessions, is very important. The development of transference phenomena is generally discouraged and visual contact is limited by the use of eyeshades for most of the session.

Most of the data used in this paper are based on observations from psycholytic therapy. Repeated sessions with LSD allow for a systematic exploration of the unconscious and a detailed study of various dynamic inter-connections between phenomena on different levels. The use of the same subject in serial sessions also eliminates the element of enormous inter-individual variability that is so typical for LSD sessions. Detailed records of all the LSD experiences of each psycholytic series, as well as of the intervals between the sessions, made it possible to utilise fully the potential of LSD as a unique tool for the investigation of the human unconscious.

I have spent many hours analysing the data from LSD sessions and trying to find a conceptual framework that would account for the most unusual observations involved. It soon became obvious that none of the existing systems of psychotherapy could explain the total range of the psychedelic phenomena. In a series of publications, I have attempted to draw conclusions from LSD research for the theory of personality and psychotherapy and to suggest a broad theoretical framework encompassing the observations from LSD sessions. During this work, it became increasingly obvious that this material has interesting implications for the understanding of a variety of cultural phenomena such as religion, mythology, philosophy, art and social movements. I was particularly impressed by the far-reaching parallels between LSD experiences and phenomena involved in various mystery religions, trance and possession states, and rites of passage.

Before we start discussing the theoretical implications of LSD research, it is necessary to demonstrate that LSD has an heuristic value as a tool for the exploration of the human unconscious and that it is legitimate to draw more general conclusions from the work with this compound. There has been a tendency among professionals to discard the experiences in psychedelic sessions as manifestations of toxic psychosis, that have little, if any, relevance for the understanding of the human mind. This is especially true for many psychoanalytically oriented psychotherapists who view the LSD experiences as a chemical phantasmagoria *sui generis* that is essentially unrelated to normal psychology and functional mental disorders. Such an attitude makes it possible to admit that psychedelic experiences cannot be explained in Freudian terms, and at the same time, maintain the belief that psychoanalysis in its present form is an adequate tool for understanding mental processes. It is not difficult for me to sympathise with this point of view since this was my own orientation when in 1956 I became interested in LSD research as a convinced and dedicated psychoanalyst. However, I found this position untenable in the light of everyday clinical observations. I now see LSD as an unspecific amplifier or catalyst of mental processes that confronts the experiencer with his own unconscious. Many reasons could be adduced in support of this point of view: I will briefly outline several of the most important facts.

A few years ago, I analysed the records from over 2,000 LSD sessions, looking for standard and invariant components of the LSD reaction. I have not been able to find a single phenomenon that could be considered a simple pharmacological effect of the drug *per se* in any of the areas studied —perceptual, emotional, ideational, and physical. Even mydriasis that is a relatively constant symptom in LSD subjects does not seem to represent an invariant phenomenon. In addition, many typical LSD experiences are indistinguishable from those induced by a variety of non-drug methods, such as spiritual practices, hypnosis, sleep and sensory deprivation, sensory overload, and new experiential psychotherapeutic techniques.

Another important observation should be mentioned in this connection. In psycholytic therapy, the content of LSD sessions changes with their increasing number in a rather characteristic and systematic way; as a result of this, different types of experience occur in a certain sequence. In the early sessions of the series, there is a predominance of aesthetic and psychodynamic experiences, in the middle part of the treatment, phenomena related to death and rebirth are prevalent, and the advanced sessions consist almost exclusively of transpersonal experiences. A similar regularity can be observed in regard to increasing dosage in psychedelic sessions.

In addition, all the LSD phenomena, including the physical manifestations, are extremely sensitive to psychological influences and can be modified by a variety of extrapharmacological factors and specific psychotherapeutic approaches. The nature of LSD sessions thus appears to represent an amplification and unfolding of various levels of the unconscious processes determined jointly by a variety of external factors, such as the personality of the therapist, the therapeutic relationship, and the elements of the setting in the broadest sense.

If we accept the basic premise, that psychedelic drugs make it possible to study the content and dynamics of the unconscious processes that are difficult to reach with less powerful techniques, the heuristic value of these substances becomes immediately obvious. This capacity of psychedelic drugs to exteriorise otherwise invisible phenomena and processes and make them the subject of scientific investigation gives these substances an unusual potential as research tools for exploration of the human mind. It does not seem inappropriate to compare their potential significance for psychiatry and psychology to that of the microscope for medicine or of the telescope for astronomy. The above insight into the nature of psychedelic drugs can also explain the unprecedented controversy about the value of psychedelics and their beneficial or destructive potential. Since they are unspecific amplifiers and catalysts of all potentialities intrinsic to human nature, their value and the outcome of experimentation depends on the uses to which these compounds are put.

Phenomenology of LSD Sessions

Analysing the records from several thousand psychedelic sessions, I was able to distinguish four major levels of the LSD experience. It is necessary to bear in mind that the content of the LSD-induced states represents a rich multidimensional network of mutually overlapping phenomena. Because of the holographic nature of psychedelic experiences any attempt at linear description and classification will necessarily involve a certain degree of oversimplification. Although such a dissection is justified for didactic purposes and has also practical clinical significance, in actual LSD sessions the elements of these experiential categories usually do not occur in a pure form, but are intimately interwoven. With these reservations we can isolate the following four levels or categories of LSD experiences: 1. Abstract and aesthetic experiences; 2. Psychodynamic experiences; 3. Perinatal experiences; and 4. Transpersonal experiences.

Abstract and Aesthetic Experiences in LSD Sessions

These experiences occur usually in the initial stages of the LSD procedure when lower and medium dosages are used, or at the very beginning or end of the first high dose sessions. With the eyes open, the individual experiences simple perceptual changes in his environment; the colours become unusually bright and beautiful, other persons and inanimate objects are geometrised, everything appears to vibrate and undulate, sensory stimuli elicit responses in inappropriate sensory areas (synaesthesias), and new forms and contents can be seen in perceived objects (optical illusions). Sometimes there is very little actual perceptual distortion of the environment, but the latter is emotionally interpreted in an unusual way. It can appear to be incredibly beautiful, comical, sensual, tender or have a fairy-tale quality.

With the eyes closed, the entoptic phenomena are distinctly enhanced. The experiencer sees colour spots, after-images, flashes of light, spirals, starlets and other types of elementary visions. Typical also are complex geometrical figures, patterns and ornaments, kaleidoscopic fireworks, as well as views of ceilings of gigantic Gothic cathedrals or cupolas of Oriental mosques (arabesques).

The aesthetic experiences seem to represent the most superficial level of the LSD experience and do not have any psychodynamic significance. They are probably produced by the chemical stimulation of the optical apparatus, and reflect its inner structure. Occasionally, some of these elements appear to have a specific emotional connotation. The subject can, for example, feel that the abstract configurations are suggestive of the soft, warm and sensuous world of the satisfied infant. They might also be experienced as disgusting and repulsive, dangerous and aggressive, or lascivious and obscene. Such a situation represents a transition from the abstract to the psychodynamic level of the LSD experience. The emotions modifying and colouring the abstract imagery belong, in such cases, to relevant biographical material of the experiencer.

Psychodynamic Experiences in LSD Sessions

The experiences belonging to this category can be understood in psychodynamic terms; they are related to important memories, emotional problems and unresolved conflicts from various life periods of the individual. Some of the experiences are the actual reliving of traumatic or unusually positive memories of real events; others seem to be screen memories in the Freudian sense, fantasies, or mixtures of fantasy and reality. In addition to these, this level involves a variety of experiences that represent relevant psychodynamic material in the cryptic form of a symbolic disguise.

Psychodynamic experiences are particularly common in psycholytic therapy of psychiatric patients. In the initial stages of treatment, they can dominate many consecutive sessions before the underlying unconscious material is resolved and the patient can move to the next level. They are much less important in sessions of persons who are emotionally more stable and whose childhood was relatively uneventful. In high dose psychedelic sessions, psychodynamic experiences usually occur at the beginning and in the termination period.

The experiences in psychodynamic LSD sessions can be, to a great extent, understood in terms of the basic Freudian concepts. Many of the principles that Freud described for the dynamics of the individual unconscious, in particular for the formation of dreams, are applicable to the dynamics of LSD sessions on this level. As a matter of fact, many of the phenomena observed in psychodynamic LSD sessions could be considered laboratory proof of the basic premises of psychoanalysis. The phenomenology of these sessions involves regression into childhood and even infancy; reliving of traumatic memories; confronting problems related to infantile sexuality and conflicts in various libidinal zones; working through the Oedipus and Electra complex; and experiencing of castration anxiety or penis envy.

However, for a more complete understanding of these sessions and of their consequences for the clinical condition of patients, as well as for their personality structure, a new principle has to be introduced, into psychoanalytic thinking. Many LSD phenomena on this level can be comprehended and some of them even predicted, if we think in terms of specific memory constellations, for which I use the term "COEX systems" (systems of condensed experience).[1] This concept emerged from the analysis of the phenomenology of therapeutic LSD sessions in the early phase of my clinical research in Prague. It proved unusually helpful for understanding the initial stage of psycholytic therapy with psychiatric patients.

A COEX system can be defined as a specific memory constellation consisting of condensed experiences (and/or fantasies from different life periods of the individual). The memories belonging to a particular COEX system have a similar basic theme or contain similar elements, and are accompanied by a strong emotional charge of the same quality. The deepest layers of this system are represented by vivid and colourful memories of experiences from the period of infancy and early childhood. More superficial layers of such a system involve memories of similar experiences from a later time, up to the present life situation. The excessive emotional charge which is attached to the COEX system (as indicated by the often powerful abreaction accompanying the unfolding of these systems in LSD sessions) seems to be a summation of the emotions belonging to all the constituent memories of a particular kind.

Individual COEX systems involve special defence mechanisms and are connected with specific clinical symptoms. The detailed interrelations between the individual parts of COEX systems are in most instances in basic agreement with Freudian thinking; the new element from the theoretical point of view is the concept of the organising dynamic system. The personality structure involves usually a greater number of COEX systems. Their character, total number, extensiveness and intensity varies considerably from one individual to another.

According to the basic quality of the emotional charge, we can differentiate *negative COEX systems* (condensing unpleasnt emotional experiences) and *positive COEX systems* (condensing pleasant emotional experiences and positive aspects of one's past life). Although there are certain interdependencies and overlappings, individual systems can function relatively autonomously. In a complicated interaction with the environment, they influence selectively the subject's perception of himself and of the world, his feelings and thinking, and even many somatic processes.

The following clinical example of an important COEX system from

---

1. The existence of governing systems as important principles for understanding the dynamics of psycholytic therapy with LSD was independently discovered and described by Leuner, 1962. He coined for them the term "transphenomenal dynamic governing systems" (transphenomenale dynamische Steurungs-systeme-tdysts). Although there are many similarities between the concept of the COEX system and that of tdyst, the terminological differentiation should be retained because of all the implications attached to the concept COEX system within the framework presented here.

psycholytic therapy of one of my patients can be used as an illustration of this concept:

Peter was intermittently hospitalised and treated in our department during two years preceding the commencement of psycholytic therapy. Intensive psychotherapy and pharmacotherapy brought only superficial and temporary relief. His major problems at that time were symptoms combining obsessive-compulsive and sadomasochistic elements. He felt almost continuously compelled to find a man with certain physiognomic features and preferably clad in black. His basic intention was to make contact with this man, tell him his life story and reveal to him his deep desire to be locked in a dark cellar, bound with a rope and be exposed to various diabolic physical and mental tortures. Unable to concentrate on anything else, he meandered through the streets, visited public parks, lavatories, railway stations and inns trying to find the proper person. He succeeded several times in persuading or bribing the individuals he selected to carry out what he requested. When this happened, he failed to experience masochistic pleasure and was instead extremely frightened and disliked the tortures. Having a special gift to find persons with marked sadistic personality traits, he was twice almost killed, several times seriously hurt and on another occasion, his partner bound him and stole his money. Beside these problems, the patient suffered from suicidal depressions, tensions and anxieties, impotence, and very infrequent epileptiform seizures.

Retrospective analysis showed that his major symptoms started during Peter's involuntary employment in Germany[2] at the time of the Second World War, when he was forced by two Nazi officers at gunpoint to engage in their homosexual practices. When the war was over, he discovered that these experiences had established in him a preference for passive homosexual experiencing of sex. Several years later, he developed typical fetishism for black male clothes. This gradually changed into the masochistic craving described above that brought him into therapy.

In a series of 15 psycholytic LSD sessions, a very interesting and important COEX system was successively manifested. Its most superficial layers were represented by recent memories of traumatic experiences that Peter had with his sadistic partners. In the first sessions of the series he visualised and relived the actual situations in great detail. As a result of the governing influence of this layer of the COEX system, the therapist was at this stage perceived as illusively transformed into the patient's past partners or various figures, symbolising sadistic aggression (butcher, murderer, executioner). The patient anticipated torture from the therapist; he saw his pen changed into a dagger and interpreted the movement of his foot as a tendency to kick him. Later he suggested that the best therapy for him would be to satisfy his desire to suffer. The treatment room and the view from the window were illusively transformed to

2. During the Second World War, the Nazis imported large numbers of young people from occupied countries to Germany and used them for slave labour in risky work situations, such as mines and ammunition factories. This was referred to by the Germans as Totaleinsetzung.

represent various settings where the patient's adventures with the sadistic partners took place.

A deeper layer of the same system was represented by Peter's experiences from the Third Reich. In the sessions influenced by this part of the system, he had visions of banners with the Nazi swastika, pompous SS military parades and large metallic eagle emblems. Innocent monotonous sounds in the room were perceived as Nazi marches, and the sound of a person walking behind the door was transformed into that of the heavy boots of German soldiers. The treatment room was changed into a prison with bars in the windows and eventually the death cell. The therapist was illusively transformed into Adolf Hitler, various Gestapo members, and SS officers. Beside these symbolic experiences, Peter also relived some of his real traumatic experiences with homosexual German officers.

The core experiences of the same system were related to Peter's childhood. In later sessions, he regressed into memories involving the punishments used by his parents. It turned out that his mother used to lock him in a dark cellar for a long time without food, and his despotic father's method of punishing him was to whip him in a very cruel way with a leather strap. The patient at this point realised that his masochistic desires were a replica of the combined parental punishments. The therapist changed in this phase into parental figures, and Peter displayed the pertinent anachronistic behaviour patterns toward him.

During the reliving of these memories, a striking oscillation of the patient's major problem was observed, but not its long-term total disappearance. Finally, he relived the agonizing experience of his birth trauma in its full biological brutality. According to his later comment, it involved exactly those elements which he expected from the sadistic treatment he was so desperately trying to get: dark closed space, restriction of all body movements and exposure to extreme physical and mental tortures. Reliving of the biological birth finally resolved his difficult symptoms.[3]

Perinatal Experiences in LSA Sessions

For the phenomena belonging to this category, no adequate explanation can be found within the framework of classical Freudian psychoanalysis. In psycholytic treatment with LSD, these levels are reached in psychiatric patients usually after a greater number of sessions. In psychedelic therapy, where higher dosages are used and the experience is fully internalised, elements of perinatal experiences can be observed frequently from the very beginning; here they occur usually between the second and fourth hour of the session when the effect of the drug culminates.

3. The reliving of the birth trauma lies beyond the realm of psychodynamics, as usually understood in traditional psychotherapy. It was included in the above case history only for the sake of its logical completion; this phenomenon belongs to the next level of the LSD experiences.

The basic characteristics of the experiences on this level and their central focus are the problems of biological birth; physical pain and agony; aging, disease and decrepitude; dying and death. Inevitably, the shattering encounter with these critical aspects of human existence and the deep realisation of the frailty and impermanence of man as a biological creature is accompanied by an agonising existential crisis. The individual comes to realise, through these experiences, that no matter what he does in his life, he cannot escape the inevitable: he will have to leave this world bereft of everything that he has accumulated and achieved and to which he has been emotionally attached. The similarity between birth and death—the startling realisation that the beginning of life is the same as its end—is the major philosophical issue that accompanies the perinatal experiences. The other important consequence of the shocking emotional and physical encounter with the phenomenon of death is the emergence of deep spiritual and religious feelings that appear to be an intrinsic part of the human personality, and are independent of the individual's cultural and religious background and programming. In my experience, everyone who confronted this area of his unconscious, developed convincing insights into the utmost relevance of the spiritual and religious dimensions in the universal scheme of things. Even hard core materialists, positivistically oriented scientists, sceptics and cynics, uncompromising atheists and antireligious crusaders such as Marxist philosophers, became suddenly interested in a spiritual search after they confronted these levels in themselves.

The sequences of dying and being born (or reborn) are frequently extremely dramatic and have many biological concomitants apparent even to the outside observer. Subjects can spend hours in agonising pain, with facial contortions, gasping for breath and discharging enormous amounts of muscular tensions in various tremors, twitching, violent shaking and complex twisting movements. The colour of their faces can be dark purple or dead pale, and their pulse rate doubled; the body temperature usually oscillates in a wide range, sweating can be profuse, and nausea with projectile vomiting is a frequent occurrence.

In a way that is not quite clear at the present stage of research, the above experiences seem to be related to the biological circumstances of birth. The LSD subjects refer to them frequently quite explicitly as reliving their own birth trauma. In addition, even in those persons who do not make this link, such experiences are frequently accompanied by images of, or identification with, embryos, fetuses and newborn children. Quite common are also various authentic neonatal feelings as well as behaviour, and visions of female genitals and breasts. From these observations and other clinical evidence, I labelled the above phenomena *perinatal experiences*. A causal nexus between the experiences of biological birth and the unconscious matrices for these experiences still remains to be established. It appears, however, appropriate to refer to this level of the unconscious as Rankian; with some modifications Rank's conceptual framework is useful for the understanding of the phenomena in question.[4]

The perinatal experiences are manifestations of a deep level of the unconscious that has not been taken into consideration in psychoanalytic speculations and is clearly beyond the reach of the classical Freudian techniques. The clinician can see phenomena from this category in a variety of acute psychotic conditions. This level can also be reached temporarily in a more controlled fashion in the course of some recent innovative experiential techniques of psychotherapy, such as gestalt therapy, marathon sessions, nude marathons, bioenergetics and primal therapy. From time immemorial powerful techniques have existed in many ancient and so-called primitive cultures that made it possible to activate this deep level of the unconscious. These methods range from the use of psychedelic plants, through trance dancing, fasting, sleep deprivation, shock and physical torture, to the elaborate and sophisticated spiritual practices developed in Oriental countries.

The perinatal phenomena represent a very important experiential intersection between individual psychology and transpersonal psychology or, for that matter, a bridge between psychology (and psychopathology) and religion. If we think about them as related to the individual's birth, they would belong to the framework of individual psychology. Some other aspects, however, give them a very definite transpersonal flavour. The intensity of these experiences transcends anything that is usually considered to be the experiential limit of the individual. They are frequently accompanied by identification with other persons, groups of persons, or struggling and suffering mankind. Also, other types of clearly transpersonal experiences frequently form an integral part of the perinatal matrices, such as evolutionary and ancestral memories, elements of the collective unconscious, and certain Jungian archetypes. The LSD experiences on this level usually have a rather complex character, combining very personal elements with clearly transpersonal phenomena.

It seems appropriate to mention in this connection a category of experiences that represents a transitional form between the Freudian psychodynamic level and the Rankian level. It is the reliving of traumatic memories from the life of the individual that are of a physical, rather than purely psychological nature. Typically, such memories involve a threat to survival

4. The Viennese psychiatrist, Otto Rank, a renegade from the mainstream of orthodox psychoanalysis, emphasized in his book, *The Trauma of Birth* (1927) the paramount significance of the biological birth for the psychological development of the individual and for various psychopathological syndromes.

BASIC PERINATAL MATRICES

	BPM I	BPM II	BPM III	BPM IV
Related psychopathological syndromes	Schizophrenic psychoses (paranoid symptomatology, feelings of mystical union, encounter with metaphysical evil forces, karmic experiences); hypochondriasis (based on strange and bizarre physical sensations); hysterical hallucinosis and confusion of daydreams with reality.	Schizophrenic psychoses (elements of hellish tortures, experience of meaningless "cardboard" world); severe inhibited "endogenous" depressions; irrational inferiority and guilt feelings; hypochondriasis (based on painful physical sensations); alcoholism and drug addiction.	Schizophrenic psychoses (sado-masochistic and scatological elements, automutilation, abnormal sexual behaviour); agitated depression; sexual deviations (sadochism, male homosexuality, drinking of urine and eating of feces); obsessive-compulsive neurosis; pregenital conversions (psychogenic asthma, tics and stammering); conversion and anxiety hysteria; frigidity and impotence; neurasthenia; traumatic neuroses; organ neuroses; migraine headache; enuresis and encopressis; psoriasis; peptic ulcer.	Schizophrenic psychoses (death-rebirth experiences, messianic delusions, elements of destruction and recreation of the world, salvation and redemption); manic symptomatology; female homosexuality; exhibitionism.
Corresponding activities in Freudian erogenous zones	Libidinal satisfaction in all erogenous zones; libidinal feeling during rocking and bathing; partial approximation to this condition after oral, anal, urethral, or genital satisfaction and delivery of a child.	Oral frustration (thirst, hunger, painful stimuli); retention of faeces and/or urine; sexual frustration; experiences of cold, pain, and other unpleasant sensations.	Chewing and swallowing of food; oral aggression and destruction of an object; process of defecation and urination; anal and urethral aggression; sexual orgasm; phallic aggression; delivering of a child; statoacoustic eroticism (jolting, gymnastics, fancy diving, parachuting).	Satiation of thirst and hunger; pleasure of sucking; libidinal feelings after defecation, urination, sexual orgasm, or delivery of a child.
Associated memories from postnatal life	Situations from later life where important needs are satisfied, (happy moments from infancy and childhood, good mothering, play with peers, harmonious periods in the family, fulfilling love relationships; trips or vacations in beautiful natural settings; exposure to artistic creations of high aesthetic value; swimming in the ocean and clear lakes).	Situations endangering survival and body integrity (war experiences, accidents, injuries, operations, painful diseases, near drowning, episodes of suffocation, imprisonment, brainwashing or illegal interrogation and physical abuse); severe psychological traumatisations (emotional deprivation, rejection, threatening situations, oppressing family atmosphere, ridicule and	Struggles, fights and adventurous activities (active attacks in battles and revolutions, hunting, experiences in military service, rough airplane flights, cruises on stormy ocean, hazardous car driving, boxing); highly sensual memories (carnivals, amusement parks and nightclubs, wild parties, sexual orgies); childhood observations of adult sexual activities; experiences of seduction and rape; in females	Fortuitous escape from dangerous situations (end of war or revolution, survival of an accident or operation); overcoming severe obstacles by active effort; episodes of strain and hard struggle resulting in a marked success; peaceful natural scenes (beginning of spring, end of an ocean storm, sunrise).

	0	1	2	3
Phenomenology in LSD sessions	...realistic recollections of "good womb" experiences; "oceanic" ecstasy; experiences of cosmic unity; the Universe seen as radiant and safe; feelings of perfect physiological functioning; *disturbances of intrauterine life*: realistic recollections of "bad womb" experiences (fetal crises, attempted abortions, diseases and emotional upheavals of the mother, twin situation); schizophrenic distortion of the Universe; paranoid ideation; visions of demons and unpleasant physical sensations ("hangover", foul tastes, disgust, feelings of being poisoned, chills, and fine muscular spasms).	...the constriction; immense physical and emotional suffering; an unbearable and inescapable situation that will never end; feelings of entrapment and encagement (no exit); various images of Hell; agonising guilt and inferiority feelings; meaninglessness and absurdity of human existance; atmosphere of dehumanised automatised society, artificial gadgets, and robots; apocalyptic view of the world (horrors of wars and concentration camps, terror of the Inquisition, dangerous epidemics, incurable diseases, decrepitude and death); ominous dark colours and unpleasant physical symptoms (feelings of compression and oppression, cardiac distress, difficult breathing, pains, alternating hot flushes and chills, sweating).	propulsion through the birth canal; life and death struggle; intensification of suffering to cosmic proportions; borderline between pain and pleasure; "volcanic" ecstasy; atmosphere of titanic fights; sadomasochistic orgies; participation in wild adventures and dangerous explorations; intense sexual feelings and erotic imagery; carnival atmosphere; scatological scenes; purifying fire; visions of Purgatory; scenes from religions involving bloody sacrifice, intense physical manifestations (pressures and pains, suffocation, muscular tension, tremors, twitches, contortions, nausea and vomiting, hot flushes and chills, ringing in the ears, sweating, cardiac distress, problems of sphincter control).	moment of birth and its specific circumstances; enormous decompression; expansion of space; images of gigantic halls; visions of radiant light and beautiful colours (heavenly blue, golden, rainbow spectrum, peacock feathers); feeling of spiritual rebirth and liberation (salvation, redemption, moksha, samadhi); appreciation of a simple way of life, intense sensory enhancement; brotherly feelings toward fellowmen; humanitarian and charitable tendencies; occasionally manic activity and grandiosity (incomplete BPM IV); pleasant feelings sometimes interrupted by the *umbilical crisis* (sharp pain in the navel, loss of breath, fear of death and castration, dynamic shifts in the body, but no external pressures).
Clinical stages of delivery				

or body integrity, such as serious operations or painful and dangerous injuries; severe diseases, particularly those connected with breathing difficulties (diphtheria, whooping cough or pneumonia); instances of near drowning; and episodes of cruel physical abuse (incarceration in a concentration camp, exposure to brainwashing and interrogation techniques of the Nazis or Communists, and maltreatment in childhood). These memories are clearly individual in nature, yet thematically they are closely related to perinatal experiences. Occasionally, the reliving of physical traumas occurs simultaneously with perinatal phenomena as a more superficial facet of the birth agony. Memories of somatic traumatisation appear to have a significant role in the psychogenesis of various emotional disorders (particularly depression and sado-masochism), as yet unrecognised and unacknowledged in most present-day schools of dynamic psychotherapy.

Most of the elements of the rich and complex content of the LSD sessions reflecting this level of the unconscious seem to appear in four typical clusters, matrices or experiential patterns. Searching for a simple, logical, and natural conceptualisation of this fact, I was struck by the astounding parallels between these patterns and the clinical stages of delivery. For both theoretical considerations and the practice of LSD psychotherapy it proved to be a very useful principle to relate the four categories distinguished above to consecutive stages in the biological process of birth and to the experiences of the child in the perinatal period. For this reason, I usually refer to the four major experiential matrices of the Rankian level as *Basic Perinatal Matrices* (BPM I–IV). It has to be emphasised that this should be considered at the present stage of knowledge only as a very useful theoretical model, not necessarily implying a causal nexus.

The Basic Perinatal Matrices are hypothetical dynamic governing systems that have a similar function on the Rankian level of the unconscious to the COEX systems on the Freudian psychodynamic level. They have a specific content of their own, namely, the perinatal phenomena. The latter have two important facets: biological and spiritual. The biological aspect of perinatal experiences consists of concrete and rather realistic experiences related to the individual stages of biological delivery. Each of the sequences of biological birth seems to have specific spiritual counterparts (experience of cosmic unity, universal engulfment, death-rebirth struggle, and death-rebirth experience). In addition to this specific content, the basic perinatal matrices also function as organising principles for the material from other levels of the unconscious, namely for the COEX systems, as well as some types of transpersonal experiences that occasionally occur simultaneously with perinatal phenomena (e.g. the archetype of the Terrible Mother and the Great Mother, group consciousness, elements of the collective unconscious or phylogenetic experiences). The individual perinatal matrices have fixed associations with certain typical categories of memories from the life of subjects; they are also related to specific aspects of the activities in the Freudian libidinal zones, and to various categories of psychiatric disorders (see the paradigm on p. 155). The deep parallel between the stages of biological delivery and the pattern of sexual orgasm makes it possible to shift the etiological emphasis in the psychogenesis of emotional disorders from sexuality to perinatal matrices, without denying or negating the significance and validity of the basic Freudian principles. Even within the new extended framework, the basic psychoanalytic rules remain useful for the understanding of the occurrences on the psychodynamic level and their mutual interrrlations.

The basic perinatal matrices will be described here in the order of the corresponding phases of delivery during childbirth. In LSD sessions, this chronological order is not maintained and different patterns of sequence can be observed. In severely disturbed patients, it usually takes a long time to work through all the later layers of traumatic experiences from an individual's history. The first perinatal matrix appearing in the more advanced sessions is usually BPM II and then BPM III, although episodes of experiences related to BPM IV and even BPM I might be observed earlier. When BPM IV is experienced in a pure and final form, this usually opens the path directly to BPM I. All the advanced sessions are then governed by various aspects of BPM I. In less disturbed individuals, positive ecstatic experiences related to BPM IV and BPM I can appear even in the early sessions, especially with higher doses and in the termination periods. The elements of the second and third matrix usually govern the first few hours of the sessions.

Perinatal Matrix I. Primal Union with Mother (Intra-uterine experience before the onset of delivery).
This matrix is related to the original condition of the intra-uterine existence during which the child and mother form a symbiotic unity. Unless some noxious stimuli interfere, the conditions for the child are optimal, involving security, protection, appropriate milieu and satisfaction of all needs. This, of course, is not always the case. There exists a broad continuum of transitions from pregnancies, where these conditions are only occasionally and for a short time disturbed (mild intercurrent diseases; dietary insults; cigarettes and alcohol; temporary stay in a very noisy environment; sexual intercourse in later months of pregnancy, etc.) to pregnancies where they are hardly ever met (chronic infections, intoxications and endocrinal or metabolic diseases of the mother; chronic anxiety, tension and emotional stress; work in an inappropriate milieu with excessive noise and vibrations; cruel treatment of mother with repeated concussions; or attempts at arti-

ficial abortion). These disturbances of pregnancy are usually considered in regard to the future development of the child only as a source of possible somatic damage. The observations from LSD psychotherapy seem to suggest that the child might experience these noxious influences also on a subjective level. We could then differentiate between the "good" and the "bad womb" in much the same way as psychoanalysts hypothesise in the case of the "good" and the "bad breast". In regard to the future stability of the personality the sum of undisturbed intra-uterine experiences during pregnancy might play an important role comparable to that of positive nursing experiences.

Undisturbed intra-uterine experiences are only exceptionally described in the early LSD sessions of an individual but are a frequent occurrence as the number of exposures increases. Some subjects describe rather realistic complex recollections of the original embryonal situation. They experience themselves as extremely small with a typical disproportion in size concerning head and body, feel the surrounding liquid and sometimes even the umbilical cord. Frequently these concrete biological elements are missing and the activation of this matrix manifests itself as the *experience of cosmic unity*. Its basic characteristics are transcendence of the subject-object dichotomy, exceptionally strong positive affect (peace, tranquillity, serenity, bliss), a special feeling of sacredness, transcendence of time and space, experience of pure being, and a richness of insights of cosmic relevance. This type of tension-free melted ecstasy can be referred to as "oceanic ecstasy". With the eyes closed, cosmic unity is experienced as an independent complex experiential pattern. With the eyes open, it results in a sense of merging with the environment and feelings of unity with perceived objects. It is basically this phenomenon which is described by Walter Pahnke's mystical categories and which Abraham Maslow refers to as the "peak experience". The experience of cosmic unity appears to be a rather important gateway to a variety of other transpersonal experiences, such as ancestral memories, elements of the collective and racial unconscious, evolutionary memories, or archetypal experiences.

Disturbances of intra-uterine life seem to have a specific phenomenology in LSD sessions. As in the case of undisturbed experiences, some subjects can report quite realistic recollections; they feel like a baby in the womb and experience different degrees and forms of distress. The nature of this distress can sometimes be identified with the use of adult cues as due to a disease of the mother, her emotional upheaval or various external noxious stimuli. These episodes of distress usually alternate with the positive experiences described above.

Beside such realistic recollections, there are other manifestations of uterine distress. The vision of the star-filled sky typical of ecstatic episodes can be covered with an ugly film. There appear visual disturbances similar to those on a TV screen, usually accompanied by various unpleasant somatic symptoms. The most frequent of these are nausea, disgust, flu feelings, chills, experiences comparable with alimentary intoxication and "hangover", headache and localised tremors of small muscles. These somatic symptoms differ diametrally from those experienced during the birth sessions. There is no external pressure on the head and the body or feelings of constriction or oppression. Nausea has a different character and usually does not result in vomiting. All symptoms are much more subtle and experienced with clear consciousness. Symbolic representations of prenatal disturbances include visions of green undersea scenes with dangerous or repulsive animals, or images of industrial areas of the world with a high degree of pollution of the air and water.

There exists some evidence that the visions of various demons and wrathful deities which appear in these sessions and seem to separate the subject from the blissful universe are also closely related to intra-uterine disturbances and embryonal crises experienced on a primitive level of consciousness. Similarly, as in the case of positive experiences, they can assume the form of demons known from different cultures or can be identified as archetypal figures. Some of the difficult experiences belonging to this category have a "past incarnation" atmosphere and are labelled by more sophisticated subjects as involving "bad karma". Some individuals experience in this context monstrous distortions of the world that strikingly resemble the descriptions of schizophrenic patients. Those LSD subjects who have relatives or acquaintances actually suffering from schizophrenia or paranoid conditions can experience at this point full identification with these persons and develop deep understanding and empathy. Psychiatrists and psychologists who tuned into this area in their LSD training sessions frequently envisioned their psychotic patients and reported unique retrospective insights into their experiential world. On the basis of rich material from the records of sessions from advanced stages of treatment, it can be hypothesised that undisturbed intra-uterine experiences seem to be the deepest model for ecstatic mystical and religious experiences of cosmic unity. The subjective concomitants of disturbances of intra-uterine life seem to represent the deepest basis for schizophrenic experiences and paranoid conditions. The closeness between these two biological situations and the easy change from one to another might explain the sometimes precarious boundary between schizophrenia and spiritual enlightenment, as well as spontaneous occurrences of religious and mystical experiences in some severely disturbed psychotics.

As far as the relation to memory mechanisms is concerned, the positive aspects of BPM I seem to represent the basis for the recording of all later life situations in which the individual is relaxed, relatively free from needs, and not disturbed by any painful and unpleasant stimuli. Reliving of memories characterised by feelings of satisfaction, security and other highly positive emotions occurs in LSD sessions in close connection with ecstatic feelings of BPM I, either simultaneously or alternating with them. The positive COEX systems associated with this matrix involve happy periods from infancy and childhood, such as full satisfaction of anaclitical needs, carefree and joyful games and playing with peers, or harmonious episodes from family life. Memories from later life that appear in this context include particularly satisfactory love relations with intense emotional and sexual gratification. Similarly important are memories of encounters with natural beauty, such as sunrises and sunsets, peaceful oceans and lakes, blue or star-filled skies, tropical islands, luscious and flourishing jungles, high mountains, romantic rivers, forest landscapes, and illuminated stalagmite caverns. Man-made creations of unusual aesthetic value have also a rather significant role in this context. Images of various beautiful paintings, sculptures, artifacts, and jewels, as well as churches, temples, castles and palaces, that the subject has seen in the past, emerge quite regularly in close connection with ecstatic feelings related to BPM I. Particularly significant seems to be the association of a special kind of music and dance with this perinatal matrix. The same is true about bathing and swimming in mountain streams, waterfalls, large clean rivers and lakes or in the ocean.

The associations for negative aspects of BPM I represent the negative mirror image of the situation described. The memories belonging to this category involve distorted communication in the family of origin; childhood dysfunctions and diseases; highly industrialised cities and other unattractive scenes; polluted air, lakes and rivers; and distasteful or distorted pieces of art.

In regard to the Freudian erotogenic zones, the positive aspects of BPM I coincide with a biological and psychological condition, when there are no tensions in any of these zones and all the partial drives are satisfied. Conversely, satisfaction of the needs in these zones (satiation of hunger, release of tension by urination, defecation, sexual orgasm or delivery of a child) results in a superficial and partial approximation to the tension-free ecstatic experience described above.

Perinatal Matrix II. Antagonism with Mother (Contractions in a closed uterine system).
The second matrix is related to the first clinical stage of the delivery. The

preceding condition that is under normal circumstances close to ideal, is disturbed. This occurs at the beginning insidiously through chemical influences and later by mechanical constrictions due to rhythmic uterine contractions. This creates a situation of vital threat and extreme emergency with various signs of intense physical discomfort. In this phase, the uterine contractions impose on the child but the cervix is closed and the way out is not yet open. The mother and the child are a source of pain for each other and are in a state of biological antagonism and conflict.

The activation of this matrix in LSD sessions results in a rather characteristic experience of "no exit" or "hell". The subject feels encaged and trapped in a claustrophobic situation and experiences incredible psychological and physical tortures. This experience is characterised by striking darkness of the visual field and rather sinister and ominous colours. Typically, this situation is absolutely unbearable and at the same time appears to be endless and hopeless; no possibility of escape can be seen either in time or in space. Usually the subject feels that even suicide would not terminate it and bring relief.

This pattern can be experienced on several different levels; these levels can be manifest separately, simultaneously or in alternating fashion. The deepest levels are related to various concepts of hell, a situation of unbearable suffering that will never end, as has been depicted by various religions of the world. In a more superficial version of the same experiential pattern, the subject looks at the situation in this world and sees our planet as an apocalyptic place full of terror, suffering, wars, epidemics, accidents, and natural catastrophes. Typical for this experience is empathy and identification with the victimised, downtrodden, and oppressed. The subject experiences himself as thousands of soldiers who have died in the battlefields from the beginning of civilisation, tortured victims of the Spanish Inquisition, prisoners of concentration camps, terminal patients, mothers and children dying during delivery, or inmates maltreated in insane asylums. He can have visions of a dehumanised world of automata and mechnical gadgets, of bizarre circus side shows, or of a meaningless "cardboard world". Existence appears to be absolutely meaningless, nonsensical and absurd, and the search for any meaning in human life completely futile. The persons experiencing this state can develop a deep understanding of existentialism, as exemplified by Jean-Paul Sartre, Albert Camus, Marcel Aymé and Søren Kirkegaard. Sartre and other existentialist philosophers and artists seem to be particularly tuned into this experiential complex, without being able to find the only possible solution, which is transcendence. Céline's books, such as *The Journey to the End of the Night*, can be used as an excellent example of the selective focus on the negative aspects of existence. In the most superficial form of this experience, the individual sees his own concrete life situation in terms of circular patterns and as completely unbearable and full of unsolvable problems.

Agonising feelings of metaphysical loneliness, alienation, helplessness, hopelessness, inferiority and guilt are a standard part of these experiences. The symbolism that most frequently accompanies this experiential pattern involves the crucifixion and suffering of Christ and his visions in the Garden of Gethsemane; the Biblical story of the expulsion from Paradise; images of hells from various religions; the concept of the Dark Night of the Soul; figures from Greek chthonic mythology such as Sisyphos, Tantalos, Ixion, or Prometheus; and Buddha's concept of suffering as expressed in his Four Noble Truths. The most important characteristics that differentiate this pattern from the following one are the unique emphasis on the role of the victim and the fact that the situation is unbearable, inescapable and eternal; there is no way out either in space or in time.

The experiences of this matrix are frequently heralded by phenomena that seem to be related to the very onset of delivery. This situation is experienced in LSD sessions as an imminent threat of a vital danger or as cosmic engulfment. There is a high amount of anxiety, but its source cannot be identified and the atmosphere of insidious danger can result in paranoid ideation. Not infrequently, the subject experiences these alarming feelings as evil influences coming from members of various secret organisations, inhabitants of other planets or as poisoning, noxious radiation and toxic gases. Intensification of this experience typically results in the vision of a gigantic and irresistible whirlpool, a cosmic Maelstrom sucking the subject and his world relentlessly to its centre. A frequent experiential variation of this dangerous engulfment is that of being swallowed and incorporated by a terrifying monster, such as a giant dragon, python, octopus, whale or spider. A less dramatic form of the same experience seems to be the theme of descent into the underworld and encounter with various monstrous entities.

The typical physical symptoms associated with this matrix involve extreme pressures on the head and body, ringing in the ears, excruciating pains in various parts of the body, difficulties with breathing, massive cardiac distress, hot flushes and chills.

As a memory matrix, BPM II represents the basis for the recording of all unpleasant life situations in which an overwhelming destructive force imposes itself on the passive and helpless subject. The most typical and frequent examples are situations endangering survival and body integrity. Thus, the recollection of sensations connected with various operations, such as appendectomy, tonsillectomy, setting of broken extremities and difficult tooth extractions, or even the complex reliving of the circumstances of such procedures, occurs quite regularly in this context. The same is true for physical diseases or injuries, excessive muscular exertion and exhaustion, experiences of imprisonment and brutal methods of interrogation, as well as those involving prolonged extreme hunger and thirst. It has already been mentioned above that diseases and situations involving suffocation seem to be of special significance from this point of view. In subjects who experienced a dramatic war situation in a passive role (siege, air-raids, captivity), or were trapped in a claustrophobic situation (coal mines, avalanche, debris of collapsed houses, underwater passage), the memories of such events also occur in LSD sessions in close association with elements of BPM II. On a somewhat more subtle level, this category also involves memories of psychological frustrations of a helpless individual, such as abandonment, emotional rejection or deprivation, threatening events and constricting or oppressing situations in the nuclear family.

In regard to Freudian erotogenic zones, this matrix seems to be related to a condition of unpleasant tension in all of them. On the oral level, it is hunger, thirst and painful stimuli; on the anal level, retention of faeces; and on the urethral level, retention of urine. The corresponding phenomena on the genital level are sexual frustration and excessive tension, as well as pains experienced by the delivering mother in the first stage of labour. If we think of the whole surface of the skin as an erotogenic area, we can also include physical pain and unpleasant sensations in different parts of the body.

Perinatal Matrix III. Synergism with Mother (Propulsion through the birth canal).

This matrix is related to the second clinical stage of the delivery. The uterine contractions continue, but the cervix stands wide open and the gradual and difficult propulsion through the birth canal begins. There is an enormous struggle for survival with mechanical crushing pressures and a high degree of suffocation. The system is not closed anymore, however, and a perspective of termination of the unbearable situation has appeared. The efforts and interests of the mother and the child coincide; their joint goal is the termination of the painful situation. In the last moment of this stage, the child can come into contact with various kinds of biological material, such as blood, mucus, urine, and even faeces.

From the experiential point of view, this matrix is rather complex; it involves a variety of phenomena on different levels which can be arranged in a rather typical sequence. In the LSD sessions, it is experienced either as reliving of the actual biological situation or in a symbolic form of the *death-rebirth struggle*. BPM III has four very distinct experiential facets, namely, titanic, sadomasochistic, sexual and scatological. The most important characteristic of this pattern is the atmosphere of a *titanic fight*.

Immense condensation and explosive release is experienced, and the subject describes feelings of powerful currents of energy streaming through his whole body. The visions typically accompanying these experiences involve scenes of natural disasters and unleashing of elemental forces, such as exploding volcanoes, electric storms, raging hurricanes, tornadoes or earthquakes, cosmic catastrophes, comets and meteors. Equally frequent are images of comparable events related to human activities, particularly to advanced technology—explosions of atomic bombs, thermonuclear reactions, dramatic scenes of war destruction, giant power plants and hydroelectric stations, high voltage electric cables and flash discharges, launching of rockets, missiles and spaceships. Some individuals describe complex scenes of destruction and havoc, such as the end of Atlantis, Herculeum or Pompeii, Martian invasion, and the Biblical Armaggedon or annihilation of Sodom and Gomorrah. Less frequently, the images involve masses of water in movement—ocean storms, enormous tidal waves, gigantic waterfalls or even the Biblical deluge.

One aspect of the experiences related to BPM III deserves special emphasis, namely, the fact that the suffering and tension involved is intensified far beyond the level which the subject used to consider humanly possible. When it reaches the absolute experiential limit, the situation ceases to have the quality of suffering and agony. The experience then changes into a wild ecstatic rapture of cosmic proportions that can be referred to as "volcanic ecstasy". In contrast to the peaceful and harmonious "oceanic ecstasy" described above, the volcanic type of ecstasy involves enormous explosive tension with many aggressive and destructive elements. It seems to be related to the Dionysian element in man in Nietzsche's sense. Subjects usually experientially alternate between the anxiety and suffering of the victims and the ability to identify with the fury of the elemental forces and to enjoy the destructive energy. In the "volcanic ecstasy" various polar sensations and emotions melt into one undifferrentiated complex which seems to contain the extremes of all possible dimensions of human experiencing. Pain and extreme suffering cannot be distinguished from utmost pleasure, caustic heat from freezing cold, murderous aggression from passionate love, vital anxiety from religious rapture, and the agony of dying from the ecstasy of being born.

Clinically, this experiential pattern seems to be related to *sadomasochism*. Visions involving sadomasochistic orgies are rather constant and typical for LSD sessions governed by BPM III. Subjects can observe and participate in tortures and cruelties of all kinds, bloody murders and executions, violent battles and revolutions, mutilations and automutilations of religious fanatics, senseless slaughtering of animals, and similar activities involving tremendous discharges of destructive and self-destructive energies.

Another important aspect of this experiential pattern is excessive *sexual excitement* that resembles the first phase of genital orgasm, characterised by a progressive increase of instinctual tension. Here it is, however, generalised to the whole body and incomparably more intense. Subjects sometimes spend hours in overwhelming sexual ecstasy, indulging in endless varieties of wild orgies. They experience scenes from Pigalle, Soho and other famous red light and night club districts of the world, observe the most ingenious strip shows, identify with Oriental harem owners and characters famous as sexual symbols such as Don Juan, Casanova, Rasputin, Poppea and Mary Magdalene. Also frequent are group orgies resembling fertility rites, Babylonian religious ceremonies involving promiscuous sex, and rhythmical sensual dances from various cultures. A particularly common element related to BPM III is the atmosphere of rich, dynamic and lascivious carnivals with their peculiar mixture of amusing, exhilarating and joyful elements with the bizarre, grotesque, frightening and macabre ones, as well as the characteristic unleashing of otherwise repressed sexual and aggressive impulses. In a way that is not quite clear at the present time, the abstract and geometrical experiences in LSD sessions seem to be sometimes associated with BPM III.

A mitigated form of this perinatal matrix involves visions and experiences of various wild adventures. The most typical of them are hunts for various large and dangerous animals; gladiator combats; fights of scuba divers with sharks or octopi; search for hidden treasures; discoveries of new continents and battles of the conquistadors with the aboriginal inhabitants; outer space exploration and science fiction type adventures; hazardous car races; parachuting, boxing, and other dangerous sports.

Several important characteristics of this experiential pattern distinguish it from the previously mentioned "no exit" experience. The situation here is not hopeless and the subject is not helpless; he is actively involved and has the feeling that his striving has a certain direction and goal, and that his suffering has a deeper meaning. In religious terms, this situation is therefore more closely related to the concept of purgatory than that of hell. In addition, the subject does not play exclusively the role of the helpless victim; he is an observer and can at the same time identify, simultaneously or in an alternating fashion, with both the aggressor and the victims; while the no exit situation involves sheer suffering, the experience of the death-rebirth struggle represents the borderline between agony and ecstasy and a fusion of both.

Two additional aspects of BPM III should be mentioned in this connection; both of them belong to the final stages of the death-rebirth struggle and immediately precede the experience of rebirth itself. The first of these could be referred to as *scatological*; it is an intimate encounter with various kinds of repulsive biological material, such as feces, urine, sweat, mucus, menstrual blood and products of putrefaction. This experience is complex and involves visual and tactile elements as well as olfactory and gustatory sensations. Subjects can have very authentic feelings of eating feces, drinking blood or urine, choking on phlegm swallowing mucus or sucking on putrefying wounds. Quite frequent in this context are also fantasies or vivid experiences of cunnilingus performed under unhygienic conditions. Subjects occasionally indicate that a logical source of these experiences appears to be the memory of contact with the maternal vagina and the biological material involved in the actual experience of delivery. In many of the deliveries conducted without the use of enema and catheter the Latin saying *inter feces et urinas nascimur* (we are born among faeces and urine) reflected a clinical reality rather than a philosophical metaphor. The last important facet of this material is the encounter with or passing through purifying fire that appears to destroy whatever is experienced as being rotten and corrupt in the individual. It usually follows the previously described scatological sequences.

The religious symbolism of BPM III is typically related to religions that use and glorify bloody sacrifice as an important part of their ceremonies. In the Judaeo-Christian tradition, the pertinent symbols from the Old Testament involve the story of Abraham and Isaac, the Deluge, destruction of Sodom and Gomorrah, and Moses with the burning bush and the tablet with Ten Commandments. From the New Testament, it is particularly Christ's humiliation, the way of the cross and suffering during the crucifixion, the Last Judgment and Armaggedon. Particularly frequent are images of ceremonies from various Pre-Columbian cultures involving human sacrifice and self-sacrifice, such as in the Aztec, Mayan or Olmec religions. Sometimes LSD subjects report elaborate scenes involving the worship of blood-thirsty deities, as exemplified by Kali, Moloch or Astarte. Visions of religious rituals and ceremonies portraying sensuality, sexual arousal and wild rhythmic dances are also quite common symbolic illustrations of the rebirth struggle. They cover a rather wide range from fertility rites, through scenes of phallic worship to tribal religious ceremonies of various African peoples.

The scatological aspects of the death-rebirth struggle can be illustrated by such images as that of Harpies contaminating the food of the helpless blind Fineus, Hercules cleaning the stables of King Augias or Tlacolteutl, "Eater of Filth", the Aztec goddess of childbirth and carnal lust who was believed to consume the sins of mankind. A frequent symbol associated with the purifying fire is the legendary bird, Phoenix.

A typical cluster of physical manifestations regularly accompanying BPM III seems to confirm the relation of this matrix to the biological birth trauma. It involves an enormous pressure on the head and body; choking, suffocation and strangulation; torturing pains in various parts of the body; serious cardiac distress; alternating chills and hot flushes; profuse sweating; nausea and projectile vomiting; increased bowel movements; problems of sphincter control; and generalised muscular tension discharged in various tremors, twitches, shaking, jerks and complex twisting movements.

As a memory matrix, BPM III is associated with recollections of active attacks in wars and revolutions, hunting for wild animals, dramatic experiences in military service, hazardous driving, parachuting or acrobatic diving, wrestling and boxing with a strong enemy. Another typical group of memories that are relived in this context involves experiences in amusement parks and night clubs, wild parties with abuse of alcohol and promiscuous sex, colourful carnivals, and other highly sensual adventures. Also, primal scenes from childhood with sadistic interpretation of sexual intercourse, experiences of seduction by adults, as well as sexual molestation and rape seem to belong to this category. It was frequently observed that female subjects reliving their own birth re-experienced, on a more superficial level, the delivery of their children. Both experiences were usually relived simultaneously, so that these women often could not tell whether they were giving birth or being born themselves.

In regard to the Freudian erotogenic zones, BPM III seems to be related to those activities that lead to sudden relief and relaxation after a prolonged period of tension. On the oral level, it is the act of chewing and swallowing of food (but also termination of gastric discomfort by vomiting); on the anal and urethral level, it is the process of defecation and urination after long retention. On the genital level, we can find striking parallels between this matrix and the first stage of sexual orgasm, as well as the process of delivering a child. Also statoacoustic eroticism seems to be related to BPM III, such as intense rocking and jolting of children, gymnastics and acrobatics.

At least a certain portion of aggression in all the erotogenic zones seems to be derived from BPM III. Oral aggression with cramps of the chewing muscles can be traced back to the frustration which the child experiences in the birth canal with its jaws locked together by external pressure. Short-cut connections can be demonstrated to exist between the elements of this matrix and anal, urethral and phallic aggression. Reflex urination or even defecation by both mother and child during delivery seems to suggest a deep involvement of these functions. A combination of libidinal feelings and painful physical sensations with extreme aggression in this phase seems to be the basic root for later masochistic and sadistic tendencies.

Perinatal Matrix IV. Separation from Mother (Termination of the symbiotic union and formation of a new type of relationship).

This matrix seems to be meaningfully related to the third clinical stage of delivery. Here the agonising experiences of several hours culminate, the propulsion through the birth canal is completed and the ultimate intensification of tension and suffering is followed by sudden relief and relaxation. After a long period of scarce supply of oxygen and various degrees of suffocation the child experiences its first breath. The umbilical cord is cut, the blood ceases to circulate in its vessels, and a new pathway is opened through the pulmonary area. The physical separation from the mother has been completed, and the child starts its existence as an anatomically independent individual.

Like the other matrices, BPM IV has a biological and a spiritual facet. Its activation in LSD sessions can result in rather concrete reliving of the circumstances of the biological birth. Its manifestation on a symbolic and spiritual level is the death-rebirth experience; this represents the termination and resolution of the death-rebirth struggle. Suffering and agony culminate in an experience of total annihilation on all levels—physical, emotional, intellectual, moral and transcendental. This is usually referred to as "ego death"; it seems to involve an instant destruction of all the previous reference points of the individual.

After the subject experiences the very depth of total annihilation and hits the "cosmic bottom", he is struck by visions of blinding white or golden light and experiences enormous decompression and expansion of space. The Universe is perceived as indescribably beautiful and radiant; aggression and evil appear distant, unimportant and ephemeral. The general atmosphere is that of liberation, redemption, salvation, love and forgiveness. The subject feels cleansed and purged and talks about having disposed of an incredible amount of "garbage", guilt, aggression and anxiety. He feels overwhelming love for his fellowmen, appreciation of warm human relationships and friendship. Irrational and exaggerated ambitions as well as craving for money, status, prestige and power appear in this state as absurd and childish, and it is difficult to believe that they once were pursued. The appreciation of natural beauty is enormously enhanced, and an uncomplicated and simple way of life in close contact with nature seems to be the most desirable of all goals. Subjects in this stage tend to discover the depth and wisdom in systems of thought that advocate this orientation towards life, such as Rousseau's philosophy, Taoism or Zen Buddhism. Anything of natural origin is experienced with utmost zest by all the widely opened sensory pathways. Feelings of love for mankind are accompanied by a sense of humility and a tendency to engage in service and charitable activities.

The experience of rebirth is frequently followed by an experience of cosmic union and seems to be closely related to the "good womb" and "good breast" experiences and happy childhood memories. The individual tuned into this experiential area usually discovers within himself genuinely positive values, such as a sense of justice, appreciation of beauty, feelings of love, self-respect and respect for others. These values, as well as motivations to pursue them and act in accordance with them, seem to be on this level an intrinsic part of the human personality. They cannot be explained in psychoanalytic terms, as reaction formations to opposite tendencies or as sublimations of primitive instinctual drives. The individual experiences them as integral parts of a higher cosmic order. It is interesting in this connection to point to the striking parallels with Maslow's (1968) concept of metavalues and metamotivations.

Ego death can be accompanied by images of various deities, such as that of the goddess Kali, Moloch, Huitzilopochtli, Shiva the Destroyer, or experienced in identification with the death and resurrection of Christ, Osiris, Dionysos, or Adonis. The symbolism typical for the experience of rebirth involves visions of radiant light that appear to come from a divine source ("clear light"), vast spaces filled with heavenly blue haze, beautiful rainbows or rainbow spectrum and displays of peacock feathers. Rather frequent are also nonfigurative images of God perceived as pure sources of energy ("cosmic sun", Brahma), or personified images of God and various deities. Some subjects see traditional Christian images of God as an old man sitting on a richly decorated throne and surrounded by Cherubim and Seraphim in radiant slendour. Others experience the union with the archetypal Great Mother or more specific versions thereof from various cultures, such as the Egyptian Divine Isis. An interesting variation of the same is the symbolism of entering Valhalla or being admitted to the feast of the Greek Gods on Mount Olympus and enjoying the taste of nectar and ambrosia. Also images of various deities representing seasonal changes of nature and vegetable cycles can occur in this context (e.g. Demeter and Persephone or Attis). Other typical visions involve gigantic halls with richly decorated columns, huge marble statues and crystal chandeliers, and beautiful natural scenery, such as luscious landscapes at springtime, panoramas of snow-capped mountains, breathtaking views of oceans calmed after a storm, idyllic pastures and flourishing meadows. Frequently there are visions representing the final victory over a powerful enemy, such as the killing of a dragon, Hydra, Chimaera, Medusa, Sphinx or other mythological creature, the overthrowing of a despotic and tyrannical ruler, or the defeat of a repressive totalitarian political regime.

Physical manifestations typical for this matrix are prolonged withholding of breath, suffocation and increasing muscular tension, followed by sudden inspiration, relief, relaxation, and feelings of perfect physiological well-being.

In regard to memory, BPM IV represents the matrix for the recording of situations characterised by a fortuitous escape from danger. In this context, subjects can relive memories from periods immediately following wars and revolutions, with particular emphasis on joyful celebrations, as well as survival in air raids, accidents, operations, serious diseases or situations of near drowning. Another typical group of recollections involves various difficult life situations which the subject resolved by his own active effort and skill. All marked successes of one's entire life can occur in connection with this matrix as if in a rapid flashback.

As far as the Freudian erotogenic zones are concerned, this matrix corresponds on all developmental levels with the condition of satisfaction following activity which discharged or reduced tension. On the oral level, it is satiation of thirst and hunger, pleasure accompanying sucking or following oral destruction of an object; on the anal level, it is the satisfaction following defecation, and on the urethral level, the relief evoked by emptying the urinary bladder. The corresponding phenomenon on the genital level is the relaxation immediately following the sexual orgasm; in females, it is also the pleasure associated with the delivery of children.

Transpersonal Experiences in LSD Sessions

The last important category of phenomena occurring in LSD sessions are transpersonal experiences. The common denominator of this otherwise rich and ramified group is the feeling of the individual that his consciousness has expanded beyond the usual ego boundaries and transcended the limitations of time and space. In the "normal", or usual state of consciousness the individual experiences himself as existing within the boundaries of his physical body (the body image), and his perception of the environment is restricted by the physically determined range of his exteroceptors. Both his internal perception (interoception) and his perception of the environment (exteroception) are confined within the usual space-time boundaries. Under ordinary circumstances the individual can vividly *perceive* his present situation and his immediate environment; he can *recall* past events and *anticipate* the future or *fantasise* about it. In transpersonal experiences in psychedelic sessions, one or several of the above limitations appear to be transcended. In some instances, the subject experiences loosening of his usual ego boundaries; his consciousness and self-awareness seem to expand to include and encompass other individuals and elements of the external world. He can also continue experiencing his own identity but at a different time, in a different place, or in a different context. In yet other cases, the subject experiences a complete loss of his own ego identity and full identification with the consciousness of somebody or something else. Finally, in a rather large group of transpersonal experiences, the subject's consciousness appears to encompass elements that do not have any continuity with his usual ego identity and cannot be considered simple derivatives of his experiences in the three-dimensional world.

This distinction as to whether or not the content of transpersonal experiences consists of elements of the phenomenal world (or "objective reality"), as we know it from our usual state of consciousness, makes it possible to divide them into two major categories. Some of the transpersonal experiences involve phenomena, the existence of which has been generally accepted on the basis of consensual validation, empirical evidence, or scientific research. In the case of ancestral experiences, phylogenetic memories or elements of the collective unconscious it is not the content that is surprising. We all know and accept that we possess human and animal ancestors and that we are part of a cultural and racial heritage. What appears so unusual and improbable is the possibility that such information could be recorded and stored in the human unconscious and under specific circumstances be transformed into complex and realistic conscious experiences. In our usual state of consciousness we are aware of the existence of other people, animals, plants, and inorganic objects as integral parts of our surroundings. We experience them, however, as totally separate from ourselves and do not accept the possibility that we could experience their consciousness. In the case of other people, we assume by inference that they have their own consciousness and awareness, but that these are inaccessible to us. As far as inorganic matter, plants, or even animals are concerned, scientists tend to deny that consciousness exists on these levels. In transpersonal experiences that involve other people, animals, plants, or inorganic matter, it is not the existence of these that is extraordinary but the fact that the individual can transcend his usual boundaries and experience himself as somebody or something else; in addition, it can be the discovery of conscious awareness on a level where it was not previously expected that comes as a surprise. The category of transpersonal experiences that involves elements from the phenomenal world can be further subdivided on the basis of whether the extension of consciousness that characterises them can be understood in terms of alteration of time or space.

There exists also a group of ESP phenomena that could be classified as "transpersonal experiences", the content of which is comprehensible in terms of "objective reality". In the case of precognition, clairvoyance, "time travel", out-of-body experiences, travelling clairvoyance, "space travel" and telepathy, it is not the content of these experiences that is unusual, but the way of acquiring certain information or perceiving a certain situation that according to generally accepted scientific paradigms is beyond the reach of senses.

The second broad category of transpersonal experiences involves elements that are not part of "objective reality" in the Western sense. This would apply to such experiences as communication with spirits of dead people, identification with archetypal figures and mythological creatures, encounters with suprahuman spiritual entities or various deities and demonic appearances, experiences in other universes or consciousness of a "Universal Mind".*

Since it represents the first attempt at a comprehensive phenomenological description of the LSD experience, the cartography described in this paper is necessarily incomplete. It is only a sketchy outline of vast territories of the human mind as yet unknown to and uncharted by traditional Western psychiatry and psychology.

In conclusion, I will briefly outline how, in my opinion, the data from psychedelic research can contribute to the study of symbolism and ritual.

1. Many cultures in various parts of the world have rituals that directly involve hallucinogenic plants with active principles similar to LSD or other substances used in psychedelic research (mescaline, psilocybin, harmaline, tryptamine derivatives, etc.). Here psychedelic research offers a unique opportunity for an experimental approach to an anthropological phenomenon. Problems such as the specificity of drug action, the possibility of programming the experience by psychological means, the importance of the set and setting, the phenomenological variations of the drug-induced state and its therapeutic potential, are all of direct relevance for the understanding of such rituals.

2. The model of the human unconscious that is emerging from psychedelic work seems to throw new light on the understanding of many rituals. The existence in the human unconscious of *a priori* matrices for a variety of specific perinatal and transpersonal experiences that can be activated by drugs or by a variety of non-drug techniques is certainly a fact of great theoretical interest. The ubiquity of perinatal phenomenology in rites of passage of different cultures, and in mystery religions of all times deserves special emphasis in this context.

3. An important aspect of psychedelic research has been the demonstration of the therapeutic potential of certain types of experiences occurring in unusual states of consciousness and their specific effect on the value system

* Detailed description and discussion of various types of transpersonal experiences can be found in: Stanislav Grof, *Realms of the Human Unconscious;* observations from LSD research. Viking Press, 1975 (Dutton Paperback, New York, 1976).

of the individual. This observation provides experimental and clinical support for the claims that ritual events and procedures involving altered states of consciousness can have a beneficial effect on the emotional and physiological well-being of the participants, and enhance social cohesion and solidarity in the community.

References

Beringer, K. 1927. *Der Meskalinrausch*, Springer-Verlag, Berlin.

Bonny, H. L., Pahnke, W. N. 1972. The use of music in psychedelic (LSD) psychotherapy. *J. Mus. Ther.*, **9**, 64.

Grof, S. 1969. Psycholytic and psychedelic therapy with LSD; toward an integration of approaches. Paper presented at the *Conference of the European Medical Association for Psycholytic Therapy*, Frankfurt A./M., West Germany.

Grof, S. 1970. Beyond psychoanalysis: I. Implications of LSD research for understanding dimensions of human personality. Presented at the First World Conference on Science and Yoga, New Delhi, India, Dec. 1970. Published in *Darshana International (India)*, **10**, 55.

Grof, S. 1970. Beyond psychoanalysis: II. A conceptual model of human personality encompassing the psychedelic phenomena. Presented as preprint at the *Second Interdisciplinary Conference on Voluntary Control of Internal States*, Council Grove, Ka.

Grof, S. 1970. Beyond psychoanalysis: III. Birth trauma and its relation to mental illness, suicide and ecstasy. Presented as preprint at the *Second Interdisciplinary Conference on Voluntary Control of Internal States*, Council Grove, Ka.

Grof. S. 1971. LSD psychotherapy and human culture (Part I), *J. Study Consciousness*, **4**, 167.

Grof, S. 1972. Varieties of transpersonal experiences: Observations from LSD psychotherapy. *J. Transpers. Psychol.*, **4**, 45.

Grof. S. 1972-3. LSD and the cosmic game: an outline of psychedelic cosmology and ontology. *J. Study Consciousness*, **5**, 165.

Leuner, H. 1962. *Die Experimentelle Psychose*, Springer-Verlag, Berlin, Goettingen, Heidelberg.

Maslow, A. H. 1964. *Religions, Values and Peak Experiences*, Ohio State University Press, Columbus.

Maslow, A. H. 1968. *Toward a Psychology of Being*, Van Nostrand Reinhold, New York.

Pahnke, W. N. and Richards, W. A. 1966. Implications of LSD and experimental mysticism. *J. Relig. Health*, **5**, 175. Reprinted in *J. Transpers. Psychol.*, **1**, 69 (1969).

Pahnke, W. N., Kurland, A. A., Unger, S., Savage, C. and Grof, S. 1970. The experimental use of psychedelic (LSD) psychotherapy. *JAMA*, **212**, 1856.

Rank, O. 1929. *The Trauma of Birth*, Harcourt, Brace and Co., New York; Routledge and Kegan Paul, London.

Stoll, W. 1947. LSD, ein Phantasticum aus der Mutterkorngruppe. *Arch. Neurol. Psychiat.*, **60**, 1, Schweiz.

9 | The Roots of Violence and Symbolism in Childhood and Adolescence

John Payne

I

We have become so accustomed to violence by both individuals and groups today, that apart from ascribing it vaguely to "conditions today" or "the effects of television" we give little thought to its cause. Recently I have had the opportunity of treating patients whose main problem was violent behaviour which was disrupting both their lives and their personal relationships. There were a number of points in common between these patients; the violence was always directed at those they loved most dearly, it either precipitated or was provoked by the withdrawal of that love, and finally it nearly always ensured that the withdrawal of love was both complete and permanent. Such behaviour is clearly purposeless, its results are contrary to everything consciously desired by the individual. The inconsistencies are so glaring that I was forced to examine the reasons for this behaviour. Was this a manifestation of instinctual behaviour? Was it caused by current circumstances? Was it a possible re-enactment of childhood or developmental experiences? Or was it provoked by current happenings symbolically standing for crucial events in the previous experience of the individual?

I want to try and establish a causal connection between violent behaviour by individuals in society and events in childhood and adolescence which can be said to have symbolic significance; symbolic significance in that these events may be causal, despite being separated by time or hidden in the unconscious. This requires a definition of symbolism, particularly private symbolism, which recognises the importance of the unconscious mind. Such is the clarity and dogmatism of Freud's writings that he towers like a giant over psychoanalytic ideas even today, while the ideas of Jung, particularly his concern with symbolism, continue to be relatively disregarded. Jung, in his book on Archetypes, said of symbols,

> Whether a thing is a symbol or not depends chiefly on the attitude of the observing consciousness, for instance on whether it regards a given fact not merely as such but also an expression for something unknown. Hence it is quite possible for a man to establish a fact which does not appear in the least symbolic to himself, but is profoundly so to another consciousness. The converse is also true. There are undoubtedly products whose symbolic character does not depend merely on the attitude of the observing consciousness, but manifests itself spontaneously in the symbolic effect they have on the observer.

Jung I believe is saying that the symbolism perceived in happenings is not only that which is obvious but also that which links directly with a person's unconscious mind. This definition of symbols I propose to employ, and it is crucial to my argument.

II

In speaking of violence it is important to distinguish between such aggression as is essential for the continuing survival of individuals or species, and abnormal aggression which may be said to constitute violence. The ethologists Konrad Lorenz (1963) and Nikko Tinbergen (1951) have made close studies of animal behaviour, both to examine the development and meaning of behaviour in animals, and also to see if this has lessons for us in explaining the behaviour of human beings. They have both been concerned to examine and understand aggressive behaviour. Lorenz has unequivocally placed aggression in what he picturesquely calls "the great parliament of instincts". And of these instincts he nominates hunger, sexuality, flight and aggression as the big four, but is yet careful to point out that these are not irresistible tyrants whose commands brook no contradiction.

Lorenz has shown that most aggression in animals is intra-specific and only becomes inter-specific, that is, members of one species attacking the members of other species, when the needs of food and survival become paramount. Nikko Tinbergen (1951) has described six functional types of aggressive behaviour in animals:

1. Territorial behaviour
2. Fighting over sexual partners
3. Pecking order
4. Fighting over food
5. Defence against predators
6. Attacks on abnormally behaving individuals.

It would require no great imaginative leap to say that these same six may also be the stimuli which provoke aggressive behaviour in human beings. I would like to examine two of these functions from Lorenz's experiments with animals. Instincts, according to Lorenz, have important functions; they promote the balanced distribution of animals of the same species over the available environment, the selection of the strongest by fights between rival aspirants, and the defence of the young. He feels, nevertheless, that these functions are not solely concerned with the preservation of the species but are an essential concomitent of motivation in that the way these activities are carried out serves to indicate the strength of these instincts in animals of the same species.

I would now like to look at two of these functions more closely from the view of animal experiments. Firstly, territorial behaviour: Lorenz found that aggressive behaviour in fishes is predominantly intra-specific and almost entirely territorial. This has the main purpose of ensuring that no territorial area becomes over-populated by an individual species, thus safeguarding the food supply of that species.

In one experiment Lorenz put twenty-four different species of brightly coloured fish into an aquarium. The fish settled in and started to flourish. It was clear that a lot of fighting and biting was going on. After a fixed period of time the number of bites on the fish were counted. With about a hundred fish in the aquarium there was a greater chance of fish biting those of another species than those of the same species, but it was nevertheless found that fish inflicted far more bites on members of the same species than they did on other species. In another experiment he put a number of members of different species into an aquarium; this resulted in vicious fights and within a short time only the strongest fish of each species remained alive.

Secondly, defence against predators, and this applies particularly to defence of the young. Lorenz carried out a number of experiments to determine the factors which provoked and the factors which dimiinished aggressive behaviour in animals mothering their young. He found that turkey hens were particularly aggressive to any creature approaching the nest. It is however crucial that they should not harm their own chicks. Lorenz and his associates found that aggressive behaviour towards the young chicks was inhibited by the cheeping of the chicks. If turkeys were rendered deaf by an operation on the inner ear their aggressive tendencies were exacerbated and non-selective. Deaf hens were mated, and when the eggs hatched it was found that deaf mother hens pecked all their chicks to death as soon as they were born, as they were unable to hear the cheeping sounds which normally prevented this savagely aggressive behaviour.

It was found that animals also showed two other important modifications of aggressive behaviour—displacement activity and appeasement gestures. Displacement activity is an aggressive gesture which does not result in aggression—a human equivalent would be shaking your fists in someone's face or crashing your hand down on the table. Appeasement gestures appear to have evolved phylogenetically to prevent needless intra-specific aggression; one particularly memorable example is the ritual presentation of the hindquarters by monkeys, and particularly baboons, towards potential enemies. Lorenz considers that smiling and laughing serve similar functions in human beings and it is well known that in small babies smiling is evoked as soon as the child is able to see other objects clearly and is quite unrelated to whether the baby feels well disposed towards the object or person. The almost universal affection felt by adults towards all small babies is directly related to their endearing propensity to smile at any human being who comes within their field of vision.

There are thus a number of conclusions that can be drawn about aggression in animals. Firstly, it appears to be instinctive. Secondly, its main purpose is the survival of a species in the broadest sense. Thirdly, much aggressive behaviour has become modified by evolution so that some actions no longer serve their original purpose and some of these modifications can be said to be highly sophisticated; this is particularly true of displacement activity and appeasement gestures.

Before I return to aggression in humans I would like to reiterate Tinbergen's (1951, p. 175) timely warning about making deductions about human behaviour directly from animal experiments,

> I should refrain from any attempt at making guesses about the nature of the subjective phenomena which may be experienced by subjects. I shall also refrain from making any but the most tentative comparison with Man since comparisons would be permissible only when the same kind of observations were used in the study of man as in that of animals.

In many studies of the motivation of human subjects, speech, by which the subject informs the investigator about his experiences, is used as an observation. Yet, as we all know, speech, though an observable behaviour pattern, is used more often to conceal true motivation than to reveal it!

It becomes clear that aggression in animals is instinctive and therefore dependent upon an appropriate trigger to elicit the response. It is also clear that in the process of evolution in the higher animals the instinct has developed a sophistication which appears in some species to suggest that they are able to employ reason. This only emphasises how complicated instinctual behaviour may become.

III

Before I discuss the roots of violence in the behaviour of human beings it is necessary to see what constitutes so-called normal aggression and what constitutes violence. Anthony Storr (1968, p. 67) writing as a psycho-analyst, asserts that it is the human being's prolonged period of dependency which requires him to be aggressive and at the same time exacerbates his aggressive instinct. He asserts that if humans lacked a powerful aggressive instinct they would remain forever dependent. He writes:

> If there were no aggressive drive towards independence children would grow up into, and remain, helpless adults as long as anyone could be persuaded to care for them. A fate which actually does befall some individuals who either lack the normal quota of assertiveness or also who have been both subjected to regimes of childhood which makes any kind of self-assertion seem a crime.

Psychologists anxious to establish a relationship between frustration and aggression have conducted experiments on small animals and babies, often consisting of periods of deprivation of food, in an endeavour to establish a firm statistical basis between deprivation of food and a vigorous reaction by the baby, either by crying or physical movement. Deprivation of food is normally successful in provoking crying and causes the baby to thrash around violently. But is the activity thus provoked any more than a cry of protest and a vigorous communication in the only way at this stage of development that is available to it? Aggression in infants is necessary to explore and master the external world, but frequently this control and mastery is extended to restricting as well as controlling other human beings.

The question that needs to be asked is: does aggression come ultimately from anger aroused by frustration or does it have a root of its own? The psychoanalytic viewpoint, while not denying the instinctual basis of much human aggressive behaviour, asserts that aggressive behaviour in infants is both spontaneous and exploratory in nature but is also associated with primitive love impulses and the satisfaction obtained in the act of feeding. From this many psychoanalysts believe that aggression is part of the primitive expression of love. This is related to the child's need to have sufficient aggressive component to survive in the act of feeding or other attacks on the mother's person. However, at a certain point in infantile development described by Winnicott (1958) as the "age before concern", the person attacked is the person most valued. In this period excited love includes an imaginative attack on the mother's body. This is aggression as part of love. If in this stage of development aggression is lost it is believed that this is accompanied by some degree of loss of the capacity to love. This illustrates the psychoanalytic concept of opposites with which this paper is very much concerned.

Additionally, Winnicott writing of aggression in relation to emotional development believed that the amount of aggressive potential that an infant carries depends on the amount of opposition that has been met with. The "opposition" of the psychoanalysts is very probably of similar quality to the "frustration" of the psychologists.

At the same time it is impossible to ignore the social and cultural climate in which children are reared. If children are reared in a climate in which violence, as opposed to controlled or healthily directed aggression is the norm, their aggressive boundaries will be pushed back so that the frontier between aggression and violence will be more easily crossed. John Baron Mayes (1969) who has done much work with teenagers in Liverpool, says:

> Toughness is a highly prized virtue and there is often a restlessness for something exciting to do. Delinquency and violence in slum rooming house areas is in the very air that people breathe.

In Pakistan it has been shown that there are more murders in Pathan country than elsewhere, and in India there are more murders in the South East Punjab where the Sikhs live. And in a study of homicide and suicide in Africa, Bohannan (1960) shows that the homicide rate among urban American negroes is at least twice the rate recorded for a number of tribes in both East and West Africa, which emphasises the importance of the cultural factor. I also know from personal experience that men who have recently been involved in war are, under certain conditions, more likely to indulge in violent behaviour than people who have not recently been exposed to this experience.

IV

Before I relate my clinical cases I feel I must refer to Freud's concept of the death instinct which, although it is no longer generally accepted, must be referred to. It seems to me to be part of Freud's basic misconception of trying to make mental processes fit a physiological/biological model and his preoccupation with instincts as the cornerstone of psychoanalytic theory (Freud, 1920). The death instinct presupposes that man's aggressive drive, instead of being directed at preservation, is directed towards his own destruction. Put simply, the argument runs that the perpetuation of life is a function of the libido and the path towards death is a function of the Ego. For Freud libido was in truth the great evil, and the Ego contained the potential for all that is good. It follows that Ego is superior to libido (which is an Id function) and therefore the "death instinct" is superior to the life instinct. This seems incomprehensible when even in animals the basic instincts are directed towards the preservation of the species; by what inconceivable developmental anomaly should man have developed an instinct which was individual and species-destructive? Even Freud's desire to make the concept of mind fit a medical biological model could not support an instinct so unbridled and self-destructive.

If I am right, most human beings wish to go on living, and only in exceptional circumstances seek to end their own lives or those of others, although the fact that there are physiological changes accompanying anger which do induce a feeling of wellbeing cannot be denied. So violence may be aggression which crosses an individual threshold. But what are the antecedents of violent behaviour, and what factors determine the threshold?

V

Clinical psychotherapeutic practice has the almost unique advantage of providing minute details of a patient's past and provides the opportunity to get to know and experience an individual in depth. Longitudinal in depth studies may provide important signposts to the origins of much human behaviour.

The two cases I wish to describe have not only had violent behaviour as the presenting problem but have been similar in that the violence was not only purposeless but counter-productive. There were sufficient similarities in the two cases to make me examine them to see if there were patterns from which we could draw general conclusions. I should emphasise that details of the case histories have been modified so as to diminish the possibility of identification.

Case I

I was asked to see a man in his middle thirties as urgently as possible because he was unpredictably assaulting his ten-month old child, was given to fits of rage, in one of which he broke one of his wife's ribs and on another occasion he smashed up household furniture. When I first saw him his wife had already made the decision to leave him because she was terrified for the safety of her baby and could no longer endure his seemingly unpredictable physical assaults.

He was a gentle-seeming, open and articulate man who appeared to love his wife and was devoted to his baby. He utterly failed to understand his behaviour. His childhood had been marked by loss and rejection but he denied that it was unhappy. When he was five years old his mother died of a cancer and his father surrendered his upbringing to his brother and his brother's wife. He says his aunt, who was childless, was overjoyed at the prospect of having a child of her own to care for, but that his uncle regarded it as an intolerable burden which he only undertook in deference to his wife's wishes. His aunt cared for him devotedly (and it is significant that he named his child after her) but his uncle lost no opportunity to demean him, to sneer at him and ridicule him for his physical awkwardness and for being what he considered "a cissy". The first occasion that he hit his wife was when he was playing bar billiards with a friend. He played exceedingly badly and his wife made mocking remarks about his woeful lack of skill. He immediately became enraged and beat her about the head in the public bar with his billiard cue.

He first attacked the baby when he went up to see it one evening in its cot after a feed—as he bent over the child to kiss it, the baby curled up its upper lip in what he interpreted as a sneer and a sign of dislike. In a fury he seized the child from the cot and beat it over the bottom and around the head. Similar incidents occurred on three or four more occasions, but on each occasion the violent attack on the baby was precipitated by the baby having appeared to sneer at her father, or on one occasion when he went up she turned her head away and would not look at him.

It was quite clear from my psychotherapeutic encounters with this man that what precipitated the feeling of rage inside him and the subsequent physical violence was the personal denigration and the depreciation of his own efforts to be independent and manly. This is what his uncle had consistently done since his adoption. For much of the time his uncle had resented his presence and the love and affection that his wife lavished upon him. This resentment was expressed either by ignoring him or by expressing his dislike for the way he was developing and for the sort of man he was struggling to become.

His childhood was thus dominated by a struggle to secure from his uncle acceptance and the recognition of his worthwhileness. It would appear that his attacks upon his own child were triggered off by what he interpreted as her non-acceptance and denigration. The link between the behaviour of his child and his uncle would seem to be convincing and in the clinical setting he acknowledged the strong symbolic connection.

During his early manhood he worked for an organisation whose political aims were dedicated to non-violence. It seems reasonable to assume that he was subconsciously aware and afraid of the violent feelings inside him.

It was also clear that on each occasion his own violent behaviour was precipitated by situations that recapitulated his own childhood; firstly, when he thought his own child sneered at him and turned away from him, and secondly when his wife mocked his games-playing ability. It would appear that both his baby and his wife were symbolically re-enacting childhood scenes with his uncle when he had then been unable to express the rage and anger that he felt towards him.

Case II

A young man in his mid-twenties came to see me because he felt he could not contain the feelings of murderousness and revenge which he harboured towards his girl friend, who had left him about three months previously. Two months after she left, when he became finally convinced she would not return, he destroyed all her clothes and personal possessions she had left in his flat but had felt too frightened to go and reclaim. He felt so distraught by this action that he immediately journeyed to see her parents to tell them what he had done and to ask for their forgiveness. A week later he came to see me and said that he was determined to murder her. He was consumed with hatred for her and acknowledged he wanted revenge. He felt she had no right to leave him and no right to withdraw her love. On another occasion he came up to leave me a note inviting me to stop him going to where the girl was now working, because he said he intended to murder her. I was fortunately able to see him immediately and have never before been so clearly aware of feelings of hatred and fury in another human being. I spent over an hour with him, and at the end of that time he looked and felt much quieter and he admitted that the murderous feelings had passed and he thought he could now cope with himself.

He says he had a happy childhood, but from the age of thirteen he became shy and withdrawn and this made him unhappy. For two years before I saw him he says he was emotionally totally numb. His father emigrated from Eastern Europe after the war and met and married his mother, who was English and came from an affluent middle class background. The father was a worker in the family business and although it was the mother's business, had the status of an employee, both in the business and in the home. Although he says his parents got on well together, they were too busy working and running the business to devote much time either to him or to his younger sister. He says he never really felt he had parents who cared. When his girl friend left him he was desolated and also unbelieving. He could not believe that the only person who had ever loved him could leave him. On one occasion he said, "If she can't cope with me, she can't cope with other people. She doesn't deserve to live." He said her parents were the only true parents he had. He was entirely dominated by feelings of revenge.

I think it is highly probable that his girl friend stood for his mother who had loved him, but who he then felt withdrew her love due to the considerable demands he made for love and affection, but I think it is possible she also stood for a part of him which was filled with rage and feelings of revenge because he felt her love towards him had been withdrawn.

Dr. Arthur Hyatt-Williams, who has done psychotherapy with murderers in Wormwood Scrubs describes what he calls a "blueprint for murder"

(Hyatt-Williams, 1964). He argues that certain people, because of happenings in their past, have a separated off murderous part inside them. This argument is based on the Kleinian theory of infantile development. If childhood or adolescent events which gave birth to this split-off murderous part become recapitulated they may violently attack the other person who symbolically stands for the individual who in their early life contributed to the production of this murderous self by depriving or appearing to deprive them of love or esteem at a crucial developmental time.

Both the cases I have described have a number of things in common. Firstly, violence or potential violence is done to someone who is close to and beloved by the person doing the violence. Secondly, this behaviour seems to be motivated by feelings of revenge. Thirdly, the person who is violent only succeeds in diminishing the affection and increasing the distance between himself or herself and the person they are violent towards. Fourthly, the event which triggers off the violence, whether it be trivial or more serious, symbolises a crucial experience at some earlier phase of the individual's development, for as Jung believes the capacity to become a symbol is individual and depends upon the observing consciousness.

Both violence and homicide appear to have similar roots and both can be explained by similar hypotheses in psychoanalytic terms. Both would appear to be triggered off by events which may symbolise important happenings in the early life of the individual. Violence is usually, and homicide often, the result of a spontaneous and uncontrollable release of rage triggered off by events of symbolic significance. If these notions of violence and homicide are valid one would expect there to be a close relationship between the murderer and his victim as much as between the person who is violent and the person assaulted.

Two cases have been cited in which there was a close relationship between the violent person and the person who was assaulted. It is likely that much violence is private violence occurring in people's homes between members of a family. In all these cases there is a close relationship between the violent person and the victim of violence. The increasing incidence and awareness of battered babies and battered wives support the contention that much violence is private and occurs between people who have close psychological and family bonds.

At the conclusion of a study on African homicide and suicide Bohannan provids a table showing the relationship between victim and assailant in a number of East and West African tribes and compares these with the same relationships between murderer and victim among American negroes and Danish killers. With the exception of the figures for one Ugandan tribe, it would appear from this study that murderers are more likely to kill people linked to them by ties of blood kinship or emotion than strangers or chance acquaintances. Remarkably, it is in a European nation that people are most likely to murder their wives, sexual partners or children. One third of Danish killers murder their children, and a fifth murder their wives or sexual partners. The Danish murderers (they are the only European nation quoted) were the only group to have their children as such a high proportion of their victims. Could it be that the removal of the strict taboos of tribal Africa or different patterns of child rearing account for the high proportion of child murder in a European country? What is clear is that the hypothesis advanced in this chapter about the likely close relationship between a high percentage of murderers and their victims is supported by these statistics.

References

Bohannan, P. (ed.) 1960. *African Homicide and Suicide*, Princeton University Press, Princeton.

Freud, S. 1920. *Beyond the Pleasure Principle*, International Psycho-Analytical Library no. 4, Hogarth Press.

Hyatt-Williams, A. 1964. *In* I. Rosen (ed.) *The Pathology and Treatment of Sexual Deviation*, Oxford University Press.

Jung, G. C. *Psychological Types*, Collected Works, Vol. 6.

Lorenz, K. 1963. *On Aggression*, Methuen, London.

Mays, J. B. 1969. *The Young Pretenders: A Study of Adolescence in Contemporary Society*, Sphere Books, London.

Storr, A. 1970. *Human Aggression*, Penguin, Harmondsworth.

Tinbergen, N. 1951. *The Study of Instincts*, Oxford University Press, London.

Winnicott, D. W. 1958. *Collected Papers*, Tavistock, London.

Representation Through Intimacy

10

A study in the symbolism of monarchy and court office in early-modern England

David Starkey

The appearance of Keith Thomas's *Religion and the Decline of Magic* has marked an epoch in the study of early-modern English history. It shows, irrefutably, that the men of that time—from the most educated and sophisticated to the least—were soaked in the occult and the irrational: they believed in astrology, witchcraft, and the direct intervention of providence in everyday life. No more will it be possible to push these aspects of the period into the margin; rather, they must figure largely in any general explanations. This applies just as much to political history as to religious history or to the history of ideas. From one point of view this has already been understood: thus Thomas himself stresses the propaganda value of the king's powers as a miraculous healer (Thomas, 1973, pp. 231–2). But there is more to it than the manipulation of opinion: as this paper will try to show, the actual instruments of government at the command of a miracle-working king are different from those available to a lounge-suited Prime Minister. The aim, then, is to explore some of the governmental consequences of divine kingship; the method will be a study of monarchical symbolism since, as religious history shows, symbolism is a particularly direct pointer to the deepest layers of belief.

Symbols were of course a highly familiar mode of expression to a fifteenth or sixteenth-century Englishman. Jousts and revels signified their meaning through a fanciful and elaborate symbolism (Hall, 1809, pp. 520, 568, 597, 688, etc.); a man's political allegiance was announced by the badge he wore in his cap or hung about his neck on a chain (cf. Tudor-Craig, 1973, illustrations 45–51 on p. 151); while on the esoteric emblems of heraldry could depend the life of the Duke of Norfolk and his son (*LP*, XXI, ii, 555/2/14/17). With the reformation, it is true, some images—those of saints and martyrs—were deliberately devalued, but others, and especially our particular concern—the symbols of monarchy—underwent a corresponding reinforcement.

Broadly, royal symbolism fell into two main categories: the material accoutrements of monarchy, and the king's own person. The former—the crown, the sceptre, the orb, and so on—are the subject of an extensive and varied literature (Legg, 1883; Schramm, 1937, etc.); the latter, on which this paper will concentrate, has experienced a comparative neglect. There is only one monograph on the topic, and even that approaches it from a very narrow point of view. In his book, *The King's Two Bodies*, Ernst Kantorowicz shows at length how corporeal symbolism was used to define the king's constitutional position—especially in England. The equation of kingship with the king's body was accepted; then two separate meanings of the symbol were distinguished. On the one hand, the ordinary sense of the word—that is, the king's mortal, fleshly body—stood for the personal, transitory aspects of monarchy; on the other, the king's body considered as the fictive entity of a "corporation sole"—that is, an undying legal "body", of which the particular sovereign was simply the temporary representative —expressed the eternal nature of the office. Clearly, since Kantorowicz is concerned with political theory, the distinction between the two bodies is of the essence. But in practice, as contemporaries usually stressed, both bodies fused in the actual person of the king "for the time being" (Plowden, 1816, p. 455a). The recognition of this fact leads to a quite different emphasis from Kantorowicz's. Only in legal discourse did the king's physical person symbolise merely the private aspects of kingship; ordinarily it was infinitely more resonant. Firm evidence is available on this point: when Stephen Gardiner was discussing the likely secular consequences (as he saw them) of ecclesiastical iconoclasm, he noted as the worst that:

> If this opinion [i.e. iconoclasm] should proceed, when the King's Majesty hereafter should show his person, his lively image, the honour due by God's law among such might continue; but as for the King's standards, his banners, his arms, [they] should hardly continue in their due reverence (Muller, 1933, pp. 274–5).

The king's body, "his lively image", is thus seen as the master-symbol, qualitatively different and hence less vulnerable than the derivative symbols of the royal standard, arms, and so on.

As the master-symbol of the office, the royal body was an essential instrument of political management. This meant that whatever his personal taste a king with any sense spent much effort on tricking out his person as a suitably magnificent emblem of royalty. And if a monarch did not, he generally paid a severe penalty. All this is well brought out by the contrast between Henry VI and Edward IV. Henry (who certainly had very little sense) incurred universal contempt by riding through London in the crucial days of 1471, clad only in an old blue gown (Myers, 1959, p. 5); on the other hand, his successful rival, Edward, was deeply concerned with the projection of his persona. He of course dressed magnificently (Nicolas, 1830, pp. 115–70); but he also went much further and (like a modern film star or pop idol) manipulated his body as an instrument of publicity:

> . . . He was easy of access to his friends and to others, even the least notable. Frequently he called to his side complete strangers, when he thought that they had come with the intention of addressing or beholding him more closely. He was wont to show himself to those who wished to watch him, and he seized any opportunity that the occasion offered of revealing his fine stature more protractedly and more evidently to on-lookers . . . (cited in Lander, 1965, p. 226).[1]

No Tudor could have done better!

But of course the symbolic role of the king's person did not stop with his own physical body. Instead, his person was multiplied by various means, of which the most obvious is artistic representation. From the earliest times royal portraits—those symbols of a symbol—had an important part to play. This is shown clearly enough by the iconography of the great seal. The seal itself took the same basic form from the Conquest to the end of the Middle Ages (and, indeed, to the present day). On the one side, there was an image of the king enthroned in majesty, full-face, and equipped with the emblems of royalty; on the other, an image of the king armed and on horseback. The first showed the king as judge; the second, as warrior-defender of his people. The whole was therefore an illustration of the versicle:

> Lo! to fight and to judge are the office of a king.

In other words, it was a double portrayal of the king's person that was used as the symbol of monarchy on its most solemn formal instrument. But the images were entirely unindividualised: only the king's name in the inscription of the seal marked it as his, rather than that of any other king (Piper, 1973, pp. 29–31). Fundamentally, then, it would be wrong to oppose such mediaeval representations of the king's person to the material symbolism

---

1. For other similar comments, see Jacob, 1961, pp. 545–6.

of the office. Rather, perhaps, we should see these "portraits" as simple lay figures on which to hang the symbols of crown, sceptre, and orb. Only, in fact, with the new technical resources of Renaissance art does the balance alter, and personality displace symbolism, or better, become a symbol in its own right.

As far as the great seal itself was concerned, the change did not occur until 1542 (Piper, 1973, pp. 29–31), but in other areas the shift was considerably earlier. Among the most notable of these was the coinage, which experienced extensive remodelling under Henry VII (1485–1509). His testoons (one shilling pieces) and groats (four-penny pieces) bear a recognisable profile, which is closely akin to the one presented by Pietro Torrigiano's polychromatic bust. The impression—like that made by the strictly comparable Roman imperial coinage—is of a slightly heightened version of reality (Chrimes, 1972, pp. 334–5; Mackie, 1952, p. 604; Grant, 1960, pp. 238–41). There exists also one realistic oil-painting of Henry (probably by Michael Sittow) but, in comparison with the coinage bust it is a modest, even understated, affair. Things (as might be expected) went much further under Henry VIII (1509–47): in part, because of the flamboyance of the King's character; and in part because Henry found an image-maker of genius in Holbein. The most grandoise and most official of his portraits of Henry was the dynastic mural in the Privy Chamber at Whitehall. In it, the King appeared with none of the formal insignia of royalty; instead, the painter took the essentials of Henry the man—huge, broad-shouldered, and thrusting—and turned them into a supremely powerful and effective image, that, even in the inferior copies which are all that survive of the complete painting, browbeats the spectator as ruthlessly as the King's fleshly presence must have done. The details of colour and texture were of course masterly, but what mattered was the overall shape: the massive trapezium of the King's body set on the splayed columns of legs (cf. Strong, 1967). Like similar representations of Marx, or Lenin, or Mao, this brilliantly simplified version of Henry's physical traits has become an independent symbol—in his case, of the whole Tudor monarchy.

The symbolic (rather than merely representational) nature of all portraits of the sovereign is driven home by the way in which they were treated. While they were never worshipped like the images of the ancient Roman emperors,[2] they were nevertheless accorded a profound respect. This fact of course played into the hands of the Roman Catholic apologists who sought to defend the use of images in Christian worship; consequently, they gave it much prominence. As early as 1538, the conservative vicar of Ticehurst in Kent held up a "King Harry groat"; pointed to the King's image on it, and said:

2. But cf. Strong, 1963, p.31

How darest thou spit upon this face? Thou darest not do it. But thou wilt spit
upon the image [in Church] . . . then thou spittest upon God (cited in Elton,
1972, p. 22).

Some thirty years later, the same argument was employed against the ico-
noclasts by Nicholas Sanders in his *Treatise of the Images of Christ and his
Saints*:

Break if you dare [he challenged his opponents] the image of the Queen's
Majesty, or the Arms of the Realm . . . (cited in Strong, 1963, p. 38).[3]

At the other end of the political spectrum, the government itself was fully
alive to the importance of the images of royalty. Under Elizabeth, indeed,
it actually made some attempt to ensure that the portraits of the Queen
which poured out of artists' studios

expressed the natural representation of her majesty's person, favour, [and]
grace (Hughes and Larkin, 1969, II, no. 56, and cf. Strong, 1963, pp. 4 ff.).

However, despite all the reverence and concern for the royal portraits, such
representations had a fairly narrow range of functions. The images used in
formal contexts (i.e. on the great seal, coins, etc.) served both as symbols of
authenticity and instruments of propaganda; in straightforward royal portraits on the other hand propaganda ruled supreme. A few lesser purposes
should perhaps be added—for example, labelling. This is seen at its clearest
in Trinity College, Cambridge, which is stamped as Henry VIII's foundation by the appearance of his statue over the great gate (Royal Commission
on Historical Monuments: England, 1959, II, plate 255). Lastly, there were
special meanings that depended on the highly particular context in which
the symbol appeared: here, the obvious example is the use of an image of
the late sovereign in his own funeral ceremonies (Kantorowicz, 1957, pp.
411–12, etc.). But that exhausts the list of symbolic significances.

So far, then, even the symbolism of the royal body has yielded few
instruments of government, as opposed to means for influencing opinion.
But the king's person could also be represented in a quite different fashion
from any that has yet been mentioned. In his discussion of the profound
difference (as he claimed) between the respect paid to royal as opposed to
sacred images, the reformer Thomas Bilson made the following comment:

The reverence given to the officers, arms, or images, which Princes send to be
set up, unto themselves, is accepted as rendered to their own persons when
they cannot otherwise be present in the place to receive it but by a substitute
or sign that shall represent their state (Bilson, 1545, p. 561).

3. For the explicitly symbolic nature of the images on the great seal, see Stephen
Gardiner's comments in Muller, 1933, pp. 274, 289.

Thus, as the indifferent listing of animate and inanimate—"officers, arms, or images"—shows, the human representative of the sovereign could be seen as just as much a symbol of his master as a royal portrait. But, despite his symbolic role, such a representative retained his inherent capacity for independent action. That is, he could be both royal agent and royal symbol, with the former role being given unique strength and resonance by the latter. The remainder of the paper will be devoted to an analysis of this hybrid agent-symbol. The analysis will fall into three principal sections: first, the political functions of the royal person itself (conceived symbolically) will be discussed; second, the major group of personal representatives of the sovereign will be isolated, and their own political role analysed; and third, the machinery—itself symbolic—by which these men were able to represent the king will be examined from the peak of its importance under the Tudors to its decline and disintegration under the Hanoverians.

I

We begin by looking more closely at the nature and function of the prime symbol, the king himself. The subject is embarrassingly rich, but for the present purpose a fairly simple scheme of classification can be used. On the one hand, stand the king's actual powers—formal and informal—that are the subject matter of the political and constitutional historian. These will concern us only obliquely. On the other hand, lies our particular province: the semi-mystical aspects of kingship. From the very beginning the institution had been sacred, and its English branch was no exception. The king's other-worldly status was firmly enunciated by his coronation: he was annointed with oil and chrism "with the which Thou [i.e. God] annointest priests, kings and prophets" (Rymer, 1818, II, p. 35); he made an offering of the sacred elements—bread and wine—"after the example of Melchisedech" (loc. cit.), who was, simultaneously, "king of Salem . . . and priest of the most high God" (Genesis, 15:18); and finally, each portion of the regalia—the crown, the sword, the rod, etc.—was blessed, and each was invested with a particular mystic significance (Rymer, 1818, II, pp. 34–5). Moreover, the sacrosanctity thus ratified through coronation coloured, and coloured deeply, the whole character of the monarchy. Two points stand out. First, like any other holy man, the king could work miracles—or rather, two particular miracles. In common with his brother king of France he "touched for the king's evil". That is, he cured (as was supposed) scrofula by the laying on of hands (cf. Bloch, 1924). And, as well, his touch endowed rings of gold and silver—called cramp rings—with a protective power against epilepsy and other muscular spasms (Thomas, 1973, pp. 235–6; Crawfurd, 1917, pp. 165 ff.). Second, again like any other sacred figure, the king was possessed of an aura or "mana". This sounds highly metaphysical, but there is explicit contemporary evidence on the point. Somewhere about 1540, John Hales wrote an unprinted treatise called an *Oration in Commendation of the Laws* . . . (BM, Harleian MS 4990). In the dedication he set out the problems which many men (clearly including the author) had in bringing themselves face-to-face with Henry VIII:

> Albeit the King's majesty [he began] be a Prince of so fatherly love toward his subjects that he forbiddeth none of them to come to his presence at time and place meet; . . . yet there ought to be in men a certain reverence mixt with gentle fear to pull them back again, remembering that they have not to do with man but with a more excellent and divine estate (ibid. fo. 1).

However, this reserve was not merely a matter of courtesy: it was often reinforced by an involuntary reaction:

> Certes, in some men nature hath wrought . . . that although they have before prepared themselves both earnestly and reverently to speak to their ruler and head; yet they have been, when they should have most drawn courage to them, so astonished and abashed, so trembling and quaking, utterly in a manner muet [i.e. dumb], as if they had been taken with the palsy, such is the majesty of a prince (ibid. fos. 1-1v).

There is of course a measure of courtly exaggeration about all this, but once that is discarded, a core of solid truth remains. Hales is describing the psychological effects of confrontation with the numinous power which clung to the "excellent and divine estate" of monarchy like a tangible and terrifying cloak. Some hundred and thirty years later, the same phenomenon was analysed with noble eloquence by Robert South in his sermon on "the peculiar care and concern of providence for the protection and defence of kings":

> God saves and delivers sovereign princes by imprinting a certain awe and dread of their persons and authority upon the minds of their subjects . . . And this is that property which in kings we call majesty, and which, no doubt, is a kind of shadow or portraiture of the divine authority drawn upon the looks and persons of princes which makes them commanders of men's fears, and thereby capable of governing them in all their concerns. *Non fero fulgur oculorum tuorum* [I cannot bear the lightning of your eyes], is the language of every subject's heart, struck with the aweful aspect of a resolute and magnanimous prince. There is a majesty in his countenance that puts lightning into his looks and thunder into his words . . . (South, 1843, II, pp. 55-6).

English kingship, therefore, like other sacred monarchies, had a double face: the beneficent (the king as healer), and the terrifying (fear of the royal presence). Or, in Frazer's own words: the king's

magical virtue is in the strictest sense of the word contagious: his divinity is a
fire, which, under proper restraints, confers endless blessings, but, if rashly
touched or allowed to break bounds, burns and destroys what it touches
(Frazer, 1963, p. 267).

But we need hardly turn to a twentieth-century anthropologist: a seventeenth-century divine, Richard Burney, hailed Charles II's restoration with
a series of ecstatic sermons in which he spelled out much the same idea:

> God has also seated the latitude of the power of kings, or the highest style of
> their prerogative in a *maledicere* [power of cursing] and a *benedicere* [power of
> blessing] . . . His Majesty as it were enters into God's mightiness, in as much
> that the King like unto God, *solus rex inter mortales possit maledicere* [only the
> king among mortals should curse] . . . This *maledicere* in a king is no pravity
> of nature, but equal, like God's justice, to a benediction, in that it preserves
> the sincere from that which is corrupt. His Majesty's wrath is potent like the
> lightning to melt the sword in the scabbard, causes the spirit of the ill-affected
> to vacillate, till he falls cursed from the tree; every man partakes of His
> Majesty's *benedicere* that keeps his soul from having any cursing thoughts of
> the King (Burney, 1660, pp. 7–9).

Numinous powers on such a scale had necessarily far-reaching consequences. First (as we have already mentioned) they were much used in
royal propaganda. In the Middle Ages, for example, their supernatural
attributes—as epitomised by touching for the king's evil—had provided the
kings of England and France with a crucial weapon in their battle with the
overweening pretentions of the papacy (Bloch, 1924). By the later Middle
Ages that particular battle had been won, but the charismatic aspects of
kingship lost none of their importance. Revolutions or intended revolutions
sought legitimacy by association with the divine: Henry IV's shaky title was
reinforced by annointing him with an opportunely-rediscovered vial of oil
that had been given by the Virgin to St. Thomas of Canterbury (Murray,
1954, pp. 179–80); Henry VII (another dubious usurper) elaborated both
the ceremony of touching for the king's evil and that of the hallowing of
cramp rings (Crawfurd, 1917); during the royalist reaction of Charles II's
reign the king's powers of healing were made more freely available than
ever before; while James II, on the eve of absolutism, seems to have thought
of reviving the blessing of cramp rings which had been abandoned at
Elizabeth I's accession (Thomas, 1973, pp. 228, 231, 236). But there is (as
we have also insisted) much more to the sacred aspects of monarchy than
the shaping of public opinion: indeed, as far as the king himself was concerned, his semi-divinity underpinned some of his most important everyday political functions.

The reasons for this lay partly in the nature of the royal administration.

England had had for some two or three centuries a small, though well-organised, bureaucracy. There were departments of state—the Chancery, the Exchequer, the Common Law Courts—with defined areas of responsibility, salaried personnel, and clear ladders of promotion. But that did not make England a bureaucratic state; the bureaucracy alone could not rule. For one thing, it was too small—numbering a few hundred at most (cf. Aylmer, 1961, pp. 470 ff.); for another, it was a purely central bureaucracy: there were scarcely any full-time salaried appointments at local level, save for the special case of the Customs administration. Instead, county government was in the hands of amateurs, of the country gentlemen who sat on the various royal commissions—of the Peace, of Sewers, etc.—through which the shires were run. Though it is easy to exaggerate the truculence of these men, they did stand in a quite different relationship with the Crown from feed servants. Their co-operation and even acquiescence could never be taken for granted; rather, they had to be won by conciliation, management and patronage. On purely institutional grounds, therefore, the formal instruments of administration were inadequate.

But the government of England was also bedevilled by another, more fundamental, issue: the fact that the fifteenth and even the sixteenth centuries had a very undeveloped concept of delegation. The common attitude was summarised by Hugh Latimer in his *Fourth Sermon on the Lord's Prayer*:

> there be some men that say "When the King's majesty himself commandeth me to do so-and-so; then I will do it, not afore" (cited in Loades, 1970, pp. 68–9).

The preacher's reply was devastating: such an assertion was

> wicked . . . and damnable; for we may not be so excused. Scripture is plain in it, and sheweth that we ought to obey his officers, having authority from the King, as well as the King himself (loc. cit.).

In the long term, the sustained Tudor propaganda campaign on obedience (of which Latimer's sermon is a distinguished product) went far towards a solution of the problem of delegated authority. But in the short term (which is what matters in day-to-day politics) the difficulty remained: too many would have joined with the men of Hoddesdon in Hertfordshire, who (in 1534) boasted after their riotous attack on a party of courtiers that

> the Marquis of Exeter was put to the worse in this town; yea, and if the best man within this realm, under the King, being the King's servant or other, do any displeasure to any of this town, he shall be set fast by the feet (PRO, SP 2/Q, no. 15 [*LP*, VII, 1120]).

Almost all, then, would obey the king in person; but many would obey no other.

Fifteenth and sixteenth-century government thus faced two essential problems: first, the feed officers on whose service it could depend were insufficient for their manifold tasks, both numerically and in their geographical distribution; and second, the measure of obedience that would be given to any royal official or to any written royal command was dangerously unpredictable. Neither problem was insoluble: indeed, both tended to yield readily enough to a direct application of the royal presence. Thus 1464 saw an extensive breakdown in public order, which neither the local administration nor royal letters could contain—let alone suppress. Edward IV's reaction was swift: between January and May he rode from Coventry to Worcester, from Worcester to Gloucester, then across country to Cambridge, and finally south to Maidstone in Kent, sitting himself as Chief Justice in all these places (Lander, 1969, p. 102). Again, three years later, Edward travelled to the north Midlands to settle in person a series of violent disputes between Lord Grey of Codnor and the Vernons (loc. cit.). Nothing shows more clearly than these examples (which could easily be multiplied) the continued dependence of English government on the immediate exercise of the king's authority, on the peculiar royal *numen* that made his command substantively different from any other.

But in a sense the use of the royal presence was no solution at all. Problems happen simultaneously—not sequentially—and no king, however fast he ride, can be in two places at once. What was needed was some device for delegating the special kingly power. One obvious method was through blood-relationship. Members of the royal family were thought to share to some extent in the monarch's semi-sacred authority (cf. Bush, 1970, pp. 37 ff.). So Edward IV made his brother, Richard of Gloucester, virtual viceroy of the North; while in the late 1520's, the administration of the Welsh Marches was devolved onto the Council of the Princess Mary, and that of the North onto the Council of the Duke of Richmond, Henry VIII's bastard son. But the elevation of Princes of the Blood was not without risk. They were too powerful, too near in succession to the throne, for any king to chance too full a confidence in them. Moreover (setting that point aside), the royal family was simply too small: there were not enough of them to cope with the multiple problems of government. So other, more flexible instruments of delegation had to be found. It is possible that a whole range of methods was employed. If so most have left no trace in the record. Instead this is dominated by one class of royal symbol-agents: the servants of the king's Privy Chamber.

II

The Privy Chamber was one of the departments of the royal household. It was, in fact, of very recent institution. The mid-fifteenth-century household had been divided into two main departments, each with its own head officer. The hall and the offices (the kitchens, etc.), together with the financial machinery of the household, formed one department, usually called the Household (proper), under the Lord Steward; while the staff of the Chamber (the collective name for the royal apartments) formed the other under the Lord Chamberlain. The latter had a double responsibility: he was in charge of both public ceremonial and the king's private service. However, in the 1490's a new development occurred. The most private of the king's apartments—the Privy or Secret Chamber—began to acquire a staff of its own, under its own head officer, the Groom of the Stool. By 1520, the Privy Chamber's organisation was fully developed, and it had secured an almost total independence from the Chamber. In effect, therefore, the household now consisted of three, not two, departments. The change was recognised and ratified by the Eltham Ordinances of 1526, which fall into three sections—Household, Chamber and Privy Chamber—corresponding to the three departments of the reformed and reconstituted household. The functions of the Household proper remained unaltered, but the Chamber retained only public ceremonial. Its other former responsibility of the king's private service had been transferred definitively to the Privy Chamber (Starkey, 1973, pp. 13–273).

Such, in brief outline, was the institutional position of the men whose activities we are about to study.

The Privy Chamber's ability to represent the king's person took many different forms. At the simplest, they could embody, on one particular issue, that absolute royal will that would not brook nay. Thus, in the autumn of 1532, Anne Boleyn, not Queen Katherine of Aragon, was going to accompany Henry VIII on his state visit to France as virtual royal consort. To underscore the fact, Henry asked Katherine to lend Anne her jewels. The queen refused pointblank, unless "le roi le lui envoyait expressement demander". This the king did, and secured compliance, "par un de sa chambre" (PRO, PRO 31/18/2/1 [LP, V, 1377]).[4] Other examples can easily be given. Ordinarily, the Court of Augmentations was itself responsible for the proper disposal of the ex-monastic lands (Elton, 1962, p. 141). However, its usual processes could be short-circuited by direct royal command, which on several occasions was transmitted by the Privy Chamber. For instance, in March 1540 Richard Browne, a Page of the King's Chamber, was granted a lease of the site of Sallam Monastery in Norfolk, free of any fine, by the king's commandment, as related by William Sherington, Page of the Wardrobe of the Robes and messenger of Anthony Denny, Chief Gentleman of the Privy Chamber (LP, XV, 436/40); in July of that

4. At this time, the French word *chambre*, when it refers to the English court, must be translated by "Privy Chamber".

year Benedict Killegrew got a lease without fine or increment, for which the king's command was carried by Denny in person (*LP*, XV, 942/121); and finally, in January 1546 a major gift to Sir Thomas Moyle was countersigned by the Chancellor of Augmentations "upon the report of your Majesty's pleasure declared to him by Sir William Herbert", Gentleman of the Privy Chamber (*LP*, XXI, i, 148/24). The striking thing is, of course, that in all these cases the mere word of a Gentleman of the Privy Chamber was sufficient evidence in itself for the king's will, without any other form of authentication whatever.

So much for simple messages. On the other hand, the Privy Chamber's representation of the king could be far less specific. Rather than transmitting a straightforward command, they would carry instead the indefinable charisma of monarchy. The point emerges most clearly in their military role. However, before that can be discussed, the king's own position as war-leader must be sketched in. This is well-expressed by a speech put into Henry VIII's mouth by Polydore Vergil. The occasion was a debate between the king and the council about the advisability of Henry's taking personal command of the expedition to France of 1513. The council were opposed to the idea, pointing out both the danger to the royal person and the need for the king's presence within the realm. But Henry overrode them, recalling grandly:

> the many triumphs over their enemies won by his ancestors when they were leading their armies in person, and, on the contrary, the losses sustained many times by the English state when battles had been fought without the King's presence (Hay, 1950, p. 197).

Henry (or better, Polydore) was not necessarily making great claims for the quality of royal generalship[5]; rather he was talking of the psychological effect of the king's presence on the troops.

But, in fact, Henry led his forces in person comparatively infrequently —certainly far less often than either Francis I or Charles V. He had, therefore, to delegate the command of his armies. In this there was a clear division of function. The supreme command in the modern sense tended to fall on a prominent nobleman—usually the Duke of Norfolk or the Duke of Suffolk. The former was a good general; the latter was probably even less competent than Henry himself. At the top level, then, the Privy Chamber had no part to play; instead, their essential contribution came at the second rank of commanders. Their activities as such are best displayed in the Scottish campaign of 1523.

The armies moved forward in the late spring. The general in command

---

5. For a very cool assessment of Henry VIII's own contribution to the campaign of 1513, see Cruickshank, 1969: *passim*, and especially, pp. 206–7.

was Thomas Howard, then earl of Surrey, but soon to become third Duke of Norfolk. Under him were the Marquis of Dorset, Sir William Compton, and Sir William Kingston. The status of Compton and Kingston is clear: the first was Groom of the Stool and head of the Privy Chamber (Starkey, 1973, pp. 69, 73–5), the second was Knight of the Body in the Privy Chamber[6] (ibid., pp. 112–14). Dorset's position, though, is more interesting. He was at that date the only marquis in England, and was also closely tied to the royal family as the son of Edward IV's stepson. These would seem qualifications enough for his post of deputy-commander, but Henry VIII appears to have felt that more was needed. Soon after his arrival in the north, Dorset wrote to the king in somewhat extravagant terms:

> Specially and most humbly thanking your Highness for that it liked the same at my departing from your Grace to admit me as one of your Privy Chamber, which was more to my comfort than if your Grace had given me either fee, land, gold, or silver (BM, Cottonian MS, Caligula B VI, fo. 325 [LP, III, ii, 2955]).

The exact reasons for Dorset's promotion to the Privy Chamber are not stated, but the timing suggests very strongly that his impending military duties and his household appointment were closely linked—perhaps, indeed, that the latter was considered a necessary, or at the least, very desirable qualification for the former.

Thus all the original deputy-commanders of the Scottish expedition were members of the Privy Chamber. While they were on active service we know nothing of their effect, but their departure brought a swift and revealing reaction. Compton spent only a short time in the north: according to Polydore, he was summoned back to court only "a few days" after setting out (Hay, 1950, p. 197). This would seem to be an exaggeration, but certainly he was home by late July (LP, III, ii, 3209). Dorset and Kingston must have returned about the same time, and Surrey was left to battle on alone. Thereafter his letters become increasingly depressed: on 24 September he sent a letter to Wolsey regretting that he no longer had the companies of Dorset, Compton, Kingston, etc. (LP, III, ii, 3360); on 1 October he wrote a formal plea for his discharge—he felt himself decayed in body as well as worn out in purse by the last four years in which he had been continually in the wars (LP, III, ii, 3384); then, eight days later, there came the full outburst, which culminated in the following passage:

> Most humbly beseeching your Grace [i.e. Wolsey] to help that some noblemen and gentlemen of the King's house and the south parts may be sent hither though they bring no great numbers with them. God knoweth, if the poorest

6. A short-lived post, created *ad hoc* in 1519.

gentleman in the King's house were here, and I at London and were advertised of these news, I would not fail to kneel upon my knees before the King's Grace to have licence to come hither in post to be at the day of battle (Ellis, 1824–46, I, pp. 223–7 [*LP*, III, ii, 3405]).

Thus loneliness and a sense of desertion had wrung from Surrey an explicit statement of the role of the royal body servants (i.e. the "noblemen and gentlemen of the King's house") in the English army. First, the fact that their position was symbolic (rather than military in a simple sense) is made clear by the earl's plea that they should be sent even "though they bring no great numbers with them". And second, one of their functions as a symbol —their effect on recruitment—is illustrated vividly by Howard's description of his hypothetical reaction to their appearance at the front had he been in London. However, clear though it is, Surrey's account has its limitations: the special role of the Privy Chamber (in comparison with the other servants of the royal household) is not spelled out; nor is the nature of their symbolic status, or anything like the full range of their symbolic functions. The first omission is, of course, covered by events: as we have seen, Surrey's original deputy-commanders were all Gentlemen of the Privy Chamber, while of the contingent sent in prompt response to his letter of 8 October, the three most prominent—the Marquis of Dorset, Sir Nicholas Carew, and Sir Francis Bryan—were again members of the Privy Chamber (*LP*, III, ii, 3434). But the broader questions of symbolism can, unfortunately, only be answered inferentially. Nevertheless, the issue hardly seems in doubt: the Privy Chamber obviously acted as symbolic representations of the king himself, and their military role, like his, was charismatic: their very presence raised the morale of the troops, and, as Surrey's depression at their absence shows, that of their commanders as well.

So far, we have discussed only partial representations of the king: either the absolute sovereign command, or the charismatic presence. However, the Privy Chamber could also combine the two and stand, in certain circumstances, as a full royal *alter ego*. This is shown most clearly in the one aspect of their symbolic role that had standing at law. Arrest without warrant or commission had been declared illegal in 37 Henry VI (1458–9), except in the king's own presence and by command of his own mouth (Pickthorn, 1934, I, p. 51 note 1). But when the Earl of Northumberland and Walter Walsh, Groom of the Privy Chamber, were sent to arrest Cardinal Wolsey in November 1530, they were given (for some reason) strict orders not to show their commission. Northumberland tried to arrest Wolsey, but the Cardinal refused to submit until he had seen the earl's warrant. An altercation began and continued for some little time; then Wolsey caught sight of Walsh and his attitude changed completely. He turned to him and said:

> I am content to yield unto you . . . [because] you are a sufficient commission yourself . . . in as much as ye be one of the King's Privy Chamber, for the worst person there is a sufficient warrant to arrest the greatest peer of this realm, by the King's only commandment without any commission (Sylvester, 1962, p. 160).

The only explanation for Wolsey's reaction is that he felt Walsh's presence fulfilled—albeit vicariously—the conditions which the fifteenth-century judges had laid down for arrest without warrant. In other words, that as one of the Privy Chamber Walsh was able to represent the very person of the king in both presence and command.

This full representation of monarchy also manifested itself in the diplomacy of the early sixteenth century. At this time, the machinery of foreign relations was undergoing profound change. Much of the revolution has been well studied (cf. Mattingly, 1955), but one important aspect stands in conspicuous neglect. This is the set of conventions that I have labelled "chamber diplomacy". Its nature can best be understood by an examination of the instructions given to Sir Richard Wingfield, the senior of the four Knights of the Body in the Privy Chamber, when he was sent as resident ambassador to the court of Francis I in February 1520. In his first audience with the French king, Wingfield was ordered to explain that although Henry:

> hath been oftentimes plentiously advertized [of Francis I's good and prosperous state etc.], as well by the French King's ambassador and others his familiar gentlemen for the time being making their abode within the King's realm, as also by Sir Thomas Boleyn [the previous English ambassador to France] . . ., yet as well for his further consolation as for to nourish and firmly entertain the said mutual amity, love, and intelligence . . . [Henry had sent one] of his right trusty and near familiars, not only to salute and visit him for the said purpose, but also to notify and declare unto him the King's entire love and affection towards him, to thintent that by renovelling of ambassadors new testimonies may be found . . . of the perseverance of fraternal love on both parts (PRO, SP 1/19, fo. 200 [*LP*, III, i, 629]).

Two assumptions underlie all this: first, that the kingdom was absorbed by the king—that is, that amicable relations between England and France (say) depended only on Henry VIII's being on good terms with his "good brother" Francis I; and second, that the best way for the two king's to preserve their friendship was to meet and embrace each other frequently. But of course that was rarely possible. The instructions, then, are grappling with the problem of providing a substitute for these personal meetings. And the one they put forward is the exchange of the kings' "trusty and near familiars" as ambassadors. Such ambassadors were negotiators only in part; much more, they were symbols of the fact that, circumstances permitting, their kings would themselves have come in their stead. However, the instructions are unclear about the precise status of the "familiars". But the point is not really in doubt. To prescribe that ambassadors should be the king's "right trusty and near familiars" was virtually the same as saying that they should be of the Privy Chamber. And so events proved. For example, between 1520 and 1526, the following were ambassadors to France: Sir Richard Wingfield, Knight of the Body in the Privy Chamber, Sir Richard Jerningham, also Knight of the Body in the Privy Chamber, William Fitzwilliam, who did not belong to the department, Sir Nicholas Carew, Gentleman of the Privy Chamber, and Sir Thomas Cheyney, Gentleman of the Privy Chamber. Thus four out of five ambassadors were of the Privy Chamber, while the one exception—Fitzwilliam—found himself almost forcibly assimilated to the rank by Francis I (BM, Cottonian MS Caligula D, VIII, fos 24–4 [*LP*, III, i, 1202]). But there is no need to rely on the weight of numbers alone: explicit evidence of the importance attached to Privy Chamber office as an ambassadorial qualification is also available. It is supplied by the corrected draft of the instructions given to Jerningham when he was sent to Francis I in August 1520. The first version was worded thus: the ambassador was to thank the French king for having sent:

> as well by letter of his own hand as by sundry of his noblemen and other his familiar servitors to visit him [i.e. Henry VIII] with comfortable words and pleasant messages, ... and for a *reciproque* ... his Highness ... hath sent [him], Sir Richard Jerningham, ... to be resident [ambassador in France].

The following alterations were then made: "his noblemen and other" was crossed out, and the phrase made to run, "by sundry of his familiar servitors of his Privy Chamber"; while after Jerningham's name was inserted the following description: "being of his Secret and Privy Chamber". The whole now read like this: that Francis was to be thanked for having sent:

> as well by letters of his own hand as by sundry of his familiar servitors of his Privy Chamber to visit him [i.e. Henry] with comfortable words and pleasant messages, and for a *reciproque* ... his Highness ... hath sent [him] Sir Richard Jerningham, being of his Secret and Privy Chamber ... (SP 1/21, fos. 20–7 [*LP*, III, i, 936]).

Thus the vagueness of the first draft was replaced by a tight institutional precision that highlights the significance of the French *chambre* (the equivalent of the Privy Chamber) and the English Privy Chamber itself: whoever the king willed could act as ambassador, but only the personnel of these two departments could represent the royal person as it were by definition.

This account of the representative functions of the Privy Chamber could be extended to cover almost all aspects of sixteenth-century government—

especially the crucial area of local government. However, there would be problems. In these other fields there is plenty of evidence of what the Privy Chamber did, but very little of how contemporaries reacted to it. In other words, the symbolic nature of their role, which can be firmly established for their activities in the army, etc., has to be inferred; it cannot be proved. This being so, there seems very little point in continuing a study that must inevitably lose all analytical quality and degenerate instead into a mere census of offices held and missions accomplished. It would be better, in fact, to turn straight away to the mechanics of Privy Chamber symbolism: that is, to a discussion of the circumstances which enabled them to represent the king.

III

Clearly, everything depended on the Privy Chamber's place within the royal household. This has already been sketched in broad outline; it must now be described more carefully.

The Eltham Ordinances of 1526 gave the Privy Chamber the following personnel: six Gentlemen, two Gentlemen Ushers, four Grooms, a Barber, and a Page. As honorific head of the department stood a Nobleman, but its actual working chief remained the Groom of the Stool, who was also counted as one of the six Gentlemen. After 1526 there was very little structural change, apart from the fact that all ranks in the department showed a fairly steady tendency to increase in numbers: in 1526, the total establishment stood at 15; by 1532 it had risen to 24, and by 1539 to 28. But at that latter figure it stabilised (Starkey, 1973, pp. 155, 182–3).

The various offices had appeared at different times, *pari passu* with the department's changing social composition. Originally, under Henry VII, the department had been staffed only by the Groom of the Stool and a handful of other grooms and pages. All were drawn from the middle to lower gentry (Starkey, 1973, pp. 24–55). However, in September 1518 the office of Gentleman was created specifically to accommodate men of the best families. Its first occupants were drawn from the highest reaches of the gentry, from the point at which that class merged almost imperceptibly into the nobility (Starkey, 1973, pp. 80–111). And to underscore the social elevation of the department, within the year the Earl of Devon (the first noble of the blood royal) was appointed to the Privy Chamber as well (Starkey, 1973, pp. 129–31). Such a standard could hardly be maintained consistently, but only a very few of the future recruits to the post of Gentleman were of less than decent gentry status.

Before the creation of the office of Gentleman (soon to be followed by that of Gentleman Usher—Starkey, 1973, pp. 116–17) there could have been relatively little differentiation of function within the department—

apart, of course, from the peculiar duties of the Groom of the Stool which will be discussed shortly. But after 1518–19 the increasingly elaborate hierarchy of office allowed for full specialisation. Overall, there was a broad functional division between the Gentlemen and the rest (which, of course, corresponded to a social distinction as well). The rest consisted of the Barber, who was simply the king's barber; the Page, who was a page in the modern sense of the word—i.e. a favoured young boy; the Grooms, who were (formally at least) the menial servants of the departments; and the Gentlemen Ushers, who were both masters of ceremonies, and in immediate command of the other lesser servants. It was, that is, in the hands of the upper servants of the department that the king's body service in the narrow sense was concentrated. The Gentlemen dressed and undressed the king; waited on him at table; brought him food or drink or anything else he required between meals; arranged the king's bed-time drink; and, finally, took turns to guard over their master's slumbers by sleeping on a pallet mattress on the floor of the Privy Chamber (Starkey, 1973, pp. 168–70). As well as these formal duties, the Gentlemen also served as the king's usual companions in his sports and pastimes: with them he jousted and masked, hunted and hawked, played tennis or cards or even shuffleboard. Henry also found among them many who could share his more cultivated tastes: some were poets and musicians, some builders and gardeners. In one or two cases, the similarity between the King and his Gentlemen went as far as close physical resemblance. The Gentlemen were, in short, more than the king's servants: they were the nearest thing he had to friends (Starkey, 1969, chapter II).

The Groom of the Stool, in his capacity as one of the Gentlemen, shared in all their duties and avocations, but, in addition, he had many important responsibilities that were his alone. These fell into two distinct categories. The first consisted of his original tasks. Their nature is implicit in his title. The earliest clear reference to the office appears in a signet warrant to the Great Wardrobe of 15 November 1497. This ordered the Keeper of the Wardrobe to supply to

> Hugh Denys, Groom of our Stool ... first a stool of timber covered with black velvet and fringed with silk. Item a cushion with two pewter basins and four broad yards of tawny cloth (PRO, E 101/413/11, fo. 37).

Now though the purpose of these articles is not stated, they can only have been intended for the construction of a close-stool or commode. The Groom was therefore, beyond doubt, Groom of the royal close-stool. As such, he was responsible for the manufacture, maintenance and transport of the stool (Starkey, 1973, pp. 251–2); and, above all, for attendance on the king when he made use of it. For example, in 1528, Thomas Heneage, who was acting as assistant to Henry Norris, the Groom proper, wrote to Wolsey to apologise for not having come to see him, but (he explained):

> there is none here but Master Norris and I to give attendance upon the King's Highness when he goeth to make water in his bed chamber (PRO, SP 1/47, fos. 56–7 [*LP*, IV, ii, 4005]).

Again, in 1539, Heneage (by this time Groom himself) reported to Cromwell that Henry had felt the beginnings of a cold; his physicians had given him a pill and a glyster (i.e. an enema), and the king had gone to bed early. He then (so Heneage continued)

> slept unto two of the clock in the morning and then his Grace rose to go to the stool, which, by working of the pills and glyster that his Highness had taken before, had a very fair siege (PRO, SP 1/153, fo. 117 [*LP*, XIV, ii, 153]).

The Groom's intimate connexion with the close-stool received official recognition at Henry VIII's death: in the inventory of the late king's goods, his numerous and lavish collection of close-stools (many covered in embroidered velvet, stuffed with swan's down, and studded with gilt nails) were bracketed together with the marginal annotation that

> all which parcels the said accountant (i.e. Sir Anthony Denny) claimeth to have by virtue of his said office of the Groomship of the Stool at the death of the late King.
> which parcels we the said commissioners do allow to the said Sir Anthony as pertaining to his said office (PRO, E 101/427/2).

The charge of the close-stool and attendance on the king when he used it were, no doubt, the sum total of the duties of the pre-Tudor Groom of the Stool. However, with the development of the Privy Chamber and his acquisition of the leading role in it,[7] the Groom had been saddled with his second and correspondingly more varied class of functions. First, the Groom was the sole servant of the royal bed-chamber and the other most private rooms: this again is made absolutely clear by the Eltham Ordinances of 1526, which provided that Henry Norris should occupy the place of Sir William Compton:

> not only giving his attendance as Groom of the King's Stool but also in his bed-chamber and other privy places as shall stand with his pleasure.

7. Here, as elsewhere, I am deliberately simplifying a complex process: under Henry VII, the Groom had been unquestionably the head officer of the Privy Chamber. However, in 1518–19 (as we have seen), for the first time men of really high social rank were put into the Privy Chamber. This meant that the Groom was now at most a first among equals. His position was not fully resolved until the early 1530's when the office of Chief Gentleman of the Privy Chamber, which carried with it the unquestioned headship of the department, was borrowed from the French court and given to the Groom. Henceforth, the two offices, though formally distinct, were invariable invested in the same person (Starkey, 1973, pp. 231–47).

Into the bed-chamber and other such rooms, none of the other servants of the Privy Chamber were "to presume to enter or follow his Grace", save by the king's specific command. At night, the Groom slept on a pallet mattress at the foot of the king's bed (Starkey, 1973, pp. 130, 264–5).

Second—and by natural extension of the first—the Groom was the king's invariable attendant wherever he went: at the beginning of the reign, when Henry rode *incognito* in a joust, his only companion was the Groom, Sir William Compton (Hall, 1809, p. 513); and at the end, in 1540, in one order of procession drawn up for the reception of Anne of Cleves, Heneage is shown completely out of precedence, riding immediately before the king himself (*LP*, XV, 10).

Third, the Groom was the king's supremely confidential messenger: above all, he handled communications between the king and queen. Thus, after Katherine Howard's arrest, Cranmer reported that about 6 p.m. she fell into another pang of grief, exclaiming that at that hour the king used to send to know how she did by Mr. Heneage (PRO, SP 1/167, fos 134–40 [*LP*, XVI, 1325]). As well, the Groom seems to have acted as intermediary between Henry and his mistresses: early in the reign, Compton was suspected of carrying on an intrigue on his master's behalf with the Duke of Buckingham's sister (*LP*, I, i, 474); while many years later, Mrs. Amadas, the wife of the Master of the Jewels, alleged that Norris was bawd between the king and Ann Boleyn (*LP*, VI, 923).

Fourth, the Groom regulated access to the king: in 1530, a delegation from Oxford, headed by the vice-chancellor, arrived at court to sue for the continuance of Cardinal College. But, "by reason of the great business that the King had and scarcity of friends", the academics were kept kicking their heels about the palace for eleven days; then Norris took pity on them, and they were with the king in a few hours (PRO, SP 1/57, fos 300–1 [*LP*, IV, iii, 6539]). Conversely, the Groom could deny the presence if he wished (e.g. PRO, SP 3/6, fo. 71 [*LP*, VI, 1352]).

Fifth, all the preceding meant that the Groom had to be permanently near the king: consequently his lodgings at court were directly under the Privy Chamber, to which they were linked by a private staircase (Starkey, 1973, pp. 265–7).

Sixth, and finally, the Groom had become a major administrative officer: he was in charge of such of the king's jewels and plate as were in daily use; of his linen, and of the furnishings and equipment of the private apartments in general. Above all, he was *ex officio* Keeper of the Privy Purse, and had, as well, important secretarial functions (Starkey, 1973, pp. 254–62, 309–56, 357–413).

The Groom's duties thus ranged from the most intimate physical attendance on the person of the sovereign to the management of the large and elaborate administrative machine on which depended the comfort of the king's daily life. Almost necessarily, therefore, the Groom occupied a special place in the royal regard. True, paucity of evidence means that we know nothing of Henry VII's relationship with his Groom, Hugh Denys, but all Henry VIII's Grooms (with the possible exception of Thomas Heneage) were prime favourites. First came Compton: in 1510 the Spanish ambassador described him as the *privado* or favourite (*LP*, I, i, 474), and a year later, in 1511, the French ambassador insisted that he enjoyed more "crédict" with Henry than anyone else (PRO, PRO 31/3/1 [*LP*, I, i, 734]). Compton's successor, Henry Norris, was "du roy le mieulx aimé" (Crapelet, 1835, p. 184); while of Anthony Denny, the last Groom of the reign, Leland wrote that whole court bore testimony to his "gratia flagrans" (Leland, 1770, V, pp. 151–2).

It would now probably be as well to pick out the main threads in this account of the Privy Chamber. It consisted of a smallish group of men who had many features in common: generally, they came from good families; were similar in tastes and disposition to the king, and stood high in his regard; above all, however, they enjoyed an institutionally-defined and exclusive intimacy with their sovereign as his body servants. All this applies equally to the Groom of the Stool, the head of the Privy Chamber, save that both his favour and his intimacy with Henry were correspondingly greater than the other Gentlemen's. Obviously, each one of these points played a part in the representative capacity of the Privy Chamber. The fact that they were in frequent and friendly contact with the king made it likely that he would employ them in his business; while the fact that they were of good family made such employment acceptable to the subject. But other members of the court shared in these sorts of qualities: what was peculiar to the Privy Chamber, what was theirs alone, was physical intimacy with the king. Only they were his body servants. On this the Eltham Ordinances are unequivocal. They ordered absolutely that "no person of what estate, degree, or condition so ever he be", who was not of the staff of the Privy Chamber, should "from henceforth presume . . . to come or repair into the King's Privy Chamber", except by the king's specific command (Bodleian, Laudian MS Miscellaneous 597, fo. 24 [*HO*, 154]). And if none but the Privy Chamber were even allowed into the apartment, much less could they wait on the king's person. Similarly, as we have seen, the supremely intimate personal services of the bed-chamber were the exclusive prerogative of the Groom of the Stool, as distinct from the other Gentlemen. The essential point can thus be expressed as a formal syllogism. Privy Chamber office is defined (through the limitation of the *entrée* to the private apartments) in terms of the right to give intimate attendance on the king; but the ability to represent the king's person in its fulness is limited to the Privy Chamber; so representation itself must depend on intimacy. Intimacy, that is, is the vehicle through which the Privy Chamber symbolise the king.

But the vehicle was itself a symbol, with two distinct sets of meanings: one sacred, the other profane. The first can best be understood by a glance at the practices of the late mediaeval church. These were dominated by a profound literalism, which stressed the need for a material channel or intermediary for the transfer of divine virtue: thus the apostolic succession was a long chain of the laying-on of hands, going back to Christ himself; while every relic had acquired its powers, either by being part of the body of a saint or martyr, or by having been in contact with such a body. And of course, the concept of a channel of grace was an awkward one: in practice it was much easier to assume that the object or action itself possessed magical properties (cf. Thomas, 1973, pp. 27–57). Naturally, the king's healing powers operated within this context: he cured scrofula, as we have seen, by actual touch—by the laying-on of hands; while in the case of the second royal miracle the position is set out fully in the Marian ritual. This described the moment of the consecration of the cramp-rings as follows:

> the king's highness rubbeth the rings between his hands, saying: "Sanctify, O Lord, these rings, . . . and consecrate them by the rubbing of our hands, which thou hast been pleased according to our ministry to sanctify by an external effusion of holy oil upon them (Crawfurd, 1917, p. 186).

The literalism is transparent: the king's hands had been annointed at his coronation and hence were holy; they then rubbed off their benediction onto the metal. Thus, though there is no formal contemporary evidence on the point, there can be little doubt that in the intimate physical contact of body service the royal charisma was felt to rub off onto the servant, who thereby became himself endowed with part of the royal virtue.

The secular symbolism of intimacy is more directly vouched for. In Sir John Harrington's *Metamorphoses of Ajax* (a "jakes" = a privy), which was published in 1596 as a puff for its author's invention of a primitive water-closet, there appears the following comment:

> it is a token of special kindness, to this day among the best men in France, to reduce a syllogism in Bocardo together. Insomuch as I have heard it seriously told, that a great magnifico of Venice, being ambassador in France, and hearing a noble person was come to speak with him, made him stay till he had untied his points [the equivalent of braces], and when he was new set on his stool sent for the nobleman to come to him at that time—as a very special favour (Harrington, 1962, p. 91).

In other words, so Harrington claimed, "reducing a syllogism in Bocardo together" was a well-understood social symbol or convention for the expression of mutual regard and confidence. True, the custom is described as French, and, by implication, as unknown and even ludicrous in England. But this last point needs careful qualification. The kind of contact that would appear to have become unthinkable between equals (for that is the situation Harrington posits) still remained possible between master and servant. Indeed, involvement in the business of evacuation was a usual feature of late-mediaeval body service. Thus John Russell in his *Book of Nurture* (*c*. 1452) includes the following instructions in his account of "the office of a chamberlain" (i.e. a bed-chamber servant):

> See the privy-house for easement be fair, soot,[8] and clean;
> And that the boards thereupon be covered with cloth fair and green;
> And the hole himself, look there no board be seen;
> Thereon a fair cushion, the ordure no man to teen.[9]
> Look there be blanket, cotton, or linen to wipe the nether end,
> And ever he clepith,[10] wait rady and entende,[11]
> Basin and ewer, and on your shoulder a towel . . .
>   (Furnival, 1868, p. 179).

Even this passage, however, suggests that the master relieved himself alone, only calling in the "chamberlain" when he required to wash his hands. But royal etiquette was different. As we have seen, the early-Tudor Groom of the Stool regularly attended the king when he made use of the stool, while as late as 1689 the groom (William III's great favourite, the Earl of Portland) was still charged with the duty. This is shown clearly by the Bed-Chamber Ordinances issued in that year, which stipulate that:

> none of our Bed-Chamber whatsoever are to follow us into our secret or privy room, when we go to ease ourself, but only our Groom of the Stool (BM, Stowe MS 563, fos. 14v–15).

Thus, *pace* Harrington, the intimacy of the Privy survived in the English court and was therefore as available for symbolic use as it was in France.

And it was indeed so used. The earliest instance I have found is in Sir Thomas More's *History of King Richard III*, which was written in about 1513, though not fully printed until 1557. The passage in question is the famous one in which Sir James Tyrell is suggested to the king as one likely to rid him of the Princes in the Tower. Richard had already ordered the Lieutenant of the Tower to kill the boys, but the lieutenant had refused.

8. = sweet (*OED*).
9. = vex or annoy (*OED*).
10. = calls (*OED*).
11. = prompt (?).

News of his refusal was brought to the king, who was alone at the time, save for "a secret page". Richard mused angrily on the lieutenant's betrayal of his confidence, asking aloud, "who shall a man trust?" The page spotted his opportunity. He had long noticed that Tyrell was an ambitious man who had been deliberately kept back by the king's two principal confidants. So, taking Richard's rhetorical question as a real one, he said:

> "Sir, . . . there lieth one on your pallet without that I dare well say to do your Grace pleasure the thing were right hard that he would refuse"—meaning this by Sir James Tyrell (More, 1963, p. 83).

Now there are, as has been pointed out (cf. Kendall, 1968, pp. 398–406 etc.), many inconsistencies and even impossibilities in this story, but its truth or falsehood is not an issue here. All that matters is the setting: More makes the conversation between Richard and his page take place while the king was "sitting at the draught". As symbolism, this is brilliant, if a little too complex for our purpose. By one deft stroke, More underlines the confidentiality of the page, the confidentiality of the conversation, and the foulness of the deed that was plotted in so foul a place. All that is missing is a direct link between the symbolism and the Privy Chamber, but that is (of course) inevitable, as in Richard III's reign the department did not yet exist.

The second example was written nearly a century after the *History of King Richard III*. It comes from John Marston's comedy, *The Parasitaster or the Fawn*, of 1606. In it, one of the characters says:

> "Thou art private with the duke; thou belongest to his close-stool" (cited in Chambers, 1923, I, p. 53 note 1).

This then is straightforward: connexion with the close-stool of a princely personage—close-stool clearly having, as in the English royal household, both a physical and an institutional sense—is used explicitly as a symbol of confidentiality.

Two examples seem very few. Others may exist, but I have been unable to find them. In any case, however, the two we have are really sufficient. More uses the privy symbolism quite casually, with no special apology or explanation. But—and this is decisive—in the second instance, the whole reference begins and ends in a dozen words that come in the middle of a quick-fire dialogue. The allusion must therefore have been instantaneously comprehensible, which in turn must mean that the symbol was either a common-place figure of speech, or at least a fairly normal usage.

All this applies directly only to the Groom of the Stool. However, body service in general clearly carried the same overall sense as attendance at the close-stool—though naturally to a lesser degree. Thus membership of the Privy Chamber *in itself* symbolised confidentiality. This emerges quite plainly from Henry VIII's instructions to Ralph Sadler when he was sent as ambassador to Scotland in 1537. The instructions directed that Sadler:

> shall, as of himself, affirm to the King of Scots, that being he of his uncle's [i.e. Henry VIII's] Privy Chamber, and of long season acquainted with his proceedings, he knoweth the King his master's true meaning, upright dealing, and proceedings to be of such reason, truth and innocency, as he wisheth all the world might know the ground and very secrecies thereof (*LP*, XIII, i, 1313).

Of course (and the instructions exploited the fact with complete cynicism) such confidentiality greatly reinforced the credibility and hence the effectiveness of the messenger.

The double operation of intimacy is now clear. On the one hand, through their bodily contact with the king, the Privy Chamber became in themselves the direct symbols or respresentations of the charismatic aspects of royalty. This was the mystical basis of their personification of the king. On the other hand, their intimate attendance on Henry served as a symbol of the high place that they held in his confidence, as men with whom he shared his inmost thoughts. This confidentiality was in turn what we could call the rational basis of their role as royal *alter ego*. But—and the fact cannot be too much emphasised—symbolism is equally significant in both the mystical and the rational forms of representation.

Such, therefore, was the machinery of Privy Chamber symbolism. But so far we have discussed the machinery without the motor. At the heart of the pattern of symbolism lay a particular attitude to the royal body service. Under Henry VIII, there is no contemporary comment—autobiographical or otherwise—on the Gentlemen's duties; instead, we must argue back from their known public standing. This is unequivocal: they were not mere powers behind the curtain or an early kitchen cabinet; on the contrary, they enjoyed the highest general esteem. Indeed, by the middle of Henry's reign the Privy Chamber was usually paired with the Privy Council itself as the second element in the constellation of power. Thus, in Cromwell's list of "certain persons to be had at this time in the King's most benign remembrance", which dates from the beginning of 1538, the Privy Council are listed first, followed immediately by "the Privy Chamber" (BM, Cottonian MS Titus B I, fo. 497 [*LP*, XIII, i, 1]). Again, two years later in 1540, the king and queen went on a short winter progress, accompanied by only four members of the Privy Council and "the Ladies, Gentlemen, and Gentlewomen of their Privy Chambers" (Nicolas, 1834–7, VII, 89[*LP*, XVI, 325]); and finally, as the king's life ebbed away in December 1546, the court was closed to all "but his councillors and three or four Gentlemen of his [Privy] Chamber" (Bergenroth, 1862–1954, VIII, 370 [*LP*, XXI, ii, 605]). All this is striking enough, but the decisive argument comes (as ever) with the extreme case. The Groom of the Stool had (to our eyes) the most menial tasks; his standing, though, was the highest: by act of Parliament of 1541 he was recognised as an officer of state of the second rank (Luders, 1810–28, III, 867); and by early 1547 he was *ex-officio* a Privy Councillor (*LP*, XXI, ii, 634/i). Clearly, then, the royal body service must have been seen as entirely honourable, without a trace of the demeaning or the humiliating.

This position was formalised by the Barons of the Exchequer in June–July 1573 when they gave judgment in Sir Thomas Wroth's case. They declared that the officers of the Privy Chamber gave service "not merely to the body natural" of the Prince (like the king's physician, or surgeon, or music-master) but "to the Majesty of the body politic, . . . which includes the body natural" (Plowden, 1816, p. 455a). That is, the Privy Chamber's private service had an acknowledged public dimension, which meant of course that it was honourable—indeed, that it demanded men of the highest station:

> for the royal Majesty requires officers of honour, who understand the honour-
> able service that is due to Majesty, and such ought to be men not only of
> accomplished carriage and deportment, but also of great skill, understanding,
> and experience (*loc. cit.*).

But of course fetching and carrying, dressing and undressing, were not the ordinary occupations of noblemen and gentlemen. Usually, such things were considered as unworthy as we should think them to be. The point was that the Privy Chamber did them for the king, and he (as we have seen) was "not . . . a man but . . . a more excellent and divine estate". The effect this had is succinctly stated in George Herbert's lines, which deal with the service of an even greater monarch than Henry Tudor:

> Teach me, my God and King,
> In all things thee to see,
> And what I do in any thing,
> To do it as for thee
>
> . . .
>
> All may of thee partake:
> Nothing can be so mean,
> Which with this tincture (for thy sake)
> Will not grow bright and clean.
>
> A servant with this clause
> Makes drudgery divine:
> Who sweeps a room, as for thy laws,
> Makes that and th'action fine (Herbert, 1953, pp. 184–5).

The title of the section of *The Temple* from which these verses are taken is *The Elixir*. In it, the name of God is seen as an agent of transformation, through which the vile becomes honourable. Similarly, the numinous powers of a king—that god upon earth—transmuted the humblest act of personal attendance into something worthy of the best blood in the kingdom. Indeed, we can go further. With the king, the ordinary social conventions were actually inverted, and the more minutely personal the attendance, the more honourable it was. This is shown clearly enough by the status of the Groom of the Stool; but the point is driven home harder by the Eltham Ordinances. These stipulate that only the Gentlemen of the Privy Chamber shall dress the king:

> and that none of the said Grooms or Ushers do approach or presume . . . to lay hands upon his royal person (Bodleian, Laudian MS Miscellaneous 597, fo. 26 [*HO*, 156]).

Thus the king's body is seen, consciously and deliberately, as sacred flesh which only those of high rank are fit to touch.

And so the argument comes full circle. Intimacy—to which we have attached so much importance—could do nothing of itself: it could function as a publicly-acknowledged symbol only so long as the divine attributes of monarchy purged the royal body service of anything which savoured of the menial or servile.

This proposition has been derived from our analysis of the Privy Chamber at the height of its importance; it can be further tested by a discussion of the history of the Privy Chamber and its successor department in the two hundred years following Henry VIII's death.

Until the late seventeenth century, the early-Tudor position remained essentially in force. Despite rebellion and revolution the reverence for monarchy continued (at least formally), while the structure of the royal household indeed experienced a change of name (the Bed-Chamber replaced the Privy Chamber under James I), but little change of substance. The fundamental continuity emerges clearly from William III's Bed-Chamber Ordinances of 1689 (BM, Stowe MS 563). These have a double importance. On the one hand, they show that the Groomship of the Stool was still very much an office of personal body service: as we have already seen, the groom was to attend the king when he relieved himself (ibid. fos 14v–15); as well, he was to put on the shirt which the king wore next to his skin; he alone (apart from the king) held the key of the private apartments; and finally, he might lodge in the King's Bed-Chamber, if he so wished (ibid. fos 5, 7v, 10). Conversely, the Ordinances established the Groomship of the Stool at the peak of its public dignity. It now stood out as the third great office of the royal household (after the Lord Stewardship and the Lord Chamberlainship), complete (like the two senior posts) with a fully developed official symbolism of its own. The symbol chosen was a "gold key on a blue ribbon", which, as the Ordinances provided, "our Groom of the Stool may wear . . . as a badge of his office" (ibid. fo. 7v). Like the other major symbols of office—the white staves of the Lord Treasurer, the Lord Steward, or the Lord Chamberlain, or the seals of the Lord Chancellor, the Lord Privy Seal, or the Secretaries of States—the key functioned in three principal ways: first, appointment to the office was symbolised by handing over the key. This point is made explicitly by the Ordinances of 1689 which state that when:

> We first constitute [the Groom of the Stool] in the said office, it shall be by Our delivery to him of a gold key . . ., which shall be a sufficient warrant to our Lord Chamberlain or Lord Steward to swear him in the said place (ibid. fo. 7v).

Second, the fact that one held the post was signalled by wearing the key. This, as we have seen, figured in the Ordinance as well. And third, dismissal or resignation was represented by the surrendering of the key back into the king's hands. This is not touched on by the 1689 Ordinance, but it emerges clearly enough from innumerable incidents throughout the eighteenth century. For instance, in 1734 Lord Chesterfield recommended a household reshuffle, for which the way should be cleared "by taking the gold key from that cypher, Lord Godolphin" (Croker, 1824, II, pp. 82–3).[12]

The symbol chosen was dignified: it was also singularly appropriate. As we have seen at length, the Groom was both in frequent and intimate attendance on the sovereign, and as well was an important agent in procuring access to the king for others. These attributes were so well expressed by the ideas associated with a key that the name of the symbol effectively replaced the name of the office in ordinary parlance (cf. Cowper, 1864, pp. 147, 155, 157, 164, 166). This usage led to many comments whose meaning vibrates interestingly between the literal (i.e. key as object and symbol) and the metaphorical (i.e. key as means of access to someone, as in "keys of my heart"). One of the most explicit of these references comes at the beginning of George I's reign, when Peter Wentworth thought that the Duke of Argyll was:

> very wise in accepting the Key to the Prince for it will give him frequenter access to court than the junto men care for (cited in Beattie, 1967, p. 3).

The use of a key as the symbol of an office of intimate attendance is a general one, to be found at widely scattered times and places. For instance, until the reign of the present Pope, the papal chamberlains had a large key

12. See also Cowper, 1864, p. 157.

embroidered on their backs, while Henry III of France, in order to increase the status of his *gentilshommes de chambre*, directed "qu'ils portassent la clef d'or pour marque de leur dignite" (Loyseau, 1701, p. 229; cf. also, Firth, 1973).

Thus in these Ordinances of 1689 the developments we have been studying reached their apotheosis: private body service and great public power and position were fused, and, simultaneously, the fusion was expressed in the vivid symbolism of the key. But the apotheosis was short-lived. In fact, its very existence depended on the customary time-lag between the occurrence of events and the full realisation of their implications. The Revolution of 1688 had shattered for ever the concept of a divine-right monarchy in England: henceforth, the king was simply first servant of the state. By the early eighteenth century this fact was beginning to sink in. The consequences for the royal Bed-chamber were immediate and striking. Two essential points stand out. First, the actual service of the royal person was abandoned by the noble Lords and Ladies of the Bed-chamber[13] and transferred instead to the department's humbler servants. This fact is (it seems to me) obscured in the standard account of the early Hanoverian court (Beattie, 1967); nevertheless, it emerges clearly enough from contemporary documents. Most precise of all is the account dictated to Dr. Arbuthnot by Mrs. Masham, sometime Bed-chamber Woman and later Groom of the Stool to Queen Anne:

> The bedchamber-*woman* came into waiting before the queen's prayers, which was before her majesty was dressed. The queen often shifted in the morning: if her majesty shifted at noon, the bedchamber-*lady* being by, the bedchamber-*woman* gave the shift to the lady without any ceremony, and the *lady* put it on. Sometimes, likewise, the bedchamber-*woman* gave the fan to the *lady* in the same manner; and this was all that the bedchamber-*lady* did about the queen at her dressing.
>
> When the queen washed her hands, the page of the back-stairs brought and set down upon a side-table the basin and ewer, then the bedchamber-woman set it before the queen, and knelt on the other side of the table over-against the queen, the bedchamber-lady only looking on. The bedchamber-woman poured the water out of the ewer upon the queen's hands (Croker, 1824, I, pp. 292–3).

Thus, there was a clear distinction between the actual body service of the Bed-chamber Woman and the largely honorific attendance of the Lady of the Bed-chamber. In the case of the Groom of the Stool—the Chief Lady of the Bed-chamber—the tendency was carried still further. For example, when the Countess of Pembroke, Lady of the Bed-chamber to Queen

13. The Queen's Bed-chamber (staffed by Ladies, etc.) paralleled the King's, and, as it happens, is much the better documented in the first half of the eighteenth century; accordingly, most of my examples will be drawn from it.

Caroline, was angling for the Groomship of the Stool, she explained that

> the uncertainty of my health, and being obliged to be, on my brother's account,
> so much in the country, would make it excessively convenient to me (Thomson,
> 1847, II, p. 248).

The impression that gives of a post with the lightest of responsibilities is
confirmed by Lady Suffolk's account of her first week as Groom of the
Stool in 1734:

> Seven nights quiet sleep, and seven easy days have almost worked a miracle
> upon me ... I shall now often visit Marble Hill: my time is become very
> much my own ... I have at this time a great deal of business upon my hands,
> but not from my court employment (Croker, 1824, II, pp. 1–3).

In short, we find a hierarchy of non-functioning, with the Women (or
Grooms) doing much; the Ladies (or Gentlemen) doing a little; and the
Groom of the Stool doing almost nothing at all.

But the development of the highest Bed-chamber offices into near sine-
cures was only the first change. There was, secondly, a clear alteration in
the attitude towards the royal body service. Lady Suffolk again provides
the test case. As plain Mrs. Howard she was Principal Bed-chamber
Woman to Queen Caroline; then, in 1731, on her husband's succeeding to
the Earldom of Suffolk, she became Groom of the Stool. Relations between
Mrs. Howard and the Queen were always delicate as the former was the
King's mistress; tension, however, came to a head when the Queen asked
her new Groom of the Stool to hold the basin in the ceremony of the royal
dressing. According to Caroline herself (as reported by Lord Hervey) Lady
Suffolk told her

> with her little fierce eyes and cheeks as red as your coat, that positively she
> would not do it (Hervey, 1848, II, p. 16).

The background to the incident is filled in by Horace Walpole's comment
in his *Reminiscences* that

> from the Queen Mrs Howard tasted many positive vexations. Till she became
> Lady Suffolk she constantly dressed the Queen's head, who delighted in sub-
> jecting her to such servile offices, though always apologizing to "her good
> Howard" (cited in Hervey, 1848, II, p. 16 note 11).

Obviously, then, as both Lady Suffolk's anger and Walpole's use of the
phrase "servile offices" shows, the monarch's body service had lost all
special quality and become a merely menial task, as humiliating and
unworthy as personal attendance on anyone else.[14]

14. See also below, p. 219 note 15.

Thus, the attitude to royal body service provides a precise index to the general attitude to kingship. Under the Tudors, Lady Suffolk's indignant reaction would have been unthinkable, because the king was simply not on the same plane as even the greatest of his subjects. Rather, he was different in substance. Under the Hanoverians, on the other hand, the monarch was still head of the social pyramid, but he differed from his peers in degree, not in kind.

The abandonment of the royal body service and the concomitant disdain for it brought its own revenge. Now that they had ceased to be the King or Queen's domestic servants, the Gentlemen and Ladies of the Bed-chamber found their relations with their sovereign becoming progressively less intimate. Already, in April 1716, the Duchess of St. Alban's, Groom of the Stool to the Princess of Wales, "huffed [her mistress] about her not being always with her" as formal etiquette demanded (Cowper, 1864, p. 109). Twenty years later, things had gone much further: as Queen Caroline was dying (in 1737) she was attended by three Woman of the Bed-chamber, while "none of her Ladies of her Bed-Chamber were admitted at all" (Hervey, 1848, II, p. 496).

Thus the first half of the eighteenth century saw a transformation in both the functions of Bed-chamber office and what, for want of a better word, can be called its ideology. From being posts of great intrinsic weight, Bed-chamber Lordships became mere indices of status won in other ways and for other reasons; they were important in themselves only because they conferred the right of access to the sovereign. The consequent tension between past duties and present situation was common to all the upper reaches of the bed-chamber, but it was particularly acute in the case of the Groom of the Stool. Moreover, the peculiar title of the post (which cried aloud for explanation) permitted the tension to come to the surface. The Groom's abandonment of personal attendance of the king of course meant that the name became an anachronism. But anachronism can be lived with. The real problem was the new attitude towards body service. This made the proper meaning of "stool" appear as an impossible vulgarism, wholly inappropriate to the dignity of the great nobleman by whom the office was always held. And so the search for a euphemism began. The earliest attempt seems to have been made by Edward Chamberlayne in his *Angliae Notitiae*, the first edition of which was published in 1669. Without a shred of justification from even the highly variable Tudor orthography, he spelled "stool" as "stole"; then, on the basis of this mis-spelling, he erected an elegant fantasy. The First Gentleman of the Bedchamber (he tells us) was called

Groom of the Stole, that is (according to the signification of the word in

Greek, from whence first the Latins, and thence the Italian and French derive it) Groom or servant of the Robe or Vestment: he having the office and honour to present and put on his Majesty's first garment or shirt every morning, and to order the things of the Bed-chamber (Chamberlayne, 1669, pp. 249–50).

Thus, the idea that personal attendance on the sovereign was honourable was still alive, but only just. In order to conform to the new sense of propriety, the publicly acknowledged content of body service had had to be changed. The lavatorial reality of the office—still clearly apparent in the Bed-chamber Ordinances of twenty years later—was suppressed, and instead attention was concentrated on the one disinfected gesture of putting on the royal shirt.

The *Angliae Notitiae*, which soon became a periodical publication (like an early *Who's Who*), enjoyed an immense success and had a corresponding influence. Accordingly, it laid down the whole pattern of interpretation of the Groomship for the next hundred years or more. But by the early nineteenth century a shift is noticeable. Dod's *Manual of Dignities* (first published in 1842) informed its readers that the office of

"Groom of the Stole" is usually combined with the duties of the Mistress of the Robes when a female sovereign is on the throne . . . The Stole is a narrow vest, lined with crimson sarcenet, and was formerly embroidered with roses, fleurs-de-lis, and crowns; but the office of Groom is a sinecure (Dod, 1842, p. 138).

And of course, though Dodd does not mention the point explicitly, the stole in question was part of the coronation regalia. This explanation of the Groomship is manifest nonsense: the Groom never had any connexion with the coronation regalia (whether the stole or anything else); and indeed, in only one coronation (that of Edward VI) did he have any official part to play at all (Leland, 1770, IV, p. 326). Thus, while Dodd's ideas about the Groom clearly derive from Chamberlayne's, they are on a different level of unreality altogether. The reason is suggested by the last line of the extract from the *Manual*, with its assertion that "the office of Groom is a sinecure". In the late seventeenth century, the fact that the Groom still had a role in body service—that he still put on the royal shirt—had given Chamberlayne's mythical etymology a solid anchorage. By the last Hanoverians, however, the Groom had long abandoned even this limited degree of personal attendance: so, in default of any discernible official functions, fantasy was given—indeed, was obliged to assume—the reins.

As a complete, inexplicable, and very well-paid sinecure, the Groomship was peculiarly vulnerable in the early nineteenth century. Popular contempt for the court (probably best exemplified in John Wade's *Extra-*

ordinary Black Book)[15] was combining with the official pursuit of economy to press for a pruning of the luxuriant royal household. In 1831, a Select Committee of the House of Commons recommended that the salaries of the leading household officers (including of course the Groom of the Stool) should be cut by between a third and a quarter—that is, in the case of the Groom, from £2,163 to £1,500. Nothing was done at the time (*British Parliamentary Papers*, 1801–52, XXIII, pp. 27 ff.), but with the accession of Victoria six years later full effect was given to the recommendations. Indeed, things went further, and, as a new Select Committee reported:

> it is not proposed to fill up the office of Groom of the Stole, or to create any analogous office in the Household of her Majesty (loc. cit.).

The decision was conveyed to the House by the Chancellor of the Exchequer, Thomas Rice, who drew a favourable comparison between the present economy, and the extravagance of the provision for Sarah, Duchess of Marlborough, under Anne. As he read out the list of offices held by the duchess—Keeper of the Privy Purse, Groom of the Stole, and First Lady of the Bed-chamber—the mention of the Groomship was follwed by "a laugh" (*The Times*, 24 November 1837, p. 3 col. 2). Since *The Times's* leader on Rice's speech made no mention of the abolition of the post, that anonymous laugh must stand as the last recorded comment on the Groomship of the Stool.

The story of the Bed-chamber in decline is therefore the mirror image of the Privy Chamber at the peak of its importance. The key to both is intimacy. As the Gentlemen, etc. of the Bed-chamber ceased to be the king's body servants, so their importance in all spheres declined—with the decline, in the case of the Groomship of the Stool, going as far as the abolition of the office. But the servants of the Chamber or Privy Chamber had suffered similar declines in the past. What was new was the monarch's loss of numinous powers: the last English sovereign to touch for the King's evil was Anne (1702–14) (Thomas, 1973, p. 228), and by the later eighteenth century even Boswell, inveterate monarchist that he was, could comment thus slightingly on that:

15. His comments on the Groomship are as follows:
Here is another of those courtly offices, which ought to be abolished, augmenting unnecessarily the expediture of the civil list. It is not sufficient to say these costly appendages are essential to support the royal dignity. The dignity of the crown is a senseless sound, unless tending to increase the respect and veneration of the people; but mere pageantry, in an enlightened age, can have no such effect: it only revolts the mind from an institution, obviously maintained in useless state, by a sacrifice of the general welfare ... To what public purport, or private gratification of the king, are the offices of groom of the stole, master of the hawks, master of the buck-hounds, master of the horse, or grooms and lords of the bedchamber? These are menial offices, and unbecoming the dignity of a nobleman, if endowed with the genuine feelings of nobility (Wade, 1832, p. 497).

superstitious notion which, it is wonderful to think, prevailed so long in this country, as to the virtue of the royal touch (Boswell, 1953, p. 32).

This loss of royal divinity[16] meant that the role of intimacy itself was devalued. It could no longer serve as a road to public greatness. Thus the Women and Grooms of the Bed-chamber (who, save under George I, were now the monarch's real body servants) never acquired any formally-acknowledged power—however great the influence that some of them (for example, Mrs. Clayton, Woman of the Bed-chamber to Queen Caroline— Thomson, 1847) might exercise behind the scenes. This failure of the lower servants of the Bed-chamber to secure promotion was decisive. It ensured that no successor department to the Bed-chamber emerged as, in similar circumstances, the Bed-chamber had displaced the Privy Chamber, and, earlier still, the Privy Chamber itself had displaced the Chamber. With the ending of this process of institutional shelling-off, the household's whole existing line of development came to an end as well. There was a brief moment of marking time at the beginning of the nineteenth century; then a violent change of direction. From about 1837 the household's establishment was drastically reduced and its departmental structure simplified until, by the end of Victoria's reign, it had become the comparatively modest and essentially private entourage that exists today.

It is now time to summarise our argument. Clearly, what we have been studying is a coherent and developed system of symbolism, centred on the human body: the king's person was the most expressive symbol of his office; the persons of his body servants were the fullest representations of their master; and finally, the mechanism by which this latter representation was achieved—the symbolism of intimate attendance—was a type of body symbolism as well. Indeed, in its "rational" aspect, it is a particularly straightforward and well-documented case of Mary Douglas's "purity rule", whereby "social distance tends to be expressed in distance from physiological origins and vice versa" (Douglas, 1973, p. 12). But though these bodily symbols are natural in their origin, their meanings are in no sense natural or inherent. Rather, as we have insisted, the functions of all these symbols—above all, the most "natural" of body service—depended on their operating within the context of a semi-divine and intensely personal monarchy. Once that context disappeared, the symbols lost their meaning. Or better, their meaning changed, for the symbols connected with the monarch's person and domestic service are still very much alive. The veil

16. Of course, as Thomas points out (1973, p. 230), belief in the thaumaturgical powers of monarchy persisted—fragmentarily—until far into the nineteenth century. But it persisted among the lower classes; the attitude of the upper classes (which alone concerns us) changed, as the text insists and Thomas (ibid., pp. 239–40) confirms, in the eighteenth century.

of silence which blankets the everyday life of royalty; the impenetrable
secrecy of the royal palaces (so different from the promiscuous crowds of
Tudor Whitehall or Hampton Court); the extraordinary anonimity of the
servants of the royal household—all symbolise, vividly and precisely, the
absolute separation between the sovereign as an individual and the sovereign as a public figure that is the key-stone of the monarchy's constitutional
position in modern England. However, the point is made most strikingly
by the most intimate bodily function of all—evacuation. In the sixteenth
century, the Groom of the Stool's highly personal job as the royal lavatory
attendant was the foundation for his rise to public power and influence.
Now, on the other hand, the monarch's relieving of him or herself is so
awesomely private that one of the usual preparations for a royal visit (so it
is rumoured) is the construction of a special WC, dedicated to the king or
queen's sole use. Thus the symbol (the close-stool or the modern lavatory)
is the same, but its meaning in the twentieth century is not merely different
from its meaning in the sixteenth century, but, in fact, is its opposite.

The study of royal symbolism has thus proved a useful exercise. First
(and the point can almost be made in passing) it has enabled us to reinte-
grate the early-modern English monarchy into the world-picture offered by
Keith Thomas. This needed doing since the accepted historical opinion on
sixteenth or seventeenth century kingship has tended to rationalise it. Thus
Professor Elton asserts that:

> Tudor divine right, and even upto a point the Bourbon monarchy of the
> seventeenth century, contained far less of that magic or mystic element that
> distinguished the newly Christianized barbarian kings. Mysticism there was,
> but attentuated; religion formed the ceremonial dress rather than the pas-
> sionate essence of post-mediaeval kings by divine right (Elton, 1973, II, p. 202).

But such a position is tenable only so long as attention concentrates on the
material symbols of monarchy; if the focus shifts, the picture changes
radically. Crown and sceptre may have degenerated into mere signs ("I
wear a crown and carry a sceptre; therefore I am to be reverenced as
King"); however, far from waning, the imputed magical (and hence symbolic) properties of the royal body survived in full and may actually have
strengthened. This means that Tudor and Stuart kingship remained theo-
cratic: the only difference was that its symbols centred round the sanctity
of the royal body (an essentially pagan notion), rather than around the
heavily Christian ceremony of the coronation. Secondly, and more immediately to our purpose, symbolic analysis has shown that the implications for
government of divine monarchy were both surprising and exotic. So much
so indeed that their absolute importance can easily be exaggerated. Sixteenth
and seventeenth-century English kings had civil servants of a recognisably

modern type: in fact, the bulk of the work of government passed through their hands. But the Privy Chamber and so on remained as instruments of last resort, to fill up the interstices in ordinary government. These agent-symbols were, that is, the characteristic (though not the most frequent) agents of the early-modern thaumaturgical king; they were also the one specific contribution that that type of monarchy made to the art of government.

References

Abbreviations used throughout the references in the text
BM   British Museum
HO   Society of Antiquaries, 1790
LP   Brewer, etc., 1862–1932
OED   *Oxford English Dictionary*
PRO   Public Record Office
I MANUSCRIPTS
   i *The Bodleian, Oxford*
      Laudian MS Miscellaneous 597
  ii *The British Museum, London*
      Cottonian MSS   Caligula B VI
                                D VIII
                   Titus   B I
      Harleian MS 4990
      Stowe MS 563
 iii *The Public Record Office, London*
      E 101   Exchequer, King's Remembrancer, Various Accounts
      PRO 31/3   Public Record Office, Transcripts, Paris Archives, Baschet's Transcripts
      PRO 31/18   Public Record Office, Transcripts, Vienna Archives
      SP 1   State Papers, Henry VIII
      SP 2   The same, Folio Volumes
      SP 3   The same, Lisle Papers

II PRINTED BOOKS
Unless otherwise noted, the place of publication is London.
Aylmer, G. E. 1961. *The King's Servants*, Routledge and Kegan Paul.
Beattie, J. M. 1967. *The English Court in the Reign of George I*, Cambridge University Press, Cambridge.
Bergenroth, G. A. 1862–1954. *et al.* (eds) *Calendar of State Papers, Spanish*, 13 vols. and 2 supplements, Longman Green and His Majesty's Stationery Office.
Bilson, T. 1545. *The True Difference between Christian Subjection and Unchristian Rebellion*, Joseph Barnes, Oxford.
Bloch, M. 1924. *Les Rois Thaumaturges*, Publications de la Faculté des lettres de l'Université, Strasbourg.
Boswell, J. 1953. *Life of Johnson* (ed. R. W. Chapman), Oxford University Press, Oxford.

Brewer, J. S. 1862–1932. *et al.* (eds) *Letters and Papers, Foreign and Domestic, of the Reign of Henry VIII, 1509–1547*, 21 vols and appendix, Longman Green and His Majesty's Stationery Office.

British Parliamentary Papers (1801–1852), XXIII.

Burney, R. 1660. *Kerdiston Doron*, Printed by J. Redmayne, for the Author.

Bush, M. L. 1970. The Tudors and the royal race. *History*, **55**, 37 ff.

Chamberlayne, E. 1669. *Angliae Notitiae, or the Present State of England*, In the Savoy.

Chambers, E. K. 1923. *The Elizabethan Stage*, 2 vols, Clarendon Press, Oxford.

Chrimes, S. B. 1972. *Henry VII*, Eyre Methuen.

Cowper, C. S. (ed.) 1864. *The Diary of Mary, Countess Cowper, Lady of the Bedchamber to the Princess of Wales, 1714–20*, John Murray.

Crapelet, G.-A. (ed.) 1835. *Lettres de Henry VIII à Anne Boleyn*, Crapelet, Paris.

Crawfurd, R. 1917. The blessing of cramp-rings. *In* C. Singer (ed.) *Studies in the History and Method of Science*, Clarendon Press, Oxford, I, 165 ff.

Croker, J. W. (ed.) 1824. *Letters to and from Henrietta, Countess of Suffolk, and her Second Husband, the Hon. George Berkeley, from 1712 to 1767*, 2 vols, John Murray.

Cruickshank, C. G. 1969. *Army Royal*, Clarendon Press, Oxford.

Dod, C. 1842. *A Manual of Dignities*, Whittaker and Co.

Douglas, M. 1973. *Natural Symbols*, Penguin, Harmondsworth.

Ellis, H. (ed.) 1824–46. *Original Letters Illustrative of English History*, 11 vols, Tiplock and Lepard, later Harding and Lepard.

Elton, G. R. 1972. *Policy and Police*, Cambridge University Press, Cambridge.

Elton, G. R. 1974. *Studies in Tudor and Stuart Politics and Government*, 2 vols, Cambridge University Press, Cambridge.

Elton, G. R. 1962. *The Tudor Constitution*, Cambridge University Press, Cambridge.

Firth, R. 1973. *Symbols Public and Private*, Allen and Unwin.

Frazer, J. G. 1963. *The Golden Bough* (abridged edn), Macmillan.

Furnivall, F. J. (ed.) 1868. *Manners and Meals in Olden Time*, Early English Text Society, **32**.

Grant M. 1960. *The World of Rome*, Weidenfeld and Nicolson.

Hall, E. 1809. *The Union of the Two Noble and Illustrious Families of York and Lancaster* [*The Chronicle*], J. Johnson, etc.

Harrington, Sir John. 1962. *A New Discourse of a Stale Subject, called the Metamorphoses of Ajax*, (ed.) E. S. Donno, Routledge and Kegan Paul.

Hay, D. (trans. and ed.) 1950. *Historia Anglicana*, by Polydore Vergil, Camden Society, 3 series, **74**.

Herbert, G. 1953. *Works*, (ed.) F. E. Hutchinson, Clarendon Press, Oxford.

Hervey, J. (Baron Hervey) 1848. *Memoirs of the Reign of George the Second*, (ed.) J. W. Croker, 2 vols, John Murray.

Hughes, P. L. and Larkin, J. F. (eds) 1964–9. *Tudor Royal Proclamations*, 2 vols, New Haven.

Jacob, E. F. 1961. *The Fifteenth Century*, Clarendon Press, Oxford.

Kantorowicz, E. H. 1957. *The King's Two Bodies*, Princeton University Press, Princeton.

Kendall, P. M. 1968. *Richard the Third*, Allen and Unwin.

Lander, J. R. 1969. *Conflict and Stability in Fifteenth-Century England*, Hutchinson.

Lander, J. R. 1965. *The Wars of the Roses*, Secker and Warburg.

Legg, L. G. W. 1883. *English Coronation Records*, Archibald Constable.

Leland, J. 1770. *De Rebus Britannicis Collectanea*, 6 vols, G. and J. Richardson.
Loades, D. M. 1970. *The Oxford Martyrs*, Batsford.
Loyseau, C. 1701. *Oeuvres*, Compagnie des Libraires, Lyons.
Luders, A. *et al.* (eds) 1810–28. *Statutes of the Realm*, 11 vols, Record Commission.
Mackie, J. D. 1966. *The Earlier Tudors*, 1485–1558, Clarendon Press, Oxford.
Mattingly, G. 1955. *Renaissance Diplomacy*, Johnathan Cape.
More, Sir Thomas. 1963. *The History of King Richard III*, (ed.) R. S. Sylvester, Yale University Press, New Haven and London.
Muller, J. A. (ed.) 1933. *Letters of Stephen Gardiner*, Cambridge University Press, Cambridge.
Murray, M. A. 1954. *The Divine King in England*, Faber and Faber.
Myers, A. P. 1959. *The Household of Edward I V*, Manchester University Press, Manchester.
Nicolas, N. H. (ed.) 1830. *The Privy Purse Expenses of Elizabeth of York*, William Pickering.
Nicolas, N. H. (ed.) 1834–7. *Proceedings and Ordinances of the Privy Council of England, 1386–1542*, 7 vols, Record Commission.
Pickthorn, K. W. M. 1934. *Early Tudor Government*, 2 vols, Cambridge University, Cambridge.
Piper, D. 1973. *Personality and the Portrait*, British Broadcasting Corporation.
Plowden, E. 1816. *Commentaries or Reports*, 2 vols, S. Brooke.
Royal Commission on Historical Monuments, England. 1959. *An Inventory of the Historical Monuments in the City of Cambridge*, 2 parts and plans, Her Majesty's Stationery Office.
Rymer, T. *et al.* (eds) 1816–89. *Foedera, Conventiones, Litterae*, 4 vols, Record Commission.
Schramm, P. E. 1937. *A History of the English Coronation*, trans. L. G. W. Legg, Clarendon Press, Oxford.
Society of Antiquaries. 1790. *A Collection of Ordinances and Regulations for the Government of the Royal Household*, Society of Antiquaries.
South, R. 1843. *Sermons Preached upon Several Occasions*, 4 vols, Thomas Tegg, etc.
Starkey, D. R. 1969. *The Gentlemen of the Privy Chamber, 1485–1547* (unpublished fellowship dissertation: Cambridge).
Starkey, D. R. 1973. *The King's Privy Chamber, 1485–1547* (unpublished Ph.D. dissertation: Cambridge).
Strong, R. 1967. *Henry VIII and Holbein*, Routledge and Kegan Paul.
Strong, R. 1963. *Portraits of Queen Elizabeth I*, Clarendon Press, Oxford.
Sylvester, R. S. and Harding, D. P. (eds) 1962. *Two Early Tudor Lives*, Yale University Press, New Haven and London.
Thomas, K. 1973. *Religion and the Decline of Magic*, Penguin, Hardmondsworth.
Thomas, A. T. (ed.) 1847. *Memoirs of Viscountess Sundon, Mistress of the Robes to Queen Caroline . . .*, 2 vols, Henry Colburn.
The Times, 1837.
Tudor-Craig, P. 1973. *Richard III* [catalogue of National Portrait Gallery exhibition, 27 June–7 Oct. 1973].
Wade, J. 1832. *The Extraordinary Black Book*, Effingham, Wilson.

11 | Moral Order and Mental Derangement

Vieda Skultans

I

> In strictness we are all mad when we give way to passion, to prejudice, to vice, to vanity; but if all passionate, prejudiced, vicious and vain people are to be locked up as lunatics who is to keep the key of the asylum? As was fairly observed, however, by a learned Baron of the Exchequer, when he was pressed by the argument, being all madmen, we must learn to do the best we can under such untoward circumstances. (*Times*, 22nd July, 1855)

This editorial from *The Times* gives a faithful account of the mid-nineteenth century view of insanity. Like the forces of anarchy and disorder, insanity was thought to be a universal presence ready to break loose. My aim is not to give a systematic account of the development of psychiatry, but to trace the evolution of certain themes on insanity and to show their relationship to other contemporary interests. For the early Victorians the remedy for both social and mental anarchy lies in self-cultivation, character and moral order.

Nineteenth century physicians saw themselves as introducing order and enlightenment in the care of the insane. This change in attitude and behaviour was seen as a favourable move away from the punitiveness of eighteenth century practice. In particular, moral management was seen as the apex of humanitarian concern and impartiality. It is undoubtedly true that the level of custodial care improved in a number of institutions for the insane as a direct result of the principles of moral management. However, moral management is not simply to be explained as the expression of increasing humanitarianism. It is also the result of a changed view of man's nature and his place in society. This view is a dualistic one which sees man's will as pitted against human desires and failings. Moral restraint was substituted for physical restraint. Thus in discarding the methods of the eighteenth century, Victorian physicians were not, in fact, abrogating their role as guardians of the moral order and agents of social control. According to Foucault (1971), during the eighteenth century order was maintained by the physical exclusion of deviants. For example, the *stultifera navis* or "ship of fools" was a familiar feature of the eighteenth century world view. Foucault gives a vivid description of how such ships were piled full of unwanted madmen and then sailed from port to port with their unacceptable human cargo. In an age which sanctifies reason, unreason or madness becomes a residual category which defies explanation and must, therefore, be physically excluded. A more complex view of man removes the need for such crude measures as physical exile and restraint. Instead, moral management gives pride of place to the will and its powers to prevent and control insanity.

From the eighteenth century onwards epidemiological enquiries link insanity with the English. Indeed, George Cheyne's famous work on nervous distempers bore the title *The English Malady* (1734). Richard Blackmore in the opening sentence of *A Treatise of the Spleen and Vapours* reaffirms the English susceptibility to nervous distempers

> If the natives of this island either from the peculiar constitution of the air they breathe, or the immoderate quantity of flesh-meats they eat, or of the malt liquors they drink or any other secret causes, are more disposed to coughs, catarrhs and consumptions, than the neighbouring nations; they are no less obnoxious to hypochondriacal and hysterical affections, vulgarly called the spleen and vapours, in a superior and distinguishing degree. And of all the chronical distempers that afflict the body, or disturb the mind, these two, consumptions and the spleen are most rife and prevalent; and either directly or by their own power, or by introducing other diseases, make the greatest havoc among the people (1725, pp. iii–iv).

Nineteenth-century physicians continue to make a generalised association between the English and insanity. More specifically, the association is between the development of civilisation and the increase of insanity. However, since, *de facto*, England is the most civilised country, she must suffer the consequences in terms of a high rate of insanity. Epidemiological speculations are fraught with conceptual difficulties and are notoriously unrealiable. However, leaving aside the question of accuracy, it is significant that the English *believed* themselves to be afflicted with a greater amount of insanity than other countries. In particular, it was thought that the stresses of urban as opposed to rural life played a significant part in aetiology. These beliefs need to be explained.

The explanation lies in the theory and practice of moral management.

This involves a changed view of man and of the nature of mental derangement. The word "moral" had a double meaning during this period. On the one hand it related to the mental or emotional as opposed to the physical. On the other hand, "moral" was used to evaluate human behaviour.

In its first use moral causes of insanity are contrasted with physical causes. Moral treatment depends upon social interaction, mutual influence and malleability of feelings. According to the second usage, moral causes of insanity include bad habits and consequently an undesirable and unprincipled character. Moral treatment consists of an appeal to the conscience, the cultivation of the will and the art of self-government. Kathleen Jones (1972) argues that these two meanings are quite distinct and that "moral management" relies upon the first meaning, except in cases where treatment is obviously bound up with religious ideas, as in the case of the Retreat at York. She says: "The term 'moral' as used by some writers of the time had a specialized meaning. 'Moral' causes were affective or emotional causes, and 'moral' treatment was treatment through the emotions. This was probably not the sense in which the Tukes used the word, since their treatment was indispensably bound up with religious and ethical teaching." (ibid., p. 100). This separation of meanings needs to be challenged. In fact, "moral management" relies upon the concurrent use of both meanings and there is a systematic ambiguity in the use of the term, whereby the second meaning is contained and hidden within the first.

The first, as well as the best-known, full length account of moral management is given by Samuel Tuke in his *Description of the Retreat, an Institution near York for Insane Persons of the Society of Friends* (1813). The Retreat was founded for the Quaker insane in 1792 by William Tuke, a Quaker and wholesale tea and coffee merchant. The Retreat became Tuke's major life interest and subsequently of his son Henry and grandson Samuel, although neither father, son, nor grandson were medically qualified. Hunter and Macalpine (1964), the medical historians, describe the family, in particular Samuel Tuke, as having wide-ranging philanthropic interests. "His philanthropy ranged from the York Dispensary and Hospital to the Faithful Female Servants' Society, from anti-slavery to Irish relief and Catholic emancipation, from popular education to prison reform, from providence societies to temperance movements. But living in the atmosphere of the Retreat, itself a family concern, he devoted himself above all to the care and conditions of the insane" (ibid., p. 2). The implications of this assimilation of an interest in the insane to wider philanthropic interests will be discussed later.

For the present the essence of the new ideas on moral management needs to be conveyed. Robert Gardiner Hill (1839) describes several interrelated principles of moral management: "But it may be demanded, 'What mode of treatment do you adopt in place of restraint? How do you guard against accidents? How do you provide for the safety of the attendants?' In short, what is the substitute for coercion? The answer may be summed up in a few words, viz. *classification—watchfulness—vigilant and unceasing attendance by day and by night—kindness, occupation, and attention to health, cleanliness and comfort, and total absence of every description of other occupation of the attendants.* This treatment in a properly constructed and suitable building with a sufficient number of strong and active attendants always at their post, is best calculated to restore the patient; and all instruments of coercion and torture are rendered absolutely and in every case unnecessary."

In order, however, that this plan may be undeviatingly pursued, several essential requisites must unite:

1. A suitable building must be provided, in an airy and open situation, with ground sufficient for several court-yards, gardens and pleasure-grounds, commanding (if possible) a pleasing and extensive prospect.
2. There must be a proper classification of patients more *especially by night.*
3. There must also be a sufficient number of strong, tall and active attendants whose remuneration must be such as to secure persons of sound character, and steady principle, to undertake their arduous duties.
4. The House-Surgeon must exercise an unremitting control and inspection, in order that the plan may never, under any circumstances whatever, be deviated from in the slightest degree (1839, p. 37).

Despite the seeming explicitness of these principles, it is not altogether clear whether coercion has been abolished and, if so, what genuine alternatives have been suggested. Control of patients still seems to be a major preoccupation. Samuel Tuke asks: "By what means the power of the patient to control the disorder, is strengthened and assisted" (1813, p. 133). Here the emphasis moves slightly from control as such to the power of self-control. The physical and social environment is chosen with a view to promoting self-control. Furthermore, treatment by domination and fear is rejected not so much on intrinsic grounds but because it is likely to have little chance of success. "The natural tendency of such treatment is, to degrade the mind of the patient, and to make him indifferent to those moral feelings, which, under judicious direction and encouragement, are found capable, in no small degree, to strengthen the power of self-restraint; and which render the resort to coercion, in many cases, unnecessary" (Tuke, 1813, p. 163). In short, internal control is proposed as a substitute for external control.

These ideas derive from the work of the French alienists. In England they were first implemented in the small utopian-inspired, privately run madhouses such as the Retreat at York. However, during the first part of the nineteenth century the principles on which they were run were widely publicised. Burrows (1828, p. 677) aptly conveys their spirit: "The confidence of his patients is the sure basis of the physician's success. A cheerful, encouraging and friendly address; kind, but firm manners, to be patient, to hear, but prudent in answering; never making a promise that cannot safely be performed, and when made never to break it; to be vigilant and decided; prompt to control when necessary, and willing, but cautious in removing it, when once imposed; these are qualities which will always acquire the good-will and respect of lunatics, and a command over them that will accomplish what force can never attain." Noble (1853, p. 314) describes the importance of cultivating individual powers of self-control: "When a person begins to recover the natural control over his ideas, he should be reminded of the power which every person possesses, and should exercise, over his own current of thought; and how by voluntary efforts, he should direct his attention to objects and pursuits calculated to establish states of mind antagonistic to his melancholy. The extent, indeed, to which an individual may modify his own sensibility by exerting a directing power over his thoughts, has a great deal to do with final and complete restoration to mental soundness, and still more with warding off threatened attacks of insanity." One of the most humane and sympathetic proponents of moral management is John Conolly. He exposes (1856, p. 13) the malpractices of the past with horror and indignation: ". . . restraints became more and more severe, and torture more and more ingenious. Among many cruel devices, an unsuspecting patient was sometimes induced to walk across a treacherous floor; it gave way, and the patient fell into a bath of surprise, and was there half drowned and half frightened to death."

In some continental asylums the patients were chained in a well and the water allowed gradually to ascend, in order to terrify the patient with the prospect of inevitable death. Other methods adopted, even within the last sixty years, for controlling the phenomena of insanity, can only be regarded as tacit acknowledgements of the general inefficiency of medicine, and of coarse determination of vain or ignorant men to effect by force what they could not accomplish by science. Conolly questions the therapeutic value of fear and violence and advocates kindness in their place. Therapeutic practice as he describes it is startling in its simplicity:

> . . . it is part of the non-restraint system to remember, whatever the state and circumstances of a newly admitted patient may be, that he comes to the asylum to be cured, or, if incurable, to be protected and taken care of, and kept out of mischief, and tranquillized; and that the strait-waistcoat effects none of these objects. Therefore, although the patients may arrive bound so securely as scarcely to be able to move, they are at once released from every

ligature and bond and fetter that may have been imposed upon them. They appear themselves generally to be surprised at this proceeding; and for a time are tranquil, yet often distrustful and uncertain in their movements. Now and then the tranquillising effect of this unexpected liberty is permanent: more frequently it is but temporary. But every newly admitted patient is as soon as possible visited by the medical officers of the asylum. They assure the stranger, by a few kind words, that no ill-treatment is any longer to be feared. This assurance sometimes gains the confidence of the patient at once, and is ever afterward remembered: but in many cases the patient is too much confused to be able to comprehend it. Few or none, however, are quite insensible to the measures immediately adopted in conformity to it.

The wretched clothes are removed; the patient is taken gently to the bathroom, and has, probably for the first time, the comfort of a warm-bath; which often occasions expressions of remarkable satisfaction. The refreshed patient is taken out of the bath, carefully dried, and has clean and comfortable clothing put on; he is then led to the day-room, and offered good and well-prepared food. The very plates, and knife and fork, and all the simple furniture of the table, are cleaner by far than what he has lately been accustomed to, or perhaps such as in his miserable struggling life he never knew before. A patient seen after these preliminary parts of treatment is scarcely to be recognised as the same patient who was admitted only an hour before. The non-restraint treatment has commenced; and some of its effects already appear (Conolly, 1856; 1975, pp. 149–50).

Despite its aspirations, the theoretical limitations and naïvety of moral management are revealed in this account.

A work which epitomises the theory of moral management is *Man's Power over Himself to Prevent or Control Insanity*. It is a tiny handbook written by the Reverend John Barlow and first published in 1843. He argues that by the proper cultivation of the mind, disease of the brain can be prevented:

Nothing but an extent of disease which destroys at once all possibility of reasoning, by annihilating, or entirely changing the structure of the organ, can make a man necessarily mad. In all other cases, the being sane or otherwise, notwithstanding considerable disease of the brain, depends on the individual himself. He who has given a proper direction to the intellectual force, and thus obtained an early command over the bodily organ by habituating it to processes of calm reasoning, remains sane amid all the vagaries of sense; while he who has been the slave, rather than the master of his animal nature, listens to its dictates without question even when distorted by disease—and is mad. A fearful result of an uncultivated childhood, or of a manhood too much devoted to the active, money getting employments of this world, which so often form the chief pursuit of life (Barlow, 1843, p. 28).

Thus the patient is no longer seen as the random victim of a mysterious process: his help is enlisted in the management of disease. The more common term is "mental derangement" rather than insanity, since this emphasises disorder and lack of government. Barlow's book is a practical manual outlining strategies of self-help in cases of derangement. It advocates discipline and moderation as a means of securing "strength of character". The importance attached to moderation and discipline is reflected in the epidemiological and aetiological speculations of the time. For example, Burrows claims that the causes of insanity are different for the rich and the poor. He writes (1828; 1975, p. 38): "The moral causes of insanity will naturally affect the rich and educated differently to the poor and uneducated. Indeed it will be found that the former with the exception of heredity insanity, are most frequently deranged from affective or moral causes, while the latter are so principally from physical causes." Maudsley (1879; 1975, p. 66), too, favours

> the accepted notion that insanity is less common among uncivilised than civilised peoples, and that there is an increased liability to mental disorder going along with an increase in complexity of the mental organisation. Certainly it is in accordance with common sense to suppose that a complex machine, like the civilised brain, which is constructed of many special and delicate parts working together in the most nicely adjusted relations, will be exposed to more risk of derangement of action and be more likely to go wrong than a simpler and coarser machine, the less various parts of which have less fine and complicated relations.

More specifically, Maudsley (1879; 1975, pp. 68–9) spells out the temptations which civilisation sets for the different social classes: "Among the lower classes of society it is for the most part a question of sobriety and temperance against intemperance and riotous living. In the classes that are above the lower, when a man sets before himself as his aim in life riches or social position, not for any good use of what he gets by his toil and cares and heart-burnings, but as an end in itself, let his business be what it will, he is pursuing a not very worthy end, and will be likely to do so in an intemperate way, if not by actually unworthy means." Thus in each case the causes of mental disorder are seen as an extreme parody of class norms, involving loss of moderation.

However, not only is loss of moderation conducive to insanity, impairment of the will is thought to be one of the central and definitive characteristics of insanity. Daniel Noble (1853, p. 11) describes the essential feature of insanity as: ". . . the destruction or impairment of moral liberty, or a notable diminution of that controlling power over self which belongs to every soundly-constituted person, since this last-mentioned feature separates insanity from those slighter perversions of the temper and those

diminished facilities of thinking which obtain in disease very generally."
According to Charles Bucknill's definition 1854, pp. 27–8) of sanity and
insanity "there are three terms, the subjected emotions, the directing intellect and the middle term of free will . . . Insanity therefore may be defined
as a condition of the mind in which a false action or conception or judgement, a defective power of the will, or an uncontrollable violence of the
emotions and instincts, have separately or conjointly been produced by
disease." Despite the tripartite division of the mind, supremacy is clearly
granted to the will which acts as mediator between the other faculties.
Countless illustrations of the importance ascribed to the will occur in the
early nineteenth century literature on insanity, including Dr. Noble's
(1853, p. 335) gentleman patient who told him that "but for strong voli-
tional efforts, he believes that he should have been insane". The importance
of the will reached a zenith in the works of the mid-century and thereafter
gradually declined.

II

What are the implications of this relationship between the will and insanity?
Since failure of will-power is equated with possible insanity, the subject
becomes one of universal concern. The problem is a shared one, having a
real relevance to both writer and reader. The problem is also seen as an
explicitly moral one, intimately related to the philosophical problem concerning the nature of man. This view of insanity is, in many ways, a
development of eighteenth-century theories. Hypochondriasis and hysteria,
or the spleen and vapours, as they were more commonly called, were
commonplace afflictions. They had both psychological and physical components: the former include lowness of spirits and general indecisiveness
and the latter include digestive disorders and general debility. The terms
hypochondriasis, hysteria, spleen and vapours had little connection with
the term insanity. This is not to say that the conditions which were so described would not at a later date have been categorised as a variety of
insanity. What it does mean is that the category of insanity did not exist in
that large way in which it was later to evolve. Kathleen Jones supports this
view of eighteenth-century ideas on insanity: "The idea of insanity as a
single social factor had not yet evolved" (1972, p. 25). Those who were
later to join the swelling ranks of the pauper insane, were not yet separated
from the indigent masses. On the other hand the middle and upper classes
suffered from a variety of distempers of an equivocal nature, certainly far
removed from insanity as conceived of in both popular and medical thought.
Thus psychological and social problems were not perceived in a distinc-
tively psychiatric idiom. Not until the latter half of the nineteenth century

when heredity comes to play an increasing part in accounts of insanity, is the affliction confined to certain categories of the population.

The subjective approach of the early part of the century follows in the footsteps of a long line of thought on insanity. For example, Robert Burton wrote *The Anatomy of Melancholy* (1621) in an attempt to graple with his own melancholic disposition. He makes his personal investment in the subject quite explicit: "I write of melancholy, by being busie to avoid melancholy . . . to ease my mind by writing, for I had gravidum cor, foetum caput, a kind of imposthume in my head, which I was very desirous to be unladen of, and could imagine no fitter evacuation than this . . . one must needs scratch where it itches" (1621; 1806, p. 7). George Cheyne also suffered from the complaints about which he wrote. He confesses to have weighed over thirty-two stone and singles out gluttony as one of the causes of insanity. His first book *An Essay of Health and Long Life* (1725) deals especially with the importance of regimen and diet in the maintenance of health. The literature of the early nineteenth century follows this tradition. Books like John Barlow's *Man's Power over Himself to Prevent or Control Insanity* (1843), Thomas Bakewell's *The Domestic Guide in Cases of Insanity* (1809) and John Abercrombie's *Culture and Discipline of the Mind* (1837) were clearly addressed to a general and not a professional readership, and these books would be consulted in situations of threatened or actual crisis.

These ideas on insanity are interesting in their own right, but they only make sense when set against the contemporary background of ideas about the individual and his potentialities. The nineteenth century was a time of great social movement. There was a feeling, on the one hand, that the established order was slipping away and, on the other, that the new social forms offered the individual unlimited possibilities. Theoretically a person could find his niche in any part of the social structure, depending, of course, on his individual inclination, effort and perseverance. In a context of mass geographical mobility, social mobility was both a real occurrence and a perpetual promise which helped mould man's image of himself. (The size of the urban population has altered relatively little since the 1870's: the movement from country to town was essentially a mid-nineteenth century phenomenon.) During this period of economic and social optimism the ranks of the middle classes swelled. This widespread social mobility and economic growth produced a highly articulated philosophy of individualism. Such a relationship between the stages of economic development and philosophic outlook is a familiar one. However, the way in which ideas about insanity fit into this general picture needs further exploration.

Much importance is attached to "energetically exercising the will". Such measures are thought to be as effective in combatting insanity as they are in securing a respectable position in society. The writing which advocates such exertions of the will to preserve individual sanity and status betrays a touching faith in man's powers to overcome internal and external constraints. The individual *is* master in his own house and can, moreover, fashion it according to his will. Each act of the will can be seen as another brick in the building. These ideas stand in sharp contrast with the late nineteenth century view of the individual. Notions of "character", "heredity" and "innate tendencies" firmly circumscribe the powers of the individual. The moral force of the individual can no longer be pitted against the social and physical world; the individual has been engulfed by these worlds.

Even a cursory glance at the literature of the early nineteenth century reveals similar preoccupations shared by educationalists, philosophers and men of letters. For example, there are many similarities between ideas about insanity and educational theory. Childhood itself was a discovery of the late eighteenth century and early children's books, like treatises on insanity, were moral tracts concerned with the inculcation of self-control and other virtues. The newly-founded public schools laid great stress on self-discipline and character-building and were also an effective path to self-advancement. Asa Briggs (1965, p. 153) writes of this feature of public schools ". . . the great social divide between landlords and businessmen was bridged. The public school consequently provided for the gradual fusion of classes and their drawing upon a common store of values." Thus character and will provide a new dimension for the measurement of individual worth, and one which surmounts both social and medical categories. This general approach is exemplified by many, very different mid-nineteenth century thinkers. John Stuart Mill wrote: "The worth of a state in the long run is the worth of the individuals composing it." His own arduous upbringing would no doubt have gained the admiration of the moral managers. Mathew Arnold, also, was concerned with the idea of perfection as an individual and inner condition. These ideas are reflected in the lesser as well as the great writers of the period. Samuel Smiles, the great populariser of the mid-Victorian ethic, prefaces his book *Thrift* (1875) with Carlyle's motto: "Not what I have but what I do is my kingdom." Both the minor and the major figures of the period express the same admiration and faith in personal power. The titles of Smiles' books aptly circumscribe the area of his interests. *Self-Help* (1859), *Character* (1871), *Thrift* (1875), *Duty* (1880) all deal with the arts of self-improvement. The physical and social worlds can be changed if the inner world is first changed. Smiles writes (1859; 1959, p. 24) "The spirit of self-help is the root of all genuine growth in the individual; and exhibited in the lives of many, it constitutes the true source of national vigour and strength. Help from without is often enfeebling in its effects, but help from within invariably invigorates. Whatever is done for men and classes to a certain extent takes away the necessity and stimulus of doing for themselves; and where men are subject to over-guidance and over-government, the inevitable tendency is to render them comparatively helpless." We are back to the arts of self-government propagated by the moral managers. Smiles was concerned with the development of character through the adoption of good habits and perseverance. Four qualities are particularly important in this process: energy, cheerfulness, prudence and industry. They are also qualities important in the control and prevention of insanity. In particular, Smiles' energy seems to be a counterpart of the physician's term "moral force". Thus an expanding and fluid social and economic structure permits us to see the individual as powerful and independent and able to bring about changes, both within himself and in the external environment. During the same period, theories of insanity evolve which attribute responsibility to the individual for the condition of his health and, indeed, for his loss of reason.

III

During this period of concern with moral management, there was an awakening of interest in two other areas: masturbation and seminal loss. This gave rise to two related diagnostic categories: "masturbatory insanity" and "spermatorrhoea". These phenomena must be seen as expressions of concern with continence in its widest sense. The disapproval of venery is but another aspect of the pursuit of moderation and discipline.

Masturbation, or, "the primal addiction" as Freud was later to call it, is one focus of anxiety. Another more general and basic area of concern is seminal loss, which may, but need not, be caused by masturbation. A generally accepted, if not clear, definition of spermatorrhoea is given by Curling in his book *A Practical Treatise on the Diseases of the Testis* (1856). He writes: "The emissions may, however, be more frequent than is consistent with health, and too readily excited, so much so, indeed, as to affect virility, and to give rise to constitutional symptoms of a serious character. These excessive spermatic discharges constitute the complaint termed spermatorrhoea" (Curling, 1856, p. 386). This loss may be voluntary as in intercourse and masturbation and involuntary as in "nocturnal pollutions" or other emissions, for example, whilst at stool. Typically the picture presented is that of a "dribbling penis". Throughout the eighteen-forties and fifties, physicians showed increasing concern that insufficient attention was paid to the dangers of seminal loss. For example, Milton (1854, p. 243) writes

It has always appeared strange to me that this affection should remain abandoned by the profession to a few solitary specialists, and for the benefit of the vile harpies who prey on this class of victims. Surgery which has wrested so much from empiricism and ignorance, seems disposed to yield up this, as if it were, debateable land, to chance, philosophy, utter neglect or quackery.

Lallemand, the French specialist on spermatorrhoea, describes (1847, p. ii) it as "A disease that degrades man, poisons the happiness of his best days, and ravages society."

In part, fear of seminal loss reflects anxiety about sexuality as such. For example, advising on the treatment and prevention of spermatorrhoea, Milton (1887, p. 170) reveals a general squeamishness on the subject: "Over and over again a patient has noticed that getting up betimes, as soon as he awoke in fact, avoids that which a longer stay in that bundle of paradoxes, the bed would have induced." However, a general coyness does not explain the particular interest in seminal loss. Seminal loss in intercourse is set apart as being rather less harmful. Spitzka (1888, p. 225), for example, writes ". . . there is a discrepancy between the results of natural and artificial excesses". And later the same author says of natural sexual excess that it has "none of the perversions or emotional anomalies so characteristic of the latter . . . Nature has so arranged that there are limits to sexual excess . . . No such limits check the onanist" (ibid., p. 225). However, it is the seminal loss involved which is considered pernicious here. For this reason male masturbation is singled out for consideration. Spitzka writes "The affects of such indulgence are less serious in the female owing to the less exhausting nature of the discharges." This indicates that it is loss of semen rather than sexual activity as such which is judged to be of greatest harm.

In fact, beliefs about seminal loss constitute a distinct syndrome. Most writers on the subject are agreed on the causes of spermatorrhoea. These include constipation, worms, piles, gonorrhoea, heat, heavy bedclothes, highly seasoned food, alcohol, intense application of the mind and excessive indulgence in sexual intercourse, usually of a promiscuous kind. The effects of spermatorrhoea are similar to those of masturbation. In general these are debilitating. In particular, there is an intimate connection between seminal loss and the condition of the brain. There is an inability to sustain mental and bodily fatigue; a heaviness in the head; giddiness; sleeplessness. Interestingly, the appetite increases, often becoming voracious. Dawson (1840, p. 6) writes "I have generally found unnatural seminal discharge accompanied with increased appetite, owing to the necessity which the system feels, of compensating the daily losses which it sustains." Long term effects, like those of masturbation, are more serious. Parched skin, loss of hair, stammering, deafness, blindness, form part of the familiar list. The picture presented is particularly interesting for the similarity which it has with Hindu preoccupations with seminal loss.

Masturbation forms a sub-category of the interest in seminal loss. The picture of the typical masturbator which emerges is one of extreme selfishness. Spitzka (1887, p. 239) describes a patient representative of this category as follows:

> His demeanour was obtrusive, mean and selfish. He sat out all my other patients on the morning he called, withdrew to the waiting-room, under indignant protests, when I represented to him that I could not keep a physician accompanying patients, who had come a great distance, waiting any longer, he having already consumed two hours. He came in repeatedly, and finally, after I had finished, he took possession of the field, and as I hurried off to my much delayed lunch, he exclaimed, "Hurry up, doctor, do not be long; I have a great deal to tell you yet. My case is of more importance than any other you ever had; I am the most important man in my family."

Maudsley (1868, p. 156) describes the consequences of masturbation begun early in life as follows ". . . we have degenerate beings produced who as regards moral character are very much what eunuchs are represented to be—cunning, deceitful, liars, selfish, in fact, morally insane; while their physical and intellectual vigor is further damaged by the exhausting vice".

Another characteristic of the chronic masturbator is his shyness, timidity, and, in particular, his inability to look others in the eye. Allnatt (1843, p. 654) describes a patient of his who ". . . entered the room with a timid and suspicious air, and appeared to quail like an irresolute maniac when the eye was fixed irresolutely upon him". David Skae (1863, p. 315), the Scottish physician, who first identified a particular brand of insanity which he termed masturbatory, also singles out similar features of the masturbator:

> . . . that vice produces a group of symptoms which are quite characteristic, and easily recognised, and give to the cases a special natural history. The peculiar imbecility and shy habits of the very youthful victim, the suspicion and fear, and dread, and suicidal impulses, and palpitations and scared look, and feeble body of the older offenders, passing gradually into dementia or fatuity, with other characteristic features familiar to all of you, which I do not stop to enlarge on, all combine to stamp this as a natural order or family.

The sad psychological portrait of the masturbator is reinforced by the physical appearance of his sallow complexion and dark ringed eyes. However, masturbation is only one among the ingredients of this character type, it is also the cause of further disabilities. General weakness is the most common result, followed by headache, backache, acne, indigestion, blindness, deafness, epilepsy and finally death. In sum, there is an inability to participate in social intercourse of any kind.

At first sight the mid-nineteenth century interest in masturbation seems incompatible with the concurrent interest in moral management. However, both presuppose self-control and, thus the two areas of interest are, in a sense, complementary. Masturbation, one of the most solitary of activities, is regarded as the arch vice precisely because of the hopes vested in the private endeavours of the individual. It is seen as the moral failure par excellence, in that it typifies loss of control.

Although interest in masturbation persists into the latter part of the nineteenth century, there is a re-interpretation of its nature. Maudsley, for example, in his early paper on masturbation in the *Journal of Mental Science* (1868) regards it with abhorrence as a form of moral degeneracy. When he comes to reconsider the subject in *Pathology of Mind* (1879) he sees masturbation much more as a function of bad inheritance over which the individual has little control. In line with this reappraisal, is the increasing insistance on surgical preventive measures as opposed to the earlier moral exhortations.

The history of both diseases has been given considerable publicity by Hare (1962), Comfort (1967) and Szasz (1971). But, interesting though these accounts are, they fail to provide a convincing explanation for the appearance and disappearance of medical and lay interest in the topic. Their accounts in outline are as follows: Hare sees the masturbatory hypothesis as illustrating the peculiar difficulty of refuting causal hypotheses in psychiatry. The reasons for its rise to popularity are: the decline of the demoniacal model of madness; the increasing interest in the effects on the mind of bodily disturbance; the increased visibility of masturbatory activity within asylums. The reasons for the persistence of belief in the masturbatory hypothesis are summarised under the headings: conservatism, poverty of scepticism and certain fallacies of reasoning. Finally, the masturbatory hypothesis is abandoned essentially because of increasing clarity and coherence of thought. For example, Hare quotes the difficulty of establishing whether masturbation is a symptom or a cause of insanity, the recognition of the widespread practice among "normal" people and the difficulty of establishing whether or not a patient has masturbated. According to Hare, each of these factors helped to expose the weaknesses of the hypothesis. In short, Hare's account relies on a rationalist and progressive view of thought. The history of medicine is one of increasing logical rigour and empirical thoroughness. This view of the development of medicine, and of the masturbatory hypothesis in particular, ignores the wider context of medical ideas and their social roots.

Comfort also explores the nineteenth century preoccupation with solitary sexual pursuits. His account is largely descriptive. However, to the extent that Comfort offers explanation, it relates to the prurient and immature personalities of the writers. Szasz (1971, p. 203) rightly takes Comfort to task for the direction of his explanations. "I disagree with Comfort, who relates both the witch-hunts and the persecution of masturbators to the mental illness of the persecutors." Comfort is demythologising one aspect of psychiatric history at the risk of setting up another set of mythologies.

Szasz's own approach is quite different. The *leitmotif* of all his writing is the social control which institutional psychiatry and its official representatives exercise. Szasz sees his task as one of unravelling the different guises under which medicine and psychiatry exert control over the individual. The identification, or rather the creation of a brand of insanity caused by masturbation and of a disease called spermatorrhoea, are just two of the guises in which medicine controls the individual. Szasz treats both conditions as attempts to control insanity. The beauty of using masturbation as an explanation of insanity is its near universality and the practical difficulty of establishing its occurrence. Thus its explanatory powers are at least equal to the possession model of insanity which Szasz claims the masturbatory hypothesis replaces.

Szasz's approach to the subject is oversimplified. It ignores many of the problems which a more detailed consideration of the two diseases present. Firstly, masturbational insanity and spermatorrhoea are just two of a number of diagnostic categories and by no means as frequent, let alone providing the universal explanation for insanity, that Szasz implies. How they relate to other explanations of insanity of the time is ignored. Secondly, to say that they replace the demoniacal model of insanity is not sufficient to account for the history of these ideas.

As Hare points out the interest in masturbation has a definite life-span, and can be given an actual date of origin. In 1710 an anonymous clergyman published a treatise on the subject of masturbation: *Onania or the Heinous Sin of Self-Pollution.* However, in England these ideas did not acquire any degree of popularity until the mid-nineteenth century. Most English works on the subject were published within the space of about forty years. The chronology of this interest requires explanation. After the appearance of *Onania* in England there is a lull in concern for over a hundred years. In 1840 there is a revival of interest. The works of Ellis (1838), Dawson (1840), Allnatt (1843), Lallemand (1847) in English translation, Milton (1854 and Curling (1856) all appeared within eighteen years of each other.

This chronology cannot be explained simply in terms of social control. Rather, beliefs about masturbation and the masturbator must be set within a wider context of values and beliefs about the nature of man. Thus the picture of the masturbator which nineteenth century physicians draw embodies the antithesis of all the valued characteristics of the period. He is the polar opposite to nature's gentleman who can get by on the strength of inner resourcefulness and outward accomplishments. He provides the prototype of uncontrolled, undisciplined behaviour. In summary, these ideas can only be fully understood in relation to more general beliefs about man and his place in society.

IV

The latter half of the nineteenth century offers a dramatically different picture of insanity. The enthusiasm and optimism of medical texts on insanity disappear. Instead, a dark note of doom and despair appears in the writing. There is no mention of moral power, acts of will or relentless self-control in the literature. Instead, the unalterable, physical basis of insanity is underlined. The great proponent of this new line of thought is Henry Maudsley whose writing appeared from the late 1860's onwards. He emphasises the inevitable unfolding of hereditary disposition or, expressed more dramatically, "the tyranny of organization". The following excerpt from *Body and Mind* (1873) is typical of much of his writing:

> It is an indisputable though extreme fact that certain human beings are born with such a native deficiency of mind that all the training and education in the world will not raise them to the height of brutes; and I believe it to be no less true that, in consequence of evil ancestral influences, individuals are born with such a flaw or warp of nature that all the care in the world will not prevent them from being vicious or criminal, or becoming insane. Education, it is true, may do much; but we cannot forget that the foundations on which the acquisitions of education must rest are not acquired, but inherited. No one can escape the tyranny of his organisation; no one can elude the destiny that is innate in him, and which unconsciously and irresistably shapes his ends, even when he believes that he is determining them with consumate foresight and skill. A well-grounded and comprehensive theory of mind must recognise and embrace these facts. (1975, p. 207).

These emotive phrases like "tyranny of organization" and "the fate made for man by his inheritance" recur throughout his books.

Maudsley is aware of the earlier importance attached to character formation, but he sees it in ways quite different from the moral managers. ". . . character is a slow and gradual growth through action in relation to the circumstances of life; it cannot be fashioned suddenly and through reflection only. A man can no more will than he can speak without having learnt to do so, nor can he be taught volition any more than he can be taught speech except by practice. It was a pregnant saying that the history of man is his character; to which one might add that whosoever would transform a character must undo a life history. The fixed and unchanging laws by which events come to pass hold sway in the domain of mind as in every other domain of nature" (Maudsley, 1874, p. 272). Maudsley (ibid., p. 289) also questions the power of the will:

I cannot but think that the moral philosophers have sometimes exaggerated greatly the direct power of the will, as an abstract entity, without at the same time having taken sufficient account of the slow and gradual way in which concrete will itself must be formed. The culminating effort of mental development, the final blossom of human evolution, it betokens a physiological development as real, though not as apparent, as that which distinguishes the nervous system of man from that of one of the lower animals. Time and systematic exercise are necessary to the gradual organisation of the structure which shall manifest it in full function. No one can resolve successfully by a mere effort of will to think in a certain way, or even, which is easier, to act always in accordance with certain rules.

Thus Maudsley, following Kant, restricts freedom to the formation of character, but denies freedom of action as such. The contemporary reader may consider that Maudsley's account gives a more realistic assessment of man's powers than that of the moral managers. Opinions here will vary according to upbringing and outlook. However, the important point is that this new approach does not reflect more acute techniques of observation of human behaviour. "Efforts of will" are by their very nature invisible. Bucknill (1854, p. 17) had earlier given an apposite summary of the problem:

> To what extent, therefore, will sound reason justify him (the physician) in maintaining the deterioration or total loss of responsibility? To arrive at a perfectly just estimate it would be necessary for him, according to the phraseology of Lord Denman, "to dive into the mind of the patient", to see what is going on below the surface, and in the mud at the bottom. This is not permitted man to do,—God only knows the heart; Omniscience alone can estimate accurately the degree of irresponsibility produced by cerebral disease, the degrees of moral freedom and responsibility left by the same.

One of the consequences of this emphasis on heredity is that it creates anxieties about the boundaries of this category which is tainted by descent. For example, Andrew Wynter (1875, p. 45) writes: "When we remember the number of persons in the country whose insanity is undoubted, it will be admitted that there is a very large number of individuals who inherit either the disease direct, or are saturated with the seeds of nervous disorders, which only require some exciting cause to force them into vigorous growth. It is this class of incipient lunatics with whom we wish to deal in the following pages . . ." This submerged category of the insane gives rise to perpetual insecurities particularly with regard to marriage. Maudsley (1874, p. 276) cautions on the need for prudence in the choice of marriage partner: "Is it right then to sanction propagation of his kind by an individual who is wanting in that which is the highest attribute of man—a sound and stable constitution? I note this as a question to be seriously faced and sincerely answered . . ." Throughout the late nineteenth century the possibility of latent insanity looms in the background. Maudsley (1879, p. 215) conveys well the terror of this idea: "The dread, inexorable destiny which plays so grand and terrible a part in Grecian tragedy, and which Grecian heroes are represented as struggling manfully against, knowing all the while that their struggles were foredoomed to be futile, embodied an instinctive perception of the law by which the sins of the father are visited upon the children unto the third and fourth generations. Deep in his inmost heart everybody has an instinctive feeling that he has been predestined to be what he is, and could not, antecedent conditions having been what they were, have been different. It was a proverb in Israel that when the fathers had eaten sour grapes the children's teeth were set on edge . . ." and so the passage continues. The mood has swung full circle from blithe optimism to full-blown pessimism.

Another consequence of the appearance of heredity is the threat of a category of hopeless degenerates. Included within this category are moral imbeciles, habitual criminals and pauper lunatics. This category constitutes "a morbid or degenerate variety of mankind, marked by peculiar low physical and mental characteristics . . . They are of weak and defective intellect, though excessively cunning . . ." (1874, p. 30). This combination of stupidity and artfulness is often remarked upon. Again in describing the animality of a particular patient, Maudsley (1873; 1975, p. 247) remarks: "He may be called an idiot of the lowest order; yet there is a mischievous brutelike intelligence in his eye." The rag-bag which is included in this category are called "morbid varieties". Maudsley (1873; 1975, p. 253) describes these varieties as follows: "Multitudes of human beings come into this world weighted with a destiny against which they have neither the will nor the power to contend; they are the step-children of nature, and groan under the worst of all tyrannies—the tyranny of a bad organisation, Men differ, indeed, in the fundamental characters of their minds, as they do in the features of their countenances, or in the habits of their bodies; and between those who are born with the potentiality of a full and complete mental development under any circumstances and those who are born with an innate incapacity of mental development under any circumstances, there exists every gradation."

What has happened in the decades which intervene between the literature extolling individual power and the writing of Maudsley? The work of evolutionists and biologists can be discerned as a background influence. However, the reassessment of man's powers to restructure his psychic economy seems permeated with an awareness of the rigidity of social boundaries. Physical laws, not education or moral effort, determine a person's place in society. The social consequences of this theoretical reappraisal are explicitly stated in the literature. "Morbid varieties of mankind" or the insane are a permanent feature of society. The physician's task is to identify the boundaries of this category and to care for the insane rather than to cure them. General William Booth (1890, pp. 204–5) epitomises these sentiments:

> There are men so incorrigibly lazy that no inducement you can offer will tempt them to work; so eaten up by vice that virtue is abhorrent to them, and so inveterately dishonest that theft is to them a master passion. When a human being has reached that stage, there is only one course that can be rationally pursued. Sorrowfully, but remorselessly, it must be recognised that he has become lunatic, morally demented, incapable of self-government, and that upon him, therefore, must be passed the seclusion from a world in which he is not fit to be at large . . . Between them and the wide world there must be reared an impassable barrier, which once passed should be recrossed no more for ever.

Booth is quite explicit about the need to erect boundaries.

So far this paper has documented ideas about insanity. How are the changes in ideas to be accounted for? During the period of massive urban growth the middle classes had increased their membership. All were admitted who possessed the right personal characteristics. By the 1870's there is a crisis of confidence, the identity of the middle classes is threatened and further economic expansion is checked. Criteria for membership of the middle classes changed from acquired characteristics to inherited ones, thus firmly closing the door to newcomers. The earlier sense of personal optimism and social progress is lost. This contraction of social and economic opportunity, in turn, affects ideas on insanity. A more detailed examination of the interlocking of social conditions and medical theory and practice is needed. This paper suggests that such a relationship exists and indicates the direction in which further research on nineteenth century psychiatry should proceed.

References

Abercrombie, J. 1837. *Culture and Discipline of the Mind*, William Whyte and Co., Edinburgh.

Allnatt, R. H. 1843. Case of atrophy of the testicle from excessive masturbation. *Lancet*, ii, p. 654.

Bakewell, T. 1809. *A Domestic Guide in Cases of Insanity.*

Barlow, J. 1843. *Man's Power over Himself to Prevent or Control Insanity*, William Pickering, London.

Blackmore, R. 1725. *A Treatise of the Spleen and Vapours: or Hypochondriacal and Hysterical Affections*, J. Pemberton, London.

Booth, W. 1890. *In Darkest England and the Way Out*, The Salvation Army, London.

Briggs, A. 1965. *Victorian People*, Penguin, Harmondsworth.

Bucknill, C. 1854. *Unsoundness of Mind in Relation to Criminal Insanity*, Longman, London.

Burrows, G. M. 1828. *Commentaries on Insanity*, Underwood, London.

Burton, R. 1621. *The Anatomy of Melancholy*, J. and E. Hodson, 11th edn. 1806, London.

Cheyne, G. 1725. *An Essay of Health and Long Life*, Strahan and Leake, London.

Cheyne, G. 1734. *The English Malady or a Treatise on Nervous Diseases of All Kinds*, Strahan and Leake, London.

Comfort, A. 1967. *The Anxiety Makers*, Panther Books Ltd., 1968, London.

Conolly, J. 1856. *The Treatment of the Insane without Mechanical Restraints*. Smith Elder and Co., London.

Curling, T. B. 1856. *A Practical Treatise on Diseases of the Testis*, John Churchill, London.

Dawson, R. 1840. *An Essay on Spermatorrhoea*, Aylott Jones, 6th edn., 1852, London.

Ellis, W. C. 1838. *A Treatise on the Nature, Symptoms, Causes and Treatment of Insanity*, Samuel Holdsworth, London.

Foucault, M. 1971. *Madness and Civilization*, Tavistock Publications, London.

Hare, E. H. 1962. Masturbational insanity: the history of an idea. *Journal of Mental Science*, **108**, pp. 1–25.

Hill, R. G. 1939. *Total Abolition of Personal Restraint in the Treatment of the Insane*, Simpkin, Marshall and Co., London.

Hunter, R. and Macalpine, I. 1964. *Three Hundred Years of Psychiatry*, Oxford University Press, London.

Jones, K. 1972. *A History of the Mental Health Services*, Routledge and Kegan Paul, London.

Lallemand, J. 1847. *A Treatise on Spermatorrhoea*, translator Henry J. McDougall, John Churchill, London.

Maudsley, H. 1868. Illustrations of a variety of insanity. *Journal of Mental Science*, **14**, pp. 149–62.

Maudsley, H. 1873. *Body and Mind*, Macmillan and Co., London.

Maudsley, H. 1874. *Responsibility in Mental Disease*, Henry S. King and Co., London.

Maudsley, H. 1874. *Mental Diseases*, D. Appleton and Co., New York and London.

Maudsley, H. 1879. *The Pathology of Mind*, Macmillan and Co., London.

Milton, J. 1854. On the nature and treatment of spermatorrhoea. *Lancet*, **I**, pp. 243–6, 269–70, 467–8, 595–6.

Milton, J. 1887. *Pathology and Treatment of Spermatorrhoea*, Henry Renshaw, London.

Noble, D. 1853. *Elements of Psychological Medicine*, John Churchill, London.

Skae, D. 1863. A rational and practical classification of insanity. *The Journal of Mental Science*, **9**, pp. 309–19.

Skultans, V. 1975. *Madness and Morals*, Routledge and Kegan Paul, London.

Smiles, S. 1859. *Self-Help*, 1959 edn., Murray, London.

Spitzka, E. C. 1887. Cases of masturbation. *Journal of Nervous and Mental Diseases,*
pp. 238–9.

Szasz, T. 1971. *The Manufacture of Madness,* Routledge and Kegan Paul, London.

Tuke, S. 1813. *A Description of the Retreat: an Institution near York for Insane
Persons of the Society of Friends,* Hunter R. and Macalpine, I. (eds.) 1964,
Dawsons of Pall Mall, London.

Wynter, A. 1875. *The Borderlands of Insanity,* Robert Hardwicke, London.

12 | Aspects of Hindu Asceticism

Audrey Cantlie

This paper is an attempt to examine the nature and implications of certain aspects of the Hindu concept of asceticism in the light of psychoanalytical theory. In the first part it is suggested that the view of *tapas* or ascetic power as transformed and stored sexuality represents a concrete type of thinking which is characteristic of a certain stage of infantile thought. The second part, more speculative in nature, relates the goal of Hindu asceticism to Freud's theory of the death instinct and, from this standpoint, examines the significance of renunciatory ideals for the organisation of the caste system.

A summary of the argument is given at the end.

Ethnographic Data

I first became acquainted with certain features of the Hindu concept of asceticism while doing anthropological field-work among the Hindus of Upper Assam. It was said that if a man does not spill his seed, either by intercourse or masturbation, he accumulates within himself a store of semen which becomes a source of magical power. This store is suffused throughout the body and shines whitely like a light so that a saintly man can be recognised by his luminosity. Intercourse is regarded as wasteful of seed because the quantity of the store is thereby diminished and a man of a religious turn of mind avoids eating "heating" foods which are believed to raise the temperature of the blood and excite the passions. Semen itself is said to come from food. As milk produces butter and butter produces ghee, so it is explained that the richest part of food becomes blood and from blood by a further distillation comes semen which is equated with the *ātman* or soul.

These ideas were not systematised in the area where I worked and possibly derive from the Tantric practices of Lower Assam. I have, to my regret, no first-hand knowledge of these and the sources for this paper are exclusively literary. It lacks as a result the basis of field-work which could show how ideas are interpreted in practice.

The belief that ascetic power (*tapas*) derives from the retention of semen is rooted deep in Hindu tradition and literature. I wish to explore one aspect of this belief by reference to the psychoanalytical concept of the "breast that feeds itself".

The Breast that Feeds Itself

The concept of the breast that feeds itself was developed by Melanie Klein in relation to her theory of primal envy. She writes: "The first object to be envied is the feeding breast, for the infant feels that it possesses everything he desires and that it has an unlimited flow of milk and love which the breast keeps for its own gratification" (Klein, 1957, p. 10). In her view the "good" and satisfying breast is the representative of the life instinct and is experienced as the first manifestation of creativeness. "The capacity to give and to preserve life is felt as the greatest gift and therefore creativeness becomes the deepest cause for envy" (Klein, 1957, p. 40). Although the feeding breast is the prototype of the envied object, the frustrating and unsatisfying breast can also be envied, for the infant may explain his deprivation by the phantasy that the breast is being withheld because it is keeping its love and milk for itself. When constitutional envy is strong, it would appear that the phantasy of the breast that feeds itself is proportionately intense together with the related phantasy of the combined parent figure locked in permanent sexual gratification.

I wish to relate this concept here, not to primal envy, but to the type of distinction made by Bion (1962, pp. 47–9) when he differentiates K in the sense of getting to know from K in the sense of being in possession of a "piece" of knowledge, the one representing the painful process of learning or acquiring knowledge, the other the supposedly painless state of possessing knowledge. Implied in the concept of the breast that feeds itself is a view of milk and gratification as a fixed store that exists without relation to the infant's needs and of the breast as the owner of that store. The capacity to give milk, love and gratification is conceived in terms similar to the ownership of inanimate objects such as money or property, which render a man rich and independent by the mere fact of their possession. The other view would be to regard the supply of milk as part of a relationship between baby and breast which is regulated by the intake of the baby as well as by the output of the breast, and to value the breast for its value in use, that is, by the measure of its capacity to provide for the needs of another.

It is characteristic of the mode of thought exemplified by the concept of the breast that feeds itself that psychical qualities are conceived on a physical model. This early tendency emerges in numerous metaphorical expressions for properties of the mind which originally derive from sense impressions of material objects, such as "clear thinking", "sweetness of temper", "sharpness of mind", "a store of wisdom", "empty-headed", and so on (cf. Bion, 1962, p. 63). Hinduism had developed techniques of meditation which aim to eliminate the distinction between psychical and physical and reach an identification of the thought of a thing with the thing thought of and of both with the thinker. In consequence knowledge of an object becomes physical possession of the object, a belief that is the basis of the supernatural powers attributed to the yogi and his mastery over the external world (Eliade, 1958, pp. 76–90).

Transferred to the genital level the phantasy of the breast that feeds itself becomes the penis that retains its own seed. Traces of this concept are to be found in certain beliefs underlying the Hindu idea of ascetic power. I wish to develop it here in relation to (1) *tapas* or the heat of asceticism, and (2) certain practices of Kuṇḍalinī Yoga.

Tapas: the Heat of Asceticism

The word *tapas* is used in the Ṛg Veda in a number of senses:

(a) In its literal sense of heat:
(O God of Fire), most full of *tapas* (*tapiṣṭha*), burning (*tápasvān*), burn him (*tápā*) with *tapas*, with your own ageless bull-like (flames) (vi, 5, 4b).
(b) As the practice of asceticism or austerities:
The gods and the Seven Sages engaged themselves in *tapas* . . . (x, 109, 4).
(c) As a creative force:
The law and truth were born from kindled *tapas*; from this, night was born and the flowing ocean (x, 190, 1).
(d) As a source of unassailable power:
Those (now dead) who were unassailable because of *tapas*, who went to the sun (i.e. to heaven) because of their *tapas* . . . (x, 154, 2).

The meaning of these passages cannot of course be known with any degree of confidence. But they suggest the germ of an association between ascetic power and sexual power which could provide a link between these apparently disparate usages. The relation between asceticism and sexuality in Hindu mythology is the subject of a recent study by Dr. Wendy O'Flaherty, *Asceticism and Eroticism in the Mythology of Śiva*. She starts from what she describes as "one of the enduring problems of Hindu mythology, the paradox of Śiva the erotic ascetic", and her work is structured as an answer to Zaehner's question: "Permanently ithyphallic, yet perpetually chaste; how is one to explain such a phenomenon?" (Zaehner, 1962, p. 113). I draw some points from her rich material to illustrate the Hindu view of ascetic power.

Tapas as Heat

Because of the equation between *tapas* and sexual *heat*, ascetic power has burning qualities. Śiva stored his ascetic power in his third eye and it was with a glance from this eye that he reduced to ashes Kāma, the god of desire, when Kāma attempted to interrupt his meditations. A number of myths illustrating the burning qualities of *tapas* were recorded by Lieutenant Francis Wilford:

> Śiva and Pārvatī parted as a result of a quarrel and each performed *tapas*. "The fires, which they kindled, blazed so violently as to threaten a general conflagration". The gods in alarm employed Kāma to wound Śiva with one of his flowery arrows (*Journal of Asiatick Researches*, vol. iii, p. 402).

> Pārvatī, angered by Śiva's attentions to the celestial nymphs, seated herself in the hollow trunk of a tree and performed *tapas* for nine years. "Fire, springing from her, pervaded with rapid violence the whole range of mountains, in so much, that men and animals were terrified, and fled with the utmost precipitation." (*Journal of Asiatick Researches*, vol. iv, p. 363.)

> Śiva and Devī came upon a region over-run with long grass which made it uninhabitable. They performed *tapas* so that the grass was burnt and the country soon filled with inhabitants. (*Journal of Asiatick Researches*, vol. iv, pp. 364–5.)

Tapas as a creative force and source of power

Because of the equation between *tapas* and *sexual* heat, ascetic power has creative qualities. Dr. O'Flaherty (1973, p. 41) writes:

> Although in human terms asceticism is opposed to sexuality and fertility, in mythological terms *tapas* is itself a powerful creative force, a generative power of ascetic heat. In a late Ṛg Vedic creation hymn, it is from *tapas* that the One is born, and the Atharva Veda *brahmacārin* creates by performing *tapas* in the ocean.

Tapas as a source of power

The practice of *tapas* endows the ascetic with supernatural powers. "The experiments of the yogis," observes Daniélou (1964, p. 220), a contemporary convert to Hinduism "have led them to the discovery that sex energy is the very energy that man can utilize for the conquest of his own self. The sexually powerful man, if he controls himself, can attain any form of power, even conquer the celestial worlds." In consequence when a mortal performed great feats of asceticism, the gods became uneasy and sent a beautiful maiden to tempt the ascetic so that he shed his seed and lost his power.

The sage Vibhāṇḍaka performed *tapas* for 3,000 years, until flames (arising from his *tapas*) penetrated Indra's heaven and seriously disturbed the gods. Indra sent Ūrvasī ("the head of celestial frail beauties") to the sage, who was "deeply smitten with the celestial nymph" when he went to bathe in the river. A doe knowingly drank the water, became pregnant, and gave birth to a human male child with two horns. (Narasimmiyengar, V.N. 1873. The legend of Rishya Sringa. *Indian Antiquary*, ii, pp. 140–3: quoted by O'Flaherty, 1973, p. 47.)

Tapas and the retention of semen

The sage Vibhāṇḍaka yielded to temptation and as a result his asceticism was destroyed. But this was not simply a moral lapse. In a more direct and quasi-physical sense abstinence is believed to build up a store of semen inside the body so that a man who sheds his seed loses his *tapas*.

After marrying Pārvatī, Śiva made love to her for a thousand years, but then he lost all of his *tejas* (burning power) and his virility was reduced. Seeing himself thus diminished, Śiva resolved to perform *tapas*, and he undertook a great vow wandering on earth, carrying a skull. (Vāmana, 34, 2–3; quoted by O'Flaherty, 1973, p. 296.)

Andhaka took his weapons and the battle began. Then Śiva said to Pārvatī, "My dear, the vow that I performed gave me powers which I have now exhausted. Therefore I, an immortal, have been attacked by mortals (demons). And this strife has come about because I lost my ascetic merit by making love to you day and night. Now I must again enter the terrible forest and perform a great vow of *tapas*." Then he went away and performed *tapas* for a thousand years. (Śiva Dharmasamhitā, 4, 127–30; quoted by O'Flaherty, 1973, p. 296.)

The luminous quality of the ascetic's body and its agreeable odour are also attributed to his internal store of semen. Daniélou (1964, p. 218) writes:

In Yoga the ashes are a symbol of the sublimated power of procreation. The semen of the man who observes perfect chastity is consumed inside his body. This burned energy is believed to give a peculiar beauty and radiance to his body. This brilliance of the Yogi is spoken of as the glow of the ashes of his semen.

The *Haṭha Yoga Pradīpikā* observes: "By preserving semen, the body of the Yogi emits a pleasing smell" (H.Y.P. iii, 88).

Kuṇḍalinī Yoga

In Kuṇḍalinī Yoga the retention of semen is only one of a number of practices designed to withdraw the powers of the ascetic into himself and extinguish the manifestations of life. The first condition of the ascetic life is the renunciation of the world. The sannyasi extinguishes his social personality by leaving his home, wife and family, giving away his possessions and performing his own funeral rites (Kane, 1941, pp. 931–2). He lights his sacrificial fires for the last time and then withdraws them into himself by swallowing the ashes (Dubois, 1936, p. 50). Thereafter he lives like an animal without fire. His possessions consist of his begging bowl, his water jar and the garment he wears and he wanders alone from place to place begging his food (Kane, 1941, p. 935). He is buried and not cremated and no mourning is to be observed for him (Kane, 1941, p. 965).

The sannyasi also separates himself from the material world of the senses by the practice of special disciplines, systematised in the various schools of yoga, designed to concentrate his powers and his attention within his own body. This results in the "de-cathexis of objects" or a total withdrawal from external object relations.

> The wise one, by restraining all his senses from their objects, and being free from all company, remains in the midst of these objects, as if in deep sleep, i.e. does not perceive them. (Śiva Saṃhitā, v, 178.)

By continued application the yogi also progressively acquires control over internal processes, both physical and mental, until he is in a position to eliminate them altogether.

> He should be neither of his inside nor of outside world; and, leaving all thoughts, he should think of nothing. (Haṭha Yoga Pradīpikā, iv, 56.)

When the sexual impulse, the breath and the mind cease to move, the manifestations of life have stopped and the ascetic becomes indistinguishable from that which was before creation began. This is the state termed liberation (mokṣa).

> The Yogi, engaged in Samādhi, feels neither smell, taste, colour, touch, sound, nor is conscious of his own self. He, whose mind is neither sleeping, waking, remembering. destitute of memory, disappearing nor appearing, is liberated. (Haṭha Yoga Pradīpikā, iv, 108, 109.)

All systems of Yoga lay stress on the beneficial effects of seminal retention which is said to cure disease, restore virility and prolong life. Certain Tantric schools, however, chiefly associated with Kuṇḍalinī Yoga, combine

---

1. This phrase was used by Dr. R. D. Laing in a talk given in 1973 to the 1952 Club describing his experiences of oriental meditation.

asceticism with sexual practices, *yoga* (discipline) with *bhoga* (enjoyment), intercourse being effected in such a manner that semen is either not emitted or, if emitted, is re-absorbed.

The "physiological" concepts underlying these practices are as follows (see Figure 1). *The suṣumnā* is a narrow channel running from the base of the spine to the hole in the top of the head. It passes through six centres where the vital forces are concentrated. The lowest of these is the *mūlādhāra* (literally "root support") situated at the door of the anus, and the highest is the *ājñā* (literally "command") situated within the skull between the eyebrows. Each is a place of union between a particular god and goddess, for the individual, being a microcosm of the universe, contains both male and female elements. Above the *ājñā* where the *suṣumnā* reaches the hole in the head is a final centre called *sahasvāra* (literally "having a thousand spokes"), the lotus of 1,000 petals containing the full moon, moist with the semen of immortality called *soma*; this is the undivided origin of all dual forms and the final goal of Kuṇḍalinī Yoga.

Bindu (semen) is believed to be distilled by the moon above the palate to the left of the space between the eye-brows. In its natural course it passes downwards through the *suṣumnā* to the *mūlādhāra*, where it is consumed by the fire of passion and discharged. The aim of Kuṇḍalinī Yoga is to reverse this process, to keep the male *bindu* fixed in its place of origin

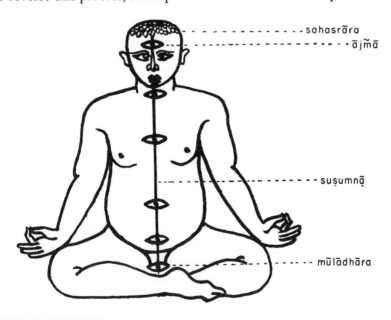

Fig. The Subtle Body.

and to draw upwards towards it through the body the female principle of desire, substituting an internal experience of coition for the external act of physical union. The upward passage of semen to the brain, where it becomes *soma*, is conceptualised by the raising of the coiled serpent Kuṇḍalinī who ordinarily lies asleep in the *mūlādhāra*, the lowest centre of the body. She is the energy (*śakti*) or creative power of the world and, as such, embodies the semen of Śiva. The postures held efficacious to rouse the sleeping Kuṇḍalinī usually include direct pressure on the genital area. As Dr. O'Flaherty (1973, pp. 261–2) puts it: "The seed must be stirred sexually before it can be absorbed mentally." By perfecting various techniques designed to generate internal heat the yogi seeks to wake Kuṇḍalinī and induce her to enter the central column of the *suṣumṇā*. These physical techniques are aids for the realisation of mental states. The yogi is instructed to imagine himself as Kuṇḍalinī on her inward journey through the body. As she rises she pierces each of the centres in turn, absorbing into herself the qualities of these centres and effecting a union there between herself and Śiva.

> This family woman (i.e. Kuṇḍalinī), entering the royal road (i.e. Sushumnā), taking rest at intervals in the sacred places (i.e. Chakras), embraces the Supreme Husband (Parashiva) and makes nectar to flow (i.e. from the Sahasrāra). (Cintāmanistava: quoted by Avalon, 1950, p. 240.)

This causes an emission of semen which she drinks. The yogi, in identification with her, partakes of the pleasure of this psychic intercourse and himself enjoys the semen.

In certain Tantric schools of the left-hand, ritual intercourse (*maithuna*) and other orgiastic rites are utilised to hasten the ascent of the Kuṇḍalinī on the grounds that the same actions which lead men to damnation can, if properly understood and practised, lead instead to salvation. Ejaculation is usually forbidden. As Eliade (1958, pp. 267–8) observes: "*Maithuna* is never allowed to terminate in an emission of semen: *bodhicittaṃ notsrjet*, 'The semen must not be emitted', the texts repeat. Otherwise the yogin falls under the law of time and death, like any common libertine." Nevertheless, some sects permit ejaculation provided steps are taken to ensure the return of the seed. These are described in the *Haṭha Yoga Pradīpikā* (iii, 82–96). *Vajrolī* is a technique for drawing the semen in again after it has been ejaculated. In *Sahajolī* semen mixed with ashes—itself a symbol of semen[2]—is re-absorbed by rubbing into the body. In *Amarolī* the semen is drunk, and can also be snuffed in. Precautions are also taken to prevent the loss of bodily emissions with procreative powers. Numerous myths tell

2. This theme is developed by Dr. O'Flaherty in her paper *The Symbolism of Ashes in the Mythology of Śiva*.

of children born from the seminal properties of sweat produced either by the sublimated seed of *tapas*, or by the heat of lust. The *Haṭha Yoga Pradīpikā* (ii, 13) instructs the yogi, after the exertion of holding his breath, not to wipe off the perspiration, but to rub it into his body to make it strong.

Modes of Thought

In attempting to trace the connection between the concept of *tapas* and the ideas and practices surrounding the conservation of semen I would like to emphasise that I am not concerned with the breast or milk or the conservation of semen as such, but with a particular mode of thought of which the concept of the breast that feeds itself can conveniently be taken as the prototype and earliest expression. The characteristic of this mode of thought is that it conceives of the processes of life using a model appropriate to the properties of inanimate things. Psychical states of thought and feeling are experienced concretely as if they were material objects, and human capacities (the capacity to give love and milk, the capacity to make love) are believed, like possessions, to be diminished rather than developed in use. "Using" is equated here with "using up": the breast is rich because it *has* milk and not because it gives milk, just as potency is conceived as the state of possessing a store of potency which is expended in the act of making love.

Lévi-Strauss (1969, p. 85) has recognised the connection between the universal properties of the mind and infantile thought which, he says, "provides a common basis of mental structures and schemes of sociability for all cultures, each of which draws on certain elements for its own particular model". The psycho-analytical concept of a breast (penis) possessed of a store of milk (semen) which can be consumed internally appears to provide the model for those aspects of Hindu asceticism described above. But the context in which these ideas emerge are different and this gives to the ideas themselves a different meaning. Melanie Klein developed her concept of the breast that feeds itself in relation to her theory of primal envy. This is not central to Hindu asceticism. Bion made a distinction between K in the sense of getting to know and K in the sense of possessing a "piece" of knowledge in relation to the process of learning from experience. The first meaning of K involves the painful recognition of not being in possession of a desired "piece" of knowledge and requires the capacity to make effort and tolerate frustration. The frustration and effort can be avoided by substituting for this state of mind K in the sense of already possessing the desired "piece" of knowledge, a way of not learning from experience. Although ascetic power is often thought of in Hindu literature in concrete and quantitative terms, it is not conceived as a state which can be achieved or maintained without the capacity for unremitting efforts. The matrix of ideas for the Hindu emphasis on the conservation of semen can more plausibly be related to Freud's concept of the death instinct.

The Death Instinct

Freud advanced his concept of a death instinct in *Beyond the Pleasure Principle*. I do not propose to recapitulate the steps of his argument, but to concentrate on the homeostatic principle which led to his final division of the instincts into two opposing groups, the life instincts and the death instincts. He starts from the observation that the tendency to re-experience even very painful events indicates a compulsion to repeat which over-rides the pleasure principle. This leads him to define an instinct as "an urge inherent in organic life to restore an earlier state of things" (Freud, 1955, p. 36). He continues (1955, p. 38): "It would be in contradiction to the conservative nature of the instincts if the goal of life were a state of things which had never yet been attained. On the contrary, it must be an old state of things, an initial state from which the living entity has at one time or other departed and to which it is striving to return by the circuitous paths along which its development leads. If we are to take it as a truth that knows no exception that everything living dies for *internal* reasons—becomes inorganic once again—then we shall be compelled to say that '*the aim of all life is death*' and, looking backwards, that '*inanimate things existed before living ones*'." To the internal forces that tend to the dissolution of the organism into its former inorganic state he gives the name of the death instinct. The libidinal forces in conflict with it that tend to the preservation of the organism he calls the life instinct. In conclusion he hazards the speculation that perhaps the sexual instinct too originates in a need to restore an earlier state of things and seeks to reunite what was formerly one. He refers here to similar speculations in Plato's myth on the origin of sexual differences in the *Symposium* and to Hindu accounts of creation which may have been Plato's source.

The opposition of life and death, characteristic of Western thought, does not occur with the same emphasis in Hinduism. According to the doctrine of transmigration, death is followed by re-birth in another life so that organic matter cannot, in the normal course, become inorganic. In Christian theology death is opposed to life and denied in the idea of life after death. The "immortality" sought by the Hindu is of a different kind. Death is here considered a quality or characteristic of life and the two are classed together as undesirable.[3] "All is suffering to the wise man" (*Patañjali's Yoga Sūtra*,

3. The equation between life and death is expressed in an early Bengali song quoted by Dasgupta (1946: 44): "Death is exactly the same as birth—there is no distinction between being and dying."

ii, 15). The aim of life is to escape from life-death into another state (or non-state) outside the categories of understanding and the universal properties of manifest things such as time, space, number, cause, quality, etc. For this to be achieved it is necessary for the individual to experience the cessation of the phenomenal world so that he can return to his unmanifest state.

In the concluding section of *Immortality and Freedom*, Eliade (1958, p. 270) discusses two aspects of yoga in relation to cosmic regression. One is the return of the seed and the other is the conjunction of opposites. He interprets the Tantric practice of re-absorbing ejaculated semen in the following way:

> In Haṭha Yoga . . . there is even supposed to be a "return of Semen"—that is, a paradoxical act, impossible to execute in a "normal" physiological context dependent upon a "normal" cosmos; in other words, the "return of semen" stands on the physiological plane, for a transcendence of the phenomenal world, entrance into freedom . . . Now, immortality cannot be gained except by *arresting manifestation*, and hence the process of disintegration; one must proceed "against the current" (*ujāna sādhana*) and once again find the primordial, motionless unity, which existed before the rupture.

The aim of the yogi is to achieve identification with that which was before creation began. In the language of the death instinct, he seeks to restore an earlier state of things. This is effected by undoing the cosmic process. All elements of reversal, therefore, have the meaning of going back in time and re-absorbing the cosmos through inversion of the process of manifestation. Because the individual is a microcosm of the universe the yogi can effect this movement within his body. Eliade (1958, p. 271) terms this the "cosmicising" of the body; alternatively it can be considered as the internalisation of the world.

> What is here is there. What is not here is nowhere. (*Visvaśāra Tantra*: quoted by Avalon, 1950, p. 50.)

> All the beings that exist in the three worlds are also to be found in the body. (*Śiva Samhitā*, ii, 4.)

> He who, leaving the Śiva (God) who is inside, worships that which is outside (viz. external forms), is like one who throws away the sweetmeat in his hand, and wanders away in search of food. (*Śiva Samhitā*, v, 71.)

The identification between the individual and the universe makes it possible to undo the cosmic process by the conjunction of opposites within the body. Life is arrested by the immobilisation of breath, thought and semen. These three are equated.

Who has brought his breath to a stop has, at the same time, brought his mental activities to rest; who has brought his mental activities to rest has stopped down his breath ... When the mind is fixed and the breathing ceases, the bindu is retained (unmoved). (*Haṭha Yoga Pradīpikā*, 4, 21, 28; quoted by Briggs, 1938, p. 344.)

The yogi relates inhalation and exhalation to day and night, so that he re-lives within his body the cosmic cycle of "days and nights" when the universe is periodically created and destroyed. When he succeeds in arresting respiration, suspending thought, and immobilising semen, he stops the phenomenal world and passes into "that non-conditioned and timeless state in which 'there is neither day nor night', 'neither sickness nor death' " (Eliade, 1958, p. 271). Similarly the union of opposites negates creation. The sun is represented within the body by the upper air (*prāna*), the moon by the lower air (*upāna*). By exercises designed to control the breath, these two airs can be brought together and united in the body. This brings about the union of the sun and the moon which represents the destruction of the cosmos. Other pairs of opposites are psychically co-joined within the body to the same effect (male with female, Śiva with Śakti or Kuṇḍalinī, semen with menstrual fluid, right with left, mind with matter, the self with the other, the individual soul with the universal soul, etc.). The paradoxical nature of these unions, if I understand Eliade, by signifying an assertion of what is not and cannot be, deny and therefore destroy what is:[4] in other words, they negate or do away with the cosmos. Here the symbolic enactment of an impossible happening is believed to make the possible un-happen.

The de-manifestation of the world and the withdrawal of the self into its source is effected in Kuṇḍalinī Yoga by the upward passage of Kuṇḍalinī from the *mūlādhāra* at the base of the spine to the thousand-petalled lotus at the top of the skull. The symbolic significance of this journey has been richly elaborated and I can give here only a few illustrative examples. In her journey Kuṇḍalinī travels backwards through the successive stages of creation, re-absorbing each into herself in the reverse order to its emergence. The major evolutionary stages are conceived as follows.[5]

What was in the beginning cannot be described for it is without characteristics (*nirguṇa*). It is sometimes referred to as *Tat* (That). In *Śaivite* theology *Tat* is usually identified with Śiva. Śiva's will to create, which is the life-force, is called Śakti. In his unmanifest state Śiva is homogeneous

---

4. A similar mechanism in reverse occurs in *Peter Pan:* ". . . every time a child says, 'I don't believe in fairies,' there is a fairy somewhere that falls down dead" (Barrie, 1928: p. 32).

5. The account of Kuṇḍalinī's journey is taken largely from Avalon's *The Serpent Power*.

and undivided, and Śakti exists within him only potentially. Creation consists in the differentiation of Śakti out of Śiva, who objectifies himself
through Śakti as the world. Śiva wills, "May I be many." With this thought
he becomes divided into Śiva-Śakti, male and female combined, and the
first element of duality appears like a single grain containing within its shell
a divided seed (Woodroffe, 1952, p. 7). As this seed ripens, a polarisation
takes place between Śiva and Śakti. Śakti assumes the form of *bindu* (literally, "a point"), the state of gathered up power (*ghanībhūtā*) which immediately precedes the burgeoning forth of the universe (Avalon, 1950, p.
55). She turns her face outwards and forwards (*unmukhin*). The seed bursts
its shell and Śiva manifests himself in creation by putting forth his Śakti.
The objectification of Śiva as the world gives rise to a false or illusory
distinction between the "I" and the "This", so that the object is experienced as other than and alien to the self. Objectified Śakti, originally homogeneous, then divides herself into the multiple forms of creation, first into
the subtle categories of Mind (*buddhi, ahamkara, manas*), and then into
the five states of Matter, etherial, gaseous, igneous, liquid and solid, each
manifestation evolving out of the one immediately preceding it. When she
has entered the last and grossest form, solid matter or earth, her creative
activity ceases and she rests in her last emanation, the earth principle.

In the body the arrangement of the vital centres (*cakras*) from above to
below recapitulates the stages of evolution so that man was created from
the head downwards, as it were, the lower centres being both the grossest
and the last evolved. The degree of alienation of the Self is also represented
in terms of distance, the centres in and near to the head involving less
differentiation between subject and object, knower and known, than the
lower centres along the spine where the object takes on an increasingly
independent existence. The forward movement of evolution (*pravṛtti*) is
represented by the downward journey of Kuṇḍalinī who with each successive manifestation travels further from the unconditioned and undivided
Śiva in the top of the skull whence she arose. This forward movement is
called *anuloma*, literally "with the hair" (or, as we would say, "with the
grain"). The object of Yoga is to reverse this process, to rouse the sleeping
Kuṇḍalinī and, in identification with her, travel backwards along the path
of creation till the universe dissolves in its source. This return process
aimed at the cessation of existence (*nivṛtti*) is called *viloma* or "against the
hair". As Kuṇḍalinī moves upwards through the central channel, she
moves backwards in time—it is said: "The *suṣumṇā* devours time"—and
pierces in turn each of the centres or lotuses along her path. These normally
hang with the head of the flower facing downwards and outwards towards
manifestation but, as she passes through, the heads turn to look backwards
towards their source. The vital powers of each centre are absorbed by

Kuṇḍalinī and carried up to the next ascending centre whence they derived, so that the process of creation is repeated in reverse order. The various forms of Matter are dissolved into one another, and then into Mind, and Mind into Consciousness till the universe collapses into a mathematical point (*bindu*) in the brain. This is the state earlier described as Śakti in her gathered-up form (*ghanībhūta*) when the "This" is again subjectified as part of the "I" and becomes a point of consciousness with it (Avalon, 1950, p. 34). Finally, when Kuṇḍalinī reaches the thousand-petalled lotus and passes again into Śiva in his undivided form, the yogi concludes his journey at his point of origin.

The return of Kuṇḍalinī can be seen as a movement from lower to higher, from later to earlier, from gross to subtle, from matter to mind, from activity to quiescence, from becoming to being, from part to whole, from the differentiated to the undifferentiated, from duality to unity, from object to subject, from earth to heaven, from effect to cause, from Śakti to Śiva, from time to eternity. The symbolism is much more elaborate than indicated here and is also worked out in relation to areas not touched upon, such as sound, colour, form and number. But the general rule is that "things dissolve into that from which they originate" (Avalon, 1950, p. 23). The retention of semen is merely one aspect of this involutionary process.

In relation to Freud's definition of an instinct as "an urge inherent in organic life to restore an earlier state of things", two points can be made. In the case of the life instinct, the Hindu conception is, as Freud noted, that the differentiation into male and female was effected by division of a single undifferentiated source so that the operation of the sexual instincts can be defined in this context in terms of restoring an earlier state. In the case of the death instnct, there is a remarkable correspondence between the goal of life as elaborated in Hinduism and Freud's formulation, already quoted, in terms of "an initial state from which the living organism has at one time or other departed and to which it is striving to return by the circuitous paths along which its development leads" (Freud, 1955, p. 38). Consistent also with Freud's view that Thanatos, as long as life lasts, can never be observed in isolation but only in combination with Eros, is the fact that the return journey is eroticised as the passionate union of Śakti with Śiva. "The Shakti Kuṇḍalinī who has been seized with desire for Her Lord is said to make swift way to Him, and, kissing the lotus mouth of Shiva enjoys Him" (Avalon, 1950, p. 238).

The symbolic significance of Kuṇḍalinī's return journey presents so close a parallel to Freud's theory that I am tempted to advance the tentative hypothesis that Hindu asceticism represents an expression of the death instinct in a disguised and qualified form. At this stage I lack any sort of conceptual framework to deal with a hypothesis of this kind, but I would like at least to attempt in a preliminary way to identify some features in the organisation of the Hindu caste system which seem to relate to an opposition to life.

The Principle of Renunciation in the Organisation of Caste

The death instinct is probably best understood as the mental counterpart of the physiological processes of ageing and death. The hypothesis that there is an instinct in man, which, albeit at the unconscious level, works towards his destruction has encountered great resistance in the West and has been rejected even by the majority of psychoanalysts. The extinction of life is, by contrast, positively evaluated in Hinduism as the highest goal of spiritual effort and mystical achievement. This corresponds with the popular view that western religions are positively oriented towards society and history and basically world-affirming whereas eastern religions are pessimistic, ascetic and world-negating. It cannot, of course, be maintained that Hinduism, as one of the oldest extant religions, has in fact neglected the things of this world, but the idea, at least, of renunciation has been elaborated as a principle of organisation which can be shown to provide the logical framework for the ordering of the caste system. I would like to develop this point through the work of Louis Dumont.

Renunciation and asceticism arose as the dominant values of movements generally regarded as heterodox, but they became, as Hinduism developed, of central importance in its orientation. Dumont's analysis of world renunciation in Indian religions concentrates on the opposition and complementarity between the renouncer as an individual-outside-the-world of caste and the man-in-the-world where the individual is not, and on the feed-back of the ideas of the renouncer as an innovator into the system. He points both to the this-worldly (Brahmanic) and other-worldly (sanyasic) dimensions of Hinduism as distinguishable "ideal types" which have increasingly combined over time, and to the progressive absorption and limitation of the renunciatory ideal in everyday practice (Dumont, 1960, pp. 45–7). I have found this model of contradiction and complementarity particularly valuable for the study of devotional sects where the analytical opposition of caste and sect, usually evident at the outset, is gradually obliterated over time as the two interpenetrate to form a single religious experience. But in the context of this paper I would like to relate the principle of renunciation to the caste system in a different way. It is recognised that some of the criteria considered relevant for caste ranking, such as vegetarianism and non-violence, owe their positive evaluation to the sanyasic ideal. If it can be shown that the concept of ritual impurity itself which, in Dumont's view, provides the very basis of the caste hierarchy, also derives from the principle of renunciation, then the relationship between renunciation and caste ceases to be one of contradiction and assumes an intrinsic character. The material in support of this view cannot be elaborated within the scope of this paper, but the main points are indicated below.

The opposition of the pure and the impure is identified by Dumont as the single principle which provides the structural basis of the caste system (Dumont, 1970, p. 43). I suggest that ritual purity does not exist except in the negative sense of denoting the absence of impurity and that this opposition should be formulated, not in terms of purity and pollution, but of the impure and the not-impure. The positive pole of Dumont's opposition, that is, ritual purity, is better understood as a negative or empty state, the absence of impurity. It is not difficult to support this formulation. The Hindu concept of ritual pollution has often been compared to the Polynesian concept of *mana*, but with a fundamental difference in its operation (Hutton, 1946, p. 162). The *mana* of the Polynesian chief is dangerous to the commoner who must in consequence avoid contact with the chief, whereas in India contact between high and low caste ordinarily has consequences only for the higher caste. Dumont makes an essentially similar point when he compares the Indian and the tribal case: ". . . the relations between superiors (who are sacred elsewhere and pure in India) and inferiors is reversed: the tribal chief is taboo, i.e. dangerous for the common people, whereas the Brahman is vulnerable to pollution by an inferior" (Dumont, 1970, p. 40). The Brahman is defiled because the impurity attaching to low caste passes across to him; the low caste man is not thereby purified because purity, being non-existent, cannot be transmitted. Pollution passes by touch, even by sight, and through permeable objects like cooked food and pottery, spreading from one to another like a contagion. Purity, by contrast, is rarely invoked except to refer to the cleansing of impurity. To take an illustration from Assam. An offering is made to the spirit of the dead within the period of mourning; the place of the offering is impure. A woman washes the ground with water and white earth. Now, she says, it is pure. The body after bath, clothes when they have been washed, bell-metal vessels heated on the fire, are called pure because water washes away impurity and fire burns it off. Purity, having no positive content with which to withstand the invasions of impurity, can be maintained only by vigilance, withdrawal and avoidance.

This re-formulation of Dumont's fundamental opposition was prompted by a passage in Lévi-Strauss's analysis of the story of Asdiwal (Lévi-Strauss, 1967, p. 32) when he contrasts the absence of food, not with the presence of food, but with the negation of its absence: that is, there is either no-food or not-no-food, there is never food. Lévi-Strauss goes on: "... we must conclude that for these natives the only positive form of existence is a negation of non-existence" (Lévi-Strauss, 1967, p. 33). Similarly in Hinduism the only positive statement that is opposed to existence is the affirmation of non-existence. In place of the evil of life the Hindu desires the blessing of not-life. Weber has commented that the holy objective "was conceived by all the highest forms of Asiatic mystical belief as an 'emptying'. This was an emptying of experience of materials of the world ... The devaluation of the world and its drives is an unavoidable psychological consequence of this" (Weber, 1958, p. 332).

Dumont relates the basis of impurity to life itself. "We acknowledge that the elementary and universal foundation of impurity is in the organic aspects of human life" (Dumont, 1970, p. 55). If we accept the qualities and conditions of life as being, at any rate, the major source of impurity, we arrive at the following equation:

$$\text{impure} \ : \ \text{not impure} \ :: \ \text{life} \ : \ \text{not-life}$$

Higher castes are, by definition, less impure than lower castes. They are also required to divest themselves to a greater degree of characteristics associated with the organic basis of life. The higher the status of a caste, the more numerous are the types of food it *cannot* eat, the occupations it *cannot* pursue, and the avoidance enjoined upon it. This aspect of caste organisation so impressed Leach that he regarded the higher castes in certain respects as "negatively privileged" and built a theory of the nature of caste society upon it (Leach, 1962, pp. 5–6). The impurity connected with "low" occupations, which are for that reason a monopoly of "low" castes such as the washerman, the barber and the tanner, clearly derive their stigma from their necessary and intimate contact with organic processes. The categorisation of food is another facet of the life/not-life polarity. "Heating" foods raise the temperature of the blood and inflame the passions, while "cooling" foods cool the blood and calm the mind. There are progressive restrictions on foods in the first category as one ascends the social hierarchy.

Dumont bases the caste hierarchy on the fundamental opposition between the pure and the impure, and on a series of lesser oppositions within this polarity (Dumont, 1970, p. 57). From another point of view it may be useful to see the caste hierarchy as a gradation. It is the degree to which a caste admits the impurity associated with life that, formally at least, determines its position in the hierarchy. If life in its organic aspect were conceived as some sort of impure substance, we would conclude that there is believed to be a greater admixture of this substance in the lower castes and progressively less in the higher castes at the upper reaches of the hierarchy.

It can be objected that things are not really like this. India is not full of under-nourished and under-privileged Brahmans and plump and privileged Untouchables. The caste order only simulates the values of renunciation; it is not in fact based upon them or certainly not based upon them alone. The techniques by which caste has accommodated the things of this world, namely political and economic power, are very differently understood by different scholars and I am concerned here with this problem only peripherally. The caste system on the ground is no doubt partly shaped by its ideology (Dumont's criteria of rank). It is also determined by other realities (Dumont's empirical factors of observation). The ideology itself is not in all respects homogeneous and the emphasis on function rather than purity in the *varna* theory is better adapted to take account of certain empirical factors. But even with these qualifications there remains a gap, sometimes wide but always detectable, between the basically ascetic values on which the system supposedly rests and the way it operates in practice. This gives to the ideology a fictive quality to which some writers have reacted by dismissing the notion of ritual status as little more than a convenient idiom for the expression of differential power. But it would be a contradiction in terms for any society to base itself on an unqualified acceptance of the principles of world renunciation and survive, and the caste system has undoubtedly shown a robust survival value. Gombrich's study of Sinhalese Buddhism is of interest here. He takes up in his conclusion "the unintended consequences of the adoption by a whole population of a religion which teaches that total renunciation of life is the only final answer to life's problems" (Gombrich, 1971, p. 326). He argues that the negative ideal of self-restraint is supplemented in practice by the positive ideal of love and that tension and accommodation between these world-denying and world-affirming tendencies has characterised the development of Buddhism almost from the outset. It is interesting in relation to Freud's dualistic theory of the instincts as Thanatos death and Eros that Gombrich has subsumed the forces opposed to the renunciatory ideal under the term "love".

Conclusion

The argument of this paper can be summarised as follows:

1. The Hindu concept of *tapas* or ascetic power as deriving from the retention of semen is paralleled, in psychoanalytical theory, by the concept dualistic theory of the instincts as Thanatos (death) and Eros that Gombrich has subsumed the forces opposed to the renunciatory ideal under the term "love".

ascetic, by conserving his semen, is believed to build up an internal store of magical power. Both beliefs are based on a mode of thought which conceives of human capacities using a model appropriate to inanimate things, i.e. it conceives of them as material possessions diminished by use. The concept of ascetic power as stored sexuality is illustrated by material from (a) Hindu mythology, where the connection is explicit; and (b) Kuṇḍalinī Yoga, where a series of techniques have been elaborated for the control and absorption of semen within the body in a more symbolic form.

2. The conservation of semen is part of an involutionary process designed to detach the yogi from the external world and withdraw his powers into himself. The aim of this process is ultimately to undo the created universe and return the self to its point of origin. There is a correspondence between the desire of the yogi to be restored to his origin and Freud's definition of the death instinct in terms of an urge inherent in organic life to return to its inorganic condition. In Kuṇḍalinī Yoga the undoing of life is effected symbolically within the body by the upward journey of the serpent Kuṇḍalinī who travels backwards through the successive stages of creation, re-absorbing each into herself in the reverse order to its emergence. The yogi, in identification with her, also repeats the history of his development backwards, as it were, till he reaches the source whence he arose. This compares with Freud's suggestion that the goal of life is "an initial state from which the living entity has at one time or other departed and to which it is striving to return by the circuitous paths along which its development leads" (Freud, 1955, p. 38).

3. This correspondence leads me to advance the tentative hypothesis that Hindu asceticism represents an expression of the death instinct in a disguised and qualified form.

4. From this standpoint an attempt is made to identify some features of the caste system which seem to relate to an opposition to life. These may be summarised as follows:

(a) Purity is an empty or negative state characterised by the absence of impurity. The opposition between the pure and the impure should be formulated as an opposition between the impure and the not-impure, a positive value being attached to the negative state of the not-impure.

(b) The goal of ascetic striving is conceived in Hinduism as an "emptying" or undoing of life. The continuation of life is negatively valued as the source of suffering and opposed to a negative or empty state of not-life, which is positively evaluated.

(c) The organic aspects of life are the chief source of impurity so that avoidance of impurity requires a withdrawal from life itself. Higher castes are by
definition less impure than lower castes. They are, therefore, required to
divest themselves to a greater degree of the qualities associated with organic
life, and the progressive restrictions on choice of occupation and diet in the
upper reaches of the hierarchy derive from this requirement. The logic of
the caste hierarchy rests on a fundamental opposition to life itself on the
basis of the following equivalences:
impure : not-impure   ::   life : not-life   ::   low status : high status.

(d) The caste hierarchy is not in fact based on an opposition to life. The social
reality of caste operates very differently from the ascetic model. Although
the principle of renunciation has given to caste its particular accent and
orientation, this has been accompanied by a corresponding shift of emphasis
from renunciation as a path of individual salvation to ritual avoidances as
the differentiating criteria of status groups. In consequence the values which
were once associated with the renunciation of the world are often chiefly
evident as "symbolic strategies" (Cohen, 1974, p. 74) in support of social
exclusiveness and other worldly interests.

Acknowledgements

I am greatly indebted to Dr. Wendy O'Flaherty for her generous assistance in
the preparation of this paper and, more particularly, for making available to me
a proof copy of her book *Asceticism and Eroticism in the Mythology of Śiva*. She
was kind enough to read the first draft of the paper and she provided a translation of the passages quoted from the Rg Veda. Without her scholarly support I
would have hesitated to venture into this field. I also wish to thank Professor
I. M. Lewis, Professor Adrian C. Mayer and Dr. Elizabeth Bott for their helpful
comments and, in particular, Professor J' Duncan M. Derrett for his careful
reading of the text and his many valuable criticisms.
     I am indebted to Miss Caroline Law for her drawing of the subtle body.

References

Avalon, A. 1950. *The Serpent Power*, Ganesh and Co., Madras.
Babb, L. A. 1970. Marriage and malevolence: the uses of sexual opposition in a
     Hindu pantheon. *Ethnology*, **2**, 137–48.
Barrie, J. M. 1928. *Peter Pan*, Hodder and Stoughton, London.
Bion, W. R. 1962. *Learning from Experience*, Heinemann, London.
Briggs, G. W. 1938. *Gorakhnāth and the Kānphaṭa Yogis*, Oxford University Press,
     London.
Cohen, A. 1974. *Two-dimensional Man*, Routledge and Kegan Paul, London.

Daniélou, A. 1964. *Hindu Polytheism*, Routledge and Kegan Paul, London.
Dasgupta, S. 1946. *Obscure Religious Cults as Background of Bengali Literature*, Calcutta University Press, Calcutta.
Dasgupta, S. 1950. *An Introduction to Tantric Buddhism*, Calcutta University Press, Calcutta.
Dubois, J. A. 1936. *Hindu Manners, Customs and Ceremonies* (trans.) H. K. Beauchamp, Clarendon Press, Oxford.
Dumont, L. 1960. World renunciation in Indian religions. *Contributions to Indian Sociology*, **iv**, pp. 33–62.
Dumont, L. 1970. *Homo hierarchicus* (trans.) M. Sainsbury, Weidenfeld and Nicolson, London.
Eliade, M. 1958. *Yoga: Immortality and Freedom* (trans.) W. R. Trask, Routledge and Kegan Paul, London.
Freud, S. 1955. *Beyond the Pleasure Principle*. S.E.xviii (trans.) J. Stracey, Hogarth Press and Institute of Psycho-Analysis, London.
Gheraṇḍa Saṃhitā. 1915. In *The Yoga Śāstra* (trans.) S. C. Vasu, Subhinda Nath Vasu, Allahabad.
Gombrich, R. F. 1971. *Precept and Practice*, Clarendon Press, Oxford.
Haṭha Yoga Pradīpikā. 1915. (Trans.) P. Sinh, Subhinda Nath Vasu, Allahabad.
Hume, R. E. 1931. *The Thirteen Principal Upanishads*. Oxford University Press, London.
Hutton, J. H. 1946. *Caste in India*, Cambridge University Press, London.
Kane, P. V. 1941. *History of dharmasastra*, vol. ii, part ii, Bhandarkar Oriental Research Institute, Poona.
Klein, M. 1957. *Envy and Gratitude*, Tavistock Publications, London.
Leach, E. R. 1962. Introduction: what should we mean by caste? In *Aspects of Caste in South India, Ceylon and North-west Pakistan* (ed.) E. R. Leach, Cambridge University Press, London.
Lévi-Strauss, C. 1967. The story of Asdiwal (trans.) N. Mann. In *The Structural Study of Myth and Totemism* (ed.) E. Leach, Tavistock, London.
Lévi-Strauss, C. 1969. *The Elementary Structures of Kinship* (trans.) R. Needham *et al.*, Eyre and Spottiswoode, London.
O'Flaherty, W. D. 1971. The symbolism of ashes in the mythology of Śiva. *Purāṇa*, xiii, **1**, 26–35.
O'Flaherty, W. D. 1973. *Asceticism and Eroticism in the Mythology of Śiva*, Oxford University Press, London.
Patañjali's Yoga Sūtras. 1924. (Trans.) Rama Prasada, Subhindranath Vasu, Allahabad.
Śiva Saṃhitā. 1915. In *The Yoga Śāstra* (trans.) S. C. Vasu, Subhindra Nath Vasu, Allahabad.
Weber, M. 1960. *The Religion of India* (trans.) H. H. Gerth and D. Martindale, Free Press, Glencoe, Illinois.
Wilford, F. 1792. On Egypt and the Nile from the ancient books of the Hindus. *Journal of Asiatick Researches*, **iii**, 295–468.
Wilford, F. 1795. A dissertation of Semiramus, the origin of Mecca . . . from the Hindu sacred books. *Journal of Asiatick Researches*, **iv**, 363–84.
Woodroffe, Sir J. 1951. *Shakti and shākta*, Ganesh and Co., Madras.
Woodroffe, Sir J. 1952. *Introduction to Tantra shastra*, Ganesh and Co., Madras.
Zaehner, R. C. 1972. *Hinduism*, Oxford University Press, London.

13 | Virgin and Mother

Paul Hershman

The ideals of Punjabi womanhood are those of virgin and mother, but nowhere in their ritual system is there any acknowledgement of the fact that in order for a virgin to become a mother is it necessary that she should have sexual intercourse and become impregnated by a man. It is therefore not without significance that the female deity *Mātā*[1] although both named and worshipped "mother" is depicted as a virgin having neither husband nor child. She is, indeed, both virgin and mother, and, through the paradoxical nature of her sexual status, has the power to bestow male children upon those who worship her. This essay is principally about the working out of this paradox and the way in which Punjabi values concerning maternal fertility and female sexuality manifest themselves through ritual in symbolic form.[2]

The cow is a second mother figure in Punjabi cosmology. It is anomolous in character, being in profane contexts treated as any other animal, but in ritual worshipped as "the mother of man". Killing a cow or devouring its

1. I should like to thank Dr. C. Shackle, of the School of African and Asian Studies, for his help in the transliteration of the Punjabi language into Roman script.

2. Gough, in an unduly neglected essay "Female Initiation Rites on the Malabar Coast" has described a similar identification of virgin and mother in an Indian ethnographic context. She employs the psychoanalytical notion of the "Oedipus Complex", and argues that it is the unconscious identification of virgin with mother, which leads to the ceremonial practice of the deflowering of a pubescent girl by a "father figure". Yalman, in a subsequent essay, "On the Purity of Women in the Castes of Ceylon and Malabar", has criticised Gough's use of a psychoanalytical framework, and instead locates the initiation rites in their sociological context, placing particular emphasis upon the facts of caste and kinship. Although Yalman's analysis is convincing, it does not, I think, invalidate Gough's account of the psychological implications of the rituals enacted and the symbols used. The values, rituals and symbolism of South India, are in many ways strikingly similar to those of Punjab.

meat is strictly taboo, and are perhaps the gravest sins that an individual may commit. I would suggest that the cow is not anomalous because of any in-built characteristics of the Punjabi system of animal classification, but rather that it occupies an anomalous and taboo position because of particular qualities which make it a suitable idiom for expressing certain Punjabi values. The cow is conceived of in Punjabi thought as particularly anthropomorphic in character, because of gestation and lactation which are very similar to the same processes in the human female; moreover it is a stall animal, living almost within the household and supplying the household members with milk. The cow is at the centre of a complex of ritual behaviour in which the contradiction is resolved between on the one hand, the positive values of motherhood and female fertility, and on the other, the impurity which Punjabis see as surrounding birth and female sexuality. Those bodily exudations which, in human women, are grossly impure and polluting become in the cow the creators of purity and the cleansers of human bodily impurity.

It is my contention that social and moral values are expressed in ritual through the medium of a symbolic code. Following Leach (1964, xiv) I accept ritual as being in a general sense "the communicative aspect of behaviour"—values form the content that such messages communicate and symbols the idiom in which these messages are expressed. In the Punjabi ethnography presented here, I hope to show this process working in a rather special way by demonstrating how contradictory values are assimilated and resolved through the mediation of symbols which are anomolous in form. In order to support this argument I will draw on ethnographic evidence which I collected during my field-work amongst Hindu and Sikh Punjabis.[3] But although most of what I say will be generally applicable to Punjabi culture as a whole, many of the rituals which I consider in detail are Hindu in nature and more specifically Brahmin.

Let me begin my analysis of the ethnography by stating two of the most basic of Punjabi moral and social values which are in apparent contradiction with one another:

1. A man is intrinsically pure and a woman impure. A woman's impurity

3. The fieldwork on which this ethnography is based was undertaken in the Jullundur Doaba region of Punjab during the eighteen months January 1972–July 1973, but I also draw upon the experience gained from sixteen months fieldwork in the Punjabi immigrant community of Southall, Middlesex. During this research I was financed by an SSRC studentship, and a small grant towards the cost of equipment from the Central Research Fund. I owe a considerable debt to Dr. H. S. Morris for his supervision of the research. I wish to thank all the members of the Department of Social Anthropology of the London School of Economics, and especially Dr. J. S. La Fontaine who made a number of suggestions which I have incorporated into the paper.

stems from the physiological processes of the female body—specifically those concerned with sexual intercourse, menstruation, birth and lactation.

2. Fertility is a dominant concern of Punjabis and unless a woman can become the mother of sons, she is not able to fulfill the criterion of what constitutes a "woman" in Punjabi society. Sons should ideally worship their mother and a woman gains status and authority through them.

I would suggest that there is a contradiction between the positive values attached to motherhood and female fertility, and the gross ritual impurity and pollution which surrounds female sexuality and the processes of birth. This contradiction is resolved principally through two dominant ritual symbols, both characteristically anomalous: first, the goddess who is both a virgin and a mother, and second, the cow which, despite being acknowledged as an animal, ritually serves as "the mother of man". Having dealt with the symbolism of the Mother goddess and of Mother Cow, I will then go on to show how Punjabi ritual employs the symbolism of birth itself, stripped of all its dirt and pollution, to empower various rites of passage. This too is the resolution of a contradiction in that birth is a socially positive force being the harbinger of new life, but it is an event surrounded in Punjabi thought by impurity and pollution. But, before going on to consider the ritual and belief of the Punjabis, it is first necessary to briefly describe the female life cycle and the contrasting attitudes towards male and female sexuality.

The Female Life-cycle and the Repression of Female Sexuality

Punjabi ritual expresses a strong difference in attitude towards male and female sexuality: while male sexuality is a socially positive force so that stored-up semen may be channelled to form spiritual power, female sexuality is something which is dark and polluting, and ultimately man-devouring.[4] Semen is regarded as the quintessential substance of male energy and a woman is considered capable of having sexual intercourse far in excess of any man;[5] so that while excessive sexual practice debilitates a man it is

4. Expressions of "vagina dentata" are commonly heard in abuse, especially in the context of an angry mother swearing at a slothful or disobedient unmarried daughter, e.g. *khasam khani* "husband eater".

The tiger, on which the Mother Goddess *Mātā* is often depicted riding, is always shown with an open, red-tongued mouth and with long white teeth.

5. Punjabi men are divided in their opinion as to whether their women enjoy sex or not. Some maintain that they have far greater appetites for it than men, while others express the view that they simply suffer it in order to have children. Paradoxically, ascetics are believed to have complete sexual control, and to be capable of lengthy acts of intercourse without ever spilling a drop of semen.

thought to have no such weakening effect upon a woman. Sex is considered something shameful and "dirty", and both partners are ritually polluted by the physical act and must bathe before they may again become pure. During menstruation, a woman enters a state of ritual impurity and is forbidden to cook or enter the cooking place. A man strictly avoids his wife during her menstrual periods and this avoidance, although ritually prescribed, is also strongly psychological in nature: Punjabi men express the greatest horror and repugnance at the idea of having intercourse with a menstruating woman. Following childbirth, a woman enters a polluted state and for a specific period of time must not leave her house, cook food or enter the cooking place. When the period of ritual impurity has elapsed, the mother is ceremonially purified by washing and drinking cow's urine "so that she may become clean inside". Only then, ritually cleansed, may she leave the house. The Punjabi word for the impurity attached to women at birth and menstruation is *chūt* and this is also applied to "untouchables", skin ulcers and contagious diseases.[6]

Punjabis begin to teach male and female children their respective sexual roles early in infancy. Boys of even four or five years old play naked, without any sense of shame, in the streets and alleyways of a Punjabi village; but the mother of even a very young baby girl constantly insists upon pulling the blouse down over her daughter's genitals. The Punjabi mother teaches her daughter to regard the vagina as something dirty which must be kept concealed, while the mother coyly teases her son about his nakedness. It is significant that in Punjabi baby-talk there is a special word for the undeveloped penis *lulī* (the word for the adult's penis being *lān*) but there is no equivalent word for the vagina of a young girl, the usual word being quite unutterable except in the most violent abuse. From an early age a Punjabi woman learns to treat the vagina as a source of shame and impurity, while a Punjabi man learns to feel pride in his penis and indeed the commonly heard Punjabi phrase *merā lan jāndai* (literally "my penis goes", the English equivalent of which would be "I can do what I fucking well like") is a phrase denoting social power expressed in a sexual idiom. Later when the girl's breasts begin to develop they too are subject to taboo and must be kept covered: the word for "breasts" *mamme* is even less commonly spoken than that for the vagina.

The sexual propensities of an unmarried woman are overtly denied but at the same time mature girls are carefully chaperoned and never allowed to stray far outside an older woman's sight. There is no ceremonial recogni-

6. From the verb *chūhṇā* "to touch". The pollution attaching to birth and menstruation is colloquially *chūt-chāt* or more formally *chūtak*. Members of "untouchable" castes are *achūt*. Closely associated are the words *jhūṭh* meaning "the impurity attatched to eating", and *cūt* which is a word for "vagina".

tion of a girl's first menstruation and an unmarried woman does not formally observe any of the strict menstrual taboos of married women. But the Punjabis have a rather ambiguous attitude towards a "menstruating virgin" and the general practice is for a mother to quietly instruct her daughter to stop cooking during the duration of her period. Interestingly, there was a traditional high caste taboo on a man eating any food whatsoever, cooked by an unmarried woman. Traditionally the line between married and unmarried women was much clearer than it is today. In the past the marriage ceremony was performed before the onset of a girl's puberty, but she remained in her father's household until she became physically mature. Only after puberty was the marriage then consummated and a woman went to live in her husband's household. Today, the age of marriage has become considerably higher, and almost all women go through a period of a number of years when they are physically mature but still unmarried. The ideal is that a woman should be a virgin at marriage, and traditionally a white sheet was employed at the time of the consummation of the marriage in order to test the bride's virginity. A woman who erred before marriage would, in the past, have been killed by either her father or her brother, the joint guardians of her honour. There was a recent case of such a killing in the village where I undertook fieldwork; but nowadays there is a general tendency towards leniency and a woman is married off to the first available groom with scant attention paid either to disparities in age or possible physical defects. As in many mediterranean and Arab societies, virginity at marriage is the ideal for women but not for men, and a Punjabi youth's sense of honour dictates that he cannot consider himself a "man" until he has had intercourse with a woman.

The unmarried woman's virgin status is not only socially desirable, but also makes her ritually pure relative to her elders, so that on particular ceremonial occasions she is worshipped as *Kanyā Devi* (the Virgin goddess) and her elders touch her feet and make her offerings. It is significant that an unmarried woman is never required to touch a person's feet, not even those of her parents. It is only after marriage and the loss of her virginity that she must touch the feet of her husband's parents. Unmarried Brahmin girls are often addressed as *Devi-ji* (respected goddess). The most revered woman in the village where I did fieldwork was an old Brahmin lady, whose betrothed husband had died before the consummation of the marriage. She lived out her days in unquestioned virginity, and was greatly respected, being treated as a living *Devi* (goddess).

Marriage is marked by a woman leaving her father's house and village, and going to live in those of her husband. There, as the most newly married "wife" she has little status and must bear the brunt of the household chores. In the first years of marriage a woman is continually journeying backwards and forwards between her father's and her husband's household. A woman's sexual relationship with her husband must be carried out in the utmost secrecy, and neither husband nor wife must show the slightest familiarity or affection in the presence of others. Traditionally a woman veiled herself from her husband in public throughout their married life, and until recently it was the custom for a woman to veil herself from her husband until the birth of the first child. A Punjabi woman also veils herself from all males who are older than her husband, and who are either his relatives or fellow-villagers. Traditionally complete sexual propriety was maintained by a woman whenever venturing outside her house, and this involved not only the veiling of the face but also the wearing of the traditional full gathered skirt, which so well disguises the curves of the female body.

As a wife, a woman has almost no status at all and if she fails to produce children, and most critically sons, a *de facto* divorce may take place, with the woman returning to live in her father's household and never again being recalled to that of her husband. It is only after the birth of the first child, which normally takes place at her father's home, that a woman may return with pride to her husband's household and become established as the mother of her husband's children. From that time on, she is no longer referred to and addressed as "so-and-so's wife" (which is something of a slur) but instead with the honorific "so-and-so's mother". Becoming a mother means that a woman has successfully made the transition from being a daughter to becoming a wife. She visits her father's household less and less frequently and becomes gradually an important part of her husband's household. This new found status is also reflected in a slight relaxation in the code of sexual modesty which takes place once a woman becomes a mother: she may openly breast-feed her child in the presence of any man, although paradoxically she may have to veil her face at the same time. The feeding of a child, whenever he demands it, is considered by Punjabis to be the primary duty of the mother, and weaning takes place at a considerably later age than in our society. Slowly the breasts become less of the tabooed area they once were, and an elderly woman feels no shame in openly displaying them.

It is only by becoming the mother of sons that a woman may hope to gain a position of status and authority. A son, unlike a daughter, must touch the feet of his parents, as also must the son's wife touch those of her husband's parents. A woman reaches her peak of potential achievement by becoming the matriarch of a joint household and exercising authority over her sons and dominating her daughters-in-law. How long this situation can last depends on the relative character of mother-in-law and daughter-in-law, but generally with the birth of the first son a woman becomes strong enough to break away and form a household of her own. As their joint sexual and child-rearing activities come to an end, husband and wife grow more and more apart and the woman has an increasing opportunity to dominate her husband and become more active in the village. As a woman grows older, there remain fewer men before whom she must veil herself, so that she enjoys considerably more freedom in the village and the kin-group. With the shedding of her shameful sexuality a woman becomes more like a man and she has the ability to exercise power according to the strength of her own personal character. Meanwhile for a man, old age is symbolised in his physical and sexual decline. Often a wife and sons quickly usurp an old man's position, and he is left to while away his days gossiping with the other old men sitting outside the village temple or shop.

As an unmarried girl, a woman is worshipped as a virgin, and as a mother she has the opportunity to gain status and authority; but as a wife, a woman has very little status at all. The situation is similar to that described by Gough in her article "Brahmin Kinship in a Tamil Village":

> The position of women in the kinship system is thus paradoxical. As mothers they are revered, but as marital partners they tend to be devalued ... The special sexual attributes of women—their menstrual and birth pollution—are much feared by men and scrupulously avoided as dangerous and ritually un-clean. Yet in myth and usually in fact, the wife is respected as the mother of sons.' (Gough, 1956, p. 841.)

Virginity and motherhood are both highly esteemed states in Punjabi society but wifehood and sexuality are those aspects which devalue a woman and make her the inferior of a man.

Mata: The Goddess who is both Virgin and Mother

I. K. Taimni in his Theosophical Society pamphlet "An introduction to Hindu symbolism" writes in the following terms about the female principle in Hindu symbolic thought

> In fact, the existence of the manifested Universe depends upon the primary differentiation of the one Reality into two polar aspects, one positive the other negative, the positive aspect being the source of all functions and the negative aspect the source of all powers ... These two opposite aspects are called Shiva and Shakti and from them arises all the functions and powers which are re-quired when a manifested universe comes into existence ... and the Devīs and Devetās can thus be paired off scientifically. This principle lies at the basis of the fact that particular Devīs are related to particular Devetas and are called their consorts. Thus Saraswati is the consort of Brahmā, Lakshmī of Vishnu and Kālī of Rudra. (Taimni, 1969, pp. 12–13.)

Taimni's account is typical of that generally found in the esoteric Hindu literature: male and female forces being depicted as opposed but complementary to one another, this being concretely manifested in the form of gods and their respective consorts. But this neat analysis in terms of binary opposition is not one with which Punjabi villagers are familiar. Indeed, although Punjabis know of the three gods Brahman, Vishṇu and Shiva, they do not synthesise them into the form of the classical Hindu trinity (creator, preserver and destroyer) and they are quite unable to name with any certainty their respective consorts. Some gods and goddesses are in fact polarised into pairs: Shiva and Parvati are well known because of the popular mythology of the birth of the elephant-headed god, Ganesh (see Hershman, 1974, p. 288); Krishna and Radha are central to Punjabi belief; and through the popularity of the Hindu epic, the Ramayana, Rama and Sita are identified as the ideal of husband and wife. But none of the goddesses Parvati, Radha or Sita would have the words *Devī* or *Mātā* employed in conjunction with their names.[7] When Punjabis use the word *Devī* (meaning goddess) or *Mātā* (which simply means "mother" but which is used to refer to "the Mother goddess") they have in mind a female deity that is far different from the "male other halves" Taimni describes. *Mātā* is a capricious female force, outside the bounds of male control, and generally only worshipped by mothers and children. Her capacities for bounteous generosity and vindictive anger are limitless: she is the giver of sons and of fortune; the sender of smallpox and of disaster; and the ingestor of male forces in the form of the tonsured hair of boys and the blood sacrifices of male animals.[8] She is depicted as a young woman riding a tiger (*sher-vālī Mātā*), wielding various weapons and objects in her eight arms,[9] her hair is unbound and powerfully free.[10] In the form of *Kalī Mātā* ("Black Mother" generally referred to in Punjab as *Kalkatte-vālī* "the Calcutta one") she is dressed completely in black. But as generally depicted in Punjab she wears the raiment of marriage: brightly coloured red clothes, red bangles upon her arms, vermillion smeared in her central hair-parting and the palms of the hands dyed a dark red.[11] Yet although worshipped as

7. It is common to hear them referred to by their first name alone without even the honorific *jī* (respected one). In song and prayer the forms Sita-Ram and Radha-Krishna are common. I am told that sometimes *Rānī* (meaning queen or girl) may be attached, e.g. Sita Rani, Radha Rani.

8. The traditional sacrifice is of a male goat, which must tremble as a sign that it is acceptable to the goddess, before it is sacrificed. I have seen a disciple possessed by the goddess make her an offering of a chalice of blood let from his arm. A recent newspaper report told of the sacrifice of a baby boy to the goddess in Rajasthan.

9. See Gough, 1955, p. 75 for some comments on the phallic symbolism surrounding the image of the South Indian Mother goddess.

10. See Hershman, 1974, for an account of the significance of hair in Punjabi ritual.

11. This image is very similar to that of the *curail* (the ghost of a woman dying in childbirth). Both are distinctly anti-male in character.

"the Mother" and dressed in the garments of marriage, *Mātā* or *Devī* is generally identified by Punjabis as a virgin, and when encountered by human beings takes the form of a beautiful maiden. There are many legends of such encounters and a particularly interesting one is given in the 1961 Census of India, where there is recorded the legendary account of the founding of the goddess's temple at Chintpurni. I give a brief summary of the legend as recounted here:

> Mai Das was a Brahmin priest, eight years old and without issue. He was on his way to his parent-in-law's one day when he passed a hilltop from which came celestial music. He climbed the hill and "witnessed a beautiful girl of about 12–14 sitting with a lion by her side and surrounded by a number of gods humming devotional songs". She revealed herself to Mai Das to be the goddess and promised him both sons and sustenance if he would stay at that place and worship her there. She instructed him that he would find water under a stone, one and a quarter hands long, and that he should take the stone and place it near a stone figure of the goddess, which he would find after she had disappeared. He was further instructed to bathe that stone figure with water. All this came to pass and he duly performed the goddess's instructions, but for some reason he set off again for his parent-in-law's. On the road he was struck blind and it was only when he had been guided back to the spot where he had first seen the goddess and begun to worship her as she had first instructed him that his sight returned. To Mai Das was born a son and it is his descendents who are temple priests at Chintpurni. (*Census of India* 1961, pp. 27–8.)

Let us leave aside the obtrusive sexual symbolism[12] of this myth and concentrate on the narrative content: the goddess appeared in the form of a virgin and offered in return for worship a son to a previously childless man. But, once he disobeyed her, she vindictively attacked him and only restored his sight after he had agreed to her request.

There are many temples of the goddess in the Punjab and she is known by as many names as there are places at which she is worshipped.[13] Most Punjabis speak of the goddess as being one of seven virgin sisters, who have a single younger brother. The imagery here evokes the many vows which

12. Such symbolism appears omnipresent and I do not think that it is only in the mind of the anthropologist. I recount the following two instances of the connection of blindness and impotence, which I encountered during my fieldwork. Firstly it is a commonly held belief amongst the Jat Sikh farmers that a man who has had sexual intercourse with an untouchable woman can never go blind. Secondly there was an illiterate peasant woman whom I interviewed in connection with her possession by spirits: she related how a guardian-snake deity used to live in her house until some ill-intentioned woman persuaded her to stop up its hole—she became blind and remained barren. It was only after she unstopped the snake's hole that her sight was restored and a son was born to her.

13. Rose, 1919, Vol. 1, pp. 318–65 gives an account of this proliferation. His account is extremely detailed and basically accurate.

Punjabi women make in order that the goddess should grant them a son.[14]
The best-known myths of the goddess revolve around the two sisters who
have their respective temples at Chintpurni and Jawalamukhi. These are
two of the most popular pilgrimage places for Punjabis, and it is at these
temples that the male tonsure ceremony is most commonly performed and
the hair offered to the goddess. Chintpurni, the younger sister (referred to
as *choṭi Mātā* "small mother"), is bitterly jealous of her elder sister Jawala-
mukhi (referred to as *baḍḍi Mātā* "big mother") and she allows nothing
brought from the temple of the elder to enter into her own domain. There
are many stories of the destruction wrought upon whole families who were
either forgetful enough, or presumptious enough, to disregard Chintpurni's
injunction. For this reason most Punjabis visit the temple of the younger
sister before going on to visit that of the elder.

During the twice-yearly festival days of *Naurāti*, Punjabis take their sons
to have the tonsure ceremony performed at the temples of the goddess. At
this time the boy is accompanied by a virgin sister whose duty it is to hold
the first lock of hair as it is cut, and to gather all the tonsured hair and make
it as an offering to the Mother goddess. The boy is then ritually bathed,
dressed in new white clothes given by his mother's brother including a
white turban speckled with yellow dye, and his old clothes are given to the
barber. During the days of *Naurāti* women make vows for sons, generally
promising to make an offering of a male goat if their prayer is answered.
During the days of the festival the virgin daughters of the temple priests,
dressed in red clothing, have the right to accost pilgrims and demand money
from them in the name of the goddess. In the evenings, young women
generally wearing red clothing, become possessed by the goddess and enter
into a state of trance in which they divine. Sometimes possession by the
goddess is exploited in a commercial manner and this seems to have been
as common in the nineteenth century (see Rose, 1919, vol. 1, p. 329) as it is
today: young virgins claiming to be living *Devī*, tour the towns and cities
of the Punjab, being possessed and divining. One recent such goddess,
whom I was privileged to observe, was named *Santoshi Mātā*. She was aged
between five and six years old and had a commercially minded father. She
appeared to have no gift more remarkable than a certain facility in shouting
jai Mātā-ji ("hail to the Mother goddess") and yet the village women
flocked to see her, and they believed absolutely in her claims and in her
powers. Another recent *Devī* phenomenon had commanded all brothers, on
pain of death, to make an offering of a red head-cloth to their sisters. She
was finally arrested by the police and was reputedly in league with a group
of merchants who had cornered the market in red cloth. The fact that she

14. There are also specific beliefs concerning the birth of a son after a string of daughters
and special rites which must be observed. See Rose, 1919, Vol. 1, p. 743.

was a fraud did not seem to outrage Punjabi morality so much as the fact that the "virgin mother" was pregnant when arrested. The Punjabis have a strangely mixed attitude towards individuals claiming to have super-natural powers: no matter how many individuals they ultimately unmask as charlatans they remain totally unshaken in their belief that some individuals do actually have divine powers.[15]

Mātā is not only a goddess who is external to the village, she also forms an integral part of the Hindu cycle of rites concerned with motherhood and female fertility. Yearly, the image of *Hoī Mātā* is freshly painted upon an inner wall of the household, the previous year's image being plastered over with cow-dung and a new smooth surface prepared of ground rice. The image of *Hoī Mātā* is stylised with the unmarried sons of the household shown in the centre of the picture. They are displayed in their wedding procession, riding with their brides in the marriage palanquin which is carried by men of the water-carrier caste. The names of all the sons of the household are carefully inscribed beside the picture. In the evening on the appearance of the first stars, offerings are made to the newly painted image of the goddess, and these are collected by women of the water-carrier caste. The household's unmarried sons touch their foreheads in obeisance to the image, and water is thrown in propitiation to the stars. At another festival which I describe elsewhere (see Hershman, 1974, p. 282) women collect a number of coloured cords in accordance with the number of sons the god-dess has granted to them, and offerings are made to *Mā Lakhmī*.[16] On the ninth day following the commemoration of the birth of Krishna (*janam ashṭmī*) Hindu women, who are the mothers of sons, observe the ritual of *ashṭmī dī kanjak* (Ashtmi's virgin girl)[17] when seven virgin children, usually six girls and a boy, are feasted and given offerings which are usually com-posed of red head-cloths for the girls. The virgin girls are regarded as personifying the goddess and the mother, who undertakes the ritual, concludes it by touching their feet.

As in other parts of India (see Mayer, 1960, p. 101; Dube, 1955, p. 95 and Pocock, 1973, p. 42), *Mātā* as we have seen also has more malevolent undertones being strongly associated with the Punjabi word for "small-pox", or more accurrately the whole group of pock diseases. Unlike Malwa and Gujarat, but like Telangana (see Dube, 1967, p. 95) smallpox is not only associated with the activities of *Sitala Mātā* (although she is known

15. For similar blends of skepticism about individuals but implicit belief in the prin-ciples concerned, see: Evans-Pritchard's *Witchcraft, Oracles and Magic among the Azande*, and Lévi-Strauss's "The Sorcerer and His Magic" in the collection of essays titled *Structural Anthropology*.

16. Punjabis here think of Lakhmi as the goddess of fortune and not as the spouse of Vishnu.

17. *Kanjak* is a female virgin, *lankṛā* a male virgin.

in Punjab and has a temple in Jullundur city). In fact Punjabis express each of the various pock-type diseases in terms of a specific *Mātā*, there being the underlying idea that when a person has a particular kind of rash he is in fact taking on the appearance of a specific *Mātā*: thus in *baḍḍi Mātā* (presumably smallpox), i.e. "big mother" the victim develops large red sores and is thought to take on the appearance of the elder sister Jawala-mukhi, while *choṭi Mātā*, i.e. "little mother" is symptomised by small red sores and the victim is thought to take on the appearance of the younger sister Chintpurni. Similarly, Punjabis classify other pock diseases as *kālī Mātā* (Black Mother) a black rash, *phullā Mātā* (flower mother) a flower-like rash . . . etc. The most deadly of all the *Mātā* diseases is that inflicted and named after the young brother of the seven sisters, *Lunḍhṛe*, when the skin erupts in large white sores. Punjabis are ambiguous in their attitudes to smallpox-type illnesses, on the one hand recognising them as contagious diseases (*chūt dī bimārī*), but on the other believing that the victim has become identified with the goddess and is ritually sacred. In some ways the Punjabis believe that the victim has "become" the goddess, not so much possessed by her, but rather that there is an identity between her body and his. I give here a list of some of the ritual observances surrounding a *Mātā illness*:

1. The vicim is isolated, remaining in the same clothes, unwashed with his hair uncombed. His ritual state is "frozen" and must be left so—the physical appearance of the goddess must be preserved and not meddled with.

2. During the illness, the victim is thought liable to mystical attack especially by sorcery. No person is allowed to visit the victim by entering directly from outside into the sickroom; they must sit for a little time out-side the room before entering. No person is allowed to visit whose mouth is not *jūṭha*, i.e. who is not partly polluted himself through having eaten before the visit.

3. Traditionally impure foods such as onion, garlic and red pulses[18] may not enter the house. In addition all pulses are taboo and also rice. Rice is served at the celebration in honour of the goddess which occurs on the first Tuesday following the victim's recovery. Food is not recooked in clarified butter in the usual way, but must be plain boiled. It is said that if the food is fried before serving in clarified butter that the victim will lose his sight.

18. Red pulses are sometimes said to be "cow's blood", just as turnips another tradi-tionally taboo food are said to be "cow's feet". Traditionally for Brahmins, at least, all the following vegetables: carrot, radish, turnip, onion, garlic, were taboo Rose writes, "for prudish reasons".

4. A sweet-smelling flower is kept at the head of the bed—being one of the goddess's symbols held in one of her eight arms. Water is also kept at the head of the bed and emptied daily at the base of the *kikkaṛ* tree (*acacia arabica*). It is unclear whether the water is emptied as a libation to the goddess or whether it is a symbolic casting out of the illness onto the sweeper caste, because they are associated with the *kikkaṛ* tree.

5. Women nightly gather in the house of the victim and sing devotional songs in honour of the goddess. If the victim fails to recover quickly then a virgin is brought, dressed in red to personify the goddess, and the victim touches her feet and makes offerings and possibly a vow. In acute illness promises are made to make the pilgrimage to the mountain temples of the goddess, and some sick people may attempt to make the pilgrimage themselves. Any bodily defects such as paralysis, skin blemishes or blindness, which are the aftermaths of an illness, according to Punjabi belief, may be healed if the victim visits the temple of the goddess and makes an appropriate vow.

6. Sohinder Singh Bedi in *Folklore of Punjab* (p. 66) remarks that traditionally anyone dying of smallpox was not cremated but immersed in water because burning the body would anger the goddess. I came across no case but according to my informants someone dying of smallpox would be buried in a deep trench because burning the body would produce a great "smell" which might infect others, it being *chūt dī bimarī*. Punjabis generally associate impurity, whether of the untouchable caste, or of birth or menstruation with "bad smells".

These rites and ritual states, as so much of Hindu ritual, are not susceptable to a simple analysis in terms of "pure" and "impure". As Srinivas has noted (1952, p. 101) the Hindu universe is divided into the sacred and the profane (i.e. the non-sacred), but the sacred in its turn is further subdivided into the "good sacred" and the "bad sacred". Hindu ritual generally employs both "good sacred" and "bad sacred", creating sanctity from a combination of both pure and impure elements.

Gau Mata (Mother Cow)

Whereas the Mother goddess, *Mātā*, is symbolic of those feminine elements which violently defy the confines of male control, *Gaū Mātā* (Mother Cow) represents a very much more domesticated and controlled image of Punjabi womanhood. "A man is the calf of a cow" (*admī gaū dā bacchā hai*) is a very commonly heard Punjabi expression, and it signifies the anomalous position which the cow occupies in Punjabi culture. In profane contexts the cow is treated as an animal, but ritually she is "the mother of man". Punjabis express the relationship between cows and men in a straightforward fashion, and they remark that just as the mother gives milk to her child so the cow gives milk to humans. But precisely because of the anomalous situation the cow occupies, Punjabi culture is at pains both to identify cows with men, while at the same time maintaining a clear distinction between them. This is well illustrated by the phonological proximity of the Punjabi words for "human child" and "cow's calf", which are at the same time clearly distinct:

> human child . . . . . *bacca*
> Cow's calf . . . . . *baccha*

The young of other animal species have specific words but in fact the word for human child *baccā* may be used in a general sense to refer to "the young" of any animal species, except the cow where the distinct form *bacchā* is always used. The line between the cow and other animal species is also clearly drawn and this is most evident in the radically different treatment of the cow and its nearest relative the buffalo. Punjabi language categorically distinguishes between the two:

	Cow	Buffalo
Adult female	*gaū*	*majh, maĭh*
Adult male	*sānh*	*māli*
Castrated male	*bald*	*jhoṭa*
Barren female		*sāṇḍhī*
Young male	*bacchā*	*kaṭṭā*
Young female	*bacchi*	*kaṭṭī*

Whereas the cow is regarded as a deity and is associated with the *Brahmaṇi* (a female Brahmin), the she-buffalo is regarded as an inauspicious and malevolent creature and often called a "black ghost". There is a special word for a barren she-buffalo *sāṇḍhī* which is close to the word *sānh* meaning a cow's bull. A barren she-buffalo is yoked and made to plough, but this would be sacrilege for a barren she-cow and there is no special Punjabi word for it.

There are a large number of contrasts which the Punjabis consciously make between cow and buffalo. The cow is a stall animal and its ox amenable to farm labour, but the buffalo is kept chained in the open and its castrated male is said by Punjabis to be wild and intractable and unsuitable for harnessing. Cow's milk is thought to be good for the intellect, while the thicker buffalo's milk is considered to be best for physical strength (goat's milk is traditionally considered impure and taboo).[19] So a number of simple oppositions may be posited to which the Punjabis themselves would certainly subscribe:

Cow	Buffalo
brain	brawn
tame, domestic, household	wild, fierce, fields
Brahmin	Farmer
good-omened	ill-omened

For non-ritual purposes Punjabis handle buffalo dung as they do cow-dung, and there are the same taboos on killing the animal, eating the meat and removing the carcass; but Punjabi ritual employs only the cow and specifically the female of the species.

In a large number of ritual contexts cows and calves are treated as if they were human beings, in a way in which Punjabis treat no other animal. It is significant that most of the ritual identification takes place in the context of birth and motherhood. At an eclipse the rope tethering a pregnant cow is loosened just as are the knots and clothing of a pregnant woman so that no constriction may malform the child. The placenta of a newborn calf is buried just as is that of a human baby, so that no harm may befall the infant because of damage suffered by the placenta. The two most common objects of sorcery are the killing of a child in order to gain its spirit for a barren womb, and the magical stopping of a cow's milk in order that the sorcerer's own dry cow may give milk. There are a number of commonly known magical procedures by which killing a cow results in its spirit being captured in the womb of a barren sorceress so that she will have a child. This can be done by cutting off the tail of a cow or feeding it specially prepared magical flour.

On other occasions the cow is ritually equated with the virgin (cf. Yalman, 1963, p. 43). The gift of a cow in charity *gaū dān* is often made at the same time as the gift of the virgin in marriage *kānya dān*. Both virgin and cow are garlanded and annointed with a red mark upon the forehead, and both are cloaked in a red embroidered cloth.

The similarities between women and cows may be overdrawn, but in both cases men clothe and feed them, and in return they supply milk and children. Both women and cows are commensal partners and eat the *jhūṭh*, the contaminated leavings of men. On the other hand *gaū grās* is performed

19. Villagers generally know that Mahatma Gandhi drank the milk of a goat and thus they acknowledge that it is also beneficial to the intellect. Generally, however, Punjabi villagers treat goat's milk with great distaste, but relish the meat of a slaughtered male animal. There is a magical belief that a "dry" cow may be cured by tethering a goat beside it—as the cow is pure and the goat impure, this is again an idea involving the juxtaposition of pure and impure elements.

daily in some households and generally on ritual occasions by others—it is
the giving of the first portion of pure untouched food to the cow, and at the
same time reverently touching its feet. Both women and cows are the pro-
viders of milk and Punjabis often link the purity of the exudations of the
cow with the nature of its diet.[20] Punjabis are shocked by the idea that a
dead mouse might get in the cow's feed and that the cow might swallow it.
Similarly while generally non-Brahmin Punjabi men are meat-eaters, even
low caste women are usually strict vegetarians. A woman is particularly
careful about the "purity" of her diet when she is producing milk for her
child. Following childbirth a special gift is made to a woman by her parents
which partly consists of a special dish which is composed mainly of clarified
butter, almonds, etc.—these types of food are especially eaten in order to
strengthen the flow of breast milk.

So in a large number of ways the cow is explicitly identified with the
imagery of mother and child. It is the treatment of the exudations of the
cow which is the most interesting. Whereas the bodily exudations of
women (including breast milk) are highly impure and polluting, the products of the cow are empowered in the opposite direction not only being
pure in themselves but also being the cleansers of human bodily impurity.
Cow-dung (*gohā*) is separated from all other faeces not only linguistically[21]
but also psychologically in that Punjabis feel no repulsion at picking up the
dung, warm and fresh, almost as it falls from the animal. The cow-dung is
mixed with mud, and patted into cakes (*pāthiã̄*) and then dried in the sun.
Cow-dung cakes are the main source of fuel and are handled freely while
cooking. Cow-dung is smeared upon the walls and floor of the house and
especially upon the cooking place. All sacred rituals are performed on a
piece of ground smeared with cow-dung, and a dying man is lowered onto
such a surface.

The ashes of cow-dung (*rākh*) are swallowed in order to cleanse the body
and especially to expel evil spirits. Cow-urine (*gaū pishab*) is drunk by
women at the end of the period of ritual pollution following childbirth in
order to cleanse themselves "inside". Similarly all the products which come
from cow's milk (*dudh*) are used at various times to purify the human body:
kaccī lassī (milk mixed with water) is used in offerings to shrines and to wash
the bones following a cremation; clarified butter (*ghī*) is rubbed into the
hair and scalp of a woman in the days following childbirth, and is also put

20. It was only when the anthropologist debated with his informants as to whether
cow-dung is "dirty" or not, that they produced the argument that the cow only eats grass
and therefore its faeces are pure whereas other animals are omniverous and so their
faeces are "dirty". However this is certainly a latent idea amongst Punjabis.
    21. Human, dog and cat faeces are *taṭṭi* or *jhaṇā*; small bird or lizard faeces are *niṭh*;
chicken *cūce*; camel *lid*; and goat *meṅgṇā̄*.

into the facial orifices of a corpse prior to burning; curd (*dahī*) is used to wash the hair and especially that of a dead person. Various sweets are made from milk which are important on ritual occasions: *khīr* (milk, rice and sugar) used at festivals, and *prasād* (clarified butter, semolina flour and sugar) which is used as a sacrament communally partaken of in temples.

While the faeces, urine and milk of human woman are highly impure and polluting, in the cow female impurity is symbolically brought under control so that the products of the cow become pure, and indeed the symbolism of the cow may be characterised as "motherhood with the impure elements of birth and sexuality removed". Human birth is a highly impure event and Punjabis employ the services of a low caste midwife, but even a high caste Punjabi shows obvious pleasure in seeing to the calving of his own cattle, and he is happy to cut the cord and bury the placenta, without any sense of shame or dirtiness. In Mother Cow the human contamination of sexuality and birth is hived off and what is left is an image of motherhood which is unambiguously pure and socially positive.

It would be wrong to leave any consideration of the cow in Punjabi ritual without mentioning the mythology of Krishna, the Pan-like god, who spent his early years as a cow-herd in romantic dalliance with the *gopiā* (cowherdesses). In the villages *Krishan rās* is often acted out by groups of Brahmin men dressing in women's clothing, and singing and dancing the parts of the *gopiā*.

The imagery of Krishna and Radha is strong in the Punjabi's mind and the village temple contains their images dressed as bride and groom, garlanded as for a wedding with the palms of their hands painted a dark red. In the esoteric Hindu literature, Krishna's love-affairs with the *gopiā* and the erotic imagery of Radha-Krishna are said to symbolise the god-force (*param-ātmā*) as the suitor of the individual soul (*ātmā*). All this is very high sounding, and Krishna is certainly a sensuous god, but his dusky form seems more concerned with human bodily fertility than the fate of the soul after death. In many of the myths of Krishna there is a central mother figure, and in one, Krishna dives into the black waters of the river Jumna in order to bring the snake *Sheshnāg* for his mother to use as a cord for her butter-churn. Krishna is both the son and the groom of woman, and the *gopiā* are little more than thinly disguised anthropomorphised cows. For the virgin cow there can be no other groom that the deity Krishna himself.

The cow is certainly a mother image in Punjabi ritual but she is a mother far different from the capricious and violently powerful goddess *Mātā*. She is a mother symbol representative of controlled feminine forces where the pollutions usually attatching to sex and birth are reversed to form life-giving, purifying power. When a cow dies, it is not the dead body which horrifies Punjabis; a devout Punjabi might bury the carcass himself using salt as is the custom in burying saints. It is not the carcass which is polluting but rather the use to which it is put; the flaying and tanning are highly impure acts and Punjabi men avert their eyes as men of the tanner caste come to drag the carcass away. It is the tanners who have all the rights to the leather and meat.[22]

Punjabis seldom consume the female animal of any species finding the idea repugnant, and to consume the cow that fed them milk is something unthinkable. In death the cow which has been the purest of objects in life becomes highly polluting[23] and the life-giving mother is in her turn used and consumed.

The Symbolism of Birth

A Punjabi child is delivered by a low-caste midwife who is responsible for the cutting of the cord and the burying of the placenta. The midwife washes the child paying particular attention in cleaning the throat, ears, eyes and nose, and then wraps the newborn infant in a cloth (see Gideon, 1962, for an account of Punjabi midwifery). During the confinement and the subsequent period of ritual impurity, mother and child are thought especially liable to attack by evil spirits, and following the birth neither are allowed to leave the house until the period of ritual impurity is passed. The mother is not permitted to breast-feed the child for approximately three days following the birth, and during this time the child is first fed with sweetened water, and subsequently with cow's milk. The Punjabis justify this practice by explaining that "the mother's milk is so thick at first, that it would damage the baby's throat", but I would interpret the practice in terms of the mother being ritually impure relative to the child. After three days have passed, the mother's breasts are ceremonially washed by a virgin with grass dipped in water, and only then is the mother allowed to suckle her child. At the end of the period of ritual impurity, the mother is ritually bathed and dressed in new clothes and her hair is ceremonially plaited by the barber's wife. She then leaves the house for the first time since the birth, carrying the child in her arms. For their services the midwife and the barber's wife receive a suit of clothes, now new but there is little doubt that these were traditionally the soiled clothes of the mother (see Rose, 1919, vol. 1, p. 749).

---

22. I doubt if many present-day "untouchable" caste members eat beef but it is likely that they did in the past. The cobbler caste *Mochi* was exclusively Muslim and therefore allowed by their religion to consume beef.

23. Today in Punjab, however, even Brahmins wear leather shoes, but people must go barefoot into temples and sacred places, and only temple priests have special wooden shoes. When hand-pumps were first introduced into the village, many orthodox Hindus refused to have them because they contained a leather washer. Now, however, their convenience has overcome prejudices based on religious grounds.

The physiology of birth is strongly reflected in the ritual of *Māiā* preceeding marriage. The etymology of the word *Māiā* is obscure but it is phonologically identical with the plural of the word *māi* meaning "mother". For several days prior to the marriage, the bride and the groom are kept confined within their respective parents' households, and during this time they are considered to be especially prone to attack by evil spirits. Special charms are made and tied, just as they are at the time of confinement and following the birth. The bride and groom remain unwashed in the same unchanged clothes. The village women daily gather at the household of both bride and groom and rub a *baṭnā* paste onto their bodies, which is an orange-yellow mixture of oil and turmeric. This paste is first rubbed on by the mother of the bride or groom, then by virgins, and lastly by other married women. After several days the skin takes on a certain sheen. The hands and feet are also dyed a bright red at the same time with *mehndī* (myrtle) especially the palms and the soles. Prakash Tandon (1972, p. 131) in his excellent account of Punjabi life quotes the following verse from a song traditionally sung during the ceremony of *Māiā*:

> Blessed be the mother who bore such a daughter,
> "In old and soiled" clothes in Mayan she put her.

On the day before the marriage, the bride and groom are ceremonially bathed respectively by the barber or the barber's wife—they put on new clothes given by the mother's brother, the barber and his wife receiving the soiled clothes. Their bodies are bathed but still retain the sheen of turmeric, and the bride wears a yellow undergarment over which is draped a large red embroidered cloth; the groom wears white clothing, including a white turban which is stained with yellow.[24]

The ceremony of *Māiā* seems to use the symbolic idiom of the physiology and ritual of birth. The new-born baby is born with a greasy layer around the skin, the *vernix*, which was described by one Punjabi woman as being like the "skin of an onion". This vernix is washed off following birth, and I would suggest it is perhaps this that is being evoked in the turmeric paste which is also washed off prior to marriage.[25] A young infant's palms and soles are bright red and again perhaps this is the symbolic referent of the dyeing of palms and soles before marriage.[26] Just as a baby is confined

---

24. Yellow is a prominent colour in Punjabi marriage. The letters on which marriage invitations are written are stained yellow. Yellow flowers are essential to the marriage rite.

25. These suggestions are at best tentative, but I feel certain that there is an evocation of the physiology of birth in these rituals. I have been told that some Indian babies have a definite yellowish tinge to their skin colour, but I do not know if this is always the case.

26. Pocock, 1972, p. 116 notes a similar custom in Gujarat: "if the first-born is a son his footprints are taken in red on a piece of paper and sent by barber to the child's father's house".

within his mother and born dirty before being bathed and wrapped in clean clothes, so a person at marriage is confined and is only washed and dressed in clean clothes prior to marriage.

The use of the rubbing of turmeric paste onto the skin as a ceremonial idiom of rebirth seems widespread in India and especially in the ceremonies leading to marriage, but it is also practised by some Muslims prior to the circumcision ceremony. Aggarwal, 1971, describes the smearing of turmeric paste both prior to marriage (p. 182) and also before circumcision (p. 175) for the Meos caste of North India. It is also described as being part of the ritual of initiation for the Jains (see Rose, 1919, vol. 2, p. 182). It is also found in non-Indian societies such as Tikopia, but here the turmeric seems more crimson than yellow. In Tikopia it is smeared on both mother and child following birth and it is a repeated motif throughout the various initiation ceremonies—"there, after being given food to eat, he is smeared on breast, neck, shoulders and sides of face and perhaps upper arms also, with the brilliant vermilion pigment of turmeric and coconut oil, which glistens like fresh blood on the skin" (Firth, 1957, p. 396).

A woman at the marriage of her son also goes through a type of ritual of giving birth, perhaps, symbolic of her attaining the new status of mother-in-law. On the night before the return of the marriage party with the bride, the bridegroom's mother drinks a mixture of milk and water (*kaccī lassī*) which has been ceremonially polluted by having elder kinswomen dip their big-toes into it.[27] Having drunk this liquid the groom's mother bathes, has her hair ceremonially plaited by the barber's wife, and puts on new clothes given to her by her brother.

At death a corpse is in many ways made to resemble a new born child. Just as there is a taboo on drinking a mother's milk in the first days of life, so a man, having drunk milk immediately before his death, is doomed to become a ghost. At the last, a man's mouth is cleansed with pure water of the Ganges, and in it is placed a green leaf of the basil plant, *Tūlsī Mātā*. The corpse is thoroughly bathed and dressed in a strip of new unbleached cotton cloth, and amongst Hindus a sacred thread is put across the body.[28] On the pyre clarified butter is smeared in the ears, nose, eyes and mouth. These acts may be seen as those of ceremonial purification, but it is also possible to interpret them as putting back those substances which were present in a new born baby.

27. This internal imbibing of polluted liquid may be symbolic of sexual intercourse. In the original Sikh initiation rituals the Guru put his big toe in a solution of sugar and water which was then drunk by the initiate. Now a two-edged dagger is used to stir the water and the liquid is then thrown on to the hair, in the eye and finally drunk by the initiate.

28. The umbilical cord of a new-born child is sometimes tied and severed with the sacred thread of an elderly man of the family.

As I have noted, both the Mother Goddess, and Krishna and Radha are shown with reddened palms and I argue that this is not only symbolic of marriage but also of birth itself. Indeed, in all these rituals the pollution is stripped away and the symbolism of birth is employed to endow various rites of passage with the generative force of power and new life.

Conclusion

In this paper I have examined some aspects of the ethnography of Punjabi ritual and I hope to have done so within the context of the theoretical proposition with which I started. I began by stating values which I considered to be in contradiction with one another: the fact that although female fertility and motherhood are socially positive values, female sexuality and birth are ritually impure and polluting. I suggested that these contradictory values are resolved through two dominant ritual symbols both anomalous in character: "the Mother goddess who is also a virgin" and "Mother Cow". In both of these the values of female fertility and motherhood are emphasised while those of the impurity of birth and sexuality are denied. The situation here is strikingly similar to that described by the Stratherns (1971, p. 197) for the Mbowamb of New Guinea:

> the spirit worshipped in the cult is female, but the cult in other ways emphasises male capacities, which are threatened by the polluting powers of women. The cult, in fact, mediated between the impurity of women and their fertility —for the *amb kor* is a spirit who comes to men as their bride and bestows increase upon them, but does not herself menstruate or bear children for she has no sexual organs.

The Punjabi's paradoxical evaluation of birth, as both intrinsically dirty and potentially powerful, is clearly seen in the rites of passage where its ritual and physiology are employed. Again, the Punjabis are not themselves consciously aware of the symbolism but to the anthropologist it would appear that birth is employed as a symbolic idiom, and that there is a clear contradiction between birth as "dirty" and birth as "powerful". As in so much of Punjabi ritual "that which is most dirty" is identical with "that which is most powerful".

Let me shed for a moment the role of naïve ethnographer and follow the example of the wise Punjabi mother who places a black mark upon the forehead of her new-born son to protect him from ghosts and the evil eye. In this paper I have employed the notion of "contradiction" without perhaps making any proper attempt to explain what I mean by it. The underlying problem is: at exactly what level does a contradiction exist—is it something of which the actors are themselves aware, or is it simply an arbitrary construct of the anthropologist; or is there perhaps a level of reality which exists somewhere between the individual actor's consciousness and the anthropologist's mind, a level which is normally termed "the social"? Indeed to even talk of "contradiction" immediately implies a notion of order and this leads to the central, but probably insoluble problem of whether order actually "exists" or whether it is something imposed through *the categories of the observer*. Leach makes a very blunt reply to this problem when he writes: "we first devise for ourselves a set of verbal categories which are nicely arranged to form an ordered system, and then fit the facts to the categories and hey presto the facts are 'seen' to be systematically ordered" (1964, p. iii).

Punjabis themselves are aware that there is an uncomfortable juxtaposition in their beliefs concerning female sexuality and motherhood, but it is only the anthropologist who can pose a "contradiction" between the negative values of female sexuality and the positive values of maternal fertility. To the Punjabis these ideas are contextually separate and apart. Similarly I have been careful to entitle this essay "Virgin and Mother" and not "Virgin-Mother". The Mother goddess whom the Punjabis worship is not a "virgin-mother", she is a virgin *and* a mother: the Punjabis conceive of the goddess in some contexts as a virgin and in others as a mother, but they never bring the two together to form a contradiction of which they themselves would be aware.

This same lack of consistency in ideas has been the subject of the recent so-called "Virgin Birth controversy" (see Leach, 1967; Spiro, 1968). From this it has emerged that the Trobriand islanders deny the male role in human conception while at the same time castrating their male pigs—they themselves see no contradiction because they do not in any context oppose the two ideas. But the ability to keep separate contradictory ideas is not only one of the characteristics of "the savage mind", it is also clearly observable in our own culture: for example in the case of the scientist who can trace man's evolution from the lower forms of life but at the same time holds the belief in an anthropomorphic god who made man in his own image; or in the case of the religious dogma of the New Testament where it is written that Christ was born the "son of god" through the immaculate conception of the Virgin Mary, but at the same time there is an elaborate genealogy tracing the descent of Christ's "father" Joseph from the house of David.

Punjabis also have many magical beliefs about the way a sorceress may capture a child for her barren womb, and they also pray to gods for children, but it would never even cross a Punjabi woman's mind that these magical and religious practices might dispose of copulation as being a necessary pre-requisite of childbirth—the two ideas simply never occur in the same context. In Punjabi ritual the symbols of the goddess who is both virgin and mother, and the cow that is both animal and "human", do not so much synthesise contradictory values through their anomalous character, but instead maintain the separateness of those values while highlighting their proximity to one another.

The contradictions exist certainly in the mind of the anthropologist and not that of the actor, but I would suggest that the order in which the anthropologist represents reality is much less arbitrary than Leach would suggest. When he first enters the field in an alien culture everything is chaotic and incomprehensible, but slowly the anthropologist begins to make sense of what he sees going on round him and he does so by consciously and unconsciously imbibing the principles by which the actors themselves order their behaviour—what the anthropologist is in fact undergoing is a highly efficient form of the learning process to which any individual born in a culture is subjected. Just as I am able to speak unheard sentences in a foreign language by learning the vocabulary and applying the principles of grammar, so I learn to react to, and to interpret previously unencountered social situations because my experience of the culture has taught me certain fundamental values which I am able to apply to new situations. The social system has an underlying order which is something more than the mere categorisation imposed by the anthropologist upon his data; individuals generally react to one another in a manner which is mutually comprehensible and new individuals born into a culture learn the same agreed set of values which ultimately condition their behaviour. When I use the notion of "contradiction" I do not mean that values are recognised by Punjabis to be inconsistent. Punjabis, like all of us, have the ability to keep contradictory ideas separate and apart by confining them to mutually exclusive contexts.

Throughout this paper I have dealt perhaps unsatisfactorily with the notion of contradiction, but ultimately I hope to have illustrated the underlying consistency of Punjabi life—a consistency which exists not merely at the level of the anthropologist's categories but at the level of Punjabi values themselves.

References

Aggarwal, P. C. 1971. *Caste, Religion and Power*, Shri Ram Centre for Industrial Relations, New Delhi.

Babb, L. A. 1970. Marriage and malevolence: the uses of sexual opposition in a Hindu Pantheon, *Ethnology*, **2**, 137–148.

Bedi, S. S. 1971. *Folklore of Punjab*, National Book Trust of India, Delhi.

Census of India. 1961. Vol. XIII, part vii-B, Punjab.

Dube, S. C. 1955. *Indian Village*, Routledge and Kegan Paul, London.

Evans-Pritchard, E. E. 1937. *Witchcraft, Oracles and Magic among the Azande*, Clarendon Press, Oxford.

Firth, R. 1963. *We, the Tikopia*, Beacon Press, Boston.

Gideon, H. 1962. A baby is born in the Punjab. *American Anthropologist*, **64**, 1220–34.

Gough, E. K. 1955. Female initiation rites on the Malabar coast. *JRAI*, **85**, 45–80.

Gough, E. K. 1956. Brahmin kinship in a Tamil village. *American Anthropologist*, **58**(5), 826–53.

Gombrich, R. 1971. Food for seven grandmothers: stages in the universalization of a Sinhalese ritual. *Man* (n.s.) **6**, 5–17.

Harris, M. 1966. The cultural ecology of India's sacred cattle. *Current Anthropology*, **7**, 51–66.

Hershman, P. 1974. Hair, sex and dirt. *Man* (N.S.) **9**, 274–98.

Leach, E. R. 1964. *Political Systems of Highland Burma*, Athlone Press, London.

Leach, E. R. 1964. Anthropological aspects of language: animal categories and verbal abuse. *In* E. H. Lenneburg (ed.), *New Directions in the Study of Language*, M.I.T. Press.

Leach, E. R. 1967. Virgin birth. *Proc. R. Anthrop Inst.* (1966), 39–49.

Lévi-Strauss, C. 1966. *Structural Anthropology*, Allen Lane, the Penguin Press, London.

Mayer, A. C. 1960. *Caste and Kinship in Central India*, Routledge and Kegan Paul, London.

Pocock, D. F. 1973. *Mind, Body and Wealth*, Basil Blackwell, Oxford.

Premchand. 1972. *Godan*, Jaico Publishing House, Bombay.

Rose, H. A. 1919. *A Glossary of the Tribes and Castes of the Punjab and North-west Frontier*, vols. 1 and 2, Lahore.

Spiro, M. E. 1968. Virgin birth, parthenogenesis and physiological paternity: an essay in cultural interpretation. *Man* (N.S.) **3**, 242–61.

Srinivas, M. N. 1952. *Religion and Society among the Coorgs of South India*, Clarendon Press, Oxford.

Strathern, A. and M. 1971. Marsupials and magic. In E. Leach (ed.) *Dialectic in Practical Religion*, University of Cambridge Press, Cambridge.

Taimni, I. K. 1969. *An Introduction to Hindu Symbolism*, Theosophical Publishing House, Madras.

Tandon, P. 1972. *Punjabi Century*, Hind Pocket Books, Delhi.

Yalman, N. 1963. On the purity of women in the castes of Ceylon and Malabar. *JRAI*, **93** (part 1), 25–58.

Index

A